CHILDREN, EDUCATION AND HEALTH

Children, Education and Health

International Perspectives on Law and Policy

Edited by
NEVILLE HARRIS
School of Law, University of Manchester

PAUL MEREDITH
School of Law, University of Southampton

ASHGATE

Published by
Ashgate Publishing Limited
Gower House
Croft Road
Aldershot
Hampshire GU11 3HR
England

Ashgate Publishing Company
Suite 420
101 Cherry Street
Burlington, VT 05401-4405
USA

Ashgate website: http://www.ashgate.com

British Library Cataloguing in Publication Data
Children, education and health : international perspectives on law and policy
1. Health education - Law and legislation 2. Health education - Government policy 3. Health education (Secondary) 4. Health education (Elementary) 5. School children – Health and hygiene 6. Children's rights 7. Sex education 8. Inclusive education
1. Harris, Neville S., 1954- II. Meredith, Paul, 1950-
344'.0769

Library of Congress Cataloging-in-Publication Data
Children, education and health : international perspectives on law and policy / edited by Neville Harris and Paul Meredith.
p. cm.
Includes bibliographical references and index.
ISBN 0-7546-4387-5
1. Educational law and legislation. 2. Right to education. 3. Right to health care. 4. Human rights. I. Harris, Neville S., 1954- II. Meredith, Paul, 1950-

K3740.C48 2005
344'.079--dc22 2005001741

ISBN 0 7546 4387 5

Printed and bound in Great Britain by MPG Books Ltd, Bodmin, Cornwall

Contents

List of Contributors

Ann Blair, Lecturer in Law, School of Law, University of Leeds, UK.

Marcia Conroy, Social Worker with the Association for Spina Bifida and Hydrocephalus, Manchester, UK.

Jan De Groof, Government Commissioner for Universities (Belgium); President of the European Association for Education Law and Policy; Professor at the College of Europe, Bruges, Belgium, and 'TIAS' (University of Tilburg), the Netherlands.

Gerald S Fain, Professor, School of Education, Boston University, USA.

Charles L Glenn, Professor, Chairman of Education Administration and Policy, Fellow of the University Professors Program, Boston University, USA.

Neville Harris, Professor of Law, School of Law, University of Manchester, UK.

Jim Jackson, Professor of Law, School of Law and Justice, Southern Cross University, Lismore, Australia.

Gracienne Lauwers, Executive Director, European Association for Education Law and Policy; Researcher at the University of Antwerp, Belgium.

Laura Lundy, Reader in the Graduate School of Education, Queen's University Belfast, Northern Ireland, UK.

Paul Meredith, Reader in Education Law, School of Law, University of Southampton, UK.

Charles J Russo, Panzer Chair in Education in the School of Education and Allied Professions and Adjunct Professor of Law at the University of Dayton, Ohio, USA.

Christa Van Wyk, Professor, Faculty of Law, University of South Africa, Pretoria, South Africa.

Charlotte Walsh, Lecturer in Law, School of Law, University of Leicester, UK.

Foreword

The crucial link between health and education and their importance for the well-being of children and of wider society are increasingly acknowledged. The education of children—mainly though not exclusively through schools—is one of the foremost means of both promoting and safeguarding the health of children and of society: schools, indeed, carry a major responsibility for the inculcation in children of not just the biological and other scientific information relating to health and well-being, but a genuine and sensitive appreciation and understanding of the social, moral and ethical issues which inevitably arise in this context.

The challenges faced by different countries across the world in the context of health vary considerably and are dependent upon a complex range of economic, social and political considerations as well as environmental, climatic and other natural factors. The scale and complexity of the AIDS epidemic, for example, will for generations have a profound impact on the economic and social fabric of society in poorer parts of Africa and Asia, where the problems posed by the disease are on an almost unimaginable scale. Ignorance is a major factor here and although the problems in such continents contrast sharply with the types of challenge faced by many wealthier regions—including obesity, alcohol and other forms of drug abuse, and many physical and psychological conditions associated with stress—here too ignorance plays its part in many of the threats to health.

There can be little doubt that these and many other challenges posed by health are of crucial importance to the economic and social well being of all countries across the world and are central to governmental policy making. But they also raise fundamental issues of individual human rights: individuals have a fundamental right to effective health care and a right to be educated in such a way as to understand the health consequences of different lifestyle choices they may face. Here the link between education and health is very clear: many lifestyle choices exercised every day by individuals carry recognised health related risks, and it is of the first importance that individuals should fully understand the nature and scope of such risks and be placed in a position where they can make informed and mature choices in relation to them. Effective education underpins so many aspects of good health, and good health as one of the most important empowering elements in the enjoyment of a fulfilled life is truly a fundamental human right, but one which is denied to so many across the world.

Health presents challenges not only at governmental level, although clearly governmental policy-making is of profound importance. International organisations such as the World Health Organisation have a vital role to play in the field of health promotion, and international Charters and Conventions such as the UN Convention on the Rights of the Child have played and will continue to play a significant role in conditioning governmental thinking and exerting pressure on governments in the development of policy and—very importantly—in the allocation of resources in this context. One should, however, also fully recognise the vital importance of those working at lower levels within government, within the education system and within the health services: indeed, the promotion of good health should be seen as going right down to the individual citizen—the teacher, the health professional and, very importantly, the individual parent and the individual child.

This book clearly recognises that the challenge posed by health raises fundamental issues as to the substantive content of the curriculum in schools, as well as in relation to the pastoral care and counselling of pupils and, in some cases, parents and teachers. Few would challenge the proposition that personal, social and health education forms an immensely important element within a broad and balanced school curriculum, although many would argue that insufficient weight and priority are attached to it in many schools. But the substantive content of the school curriculum in this context raises many intractable and highly contentious ethical and moral dilemmas which must be recognised, but for which it may well be impossible to offer any satisfactory solution.

Nowhere is this more apparent than in the context of the sex education curriculum and—no less important—the pastoral care and counselling of pupils in respect of their sexuality. It is by no means universally accepted, however, that schools have a legitimate role in the provision of sex education at all: many parents would take the view in all sincerity that the provision of sex education and counselling over issues of sexuality should be carried out exclusively within the family, that parents have a deep moral right and duty to bring their children up within the framework of their own culture, conscience and religious convictions, and that the public education system has no legitimate role to play in this context—or only a very limited role in terms of inculcating a sound knowledge and understanding of essential biological facts. Many, on the other hand, would take the view that schools should play a most important role in broadening children's perspective, in exposing their minds to the enriching experience of diverse approaches and giving them the widest possible range of educational experience consistent with a balanced, objective and critical presentation of issues. There is little common ground between these fundamentally different approaches, and it is almost certainly the case that no consensus will ever be attained in this context. But educational policy makers and teachers must recognise and respect this diversity of views and act with genuine sensitivity in this important and delicate area. What is clear is that sex education provides a fascinating study of policy-making in an extremely difficult context, as several of the chapters in this volume demonstrate.

Many other crucial issues relating to health and education are tackled in this volume: the editors have been fortunate to be able to include contributions by leading authors from a wide range of different educational systems across the international community, focusing on many key issues of concern. A major strength of the book is that the authors have adopted widely divergent approaches, and have not hesitated to express controversial views in approaching the issues. This is a highly thought-provoking volume and a most welcome contribution to the debate.

Jan De Groof
President,
European Association for Education Law and Policy,
Professor of Law, The College of Europe, Bruges

Preface

States, through their institutions and policies, exercise a fundamental responsibility for safeguarding and promoting the health of their populations. Child health is a particular concern, and while infant mortality rates have fallen continually throughout the past century across the developed world, they remain high in less developed areas. Wars, famine and the continual presence of diseases such as malaria (despite some scientific advances of late) in transitional states put the less severe health risks in the developed world into perspective. New threats are, however, constantly emerging; since the 1980s there has been HIV/AIDS, which, as Christa Van Wyk explains chapter 9 in this collection, affects directly or indirectly the millions of children in South Africa who live as members of families containing one or more infected individuals, including, in many cases, the child him or herself.

The growing international recognition of the importance of better health promotion is reflected in the range of legislative obligations placed upon and/or accepted by states. As Laura Lundy explains in the book's opening chapter, this responsibility is underscored by the international human rights framework and especially, in the case of children, the UN Convention on the Rights of the Child. Both internationally and within states sexual health is an area of particular concern. Teenage pregnancy and sexually transmitted diseases (STDs) among young people continue to beset many countries. As Gracienne Lauwers explains in chapter 7, the Russian Federation has a huge problem with sexually transmitted diseases and pregnancy among young people and, as elsewhere, is looking to the education system for some solutions. Indeed, it is a common theme of this book that in many states the role that schools and other educational institutions are expected to play in safeguarding health is growing. As Ann Blair explains in chapter 6, in an evaluation of the principles that underlie the state's growing attempts to regulate for better sexual health, 'education seems to be, at least for the moment, the best vaccine we have'.

The question is then: how should law and policy be framed? In the area of sex education in particular, issues of private morality, personal freedom and public welfare can come into conflict. In their respective chapters, Charles Glenn, in relation to the United States (chapter 4), and Paul Meredith, covering developments in England (chapter 5), highlight the problems that are faced by legislators in seeking to provide an appropriate legal framework in a pluralistic society where the health needs of often sexually active young people tend to play against the particular moral values held by parents and espoused by political ideologues. In England, which has a well-developed statutory framework, this conflict is partly resolved through the rather unsatisfactory means of conferring a right upon individual parents to withdraw their children from sex education at school.

Prevention, as already noted in relation to sexual health above, is another common theme in the book. It is linked to the notions of protection and risk. Education may have a crucial role in preventing ill-health, through sex education or, for example, the promotion of better diets and exercise, as Gerald Fain explains in chapter 11, evaluating health promotion in American schools. But the school environment itself can pose health risks, mirroring the risks in wider society. One area of particular concern is the threat to the mental and physical health of children caused by bullying by fellow pupils; in chapter 2, Neville Harris discusses the incidence of bullying in schools in the UK, highlights the evidence on its effects and assesses the various and wide-ranging legal responses to it. Another risk concerns society's so-called 'drugs culture,' from which schools and school pupils are by no means immune. This is a particularly difficult nut to crack; as Charlotte Walsh explains in chapter 3, drugs education seems to have had 'minimal primary preventive effects' and the UK government is struggling to find the right legal response to a pervasive problem.

Health also becomes important in the context of access to education. Illness or incapacity threaten to limit opportunities to receive schooling. The law in many states will generally aim to ensure a child's inclusion in the education system regardless of, for example, his or her state of health or disability. In England and Australia, for example, the authorities are not only placed under non-discrimination duties but are also under positive (albeit conditional) obligations, as Marcia Conroy and Jim Jackson explain in chapter 10. If the child's ill-health poses a very serious risk to other children, such as where there is a highly contagious disease such as measles or SARS, isolation may be necessary. Similarly, degrees of disability and the need for a highly specialised learning environment will vary between disabled children, so that it is not possible to include all in mainstream education. Inclusion is nonetheless a very important principle and yet, as Marcia Conroy and Jim Jackson's chapter illustrates, there remain significant barriers to, and differences internationally in the progress towards, equality of access to education for children with a disability, including those with behavioural problems.

Inclusion is also threatened by social and professional attitudes towards HIV-infected pupils. In chapter 8, Charles Russo highlights the over-emphasis on the perceived legal and health risks arising from the presence of infected pupils within schools in the United States. Christa Van Wyk shows in chapter 9 that the presence of HIV infection and AIDS, and the attendant infection risks, are facts of life in South Africa's schools. However, as she explains, despite the fact that '[c]hildren with HIV have the right to attend any public school and their needs should, as far as is reasonably practicable, be accommodated in the school,' a nursery school has refused to admit an HIV-infected child, lest she bite another pupil, and as yet unresolved litigation has ensued.

Given the breadth of the subject, it has been impossible to cover all aspects of children's education and health. We nevertheless hope that the book will raise awareness of some of the more problematic issues in the relationship between these two important spheres of responsibility. We are also hopeful that the book highlights the importance that needs to be paid to health in the context of education in order to safeguard and promote the rights of children, developmental as well as protective.

All bar one of the papers contained in this collection were originally presented at the annual conference of the European Association for Education Law and Policy (ELA) at the University of Manchester in November 2003, which explored the theme of Education, Health and the Law. All were updated for this collection and we are grateful to all the contributors, including Charlotte Walsh, whose paper was specially commissioned by the editors for this collection, for their hard work in preparing them. Given the controversial nature of some of the issues covered by the book we should add the caveat that the views expressed by individual authors do not necessarily coincide with those of the editors.

We also extend our gratitude to Professor Jan De Groof, President of ELA, and his assistant Gracienne Lauwers, for their support in the development of the conference and in giving us encouragement to bring this book to fruition.

Neville Harris and Paul Meredith
2005

Table of Cases

Table of Statutes and Other National Instruments

Table of International Instruments

PART I
THE INTERNATIONAL HUMAN RIGHTS FRAMEWORK

Chapter 1

Schoolchildren and Health: The Role of International Human Rights Law

Laura Lundy

Introduction

The relationship between the right to education and the right to health is a perfect example of the indivisibility and interdependence of human rights obligations. The right to health and the right to education, like many socio-economic rights, are inextricably linked. It can be as difficult for a person to sustain a healthy lifestyle without the knowledge with which to make informed decisions as it can be for someone to derive benefit from education if he or she is struggling with poor health. An investment in one area pays dividends in the other. Moreover, a denial of the right to education and/or the right to health has the potential to restrict the enjoyment of other fundamental rights such as the right to freedom of expression and/or association. Both rights have the capacity to multiply the enjoyment of other rights when protected and to undermine their enjoyment when denied. The key objective of this chapter is to provide a review of what international human rights law can contribute to the protection and enhancement of the health of schoolchildren. With a view to this, the chapter documents the international human rights principles which pertain to the issue of health and schools and provides a critique as to how effective these provisions are in practice in advancing the well-being of schoolchildren.

The Scope of the International Human Rights Obligations

International human rights law is relevant to the health of schoolchildren in a number of key respects. First, both the right to education and the right to health, as expressed in the international covenants, are understood to include a right to health education. Secondly, when a child attends a publicly-funded school, a range of other provisions apply, the focus of which is to ensure that the child is safe and well while at school. Thirdly, international human rights law provides a range of guarantees in relation to the education of children with health-related disabilities. Finally, children enjoy a number of autonomous rights, including the right to have their views given due weight in matters affecting their health and education. All of these issues are addressed in the convention dedicated to the specific rights of children—the United Nations Convention on the Rights of the Child ('the CRC'). However, children, as human beings, are the beneficiaries of a range of provisions contained in all of the other international human rights covenants. The provisions relevant to pupils' health do not always appear neatly in dedicated sections of the international covenants. Instead, they are peppered throughout the human rights treaties. In an effort to catalogue the human rights obligations which are significant for the purposes of this chapter, the relevant protections have been categorised under four core themes: the right to health education; the right to protection from harm; the right to inclusion; and the right to participate in decision-making.

The Right to Health Education

The Director General of the World Health Organisation has stated that: 'An effective school health programme... can be one of the most cost effective investments a nation can make to simultaneously improve education and health.'[1] However, few of the international covenants make explicit reference to a person's right to health education.[2] Instead, the right to health education can be inferred from broader statements about the goals of education. For instance, the CRC states that education shall be directed to: 'the development of the child's personality, talents and mental and physical abilities to their fullest potential.'[3] The United Nations Committee on the Rights of the Child has said that this provision is aimed at ensuring that 'essential life skills are learnt by every child and that no child leaves school without being equipped to face the challenges that he or she can be expected to be confronted with in life' requiring 'life skills such as the ability to resolve conflicts in a non-violent manner; and to develop a healthy lifestyle, good social relationships and responsibility.'[4] The CRC also contains specific rights to: 'seek, receive and impart information'[5] and requires State Parties to 'ensure that the child has access to information and material from a diversity of international sources, especially aimed at the promotion of his or her social, spiritual and moral well-being and physical and mental health.'

---

1 Source: www.who.int/school_youth-health/en/.

2 The key exceptions are the African Charter on the Rights and Welfare of the Child which requires State Parties to 'develop preventative health care and family life education' (Art14 (20(f)), and the Convention on the Elimination of all Forms of Discrimination against Women which requires State Parties to ensure: 'access to specific educational information to ensure the health and well being of families...' (Art 10 (h)).

3 Art 29 (1)(a).

4 United Nations Committee on the Rights of the Child, *General Comment No. 1 (2001): The Aims of Education*, UN/CRC/GC/2001/1, para 9.

5 Art 13.

While the right to education appears in all of the key international human rights treaties, the right to health is not as common nor as well-established.[6] For instance, the Universal Declaration on Human Rights does not contain an explicit right to health although it does afford everyone a right 'to a standard of living adequate for the health of himself or his family.'[7] The most specific formulation of the right is contained in the International Covenant on Economic, Social and Cultural Rights which states that everyone has the right 'to the enjoyment of the highest attainable standard of mental and physical health.'[8] A similar provision is contained in the CRC,[9] the American Convention on Human Rights[10] and the African Charter of Human and People's Rights.[11] The Committee on Economic, Social and Cultural Rights has stated that this includes 'the right to seek, receive and impart information and ideas concerning health issues.'[12] Moreover, it has stated that adolescents should be given the opportunity: 'to participate in decisions affecting their health, to build life skills, to receive counselling and to negotiate the health-behaviour choices they make.'[13] The revised European Social Charter (1996) also places emphasis on providing individuals with the resources to make healthy life-style choices through the provision of: 'advisory and educational facilities for the promotion of health and the encouragement of individual responsibility in matters of health.'[14]

The range of relevant human rights obligations has facilitated considerable discussion of health education issues in international fora. For the most part, the attention of the international community has been focussed on issues relating to sex education, most notably increases in rates of teenage pregnancy and the spread of sexually transmitted diseases. In July 2003, in an event to mark World Population Day, there was an explicit call for the protection of adolescents' right to health, information and services. The President of the United Nations General Assembly stated:

---

6 The Special Rapporteur on the Right to Health considers that it 'may take some years before the right to health enjoys the same currency as more established human rights': Report of the Special Rapporteur Paul Hunt, submitted in accordance with Commission resolution 2002/3, *The right of everyone to the enjoyment of the highest attainable standard of physical and mental health* (Geneva: United Nations, 2003) E/CN.4/2003/58, para 38.

7 Art 25.1.

8 Art 12.

9 Art 24(1).

10 In the Additional Protocol (1988).

11 Art 14(1).

12 United Nations Committee on Economic, Social and Cultural Rights, *General Comment: The right to the highest attainable standard of health*, E/C.12/2000/4 CESCR, para 12(b).

13 Ibid, para 23.

14 Art 11.2.

> Adolescence is a uniquely vulnerable period of life. It is a time when many young people confront sexual and reproductive health issues for the first time. They must deal with new pressures and new risks. And unless they are given the necessary support, they may not be able to make the informed decisions that lead to healthy lives.[15]

There can be little doubt that the most pressing concern facing the international community is the spread of HIV/AIDS.[16] States Parties are under a specific obligation to take measures for the 'prevention, treatment and control of epidemic, endemic, occupational and other diseases.'[17] The significance of education in tackling the HIV/AIDS crisis is repeatedly emphasised. The Committee on the Rights of the Child has issued a General Comment on HIV/AIDS which states that: 'education can and should empower children to protect themselves from the risk of HIV infection.'[18] A fundamental difficulty is the fact that many children do not have access to school at all and do not therefore have access to the information which they need. The Secretary General of the United Nations, Kofi Annan, has observed that without the benefit of education, children 'pay many times over the deadly price of not going to school.'[19] Moreover, the incidence of HIV/AIDS in the adult population can exacerbate the problem of non-school attendance, forcing orphans into parenting roles and depriving children of their teachers through AIDS-related deaths.[20]

Even where children do attend school, they do not always receive the information they require to protect themselves. The Committee on the Elimination of Discrimination against Women has expressed concern about the fact that adolescent girls are frequently denied access to the information necessary to ensure sexual health. It has emphasised that sexual and reproductive health education should be provided without discrimination 'by properly trained personnel in specially designed programmes that respect their right to privacy and

---

15 UN High Commissioner for Human Rights, Press Release, 11 July 2003. United Nations Committee on the Rights of the Child has also published a General Comment on the issue of adolescent health, *General Comment No. 4 (2003): Adolescent Health and Development in the context of the Convention on the Rights of the Child,* CRC/GC/2003/4.

16 The United Nations High Commissioner for Human Rights identified it as one the most pressing global concerns for public health and human rights: *Message on World AIDS Day,* 1 December 1999.

17 *International Covenant on Economic, Social and Cultural Rights* Art 12(c). Art 11(3) of the revised European Social Charter (1966) contains a similar provision.

18 United Nations Committee on the Rights of the Child, *General Comment No. 3 (2003): HIV/AIDS and the Rights of the Child,* CRC/GC/2003/1, para 18.

19 Address by the Secretary General of the United Nations, at the World Education Forum on 26 April 2000.

20 This is a problem in a number of African countries, such as Zambia. See, United Nations Committee on the Rights of the Child, *Concluding Observations: Zambia (*2003) CRC/C/15/Add.206.

confidentiality.'[21] The Committee on the Rights of the Child has repeatedly drawn attention to inadequacies in the content and coverage of sex education programmes.[22] Further obstacles can arise as a result of parental objections to the content of sex education programmes. This issue has been highlighted by the UN Special Rapporteur on the Right to Education who has stated that:

> Calls for children's right of access to information necessary for their self-protection are as numerous as are the objections and children pay a high price for disagreement amongst adults.[23]

Although the extent of parental influence over the content of school curriculum issues can be contentious, the position in international human rights law is clear. Children have a right to an effective education, and this trumps parental rights to have their children educated in accordance with their wishes. This point was clearly established in *Kjelsden, Busk Madsen and Pedersen* v *Denmark* (*Kjelsden*), where the European Court of Human Rights considered that a system of compulsory sex education did not interfere with a parent's right to have his or her child educated in accordance with his or her religious or philosophical convictions provided that the information was presented critically, pluralistically and objectively.[24] In spite of this, many countries continue to give parents an absolute right to withdraw their children from sex education classes, potentially negating children's right to education, to receive information and to have their views given weight. In view of this, the Special Rapporteur on the Right to Education has called for a careful examination of existing practices with a view to distilling the best options for promoting rights-based processes of teaching and learning in the best interest of each child.[25]

Although sex education has been the major focus of the international bodies, other health issues which impact on children have been highlighted. For instance, the Committee of Ministers of the Council of Europe has adopted a resolution on road safety education which called on member states to give road safety instruction systematically and in a stipulated number of hours.[26] The Committee on the Rights of the Child has also expressed concern that road traffic accidents

---

21 United Nations Committee on the Elimination of Discrimination against Women, *General Recommendation No. 24: Women and Health (Article 12)*, 2 February 1999, para 18.

22 See, for example, its criticism of Libya: United Nations Committee on the Rights of the Child, *Concluding Observations: Libyan Arab Jamahirya* (2003) CRC/C/15/Add.209.

23 Report of the Special Rapporteur on the Right to Education, submitted pursuant to Commission on Human Rights resolution 2002/23, *The Right to Education* (Geneva: United Nations, 2003). E/CN.4/2003/9, para 45.

24 (1976) 1 EHRR 711.

25 Above n 23.

26 Committee of Ministers Resolution (64)12.

affect adolescents disproportionately and has recommended that states should adopt programmes to improve road safety including driver education for young people.[27] The issue of substance abuse also receives considerable attention. Article 33 of the CRC requires states to take educational measures to 'protect children from the illicit use of narcotic drugs and psychotropic substances.' The Committee on the Rights of the Child has repeatedly emphasised the need for national educational strategies to prevent tobacco, alcohol and drug abuse among school children.[28] Moreover, the Parliamentary Assembly of the Council of Europe has made formal recommendations in relation to education for health and drug misuse.[29]

The Right to Protection from Harm: Ensuring Children's Safety and Well-Being While they are at School

The Committee of Ministers of the Council of Europe has stated that an essential element of an effective school health programme is: 'The ethos established at school or health in school. It is necessary to ensure that life within the school is consistent with the aims of the health education programme; it should ensure physical and mental health and good social relations.'[30] It is somewhat unfortunate that, while children need to be educated in order to stay healthy, attending school can in certain circumstances place children's well-being at risk. There are a number of factors which can increase children's vulnerability to illness or harm when they are at school. One of the most obvious is where the school buildings themselves are unsafe. The Committee on the Rights of the Child has observed that all states are required to 'provide well-functioning school and recreational facilities which do not pose health risks to students, including water and sanitation and safe journeys to school'[31] and has highlighted various instances where school estate places pupils at risk.[32] Other aspects of school life which may threaten children's well-being include unsafe practices and potentially inadequate supervision. The CRC requires states to protect children from injury[33] and to 'take appropriate measures to ensure that all segments of society, in particular parents and children, are informed, have access to education and are

---

27 Above n 15, para 21.

28 See, for example, its criticism of Denmark: United Nations Committee on the Rights of Child, *Concluding Observations: Denmark (*2003) CRC/C/15/Add. 151.

29 Recommendation 1169 (1991). *Recommendation on education for health and drug misuse in the member states of the Council of Europe and the European Community.*

30 *Recommendation No. R (88) 7, Recommendation on school health education and the role and training of teachers.*

31 Above n 15, para 17.

32 See, for example, its criticism of the lack of water, sanitation and electricity in schools in conflict-affected areas of Sri Lanka: United Nations Committee on the Rights of the Child, *Concluding Observations: Sri Lanka (*2003) CRC/C/15/Add.207.

33 Art 19(1).

supported in the use of basic knowledge of... hygiene and environmental sanitation and the prevention of accidents.'[34] The revised European Social Charter also requires states to take measures to prevent accidents.[35] The Special Rapporteur on the Right to Education has criticised China for exposing children to danger by allowing them to undertake work at school as means of compensating for a shortage of funds.[36]

Finally, children's vulnerability is increased at school through exposure to strangers, both adults and other pupils, whose actions may cause them harm. The most relevant human rights obligation in this area arises under Article 19 of the CRC which states that:

> States parties shall take all appropriate legislative, administrative, social and educational measures to protect the child from all forms of physical or mental violence, injury or abuse, neglect or negligent treatment, maltreatment or exploitation, including sexual abuse, while in the care of parents(s), legal guardian(s) or any other person who has the care of the child.

States Parties are required to include effective procedures for the identification, reporting, referral, investigation, treatment and follow-up of instances of child maltreatment and, as appropriate, for judicial involvement. Likewise the United Nations Commission on Human Rights has urged all states to 'take measures to protect pupils from violence, injury or abuse, including sexual abuse and intimidation in schools, to establish complaint mechanisms that are accessible to children and to undertake thorough and prompt investigations of all acts of violence and discrimination.'[37]

The area in which human rights law has made the biggest impact to date has undoubtedly been in relation to physical abuse within schools. The Universal Declaration,[38] ECHR[39] and CRC[40] all provide children with an absolute right not be subjected to torture, inhuman and degrading treatment. The interpretation of this provision, most notably by the ECHR, has effectively ended the use of corporal punishment in schools in many countries.[41] However, an issue which is receiving increasing attention is the protection of children from inter-pupil violence at school. The UN Special Rapporteur on the Right to Education, has

---

34 Art 24(2)(e).

35 Art 11(3).

36 Forty-two children and their teachers were killed when there was an explosion at their school while they were manufacturing fire-crackers. UN Special Rapporteur on the Right to Education, *Mission to the People's Republic of China*, E/CN.4/2004/45/Add.1, para 14.

37 *Resolution 2003/86 on the Rights of the Child.*

38 Art 5.

39 Art 3.

40 Art 37.

41 See, for instance, *Costello-Roberts v UK* (1993) 19 EHRR 112.

highlighted the impact of gun crime in schools in the United States. She has identified a need for schools to teach children to separate reality and virtual reality, observing that: 'It is adults who help children separate fact from fiction, and children take their emotional cue from adults.'[42] Moreover, a recent report has highlighted widespread physical violations against lesbian, gay, bisexual and transgendered students in schools in the United States.[43]

Article 19 of the CRC, which is set out above, requires states to protect children from 'mental violence.' Protection from mental abuse in other international covenants is not explicit, but instead derives largely from the general right to health, dignity and/or the right to be protected from degrading treatment. Perhaps the most relevant instance of this in relation to schools is the psychological impact of bullying. The Committee on the Rights of the Child has criticised the high incidence of bullying in schools in a number of State Parties including Spain, the United Kingdom, Switzerland, Germany and Denmark. Moreover, an issue which is beginning to receive attention is the mental health implications of stress caused by the over-work of pupils.[44] For instance, both the Committee on Economic Social and Cultural Rights and the Committee on the Rights of the Child have expressed concern about 'the frequently excessively competitive and stressful nature of all levels of education in Japan, which results in school absence, illness, and even suicide by students.'[45] Article 31 of the CRC, which gives children a right 'to rest and leisure, to engage in play and recreational activities appropriate to the age of the child and to participate freely in cultural life and the arts,' may also be relevant to the issue of sustained academic pressure.

The CRC contains specific provisions in relation to protection from sexual abuse. Article 34 requires State Parties to undertake to protect the child from all forms of sexual exploitation and sexual abuse, including 'the inducement of a child to engage in any unlawful sexual activity.' The Committee on the Rights of the Child has recommended that states adopt special measures to protect children who are most vulnerable to sexual abuse, such as children who have learning difficulties.[46] One way of protecting children from sexual abuse is to make sure that they attend school, as it is children outside the education system who are most vulnerable to sexual exploitation. However, it is recognised that children

---

42 UN Special Rapporteur on the Right to Education, *Mission to the United States of America*, E/CN.4/2002/60/Add.1, para 63.

43 Human Rights Watch, *Hatred in the Hallways: Violence and discrimination against lesbian, gay, bisexual and transgender students in US Schools* (New York: Human Rights Watch, 2001).

44 K. Tomaševski, *Education Denied: Costs and Remedies* (London: Zed Books, 2003), cites the example of Singapore, where one survey noted that children's greatest fear was failing examinations, placed ahead of their parents' death.

45 United Nations Committee on Economic, Social and Cultural Rights, *Concluding Observations: Japan* (2001) E/C.12/1/Add.67, para 31.

46 Above n 15, para 12.

also need protecting when in school. Instances of widespread sexual abuse in the school system have been highlighted by the international reporting bodies. The Committee on the Rights of Women has been particularly pro-active in identifying and criticising states where there is widespread sexual abuse of girls.[47] Likewise, non-governmental organisations have drawn attention to instances of institutionalised sexual harassment and abuse. For example, Human Rights Watch, an international non-governmental organisation, has recently published research documenting sexual violations against girls in South African schools.[48]

The Right to Inclusion: Access to Education for Children with Health-related Problems

Disability and ill-health are not necessarily the same thing.[49] Nonetheless, many children who are disabled have health problems which impact on their education. These children may derive some protection from the rights afforded to people with disabilities in international human rights law. For instance, Article 23 of the CRC states that assistance should be provided to ensure that the child has effective access to and receives education 'in a manner conducive to the child's achieving the fullest possible social integration and individual development.' In a similar vein, the Standard Rules on the Equalization of Opportunities for Disabled People, which have been adopted by the UN General Assembly, provide that 'States should recognize the principle of equal primary, secondary and tertiary educational opportunities for children, youth and adults with disabilities, in integrated settings.'[50] A survey by the United Nations Special Rapporteur on Disability on the operation of the Standard Rules highlighted the fact that many states have no legislation dealing with special educational needs; and that in other countries schooling for children with special educational needs is still provided predominantly in segregated environments.[51] The Committee on the

---

47 See, for example, the criticisms of the Committee on the Elimination of Discrimination against Women in its first report on Uganda: CEDW, A/50/38 31 May 1995, paras 335-336.

48 Human Rights Watch, *Scared at School: Sexual Violence against Girls in South African Schools* (New York: Human Rights Watch, 2001).

49 There is no internationally accepted definition of disability. However, the *Standard Rules on the Equalization of Opportunities for Disabled People,* annexed to General Assembly resolution 48/96 (1993), states that: 'people may be disabled by physical, intellectual or sensory impairment, medical condition or mental illness. Such impairments, conditions or illnesses may be permanent or transitory in nature' (para 17).

50 Rule 6.

51 Final report of the Special Rapporteur of the Commission for Social Development *Monitoring the implementation of the Standard Rules on the Equalization of Opportunities for Persons with Disabilities* (Geneva: United Nations, 2003) A/52/56 annex.

Rights of the Child has drawn attention regularly to instances where disabled children have no access to education or where they are simply institutionalised.[52]

In situations where there is specific educational provision made for children with disabilities, the key human rights issue tends to be whether such education is provided in mainstream schools or in special educational units i.e. focussing on the principle of integration. Both the ECHR and CRC are widely recognised as being relatively weak on this issue.[53] However, the European Social Charter gives persons with disabilities the right to independence, social integration and participation, 'irrespective of age and the nature and origin of their disabilities,' and requires states to undertake the necessary measures to provide persons with disabilities with education 'in the framework of general schemes wherever possible, or, where this is not possible, through specialised bodies.'[54] In the case of *Autism-Europe v France*, the European Committee of Social Rights upheld a complaint that France had breached this provision when it was considered in combination with Article E of the Charter which prohibits discrimination.[55] The Committee found that educational provision for children with autism in both mainstream and specialised schools in France was much lower than that for other children, whether disabled or not. It stated that the implementation of the Charter requires: 'not merely legal action but practical action to give full effect to the rights recognised in the Charter.'[56]

There is ongoing work to prepare a draft United Nations Convention on the Rights of Persons with Disabilities. In the meantime, the United Nations Special Rapporteur on Disability has advocated the incorporation of the recommendations in the Salamanca Statement and Framework for Action on Special Needs Education,[57] which provides that children with disabilities should have access to regular schools which can accommodate them within a child-centred pedagogy capable of meeting their needs. The Committee on Economic, Social and Cultural Rights has stated that in order to implement such a genuinely inclusive approach: 'States should ensure that teachers are trained to educate children with disabilities within regular schools and that the necessary equipment and support are available to bring persons with disabilities up to the same level of education as their non-disabled peers.'[58]

---

52 See, for example, its report on the Solomon Islands: United Nations Committee on the Rights of the Child, *Concluding Observations: Solomon Islands* (2003) CRC/C/15/Add.208.

53 For a critique of the CRC, see M. Freeman, 'The Future of Children's Rights' (2000) *Children and Society*, 14, 277-293.

54 Art 15.

55 Complaint No. 13/2002.

56 Ibid, para 52.

57 *Salamanca Statement on Principles, Policy and Practice in Special Needs Education* (Paris: UNESCO, 1994) ED-94/WS/18.

58 United Nations Committee on Economic, Social and Cultural Rights, *General Comment No. 5 (1994): Persons with Disabilities*.

One of the most frequently highlighted concerns in this context is the ongoing discrimination against children with HIV/AIDS, an issue explored in subsequent chapters of this book. The Committee on the Rights of the Child has highlighted a number of countries where children with HIV/AIDS are denied access to schools.[59] Education has a role to play in combating ignorance about HIV in order to reduce the stigmatisation which accompanies the disease. However, an additional difficulty is that discrimination on these grounds often falls outside domestic equality legislation.[60] In particular, protection can be lost in legal arguments about whether HIV and/or AIDS falls within the definition of 'disability' in domestic legislation. Although HIV/AIDS is not covered expressly in the international covenants, the United Nations has emphasised that: 'discrimination on the basis of HIV or AIDS status, actual or presumed, is prohibited by existing international human rights standards, and the term "or other status" in non-discrimination provisions in international human rights texts should be interpreted to cover health status, including HIV/AIDS.'[61] This means, for instance, that HIV/AIDS discrimination in access to education is prohibited by Article 14 of the European Convention on Human Rights taken in conjunction with the right to education in Article 2 of Protocol 1.

The Right to Participation: Giving Children's Views Due Weight

Article 12 of the CRC requires States Parties to 'assure to the child who is capable of forming his or her own views the right to express those views freely in all matters affecting the child, the views of the child being given due weight in accordance with the age and maturity of the child.' This applies to all decisions, including those which pertain to their health and/or their education. The right could be particularly significant in relation to sex education programmes, since participation in these often requires parental consent. The fact that the UK gives parents an absolute right to withdraw their children from sex education classes irrespective of the views of the child has been the subject of criticism by the Committee on the Rights of the Child.[62] More generally in the school

---

59 See, for example, its criticism of Jamaica: United Nations Committee on the Rights of the Child: *Concluding Observations: Jamaica (*2003) CRC/C/15/Add.210.

60 Almost 40 per cent of countries do not have anti-discrimination legislation protecting people living with HIV/AIDS: UNAIDS press release for the *11th International Conference for People Living with HIV/AIDS*, Uganda, 26 October 2003.

61 Commission on Human Rights Resolution 2003/47*: The Protection of human rights in the context of human immunodeficiency virus (HIV) and acquired immunodeficiency syndrome (AIDS)*. The Committee on the Rights of the Child has made the same observation: United Nations Committee on the Rights of the Child, *General Comment No. 3 (2003): HIV/AIDS and the Rights of the Child,* CRC/GC/2003/, para 9.

62 *Concluding Observations of the Committee on the Rights of the Child: United Kingdom of Great Britain and Northern Ireland* (1995) CRC/C/15/Add .34, para 14. The parental right of withdrawal from sex education was not mentioned specifically in

environment, Article 12 requires systematic attempts to ensure that pupils' voices are heard in the major decisions in the school, through the establishment of appropriate mechanisms for consulting with pupils such as student councils. This could have significant implications for the content of health education programmes (particularly on topics such as drugs or sex) which should not just reflect the views of adults who design or teach the programmes about what children should learn, but also the views of the pupils as to what they wish or need to know.

The Impact of the International Human Rights Standards

International human rights law has sufficient scope to advance children's rights on most health and education related issues. The coverage and substance of the rights are not at issue. What can be questioned is whether the international frameworks actually make a difference at a local level. The difficulties in measuring the impact of human rights treaties are considerable.[63] However, it is evident that their capacity to secure change within individual countries is made more difficult by the fact that both the right to education and the right to health suffer from two characteristics which are common to all socio-economic rights: indeterminacy and resource-dependence. Many international human rights provisions are worded in very general terms, sometimes to the point of vagueness. This is especially true in relation to socio-economic rights. The potential impact of these rights is considered to be so significant that they can be negotiated into an increasing level of abstraction in order to secure agreement amongst the signatories. The eventual wording of the right to education in the ECHR as a negative formulation (i.e. 'no-one shall be denied the right to education') is a particularly good example of this.[64] What can emerge is a type of 'lowest common denominator' phrasing which encourages as many states as possible to sign up in spite of their concerns about the budgetary implications of ensuring the right for all citizens.

In recognition of the fact that resources are a crucial factor in the implementation of socio-economic rights, states are usually expected to implement them progressively. The concept of progressive realisation derives

---

the 2002 report on the United Kingdom even though there has been no change to the law since the Committee last reported.

63 See, O. Hathaway, 'Do Human Rights Treaties Make A Difference?' (2002) *Yale Law Journal*, 112, 1935-2025 for an argument that ratification is associated with worse human rights practice. This is critiqued in R. Goodman and D. Jinks, 'Measuring the effects of human rights treaties' (2003) *European Journal of International Law*, 14, 171-183.

64 For a discussion of the negotiation process, see, D.J. Harris, M. O'Boyle and C. Warbrick, *The Law of the European Convention on Human Rights* (2nd edn) (London: Butterworths, 2001).

from the International Covenant on Economic, Social and Cultural Rights, Article 2 of which requires State Parties 'to take steps ... to the maximum of its available resources, with a view to achieving the full realization of the rights recognized in this present Covenant by all appropriate means, including particularly the adoption of legislative measures.' The CRC is arguably more limited still as it requires states to implement economic and social rights 'to the maximum extent of their available resources and, where needed, within the framework of international cooperation.'[65] Effectively, this means that what can be expected of the state will vary in particular contexts and over time. For sceptics, this is simply a get-out which allows states to be human-rights compliant, regardless of the levels of protection they offer. It has also been questioned whether the rights are so contingent upon resources that they are 'deprived of any normative significance.'[66] However, as the Special Rapporteur on the Right to Health has stressed: 'progressive realization means that states have a specific and continuing obligation to move as expeditiously and effectively as possible towards the full realization of the right to health.'[67] Moreover, he has emphasised that progressive realisation entails a number of basic and immediate commitments: the principle of minimum core content (i.e. that people cannot be deprived of the basic assistance they need to live in dignity) and the principle of non-regression (i.e. that the state cannot act in such a way as to make the prevailing conditions worse). In addition, there is an immediate obligation to ensure that there is no discrimination in terms of access to the services and assistance provided, however limited that may be. Nonetheless, a crucial factor in the success of a strategy of progressive realisation is a set of enforcement mechanisms which ensure that compliance is being independently monitored and that there is sustained international pressure to advance. The efficacy of three of these mechanisms—complaints mechanisms, monitoring by the United Nations treaty bodies and Special Rapporteurs—is assessed below.

Complaints Mechanisms

The scope for individuals to make complaints about breaches of international human rights law is very limited.[68] A notable exception is the European Convention on Human Rights. Although there have been very few cases involving schools which have been considered by the European Court of Human

65 Article 4. For a critique of this, see J. Todres, 'Emerging Limitations on the Rights of the Child: The United Nations Convention on the Rights of the Child and its early case law' (1998) *Columbia Human Rights Law Review,* 30, 159-200, at 177.

66 P. Alston and G. Quinn, 'The Nature and Scope of States Parties' Obligations Under the International Covenant on Economic, Social and Cultural Rights' (1987) *Human Rights Quarterly, 9,* 159-229.

67 Above n 6, para 27.

68 The International Covenant on Social, Economic and Cultural Rights does not yet have procedure for individual or group complaints.

Rights, two of these have resulted in significant decisions which are directly relevant to the issue of pupils' health. The Court's decision to uphold a system of compulsory sex education in *Kjelsden, Busk Madsen and Pedersen v Denmark*[69] (noted above) has been criticised for its restrictive approach to parental rights, but it could also be construed as a landmark decision for children's right to health-related education. Moreover, the Court's decision that parents had the right to object to corporal punishment in *Campbell and Cosans v United Kingdom*, paved the way for the abolition of corporal punishment in many European states.[70] Other applications, particularly those which have significant spending implications for government, have not fared as well. In particular, a series of applications by parents seeking to secure education in mainstream schools for children with special educational needs have been deemed inadmissible by the European Commission on Human Rights.[71]

Individual cases on the right to health at an international level are rare: the conventions in which the right to health appears rarely make provision for individual complaints. Nonetheless, the ECHR is being used in ever more imaginative ways to advance rights not specifically protected with the text. For example, in *Lopez Ostra v Spain* the European Court of Human Rights accepted that environmental harm to human health (caused by contamination from a waste treatment plant) may constitute a violation of the right (under Article 8) to a home and family life.[72] In the light of this, it is possible to envisage a successful argument about unsafe school buildings violating the right to education. Moreover, cases involving arguments about the right to health are likely to increase. The Special Rapporteur on the Right to Health has indicated his intention to examine the legal frameworks 'with a view of clarifying the contours and content of the right to health and identifying good practice in relation to its implementation.'[73] An increasing number of national constitutions are including provisions on the right to health or access to health care and much can be learnt from the interpretation of these in the domestic courts. It can be anticipated that, as the jurisprudence of the national judicial authorities and courts such as the European Court of Human Rights evolves, other issues are likely to emerge. For instance, given the considerable progress which is being made in the field of children's participation rights, it is possible that children will begin to initiate human rights challenges based on the quality of their education or school environment; complaining about discriminatory treatment; or arguing that there has been a breach of their right to freedom of conscience or to receive information when parents withhold them from health education classes on the basis of religious objections to the content of the course of study.

---

69 Above n 24.

70 (1982) 4 EHRR 293.

71 See, for example, *PD & LD v UK* (1989) 62 DR 292.

72 [1994] IIHRL 106.

73 Above n 6, 39.

An interesting development in this area is the collective complaints procedure under the revised European Social Charter (1996). This allows designated non-governmental organisations to file complaints against State Parties for breaches of the Charter. For instance, in the first case of this kind, *International Commission on Jurists v Portugal*, the European Committee of Social Rights considered that there had been a breach of Article 15 (which prohibits the employment of children under 15) when children worked in a sector which had negative consequences on their health and development.[74] In *Autism-Europe v France*, discussed earlier, the Committee found inadequate levels of educational provision for people with autism to be in breach of Article 15 and 17 of the European Social Charter when considered in combination with Article E which prohibits discrimination.[75] More recently, the World Organisation Against Torture (OMCT) has lodged five complaints (against Belgium, Portugal, Italy, Ireland and Greece) arguing that the failure to protect children from corporal punishment is a breach of Article 17 of the revised Charter (which includes the right to economic and social protection).[76] The benefit of this kind of depersonalised 'representative action' is apparent; it does not depend on the existence of an affected individual who is sufficiently motivated to tolerate the stress, delay and personal expense which often accompanies the process of pursuing an individual complaint.

Monitoring by the United Nations Treaty Bodies

One of the main human rights implementation mechanisms is the system of periodic reporting on State Party compliance by the United Nations Treaty Bodies—committees attached to specific United Nations conventions. These have addressed a number of health and education-related issues. For example, the wide range of socio-economic rights protected in the International Covenant on Economic, Social and Cultural Rights has enabled the Committee on Economic, Social and Cultural rights to take a multi-layered view of health and education related issues. For instance, in its commentary on Poland, the Committee recommended: 'the adoption of legislation in order to regulate child labour in rural areas in such a way that the right to health and right to education of working children are fully protected.'[77] Other Committees can focus on issues relevant to particular groups. The Committee on the Elimination of Discrimination Against Women regularly highlights issues relating to teenage pregnancy and the sexual abuse of girls and the Committee on Racial Discrimination has criticised differential provision for particular minority groups.

74 Complaint No. 1/1998.

75 Complaint No. 13/2002.

76 Complaint Nos. 17- 21/2003.

77 United Nations Committee on Economic, Social and Cultural Rights, *Concluding Observations: Poland* (2002) E/C.12/1/Add.82, para 23.

The most relevant reporting structure in the context of this discussion is undoubtedly that of the Committee on the Rights of the Child. It is not surprising that health and education issues are prevalent in all of the reports of the CRC committees.[78] The precise focus of criticisms varies considerably, as can be seen from a review of the issues highlighted in some of the most recent country reports:

Indonesia: violence, abuse and neglect, including sexual abuse in schools; high levels of bullying and fighting among students; widespread corporal punishment; lack of education on HIV/AIDS and sexually transmitted diseases; drug abuse.[79]

Guyana: corporal punishment in schools; lack of integration into mainstream education of children with disabilities; need to address the issue of malnutrition through education; high levels of teenage pregnancy and drug abuse; high rates of HIV/AIDS among children.[80]

Germany: a growing problem of violence at school; widespread abuse of drugs, alcohol and tobacco among children; high incidence of suicide among children and adolescents.[81]

The Kingdom of the Netherlands (Netherlands and Aruba): a need to improve the physical accessibility of mainstream schools in Aruba; prevalence of drug and alcohol abuse; primary education is not compulsory in Aruba.[82]

Japan: the fact that corporal punishment in schools, although illegal, is widely practised; lack of integration of children with disabilities in the school system; prevalence of mental and emotional disorders among adolescents; high levels of youth suicide; the negative effect on children's physical and emotional health of the excessively competitive education system; bullying.[83]

---

78 For an overview of its work in the area of children's health see, J. Doek, 'Children and Their Right to Enjoy Health: A Brief Report on the Monitoring Activities of the Committee of The Rights of the Child', (2001), *Health and Human Rights*, 5/2, 155-173.

79 United Nations Committee on the Rights of the Child, *Concluding Observations: Indonesia (*2004) CRC/C/15/Add.223.

80 United Nations Committee on the Rights of the Child, *Concluding Observations: Guyana (*2004) CRC/C/15/Add.224.

81 United Nations Committee on the Rights of the Child, *Concluding Observations: Germany (*2004) CRC/C/15/Add.226.

82 United Nations Committee on the Rights of the Child, *Concluding Observations: The Kingdom of the Netherlands (Netherlands and Aruba) (*2004) CRC/C/15/Add.227.

83 United Nations Committee on the Rights of the Child, *Concluding Observations: Japan (*2004) CRC/C/15/Add. 331.

San Marino: high levels of obesity among children.[84]

Canada: corporal punishment is not unlawful; high rates of suicide and substance abuse among Aboriginal population.[85]

New Zealand: a prevalence of child abuse; high levels of youth suicide, teenage pregnancies and alcohol abuse; lack of integration of children with disabilities into mainstream education.[86]

Pakistan: widespread corporal punishment in schools; limited integration of children with disabilities in schools; very poor health situation of children generally; lack of adequate health education; violence and sexual abuse in 'madrasas' (an alternative non-public form of education); high rates of drug abuse.[87]

Madagascar: corporal punishment of children is not unlawful in schools; need for better reproductive health education and mental health services for adolescents; limited access to education for children with disabilities; lack of playgrounds at schools.[88]

In almost all of its reports, the Committee on the Rights of the Child will draw attention to deficiencies in sex education programmes, adolescent health strategies and the measures adopted to secure the inclusion of children with disabilities. However, in the developing world or in countries which have a high incidence of poverty (as is the case in many of the countries set out above), the Committee's concerns often focus on problems with malnutrition, access to safe water and economic and sexual exploitation. In contrast, a review of the Committee's comments in more affluent societies highlights a different set of concerns. Thus, concerns about eating disorders and obesity replace those about malnutrition; the psychological effects of bullying or examination stress are highlighted rather than the psychological effects of child soldiering; high rates of suicide are criticised rather than high rates of infant mortality; and road traffic accidents are noted as disproportionately high instead of deaths from violence in

84 United Nations Committee on the Rights of the Child, *Concluding Observations: San Marino* (2004) CRC/C/15/Add. 214.

85 United Nations Committee on the Rights of the Child, *Concluding Observations: Canada* (2004) CRC/C/15/Add. 215.

86 United Nations Committee on the Rights of the Child, *Concluding Observations: New Zealand* (2004) CRC/C/15/Add. 216.

87 United Nations Committee on the Rights of the Child, *Concluding Observations: Pakistan* (2004) CRC/C/15/Add. 217.

88 United Nations Committee on the Rights of the Child, *Concluding Observations: Madagascar* (2004) CRC/C/15/Add. 218.

the home or institutions. This can be seen in the criticisms of a selected number of European countries set out below:

Cyprus: the impact of enforced separation from parents by children having to attend boarding schools at secondary level due to the island's separation in 1974; high levels of adolescent consumption of alcohol, tobacco and drugs; integration of children with disabilities.[89]

United Kingdom: a prevalence of violence, including sexual violence in schools; high rates of teenage pregnancy; high rates of suicide; fact that homosexual and transsexual young people do not have access to appropriate information.[90]

Spain: widespread bullying; the negative impact of terrorism.[91]

Switzerland: bullying; high rates of adolescent suicide; road traffic accidents; drug abuse.[92]

Greece: road traffic accidents; high rates of domestic poisoning; high incidence of tobacco and alcohol use; institutionalisation of children with disabilities; wide use of abortion; lack of gymnasium and sports facilities; petrol and glue sniffing.[93]

Portugal: a high incidence of teenage pregnancy; lack of information on abortions; high incidence of AIDS/HIV including mother to child transmission; lack of investment in physical activities for children in school; substance abuse.[94]

Denmark: high incidence of eating disorders, drug, alcohol and tobacco abuse and suicides; bullying and sexual abuse in schools.[95]

---

89 United Nations Committee on the Rights of the Child, *Concluding Observations: Cyprus* (2003) CRC/C/15/Add.205.

90 United Nations Committee on the Rights of the Child, *Concluding Observations: United Kingdom of Great Britain and Northern Ireland* (2002) CRC/C/15/Add.188.

91 United Nations Committee on the Rights of the Child, *Concluding Observations: Spain* (2002) CRC/C/15/Add.185.

92 United Nations Committee on the Rights of the Child, *Concluding Observations: Switzerland* (2002) CRC/C/15/Add.182.

93 United Nations Committee on the Rights of the Child, *Concluding Observations: Greece* (2003) CRC/C/15/Add.170.

94 United Nations Committee on the Rights of the Child, *Concluding Observations: Portugal* (2001) CRC/C/15/Add.162.

95 United Nations Committee on the Rights of the Child, *Concluding Observations: Denmark* (2003) CRC/C/15/Add.151.

Ireland: high incidence of teenage suicide; drug and alcohol abuse; early pregnancies.[96]

It is generally recognised that the enforcement and monitoring mechanisms of the United Nations Treaty System are in need of an overhaul.[97] The periodic reporting system has particular weaknesses: there is a back-log of reports; the reports themselves often lack detail; and there are insufficient resources to ensure adequate follow-up of the recommendations.[98] Nonetheless, Landsdown has observed that the Committee's success has exceeded expectations since it has 'sought to enhance the understanding of the indivisibility of the human rights of children, has strengthened the relationship between the international and national monitoring systems; and has engaged NGOs as critical actors in promoting and monitoring children's rights.'[99] While the Committee cannot guarantee compliance, its Concluding Observations have a major role to play in focusing States Parties' (and world) attention on the key weaknesses in their implementation strategies. Moreover, the extensive range of issues raised by the Committee on the Rights of the Child is indicative of one of the key strengths of the CRC, namely its scope. It is at this point that the indeterminacy of many of the provisions has its advantages, allowing the Committee sufficient leeway to address a wide range of issues in their specific social context. Moreover, in all of its Concluding Observations the Committee reports on progress under specific headings which include: resources; co-ordination; the national plan of action; independent monitoring; data collection and training and dissemination. There are repeated calls for individual states to increase health and education spending; to produce a National Children's Strategy; and to establish an office or body for the protection of children's rights such as that of a Children's Commissioner. The advances which can be made in children's rights at these macro-levels are potentially of huge significance when decisions are made within the specific policy and legal contexts of health and education.

The UN Special Rapporteurs

The United Nations has the power to appoint Special Rapporteurs to report on human rights compliance within particular themes. It has recently appointed a

---

96 United Nations Committee on the Rights of the Child, *Concluding Observations: Ireland* (1998) CRC/C/15/Add.85.

97 See, A. Bayefsky, *The UN Human Rights Treaty System: Universality at the Crossroads* (The Hague: Klewer Law International, 2001).

98 See, Z. Kedzia, 'United Nations Mechanisms to Promote and Protect Human Rights,' in J. Symonides (ed.), *Human Rights: International Protection, Monitoring and Enforcement* (Aldershot: Ashgate, 2003), 3-90, at pp 30-37.

99 G. Landsdown, 'The Reporting Process Under the Convention on the Rights of the Child', in P. Alston and J. Crawford (eds), *The Future of the UN Human Rights Treaty Monitoring*, (Cambridge: Cambridge University Press, 2000), 113-128, p 127.

Special Rapporteur on the Right to Health. He has acknowledged that the right to health includes a right of: 'access to health related education and information, including on sexual and reproductive health.'[100] However, given the scale of the task which confronts him, he has decided to focus initially on the impact of poverty on the right to health and on the impact of discrimination and stigma rather than on the education-related dimensions of the right. This may be partly due to the fact that the UN Special Rapporteur on the Right to Education (appointed in 1998) had repeatedly highlighted health-related issues in her general reports to the United Nations and in the reports of her missions to individual countries. The health-related issues highlighted by her in some of her *in situ* reports are summarised below.

Uganda The Special Rapporteur praised Uganda for its success in halting the spread of HIV infection through a concerted educational strategy.[101] Her criticism was directed to the ongoing use of corporal punishment in schools, expressing her concern about the effects of the 'exposure of Ugandan children to violence whether it is manifested in corporal punishment in the family and in school, or in abuse of children in armed conflicts' and her hope that there would be an initiative 'to rupture inter-generational transmission of such a culture of violence.'[102]

England The Special Rapporteur highlighted the high numbers of teenage pregnancies and related that to the lack of consistency in sex education in state schools (in particular the fact that parents can opt children out of sex education and that primary schools do not have to provide sex education at all). She argued that the obstacles which were cited as preventing the introduction of compulsory sex education had been overcome in other countries and that: 'Governmental human rights obligations stemming from the best interests of the child and the goal of gender equality impose upon the government the obligation to take the lead in overcoming such obstacles.'[103]

Indonesia The Special Rapporteur expressed concern about the fact that very few children with disabilities attend regular schools. Moreover, only 0.1 per cent of

---

100 Above n 6, para 23.

101 UN Special Rapporteur on the Right to Education, *Mission to Uganda*, E/CN.4/2000/6/Add.1, para 86. She was, however, critical of the policy of excluding child mothers from school.

102 Ibid, para 84.

103 UN Special Rapporteur on the Right to Education, *Mission to the United Kingdom of Great Britain and Northern Ireland (England)* 18-22 October 1999, E/CN.4/2000/6/Add.2, para 80.

children attended special schools in spite of statistics indicating that the global average of children with special needs in the population was one in ten.[104]

The United States The Special Rapporteur highlighted concerns with 'premature sexuality' criticising the US's domestic and international policy on this issue: 'Internationally, the United States has been curtailing foreign aid lest it facilitate access to abortion and domestically, advocating abstinence rather than sex education. That such advocacy hurts rather than helps is shown by the large numbers of new HIV infections and high rates of child pregnancy.'[105] She also drew attention to the high levels of violence in schools. In her view, 'in-school and out-of school messages often conflict. Studies into violence have revealed that youth who observe adults accepting violence as a solution to problems are apt to emulate that violence.'[106]

The United Nations Special Rapporteur system is widely regarded as an important weapon in the arsenal of human rights monitoring mechanisms. It gives independent experts the opportunity to take multi-disciplinary perspectives on a specific area of concern with individual countries. The Rapporteurs are, however, devoid, of any specific powers of investigation or enforcement, which some would suggest hampers their efficacy. The Special Rapporteur on the Right to Education has recently resigned, citing her frustration at the obstacles and difficulties in carrying out her mandate.[107] Moreover, the Secretary General of United Nations has advocated changes to improve the quality of the reports and the administrative and specialist support available to the Rapporteurs.[108] In spite of the acknowledged weaknesses, the UN is committed to retaining the role of the Special Rapporteur, thus enabling immediate, independent and *in situ* investigations on issues of specific concern, something which is not feasible within the periodic reporting procedures attached to the CRC.

Conclusion

A global survey of the state of children's health begs the question whether the international covenants or the extensive efforts which go into reporting on human rights compliance within individual countries actually make any difference to the

---

104 UN Special Rapporteur on the Right to Education, *Mission to Indonesia*, E/CN/4/2003/9/Add.1.

105 UN Special Rapporteur on the Right to Education, *Mission to the United States of America*, E/CN.4/2002/60/Add.1, para 31.

106 Ibid, para 62-63.

107 *Report of the Special Rapporteur on the Right to Education* (Geneva: UN, 2004) E/CN.4/2004/45.

108 UN Secretary General, *Strengthening of the United Nations: an agenda for further change* (Geneva: UN, 2002). A/57/387, paras 56-57.

quality of children's lives in and out of school. Some of the statistics published by the World Health Organisation make for bleak reading:

- Injury is the leading cause of death and disability among school-age youth.
- One out of two young people who start and continue to smoke will be killed by tobacco-related illness.
- Worldwide, five per cent of all deaths of young people between the ages of 15 and 29 are attributable to alcohol use.
- In some countries, up to 60 per cent of all new HIV infections occur among 15-24 year olds.[109]

There is an apparent gulf in the rhetoric of the international human rights covenants and the reality of many children's lived experience. One of the difficulties is that the right to education and the right to health are not only co-dependent but they are also contingent upon the ability of the state to fulfil its obligations in relation to a third key socio-economic right—the right to an adequate standard of living.[110] The biggest challenge for many countries in securing education, health and their associated benefits is the challenge posed by poverty, whether that manifests itself country-wide or within certain social groups or regions:

> Children are hardest hit by poverty because it strikes at the very roots of their potential for development—their growing bodies and minds.[111]

The Special Rapporteur on the Right to Health has indicated that one of his key priorities for office will be to focus on the relationship between poverty and ill-health. He has observed that 'ill-health is both a cause and consequence of poverty: sick people are more likely to become poor, and the poor are more vulnerable to disease and disability.'[112] The same might be said about the relationship between education and poverty. Those who have not received an adequate education are most likely to be poor and the poor are least likely to be able to access and derive full benefit from education. Moreover, as was observed earlier, inadequate education can lead to ill-health just as ill-health can impinge on a child's capacity to benefit from education. Denial of rights in any one of the

---

109 Source: www.who.int/school_youth-health/en/.

110 Art 11 of the International Covenant on Economic, Social and Cultural Rights recognises the right of everyone to 'an adequate standard of living for himself and his family, including adequate food, clothing and housing, and to the continuous improvement of living conditions.'

111 United Nations, *A World Fit For Children* (Geneva: UN, 2002) S-27/2 annex. para 18.

112 P. Hunt, 'The UN Special Rapporteur on the Right to Health: Key Objectives, Themes and Interventions' (2003) *Health and Human Rights*, 7, 1-27, 6.

three areas will inevitably diminish a child's capacity to derive full enjoyment of the others. However, it is arguable that the inevitability and potentially devastating impact of poverty makes the argument for securing specific rights within the areas of health and education even more compelling. Human rights law cannot guarantee that all children will have access to an adequate standard of living any more than it can ensure that they stay well in and out of school. What it can do is to set standards which can be harnessed by those wanting to effect change, albeit that advances might at times be piecemeal or incremental. In this respect, international human rights principles can be deployed in a number of ways, both within individual jurisdictions and internationally.

First, within individual jurisdictions, the human rights principles can be used as a blue print to shape new laws and practices. The ratification of human rights treaties is seen to play an important role in building human rights cultures within individual states by 'increasing the salience and legitimacy of human rights norms.'[113] In particular, the principles can be used to guide the content of new laws on specific issues such as the substance of sex education programmes or on ensuring inclusion rights for children with disabilities. Moreover, even where the international provisions are not directly enforceable in the domestic courts, their legal significance is enhanced by the general principle that the obligations may be used to interpret domestic legislation on the presumption that the state will not have intended to legislate in such a way that it is in breach of its international obligations. Additionally, the principles underlying the CRC should be used to secure children's participation in the process with the result that their interests and views are mainstreamed into the policy and pre-legislative debates. Moreover, the international framework is of particular significance when new constitutional arrangements are being drawn up. A good example is the high profile given to socio-economic rights in the South African Final Constitution, resulting in a justiciable right of access to health care.[114] Moreover, in Northern Ireland, there is currently a major consultation on the content of a proposed Bill of Rights to supplement the rights in the ECHR. The proposals, which include a specific right of access to health care, have been tailored directly from the relevant international human rights covenants.[115] The major advantage of the

---

113 R. Goodman and D. Jinks, op cit n 63.

114 See J. Sarkin, 'The Drafting of South Africa's Final Constitution from a Human Rights Perspective' (1999) *American Journal of Comparative Law,* 47, 67-87.

115 The proposed right to health reads as follows:
'1. Everyone is entitled to the highest attainable standard of physical and mental health and well-being.
2. Government shall take all reasonable steps to promote good health and well-being, and to ensure adequate prevention and treatment of ill-health.
3. Equality of access to health promotion, treatment and prevention of ill-health shall be assured.
4. Everyone has the right to be consulted about decisions which affect his or her physical or mental health.

constitutionalisation of international norms is that it paves the way for challenges in the domestic courts.[116]

Secondly, the standards can be harnessed by non-governmental organisations and others campaigning for change to highlight gaps in provision within specific jurisdictions. NGO involvement is seen as a crucial element in the implementation of human rights, fulfilling a number of basic but essential roles, most notably the monitoring and identification of breaches. International NGOs such as Save the Children and Human Rights Watch regularly publish reports highlighting abuses of schoolchildren's rights world-wide. For example, Human Rights Watch has recently published reports highlighting violence against gay and lesbian pupils in schools in the United States and the sexual harassment and abuse of girls in the South African school system.[117] The backing of the international human rights covenants allows non-governmental organisations to engage in rights-based rather than needs-based advocacy. The claim that there has been a breach of international human rights law—sometimes evidenced by the comments of the independent treaty monitoring bodies—can add both legal and moral weight to the argument for change. The possibility of doing this in a cross-jurisdictional way, presented by the European Social Charter, is an exciting new development.[118]

The significance of the international provisions at a global level operates in various ways. First, the international standards combine to create a international normative framework which is influential both horizontally (inter-state) and vertically (through its influence on domestic practice). In this respect, the international human rights documents have what has been described as a 'global expressive function.'[119] A second key contribution derives from their capacity to prompt States Parties to reflect critically on their current practices and to attempt to improve upon existing levels of provision. Many countries will be minded to comply with their international promises as a direct result of the political embarrassment which accompanies the public disclosure of non-compliance. The

---

5. Everyone has the right to have equal and free access to sexual and reproductive health care and to information and education relating to sexual and reproductive matters at all levels, free of coercion, discrimination or violence.'

116 J. Dugard, 'The Role of Human Rights Treaty Standards in Domestic Law - The South African Experience, chapter 12 in P. Alston and J. Crawford (eds), *The Future of the UN Human Rights Treaty Monitoring*, (Cambridge: Cambridge University Press, 2000), 269-286.

117 Human Rights Watch, *Hatred in the Hallways: Violence and discrimination against lesbian, gay, bisexual and transgender students in US schools* (New York: Human Rights Watch, 2001); Idem, *Scared at School: Sexual Violence against Girls in South African Schools* (New York: Human Rights Watch, 2001).

118 See the collection of actions taken by the World Organisation Against Torture under the collective complaints procedure in the revised European Social Charter, described above at note 75.

119 Above n 63.

various systems for the identification and exposure of breaches of human rights discussed above maintain pressure on individual states to comply with the international norms. The significance of the world-wide 'name and shame' strategy which characterises the reports of the UN treaty bodies and Special Rapporteurs cannot be underestimated, particularly where the country in question is trying to forge new economic and political alliances. However, perhaps their most significant contribution at a practical level lies in their capacity to marshal inter-state cooperation on the major global challenges to the protection of human rights, such as the spread of HIV/AIDS. This is not just a lofty political aspiration—it is in itself a binding international human rights obligation. The International Covenant on Social, Economic and Cultural Rights requires each State Party to take steps to ensure the rights contained within it 'individually and through international assistance and co-operation, especially economic and technical, to the maximum of its available resources.'[120] The CRC also requires measures to be taken 'where needed, within the framework of international co-operation.'[121] The Committee on the Rights of the Child regularly criticises wealthier countries for failing to place sufficient proportions of GDP into international development.[122] It also guides countries who are struggling with compliance towards the technical assistance which can be offered by organisations such as UNICEF, the WHO and UNAIDS.[123]

The Vienna Declaration issued at the 1993 World Conference on Human Rights emphasised the pressing need for international co-ordination on children's rights, observing that 'the rights of the child should be a priority in the United Nations system-wide action on human rights.'[124] In 2002, in 'A World Fit For Children', the global community agreed a set of specific targets for improving children's lives. In doing so, it was emphasised that the stated objectives were not just well-intentioned aspirations but realistic and attainable objectives:

> Promoting healthy lives including good nutrition and control of infectious diseases, providing quality education, protecting children from abuse, exploitation, violence and armed conflict, and combating HIV/AIDS are achievable goals and are clearly affordable for the global community.[125]

---

120 Art 2.

121 Art 4.

122 Above n 81, para 21-22. The Committee expressed concerned over Germany's low allocation of GDP to overseas development assistance and encouraged it to increase its contribution to the UN target of 0.7 per cent.

123 J. Doek, 'Children and Their Right to Enjoy Health: A Brief Report on the Monitoring Activities of the Committee of The Rights of the Child' (2001), *Health and Human Rights*, 5/2, 155-173.

124 United Nations, *The Vienna Declaration and Programme of Action* (Geneva: UN, 1993) A/Conf.157/23, para 21.

125 Above n 111, para 48.

A crucial dimension to the success of this strategy is the need to share and disseminate good practice, a finding which underlines the value and significance of this essay collection.

PART II
SPECIAL RISK FACTORS: BULLYING AND DRUGS

Chapter 2

Pupil Bullying, Mental Health and the Law in England

Neville Harris

Introduction

> Bullying is harmful to all involved, not just the bullied, and can sometimes lead to self doubt, lack of confidence, low self esteem, depression, anxiety, self harm and sometimes even suicide.[1]

This statement was made by the Anti-Bullying Alliance, which represents 40 children's charities in the UK. The Alliance, formed in July 2002, aims to give greater weight, through collective representation, to independent campaigns to ensure that there is a more secure and healthy environment for children's education and development. Bullying is both an educational and a social problem, but its most serious effects are to the health of pupils and particularly their mental health. It takes many forms, but of particular concern is the evidence that some bullying has racial or homophobic overtones.[2] The impact of bullying has been well researched and some of the evidence is highlighted in this chapter. Evidence that an increasing number of school pupils have problems such as anxiety and depression[3] and that this is causing considerable difficulties not only for the pupils themselves but also schools, who are responsible for the management of pupil behaviour and (jointly with local education authorities (LEAs)) for the welfare of pupils, has made the remediation of bullying particularly urgent.

Bullying of school pupils by their peers is a world-wide problem; and it has been highlighted in a number of reports on European states by the UN Committee

---

1 Anti-Bullying Alliance, *Statement of Purpose* (London: Anti-Bullying Alliance, 2003).

2 N. Douglas et al, *Playing it Safe: Response of Secondary School Teachers to Lesbian and Gay Pupils, Bullying, HIV and AIDS Education and Section 28* (London: Health and Education Research Unit, Institute of Education, University of London, 1998). See A. Mulholland, 'Tackling homophobic bullying in schools', *Sex Education Matters*, Winter 2003, pp 5-6 for discussion of an initiative to deal with the problem in North-West England.

3 Office for Standards in Education (Ofsted), *The Education of Pupils with Medical Needs* HMI 1713 (London: Ofsted, 2003), para 11.

on the Rights of the Child.[4] In the UK, various initiatives have been introduced by the government over the past decade. The children who experience bullying today might be seen as providing evidence of the failure of these policies. Indeed, according to Harber, some of the blame rests with schools: they are 'implicated in violence by omission in relation to bullying.'[5] Nonetheless, bullying has proven to be an entrenched problem, often resistant to outside pressure.

Increasingly, the law in England is playing its part in efforts to control bullying and compensate its victims. In addition to the legislation that imposes obligations on schools to take steps to prevent misbehaviour generally and bullying specifically, there are other areas of the general law relevant to bullying and its effects, notably criminal law and tort. Case-law developments in relation to the latter show that irrespective of the moral and social arguments for dealing with bullying there are increasingly powerful legal imperatives for doing so. The framework of rights laid down under international treaty obligations, especially the European Convention on Human Rights (whose principal provisions have, in effect, been incorporated into English Law) and the afore-mentioned UN Convention on the Rights of the Child, are also highly relevant in this context. By threatening health and general well-being, bullying also prejudices full enjoyment of the right to education by undermining the child's capacity to learn in school.

Definitions and Forms of Bullying

The word 'bullying' appears in only one place in education law in England, in section 61 of the School Standards and Framework 1998. This sets out the responsibilities of head teachers regarding the taking of disciplinary measures within a school (see below) and includes, within the measures to be taken, ones aimed at 'encouraging good behaviour and respect for others on the part of pupils and, in particular, preventing all forms of bullying among pupils.' But the term 'bullying' is not defined. In a leading Court of Appeal judgment, Judge LJ said: 'There is no magic in the term bullying'[6] and the courts have not regarded it as necessary to provide a definition.

Looking beyond the legal sphere, researchers' and educational practitioners' definitions of bullying may diverge. Indeed, teachers and education authorities may well adopt their own definitions of bullying when devising strategies for

---

4 P K. Smith and S. Sharp, *School bullying: insights and perspectives* (London: Routledge, 1994); R. Forero et al, 'Bullying behaviour and psychosocial health among school students in New South Wales, Australia: cross sectional survey', *British Medical Journal* (1999) 319: 344-348; C. Harber, *Schooling as Violence* (London: Routledge Falmer, 2004), 47-49. As regards UN Committee on the Rights of the Child reports, see chapter 1 by Laura Lundy.

5 C. Harber, above n 4, p 47.

6 *Bradford-Smart v West Sussex C.C.* [2002] ELR 139 at para [38].

prevention and in formulating policies relating to the enforcement of discipline. When researchers conduct ethnographic studies of bullying or 'peer-victimisation,'[7] differential definitions of the phenomenon contribute to variations in their findings, although another factor is the variable levels of reporting by victims in different schools.[8]

According to Thompson, the various academic studies of bullying see bullying as

> essentially a type of aggressive behaviour, involving a systematic abuse of power, and occurring over a prolonged period of time. Scandinavian researchers would also add that it is characterised by a group of people bullying a single individual. Some British researchers would disagree with this, claiming that if one individual exercises the systematic abuse of power over another individual, then this should also be seen as bullying.[9]

Bullying is widely considered to be characterised by deliberately hurtful behaviour, including aggressive conduct (whether physical, verbal or exclusionary), which is difficult for victims to defend themselves against.[10]

Government guidance to schools is somewhat contradictory as regards the need for behaviour to be repetitive. Guidance dealing with anti-bullying strategies says that bullying is considered to be 'repeated often over a period of time.'[11] On the other hand, the guidance on pupil inclusion, like the 1994 guidance on discipline that it replaced,[12] notes that bullying is '*usually* part of a pattern of behaviour rather than an isolated incident.'[13] When, in *Faulkner v London Borough and Enfield and Lea Valley High School*,[14] Judge Wilkie QC said that 'persistence... is a prerequisite for bullying as defined in the relevant [Department for Education] guidance,'[15] that was not strictly correct, because the guidance did not state that isolated incidents were necessarily excluded from the definition. The Office for Standards in Education (Ofsted) notes that bullying can be 'one-off

---

7 H. Mynard, S. Joseph and J. Alexander, 'Peer-victimisation and posttraumatic stress in adolescents' *Personality and Individual Differences* (2000), 29, 815-821.

8 D.A. Thompson, 'Bullying and Harassment in and out of School', in P Aggleton, J. Hurry and I. Warwick, *Young People and Mental Health* (Chichester: John Wiley and Sons, 2000), 197-210.

9 Ibid, p 198.

10 Department for Education and Skills, *Bullying: Don't Suffer in Silence* (London: Department for Education and Skills, 2002), para 1.

11 Ibid. See also, Scottish Executive, *Protecting Children – A Shared Responsibility* (Edinburgh: Scottish Executive, 2003), para 165.

12 Department for Education and Employment (DfEE), *Pupil Behaviour and Discipline,* Circular 8/94 (London: DfEE, 1994).

13 Department for Education and Skills, *Social Inclusion: Pupils Support* (Circular No. 10/99), para 4.29 (emphasis added); DfEE, above n 12, para 55.

14 [2003] ELR 426.

15 Ibid, para 66.

or sustained.'[16] In practice, most bullying does tend to be repetitive: in one survey of pupils, 85 per cent of victims said that they had been bullied at least twice per week.[17]

The absence of an overarching definition in official publications is probably deliberate, in the interests of maximising flexibility. As Watkins and Wagner say: 'Definitional nit-picking could divert a school's energies away from acting.'[18] They say that around 80 per cent of bullying is carried out by groups or by individuals who have a group audience and that it can include a range of behaviours. Direct forms can involve *physical aggression*, such as hitting, kicking and taking or damaging personal property, or *verbal abuse*—name-calling, nasty teasing or spreading rumours. According to a survey of primary school pupils carried out in 1999, 46 per cent of pupils had experienced such 'relational bullying' in the previous six months.[19] (One direct form of bullying, extortion, seems not to fit easily into either of the sub-categories.[20]) There are also indirect types involving *forms of exclusion*—deliberately ignoring someone or failing to include them in social activities.

In the research study by the Thomas Coram Research Unit, published in 2003,[21] nearly 1,000 Year 5 and 8 pupils were asked to define bullying. Verbal and physical abuse, theft, threatening behaviour and coercion were all mentioned by pupils; and the pupils also saw bullying as *intended* to cause distress or harm. Name-calling was identified as the most common form of bullying experienced, a finding mirrored by other studies.[22] In a Northern Ireland study, however, researchers reported that girls tended to use 'indirect or psychological methods of peer intimidation, which they may not necessarily construe as bullying.'[23] The

---

16 Office for Standards in Education (Ofsted), *Bullying: Effective Action in Secondary Schools* HMI 465 (London: Ofsted, 2003), para 14.

17 V. Chaudhary, 'Children expect bullying at school,' *The Guardian*, 22 January 1998, reporting on a survey of 1,000 pupils commissioned by *Family Circle* magazine and presented to the Secretary of State for Education and Skills.

18 C. Watkins and P. Wagner, *Improving School Behaviour* (London: Paul Chapman, 2000), p 49.

19 Quoted in D. Charter, 'Why schoolboy Flashman was a happy bully,' *The Times* 14 December 1999.

20 D.J. Stewart and A. E. Knott, *Schools, Courts and the Law* (Frenchs Forest: Pearson Education, 2002), p 124.

21 C. Oliver and M. Candappa, *Tackling Bullying: Listening to the views of children and young people* (London: Department for Education and Skills, 2003).

22 eg. R. Forero et al, 'Bullying behaviour and psychosocial health among school students in New South Wales, Australia: cross sectional survey', *British Medical Journal* (1999) 319: 344-348; K. Collins, G. McAleavy and G. Adamson, 'Bullying in schools: a Northern Ireland study' (2004) *Educational Research*, 46(1), 55-71, which found name-calling, making fun of a person or teasing in a hurtful way as the most common form of bullying.

23 K. Collins, G. McAleavy and G. Adamson, above n 22, p 68.

study also found that in post-primary education many incidences of name-calling and gestures directed at pupils conveyed a sexual meaning, which was 'not surprising, as this type of bullying, often having connotations relating to sexuality, either confirmed or perceived, has become an established method of intimidation and harassment.'[24] A minority of pupils in the Thomas Coram research also reported racist, sexist and homophobic taunting. Social isolation and exclusion are also commonly referred to in studies. A new form of bullying has also emerged in recent years, the practice of 'text bullying' via mobile phones or email, enabling some pupils 'to taunt their victims around the clock.'[25]

Bullying overlaps with kinds of behaviour often referred to, or officially labelled, as 'harassment.' Both racial and sexual harassment occur in wider society, such as the workplace, but they also manifest themselves in the behaviour of school pupils. The government's current guidance to schools on managing pupil behaviour distinguishes bullying from racial and sexual harassment and gives rather more attention to the undesirable consequences of the former than it does to the effects of the latter. As Thompson points out, however, harassment is a form of bullying relationship, with similar potential effects on the mental health of victims.[26] The Thomas Coram research referred to examples of 'sexualised bullying'; five per cent of the Year 8 pupils (mostly girls) experienced unwanted sexual touching.[27] These forms of harassment have a specific meaning under the law relating to employment, public order or domestic violence, including the criminal law. This reinforces the way that what we might in general terms refer to as bullying, and categorise as a social problem, may need to be conceptualised and dealt with as a form of criminality in some cases.[28]

This is particularly so where the more severe forms of bullying are concerned. Relatively serious criminal offences, typically involving various forms of assault (including sexual assault), may well be involved. Indeed, Furniss concludes that 'tools exist to tackle most forms of bullying (ostracism would be one exception) using the criminal law.'[29] Some forms of behaviour may also be properly categorised as social or community crimes, for which the law in England now provides new forms of penalty designed to reinforce the notion of social responsibility. For example, the Crime and Disorder Act 1998 enables a local authority or the police to apply for an anti-social behaviour order where any person aged ten or over has acted in an 'anti-social manner... in a manner that

---

24 Ibid.

25 A. Blair, 'School bullies turn to text messages', *The Times*, 21 June 2004; see also ChildLine, Press release, 'Bullying – biggest ever rise in calls to ChildLine,' 25 August 2004: www.childline.org.uk.

26 D.A. Thompson, above n 8, p 200.

27 Above n 21.

28 C. Furniss, 'Bullying in schools: it's not a crime-is it?' (2000) *Education and the Law*, 12(1), 9-21.

29 Ibid, p 19.

caused or was likely to cause harassment, alarm or distress to one or more persons....' and it is necessary to protect persons in the area.[30] A 'parenting order' could be made by the court (requiring the parent to take specific steps such as attend a parenting programme: see below). Under provisions in the Anti-social Behaviour Act 2003 that came into force in 2004 (discussed below), such an order could be applied for separately by the authorities in cases where a misbehaving pupil has been excluded from school. In any event, most incidences of bullying, when detected or reported, are likely to be dealt with at the school level through disciplinary sanctions. While the police will need to involved if a crime is thought to have taken place, it seems from research that there is a general reluctance by schools to report bullying to them; the main reason is that schools prefer to rely on their own disciplinary procedures that can be more easily tailored to the individual child.[31] Schools might also be worried about their reputation, or about complaints from parents, if the police decide that no action is warranted. Involvement of an outside agency might also be time-consuming for school staff. This leads to concerns that insufficient regard is paid to the interests of children who are the victims of bullying.

From a legal perspective, therefore, the umbrella term 'bullying' can refer to conduct ranging from simple indiscipline through to anti-social behaviour and crimes of varying degrees of gravity.

The Incidence of Bullying

In 2002 the UN Committee on the Rights of the Child recorded that it was 'concerned at the widespread bullying in schools' in the UK.[32] How prevalent is bullying? There have been a number of studies over the past two decades, many of them influenced by the research studies by Olweus in Norway.[33] The results have varied, but the overwhelming conclusion is that the incidence of bullying is high, although the level varies considerably between schools and age groups.

A research study by Whitney and Smith influenced the government's first significant guidance to schools, in 1994.[34] The researchers asked 2,600 primary school pupils and 4,135 secondary school pupils whether they had experienced bullying: 27 per cent of the primary school pupils and 10 per cent of the secondary school pupils had experienced bullying at least some of the time.[35] The

---

30 Section 1(1)(a) and (b).

31 Furniss, above n 28.

32 *Concluding Observations of the Committee on the Rights of the Child: United Kingdom of Great Britain and Northern Ireland*, CRC/C/15/Add.188, para 47.

33 See generally D. Olweus, *Bullying at School: what we know and what we can do* (Oxford: Blackwell, 1993).

34 Above n 12.

35 Cited in ibid, p 25.

researchers also discovered that while bullying decreased with age (a finding mirrored by the most recent research studies, outlined below), it could take particularly serious forms among older pupils. They also reported that a propensity to commit bullying is not dependent on social class.

Other research has tended to find bullying to be far more prevalent. For example, a major study by the Commission on Children and Violence, supported by the Gulbenkian Foundation, reported in 1995 that 580 children in every 1,000 experienced bullying of one kind or another in schools.[36] A subsequent study, in the late 1990s, found that between 40 per cent of secondary school pupils had experienced bullying at some time,[37] while another found that approximately 33 per cent of 12-16 year olds had been bullied in the previous six months.[38] Another study, by Katz et al[39] for the charity Young Voice, carried out in 2000, surveyed nearly 3,000 pupils: 60 per cent of boys and 54 per cent of girls said they had been victims of bullying. In around a quarter of these cases the bullying had been serious. As many as 35 per cent of boys and 26 per cent of girls in the survey admitted they had been involved in bullying someone else.

The rate of school bullying is reported to have doubled in the past ten years, despite a range of government strategies including a requirement that schools devise and implement an anti-bullying strategy.[40] While physical attacks on girls by girls are still less frequent than boy on boy attacks, they are increasing.[41]

Recently two large studies were conducted—one by the Thomas Coram Research Unit, published by the Department for Education and Skills,[42] and the other by Collins, McAleary and Adamson in Northern Ireland.[43] The Thomas Coram research was sponsored by the children's charity ChildLine, which provides a confidential telephone helpline for children who are victims of various forms of abuse. In August 2004 ChildLine reported a 42 per cent annual increase (from 21,000 to 31,000) in the number of children counselled by the organisation about bullying.[44] In Scotland, 27 per cent (6,119) of the telephone calls in 2000-01 were about bullying.[45] The Thomas Coram research was based on a survey of

---

36 Commission on Children and Violence, *Children and Violence* (London: Calouste Gulbenkian Foundation, 1995).

37 Mynard et al., above n 7.

38 A. Flood-Page et al, *Youth Crime: Findings from a 1998/1999 Youth Lifestyles Survey* (London: Home Office, 2000).

39 A. Katz, A. Buchanan and V. Bream, *Bullying in Britain* (London: Young Voice, 2001).

40 See H. Studd, 'Cruel behaviour is getting worse', *The Times* 28 November 2001.

41 Above n 10, para 10.

42 C. Oliver and M. Candappa, above n 21.

43 K. Collins, G. McAleavy and G. Adamson, above n 22.

44 ChildLine, Press release, 'Bullying—biggest ever rise in calls to ChildLine,' 25 August 2004: www.childline.org.uk.

45 ChildLine, *An analysis of calls to ChildLine on the subject of child abuse and neglect* (ChildLine Scotland, 2003).

nearly 1,000 children. Over half of the children reported that bullying was a problem in their school. Rates of reported bullying varied across age ranges: 51 per cent of Year 5 (9-10 years) pupils reported being bullied as against 28 per cent year 8 (12-13 years) pupils. Among Year 8 pupils, bullying was more likely to be experienced among ethnic minority children. The Northern Ireland research was carried out in 60 primary and 60 post-primary schools and covered nearly 2,500 pupils in years 6 (10-11 years) and 9 (13-14 years). In this study, 40 per cent of primary school pupils and 30 per cent of post-primary pupils had been bullied to some degree in the previous couple of months, although a majority had been bullied only once or twice.[46]

Researchers have also examined the characteristics of those bullied, to identify the risk factors. As some of the above data showed, there is much evidence that boys are more likely than girls to be bullied at school. The Thomas Coram and Northern Ireland research, however, found broadly similar rates of bullying for both genders. Ethnicity, cultural background and sexuality[47] have already been referred to as potential risk factors, but what of the popular assumption that bullied children tend to be physically weak or feeble, very tall or small, or considerably overweight or thin? It seems that physical characteristics are not risk factors in themselves but only in so far as they become associated with social isolation.[48] Indeed, researchers have found an inverse relationship between the number of friends a pupil has and the likelihood of the pupil being bullied.[49] Thus it is widely recommended that policies should be aimed at reducing social isolation by promoting pupils' integration through the development of better skills of social interaction and the capacity to form friendships and join social groups both within and outside school.[50]

Children suffering from disabilities are at greater than average risk of being bullied, and usually about their disability.[51] The measures taken by the government in the Special Educational Needs and Disability Act 2001[52] to increase the proportion of children with disabilities being educated in mainstream schools may inadvertently have increased this risk. The Disability Discrimination Act 1995, which the afore-mentioned 2001 Act extended to schools, provides[53] that it is

---

46 Above n 22, p 58.

47 N. Douglas et al, 'Homophobic bullying in secondary schools in England and Wales—teachers' experiences' (1999) *Health Education*, 99(2), 53-60.

48 Thompson, above n 8, p 204.

49 K. Collins, G. McAleavy and G. Adamson, above n 22, pp 58 and 62.

50 C. Oliver and M. Candappa, above n 21.

51 Above n. 10, para 24.

52 See in particular s 1.

53 Section 28(2).

unlawful for the body responsible for the school to discriminate against a disabled pupil in the education or associated services provided for, or offered to, pupils in the school by that body.

A school that did not include disabled children in its anti-bullying policies (their inclusion is now recommended in the Department for Education and Skills' guidance[54]) would run the risk of being in breach of this provision.

Reporting of Bullying

Many teachers underestimate the amount of bullying that is occurring in or around school, and this seems largely to be due the covert and disguised nature of much of the bullying that is taking place.[55] Furthermore, by virtue of the kind of threat to which bullying subjects the individual, it often goes unreported by the victim. Teachers 'are often the last people to find out that bullying has taken place.'[56] It would appear that victims are far more likely to tell their parents than the school about the problem.[57] The Thomas Coram Research Unit survey[58] found that nearly 70 per cent of Year 8 pupils would not find it easy to talk to their teachers about any bullying they had experienced. It was found that there were concerns among pupils that confidentiality would be breached, no action would be taken, or the victim might be subjected to retaliation for daring to speak out. A further factor is that children can simply become inured to violence, especially when it also occurs at home, or might downplay it as part of their coping strategy.[59] (In the long term, personal coping strategies at school appear not to protect against later victimisation in the workplace.[60])

The government's guidance on pupil inclusion stresses the importance of encouraging pupils to report incidences of bullying to staff or older pupils they feel they can trust and recommends that schools should not be complacent if reported incidences of bullying are low, because it does not prove that bullying is not taking place.[61] According to the Thomas Coram research, however, pupils receive 'mixed messages' from schools. They are encouraged to report bullying, but often feel that they are disbelieved or not listened to when they do or that the school will not be able to protect them from retaliatory action. The report

---

54 Above n 10, para 25.

55 Watkins and Wagner, above n 18, p 50.

56 Ibid.

57 V. Chaudhary, above n 17.

58 Above n 21.

59 Furniss, above n 28, p 21.

60 P.K. Smith et al, 'Victimisation in the school and the workplace: Are there any links?' (2003) *Br. Jnl of Psychology* 175-188.

61 Department for Education and Skills, *Social Inclusion: Pupil Support* (Circular 10/99) (London, Department for Education and Skills, 1999), para 4.29.

recommends that schools should develop strategies that seek to minimise the risks from pupils' reluctance to tell teachers about bullying, through the development of confidential sources of advice and support within schools and in local communities (for example through arrangements for outside counselling services to hold consultations outside school hours).

Ofsted's survey of anti-bullying strategies in schools led it to conclude that a dual approach is needed.[62] While encouraging pupils to report bullying is necessary, it is also important that staff become alert to the signs of bullying. For example, teachers in the survey mentioned previously extroverted pupils becoming withdrawn; pupils becoming unwilling to participate in group work; physical signs such as cuts bruises or dishevelled appearance during the school day; damage to books or other property; and the unaccountable or repeated loss of bags, books or possessions (including money).

Bullying and Mental Health

The fact that many victims of bullying suffer various psychological consequences is well understood. Bullying can result in a number of psychological problems for its victims, often with physical manifestations. For example, it is known to cause anxiety, loss of self-esteem and loss of confidence, with physical problems such as sleeplessness, bed-wetting and loss of appetite. Mynard et al found that bullying was associated with lower self-worth and increased posttraumatic stress: indeed, 37 per cent of those who reported having been bullied had significant levels of such stress.[63] Psychosomatic problems such as stomach aches or headaches are also possible, leading one group of researchers to conclude that health professionals seeing children with health problems of this kind should enquire whether the child has been bullied.[64] Victims may also suffer faints or vomiting.[65] The victim's education may well suffer; indeed as a person suffering from anxiety, depression or phobia, a victim of bullying may find it very difficult to remain in or return to school.[66] Bullying is also implicated in some cases of truancy. In one survey one-third of girls and a quarter of boys reported anxiety and fear in respect of attending school, due to bullying.[67] In addition, there can

---

62 Ofsted above n 16, pp 13-14.

63 Above n 7.

64 K. Williams et al., 'Association of common health symptoms with bullying in primary schools' (1996) *British Medical Journal* 313, 17-19.

65 Above n 10, para 13.

66 Ofsted, above n 2, para 89. The association of bullying with school phobia is explored in M. Csóti, *School phobia, panic attacks and anxiety in children* (London: Jessica Kingsley, 2003).

67 Cited in Social Exclusion Unit, *Truancy and School Exclusion* Cm 3957 (London: The Stationery Office, 1998), para 1.10.

be long-term psychological effects such as difficulties in forming relationships and trusting other people.[68] Bullying is also linked to suicide.[69]

The devastating effects that bullying can have on its victims are illustrated by two reported cases. The first is the case of Elaine Swift, a 15 year old girl who, having donated bone marrow to save her young sister with leukaemia four years previously, was mercilessly bullied by her school-friends after the local media praised her bravery. The bullying included having a lighted match thrown into her hair. She committed suicide by taking an overdose.[70] There is also the case of Rebecca Hayworth. She was a victim of name-calling. She had the door shut in her face by other pupils. She was victimised, blamed by other pupils for things she had not done and was laughed at. She developed anorexia nervosa, brought on by the bullying, and spent four months in hospital. Her parents blamed the school. Her mother was quoted as saying: 'I would like to see teachers and schools made accountable for bullying because at the moment it goes on unnoticed and ruins lives.'[71]

It is not always possible to predict the impact of bullying in individual cases. As a recent Ofsted report notes: '[N]ot all children and young people subjected to bullying experience serious effects as a result; some are able to put it behind them. But for some, the effects of bullying in school can last well into adulthood.'[72] As we have seen, there is a risk that some of the most adversely affected bullied children may not survive that long.

It is important to acknowledge that bullies also tend to have mental health problems. The study by Katz et al[73] found that depression affects both victims and those perpetrating the bullying. While eight per cent of pupils as a whole felt depressed, 24 per cent of bullied children felt depressed often, as did 20 per cent of bullies. While it may be difficult to feel much sympathy for the perpetrators of bullying, a study in Finland concluded that both bullies and the victims of bullying are at increased risk of depression and severe suicidal ideation.[74] Both this and a study in Australia by Forero et al,[75] point to the need to focus attention on the mental health problems of bullies as well. Scottish Executive guidance

68 See D. Thompson, above n 8, pp 201-202.

69 Royal College of Psychiatrists, *Mental Health and Growing Up—The Emotional Cost of Bullying* (3rd edn) (London: Royal College of Psychiatrists, 2004); see also N. Marr and T. Field, *Bullycide. Death at Playtime* (London: Success Unlimited, 2001).

70 H. Studd, 'Bullies drive girl who saved sister to suicide', *The Times*, 28 November 2001. This article reports a number of other suicides in response to bullying.

71 V. Chaudhary, 'Fear followed name calling', *The Guardian*, 22 January 1998.

72 Ofsted, above n 16, para 21.

73 A. Katz, A. Buchanan and V. Bream, above n 39.

74 R Kaltiala et al, 'Bullying, depression and suicidal ideation in Finnish adolescents: school survey' *British Medical Journal* (1999) 319: 348-351.

75 R. Forero et al, above n 22.

notes that children who abuse others require 'comprehensive assessment and therapeutic intervention by skilled childcare professionals.'[76]

Bullying and the Rights of the Child

To the many children's organisations which support anti-bullying campaigns, the issue of bullying takes its place alongside child abuse by adults and the continuing legality of corporal punishment by parents, as posing the greatest threat to the rights of the child. Since October 2000, the incorporation of the European Convention on Human Rights in the UK via the Human Rights Act 1998 has strengthened the rights of children to greater protection from bullying and created a greater imperative for public authorities and government to deal with it.[77] The protection afforded by international law to health in general and in the specific context of education is discussed by Laura Lundy's chapter in this collection. The following provisions are of particular relevance to bullying and its effects in schools in the UK.

The European Convention on Human Rights (ECHR)

Article 2 of the Convention protects the right to life. As bullying is associated with suicidal ideation (albeit in a very small proportion of cases), one might assume that the need for public authorities, including schools in the public sector, to take reasonable steps to tackle it must in part stem from the positive duty on the state to protect the right to life,[78] especially where a child is known to be at particular risk. However, apart from in the medical context, this principle has so far only been applied to protection (by the police) against the acts of others that threaten life.[79] It seems to be the case that there could well be a positive obligation on the police or prison authorities to protect those in custody from the risk of suicide,[80] but it is perhaps unlikely that the equivalent risk to victims of bullying at school would place schools in an analogous position.

Article 3 of the Convention provides that 'No one shall be subjected to torture or to inhuman or degrading treatment or punishment.' It is clear that

---

76 Scottish Executive (2003), above n 11, para 166. The poor long term psychosocial outcomes for young people who exhibit conduct problems, including bullying, were among the findings of S. Collishaw et al, 'Time trends in adolescent mental health,' (2004) *Jnl of Child Psychology and Psychiatry*, 45(8), 1350-62.

77 The current anti-bullying guidance to schools emphasises that 'Head teachers will need to satisfy themselves that their policies comply with the Human Rights Act 1998': above n.10 at para 2.

78 *Osman v UK* [1999] 1 FLR 193 [1999] EHRLR 228; *R (on the application of Pretty) v Director of Public Prosecutions* [2002] 1 All ER 1.

79 *Osman v UK* [1999] 1 FLR 193; 1999] EHRLR 228.

80 See K. Starmer, *European Human Rights Law* (London: LAG, 1999), p 455.

bullying is a form of degrading treatment, which includes any treatment that induces apprehension of fear, anguish or diminished self-worth and is capable of being humiliating.[81] The state may be in violation of this principle if it does not provide adequate safeguards to prevent torture or inhuman or degrading treatment by others.[82]

Article 8 protects 'the right to respect for... private and family life,' which has been held to include respect for the individual's personal integrity and thereby for his or her protection from acts or omissions that might affect his or her mental well-being. In *Benaid v United Kingdom*[83] the European Court of Human Rights accepted that mental health is integral to private life and that mental stability is an indispensable element in the enjoyment of the Article 8 right. In *The Queen on the application of N v The Secretary of State for the Home Department*[84] Silber J held that a Libyan man whose asylum application was so delayed by the omission of the Home Office that he developed a major depressive disorder brought about through prolonged fear and anxiety had his rights under Article 8 interfered with, so an award of damages was justified. While the Court of Appeal in this case subsequently criticised Silber J's conclusion, holding that if maladministration happened to cause harm to mental health that could not reasonably have been foreseen there would be no breach of the Article,[85] it nevertheless confirmed that if 'a public authority commits acts which it knows are likely to cause psychiatric harm to an individual, those acts are capable of constituting a breach of Article 8.'[86] One can reasonably assume that 'acts' would include omissions, so that if a school knows that a pupil is at risk of suffering mental harm due to bullying, for example because he has suffered it in the past, then the failure to take adequate steps to deal with it could well give rise to a breach of Article 8 and consequential liability in damages. This is especially so because Article 8 may require positive action by the state. For example, a complaint that a suicidal prisoner was not properly observed, counselled or treated has been declared admissible.[87] In conclusion, bullying interferes with privacy and family life and so the authorities may well be obliged under Article 8 to protect a child from it and its effects.

---

81 H. Mountfield, 'The Implications of the Human Rights Act 1998 for the Law of Education' (2002) *Ed Law* 146-158, p 152, citing *Ireland v United Kingdom* (1978) 2 EHRR 25.

82 *A v United Kingdom* (1999) 27 EHRR 611.

83 (2001) 31 EHRR 1, at 47.

84 (2003) WL 117120 (QBD (Admin Ct)), judgment 14 February 2003.

85 *Anufrijeva and another v Southwark London Borough Council; R (on the application of N) v Secretary of State for the Home Department; R (on the application of M) v Secretary of State for the Home Department* [2003] EWCA Civ 1406, [2003] All ER (D) 288 (Oct), at para 142.

86 Ibid, para 143.

87 *Keenan v UK* (1998) 26 EHRR CD 64.

The only provision in the ECHR specifically concerned with education is Article 2 of Protocol 1. This provides that 'No one shall be denied the right to education,' which, according to *Belgian Linguistics*,[88] means effective education. Therefore, a person whose capacity to receive education is sufficiently prejudiced through the psychological effects of bullying might well be able to show an interference with this Convention right. This could also be linked to Article 14, which protects other Convention rights where affected by discrimination.

The UN Convention on the Rights of the Child

Several provisions of the UN Convention on the Rights of the Child, which has not been incorporated into UK law but is often referred to the by courts when giving consideration to legal rights and obligations, and also generates international political imperatives for national action, are also relevant to the child's right to freedom from bullying.

Article 3 provides that States Parties must

> undertake to ensure that the institutions, services and facilities responsible for the care or protection of children conform with the standards established by competent authorities, particularly in the areas of safety, health, in the number and suitability of their staff, as well as constant supervision.[89]

It also states that 'the best interests of the child shall be a primary consideration' in relation to all actions concerning children, including those taken by public authorities and courts.[90]

Article 12 requires states to assure to the competent child 'the right to express those views freely in all matters affecting the child', with the child's views to be given 'due weight in accordance with the age and maturity of the child.' This has a particular significance in relation to the development of anti-bullying strategies and is discussed more fully below.

Article 19(1) has an obvious relevance to bullying since it requires the state to take 'all appropriate legislative, administrative, social and educational measures to protect the child from all forms of physical or mental violence, injury or abuse.... While in the care of parent(s), legal guardian(s) or any other person who has care of the child.'

The right to education is recognised by Article 28, which also calls on states to take various measures including that of encouraging regular attendance at schools and the reduction of drop-out rates. Again this reinforces the need to prevent bullying, as it is a factor in some cases of absence from school. The various objectives which education should be directed towards are set out in

---

88 *Belgian Linguistics (No 2)* (1979-80) 1 EHRR 252.
89 Article 3(2).
90 Article 3(1).

Article 29. They include the development of the child's personality, talents and mental and physical abilities and the preparation of the child for a 'responsible life in a free society, in the spirit of understanding, peace, tolerance, equality of sexes, and friendship among all peoples, ethnic, national and religious groups and persons of indigenous origin.' This clearly implies that misbehaviour such as bullying should be actively deterred.

Article 37 parallels Article 3 of the European Convention on Human Rights above in proscribing inhuman or degrading treatment or torture, while Article 39 calls for support for its victims, requiring States parties to take

> all appropriate measures to promote physical and psychological recovery and social reintegration of a child victim of: any form of [inter alia]... abuse; torture or any form of cruel, inhuman or degrading treatment or punishment... Such recovery and reintegration shall take place in an environment which fosters the health, self-respect and dignity of the child.

The Effect of these Provisions

In combination, these provisions seem to create obligations for ratifying states to ensure that children are educated in a non-threatening and conducive environment, one where bullying is dealt with and, under the United Nations Convention on the Rights of the Child at least, education itself aims to promote good behaviour and to deter all forms of bullying and harassment. The UN Committee on the Rights of the Child in its *Concluding Observations* (2002) on the UK's implementation of the Convention drew specific attention to the need for the government to take further steps to prevent bullying and other forms of violence in schools and to include children in the development and implementation of strategies.[91]

In September 2003 the Government began a new campaign against bullying in schools (see below), reinforced by a publicity campaign which included a short film which can be downloaded from the Department for Education and Skills website and which was also to be shown on national television, and the issuing of a 'Charter for Action' for schools. The Department has said that it wants pupils to assist schools in improving the identification and reporting of bullying and it has stated that pupils should be involved in the development and implementation of anti-bullying policies.[92] This is consistent with the principle in Article 12 of the UN Convention on the Rights of the Child, which has recently been advanced through a new duty on LEAs and school governing bodies under the Education Act 2002, section 176, to have regard to any guidance issued by the Secretary of

---

91 Above n 32, para 47(e).

92 Chief Secretary to the Treasury, *Every Child Matters* (London: The Stationery Office, 2003), para 2.44. This is also highlighted in the notes accompanying the 'Charter for Action' referred to above.

State 'about consultation with pupils in connection with the taking of decisions affecting them'; the draft guidance refers specifically to consultation in respect of behaviour policies in schools.[93] Both a recent Ofsted evaluation of schools' success in dealing with bullying[94] and the Thomas Coram research[95] note that the most successful approaches were found in schools which took full account of pupils' views and canvassed their opinions.

Specific Legal Obligations and Powers and Policy Initiatives Concerning Bullying in School

Maintenance of Discipline and Prevention of Bullying

Governing bodies and head teachers of schools have specific statutory responsibilities concerning the development and implementation of disciplinary policies and enforcement measures.[96] As mentioned above, these include, in the case of head teachers, a duty to 'encourage good behaviour and respect for others on the part of pupils and, in particular, preventing all forms of bullying among pupils.'[97] As bullying affects the welfare of pupils, it is also covered by the statutory duty on school governing bodies to make sure that 'their functions relating to the conduct of the school are exercised with a view to safeguarding and promoting the welfare of children who are pupils at the school.'[98]

The focussing of government attention on the problem of bullying in Britain's schools was originally part of the drive to improve educational management, school standards and discipline. While these are still primary aims, the initiatives can also reasonably be seen now as part of the wider policy of increasing social inclusion and protecting the interests of vulnerable children. A sequence of initiatives in England commenced in 1994, when a guide for schools, *Bullying: don't suffer in silence,*[99] was published. Parallel developments occurred in Scotland, starting with the Scottish Schools Anti-Bullying Initiative in 1993.

---

93 Department for Education and Skills, *Working together: Giving children and young people a say* (London: Department for Education and Skills, 2003) (www.dfes.gov.uk/consultations).

94 Ofsted, above n 16, para.37.

95 Above n 21.

96 School Standards and Framework Act 1998, s 61. See generally, N. Harris, 'The legislative response to indiscipline in schools in England and Wales' (2002) *Education and the Law*, 14(1/2), 57-76.

97 School Standards and Framework Act 1998, s 61(4)(b).

98 Education Act 2002, s 175. See also the guidance on this duty, Department for Education and Skills, *Safeguarding Children in Education* (DfES/0027/2004) (London: Department for Education and Skills, 2004), which notes that this duty sits alongside specific duties concerned with tackling bullying.

99 (London, HMSO, 1994).

Various resources were distributed to Scottish schools, placing an emphasis on the development of a whole school anti-bullying policy to which staff, pupils and parents should be committed. Most schools in Scotland are now reported to have specific anti-bullying strategies. In January 1999 it was announced that an anti-bullying network was being established which would enable Scotland's schools to share good practice and participate in providing training and consultancy. The Scottish Office funds a 'Bullying Helpline,' a free confidential service for children and young people.

In England, following the implementation in September 1999 of the new statutory duty on head teachers of schools to determine measures to prevent bullying (above), the Government launched in 2000 a new version of *Bullying: Don't suffer in silence*. An independent evaluation of the guidance was subsequently carried out.[100] It found that since the guidance was issued, more schools (up from 49 per cent to 67 per cent) adopted a separate anti-bullying policy, as recommended, as opposed to dealing with bullying only within a more general behaviour policy. Recommended strategies—such as active listening/counselling, encouraging 'circles of friends,' working with parents, drama/role play exercises, and improving the physical environment in schools—have all been found useful by schools. While six per cent of schools felt that there had been an increase in bullying since the new edition of the guidance was implemented, 46.6 per cent considered there to have been a fall, although the remaining 47.4 per cent felt that there had been no change.

The 2000 guidance was further amended in September 2002.[101] The central element is the 'whole school policy' on bullying. This new version of the guidance deals with homophobic bullying (which was referred to by six per cent of schools' anti-bullying policies[102]) and highlights a new form of bullying, involving abusive or threatening mobile phone text messages (noted above). It also emphasises the need for schools to monitor levels of bullying in order to gauge the success of their policies. It highlights ways that bullying can be dealt with via the school curriculum, to raise understanding and build an anti-bullying ethos,[103] and through strategies such as co-operative group work, 'circle time' for younger children (the teacher forms a circle in which s/he and the pupils talk for about 20-30 minutes about relevant issues, eg relationships, anger, fighting and bullying), befriending, and mediation by adults and peers.[104] Other recommended measures include assertiveness training for pupils and, in cases where bullies are unresponsive to preventive strategies, sanctions at various levels up to and

---

100 P Smith and M. Samara, *Evaluation of the DfES Anti-Bullying Pack* DfES Brief RBX06-03 (London: DfES, 2003).

101 Above n 10.

102 Ibid, para 22.

103 See also Ofsted above n 94, paras 46-48.

104 See ibid, part 4.

including exclusion.[105] The guidance calls on schools to work with parents to prevent bullying. Finally, it focuses on the school environment to ensure that there are safe and healthy spaces for purposeful recreation. Further research will be needed to evaluate this latest version of the guidance.

Reference was also made earlier to the UK Government's renewed anti-bullying campaign launched in September 2003. This aims to facilitate improved responses to bullying, including greater participation by children and young people themselves in the design and implementation of anti-bullying strategies.

It is perhaps unrealistic to expect anti-bullying strategies to eliminate all bullying. In some instances, therefore, a parent who considers that the school is not able to prevent it might consider moving their child to another school. That will not, however, always be possible. In one recent case[106] a parent withdrew his 15-year-old son from school after it was alleged that the boy had been bullied. An attempt to secure a place at another school failed, as that school had no vacancies. The boy's solicitor requested that the LEA make special alternative provision for the boy under its statutory duty. Section 19(1) of the Education Act 1996 requires LEAs to make appropriate educational arrangements, in the form of suitable full-time or part-time education, for pupils of compulsory school age (5-16 years) who 'by reason of illness, exclusion from school or otherwise, may not for any period receive suitable education unless such arrangements are made for them.' The authority, however, took the view that the child was able to attend his present school and refused to make any special alternative arrangements. The father applied for judicial review. Although the boy had seen a psychiatrist the court held that the psychiatrist's report did not establish that there was a mental illness preventing the boy from attending school. But the boy's counsel argued that the duty in section 19 was not restricted to cases of illness, since it referred to 'exclusion, illness *or otherwise*' (emphasis added). He contended that the duty should be construed in the light of Article 8 of the ECHR, which encompasses respect for a person's psychological integrity, and Article 3 of the UN Convention on the Rights of the Child (the best interests principle—above).

The judge accepted that the duty under section 19 to make alternative educational arrangements could apply to persons with behavioural difficulties, if sufficiently serious, which in fact was not felt to be the case here. The judge therefore left undecided the human rights arguments. He said that the father was motivated by a genuine concern for his son, but 'it is for the school to ensure that adequate standards of behaviour are applied' and it had a statutory power of exclusion open to it.[107] The judge nonetheless acknowledged that if, in such a case, it could be shown that the head teacher's or LEA's conclusion regarding the seriousness of any illness or behavioural problems was irrational, such a decision

---

105 See ibid, para 48.

106 *The Queen on the application of G v Westminster City Council* [2004] ELR 734.

107 Ibid, at para 35.

could be judicially reviewed.[108] The Court of Appeal also dismissed the claim.[109] Lord Phillips MR, giving the judgment of the court, said that that it was reasonable for the parent to try to move the boy to another school but not to withdraw him from his present school in the absence of an alternative.[110] A significant factor in this case was that the school was prepared to take special measures to help the boy. Lord Phillips MR nonetheless said that where

> a school is unable to prevent a child being subjected to persistent bullying it may be reasonable for the parents to withdraw that child from the school. In such circumstances it will not be reasonably practicable for the child to continue to attend that school.[111]

Lord Phillips MR acknowledged that Article 8 of the ECHR can impose positive obligations on a state, but felt that the positive obligations owed by the education authorities under domestic law went beyond anything imposed by the Article, which therefore did not add anything to G's case.[112]

If the child had been attending an independent (private school) this would have been a contractual issue. In one recently reported case[113] a pupil's parents withdrew him from an independent school at which the boy had been bullied. The school then sued for unpaid fees. The judge ordered the parents to pay up to the end of the term in which the boy had left, a total of £855. The parents complained that the head teacher had been somewhat dismissive of the behaviour of other boys towards their son, but the judge found the parents rather than the school to have been in breach of contract. In a case such as this the onus of proof will be on the parents to show, on the balance of probabilities, that the child had been bullied, which will often be very difficult from such an external position. Note that since 1 September 2003 new regulations prescribing school standards for the independent sector in England have been in force.[114] The standards include provisions on the welfare, health and safety of pupils, one of which requires each school to 'draw up and implement effectively a written policy to – (a) prevent bullying, with regard to [Department for Education and Skills] Guidance "Bullying: don't suffer in silence".'[115] These regulations are made

108 Ibid, at para 34.

109 *R (G by his father and litigation friend R(G) v Westminster City Council* [2004] ELR 135, CA.

110 Ibid, para 21.

111 Ibid, para 49.

112 Ibid, para 39.

113 See G Owen, 'Parents told to pay bullied boy's fees,' *The Times*, 22 February, 2003.

114 Education (Independent School Standards) (England) Regulations 2003 (SI 2003/1910).

115 Schedule, para 3(2). The policy must be supplied to the registration authority in accordance with the Education (Provision of Information by Independent Schools) (England) Regulations 2003 (SI 2003/1934).

under the Education Act 2002 powers. Provision is made for enforcement of standards, including sanctions (such as de-registration) for default.[116]

Bullying and the Duty of Care

The first reported negligence claim in respect of a school's failure to prevent bullying was brought in the UK ten years ago by a 20-year-old woman who claimed she was suffering psychological effects from persistent bullying she had received at school; but it was unsuccessful, largely because a causal link was not established.[117] There has since been a definitive judgment, by the Court of Appeal, in *Bradford-Smart v West Sussex County Council*,[118] to the effect that a school's duty of care at common law extends to taking reasonable steps to prevent bullying within the school, including one-off acts of aggression and the persistent targeting of one individual. While holding that schools are not responsible for acts committed by pupils on other pupils while outside their field of control (such as when out in their home neighbourhood), the court acknowledged that there might be circumstances (although such cases would be 'few and far between') when a school's failure to exercise its disciplinary powers in respect of action taken by one pupil against another outside school could amount to breach of the duty of care. Relevant factors would be whether the effects of the incident carried over into school and whether a reasonable head teacher would consider it necessary to investigate it in the light of the deleterious effects.[119] The court noted Auld LJ's statement in *Gower v London Borough of Bromley* in 1999 that the teacher's duty of care included 'a duty to take such care of pupils in their charge as a careful parent would have in like circumstances, including a duty to take positive steps to protect their well-being.'[120]

The circumstances surrounding bullying are such that, as Judge LJ said in *Bradford-Smart*, '[b]ullying may be either a "health and safety" or an "educational" issue or both,' giving rise to physical or psychiatric injury. It could cause 'educational under-achievement and consequent psychiatric injury or economic loss.'[121] Previous cases over many years in the UK[122] (and in Australia[123]) have held that the health and safety duty demands both reasonable supervision of pupils who are liable to misbehave and injure other pupils and

---

[116] Education Act 2002, s 165.

[117] *Walker v Derbyshire County Council*, *The Times*, 7 June 1994.

[118] [2002] ELR 139.

[119] Per Judge LJ at paras 34 and 36.

[120] [1999] ELR 356 at 359.

[121] Above n 118, at para 31.

[122] See, for example, *Beaumont v Surrey County Council* (1968) 66 LGR 580; *Porter v City of Bradford Metropolitan Borough Council*, 14 January 1985, Lexis.

[123] See *Haines v Warren* (1987) Austr. Torts Reports ¶80-115, Court of Appeal, New South Wales, cited in D.J. Stewart and A.E. Knott, *Schools, Courts and the Law* (Frenchs Forest: Pearson Education, 2002), pp 125-127.

proper systems for controlling behaviour. *Bradford-Smart* has, in the context of bullying, taken the law one very important stage further, following on from the House of Lords' decision in *Phelps*,[124] which confirmed that teachers and others owe a duty of care over matters within their professional field of competence.

In *Bradford-Smart* the court also noted that a claimant would have to show a causal connection between the breach of duty by the school and the injury or loss complained of. The failure to establish that connection was fatal to the complaint in *Faulkner v London Borough of Enfield and Lea Valley High School*.[125] Two sisters had been victims of bullying at school, in the form of abusive name-calling, hair pulling, shoving and spitting and had suffered clinical depression and posttraumatic stress disorder as a consequence of an assault at school and its aftermath. However, the court found that the psychological harm did not flow from any breach of the duty of care on the part of the school. The court found that the systems and arrangements for discipline and to counteract bullying were not perfect but were reasonable to discharge the duty of care.

The prospects of liability in such cases are limited by the difficulty in acquiring cogent evidence to substantiate a breach of the duty of care, to demonstrate that the standard of care fell below that which could reasonably be expected of a competent and responsible member of the profession,[126] or to establish a causal link to the harm or injury suffered. In cases where the injury is psychological, it is necessary to show that it takes the form of a clinically-recognised mental health problem.[127]

Exclusion for Bullying

The power to exclude a pupil for a fixed period or fixed periods of no more than 45 school days in aggregate in any school year, or permanently, is likely to be used in cases where more serious and irremediable forms of bullying have

---

124 *Phelps v London Borough of Hillingdon; Anderton v Clwyd County Council; G v London Borough of Bromley; Jarvis v Hampshire County Council* [2000] ELR 499; [2000] 3 WLR 776; [2000] 4 All ER 504, HL. See further See further P. Craig and D. Fairgrieve, '*Barrett*, Negligence and Discretionary Powers' [1999] PL 626; N. Harris, 'Liability under Education Law in the UK—How Much Further Can it Go?' (2000) *European Jnl for Ed Law & Policy*, 4(2), 131-140; R. McManus, 'The House of Lords' ruling in *Phelps v London Borough of* Hillingdon and its implications' (2000) *Ed Law Jnl,* 1(4), 200-205; A. Mullis, '*Phelps v Hillingdon London Borough* Council. A rod for the hunch-backed teacher' (2001) *CFLQ*, 13(3), 331.

125 [2003] ELR 426.

126 See, for example, *Carty (by his litigation and next friend Dorothy Brown-Carty) v London Borough of Croydon* [2004] ELR 226, applying the test in *Bolam v Friern Hospital Management Committee* [1957] 1 WLR 582.

127 *Phelps* op cit; *Robinson v St Helens Metropolitan Borough Council* [2002] ELR 681.

occurred.[128] In some cases the involvement of parents in preventing future bullying by an excluded pupil may now be included in a parenting contract between the parents and the LEA or school governing body or directed via a parenting order made by a magistrates' court.[129] Under the terms of the contract or order the parent would be expected to attend counselling or guidance sessions. The effectiveness of such measures is yet to be assessed, but there is evidence that, in the case of young criminal offenders, participation in parenting programmes (whether voluntary or via parenting orders) has improved parents' confidence in coping with their misbehaving children but has not had a measurable overall impact to date on the young people's behaviour (despite a lower recorded reconviction rate).[130]

The use of the power of exclusion in any particular case is a matter for the discretion of the head teacher, but he or she is required by law[131] to have regard to official guidance on this sanction.[132] The guidance indicates that this sanction should be employed only in response to a serious breach of the school's behaviour policy and if allowing the pupil to remain at school would seriously harm the education or welfare of the pupil or others at the school.[133] It advises that permanent exclusion should normally be used only as a last resort, where all other available strategies have been tried and have failed, but that it may, exceptionally, be appropriate in the case of a first or single offence, such as one involving serious actual or threatened violence against another pupil or a member of staff, sexual abuse or assault,[134] or carrying an offensive weapon, any of which

---

128 The power is set out in the Education Act 2002, s 52, and the Education (Pupil Exclusions and Appeals) (Maintained Schools) (England) Regulations 2002 (SI 2002/3178) ("the Exclusions Regs").

129 Anti-social Behaviour Act 2003, ss 19-21. The order is made under the Crime and Disorder Act 1998, s 8, as amended. See also the Education (Parenting Orders) (England) Regulations 2004 (SI 2004/182).

130 Youth Justice Board for England and Wales, *Positive Parenting – the National Evaluation of the Youth Justice Board's Parenting Programme* (London: Youth Justice Board, 2002), pp 49-51.

131 Education Act 2002, s 52(3)(c); Exclusions Regs, reg 7.

132 In *The Queen on the application of P v Oxfordshire County Council Exclusions Appeals Panel and the Secretary of State for Education and Employment* [2001] ELR 631, Turner J explained that the guidance had altered the burden of response to violent behaviour so that the panel normally had to uphold the exclusion in such a case, whereas previously it had a broad discretion whether to uphold or overturn the exclusion as it saw fit.

133 Department for Education and Skills, *Improving Behaviour and Attendance: Guidance on Exclusion for Schools and Pupil Referral Units* (London, Department for Education and Skills, 2004), part 2 para 9. This version dates from July 2004.

134 In *The Queen on the application of C v Sefton Metropolitan Council Independent Appeals Panel and the Governors of Hillside High School* [2001] ELR 393 C, a pupil aged 15 lost his temper with another pupil, W, whom he saw as a rival, and pushed W through a classroom door with such force that W had to go to hospital. Scott Baker

could be involved in a bullying case.[135] While the parent, or pupil if aged 18 or over, has a right to appeal to an independent appeal panel (IAP) if the governing body upholds a permanent exclusion,[136] the guidance now advises that if a pupil has been excluded permanently for one of the above offences or for 'persistent and defiant misbehaviour including bullying (which would include racist or homophobic bullying),' the governing body or an [IAP] would not normally be expected to reinstate the pupil.[137] The guidance appears to compromise, to some extent, the independent judicial function of the appeal panels, but the courts have rejected challenges argued on that basis.[138]

Cases where exclusion has resulted from violent conduct, including sexual bullying, have raised difficult issues concerning the depth of the investigation and the standard of proof. A considerable body of case-law has developed around this subject. One of the issues concerns the evidence of those who claim to be the victims of bullying. While the courts have accepted that it may be sufficient for the appeal panel to rely on witness statements rather than hearing from every witness in person,[139] it has been argued that unsigned or anonymous witness statements should not be relied upon by the panel, especially when the witnesses are not present to be cross-examined. But in one case[140] the High Court held that the IAP was entitled to rely upon unsigned statements from the alleged victims of bullying. The judge, Collins J, said it was understandable that victims of bullying did not want to be identified. When the case reached the Court of Appeal[141] the court reached a similar conclusion and laid down guidelines on the use of anonymous witness statements. Schiemann LJ referred to the need for 'singular care,' because the anonymous statement could be made by a 'well-known liar' or a person with a biased motive.[142] Sedley LJ said that more general allegations, of the sort made in the statements in the case itself, although requiring to be approached cautiously when anonymous, might be admitted if the panel considered them relevant and had made an informed and careful judgment of the balance of fairness and unfairness that was involved when relying on such

---

J concluded that it was not unreasonable for the appeal panel to uphold an exclusion ordered because of a serious one-off incident.

135 Above n 133, paras 11 and 12.

136 See above n 128.

137 Ibid, para 14.

138 *The Queen on the appln of S v London Borough of Brent and others*, 9 May 2001 (unreported); *The Queen on the application of P v Oxfordshire County Council Exclusions Appeals Panel and the Secretary of State for Education and Employment* [2001] ELR 631; *S, T and P v London Borough of Brent Etc* [2002] ELR 556, CA. The case law concerns similarly expressed previous versions of the guidance.

139 *The Queen on the application of C v Sefton Metropolitan Council Independent Appeals Panel and the Governors of Hillside High School* [2001] ELR 393.

140 *The Queen on the appln of N v Head Teacher of X School & Others* [2002] ELR 187.

141 Under the name *R (T) v Head Teacher of Elliott School* [2003] ELR 160.

142 Ibid, at para [24].

statements.[143] The pupil in this case, T, had been excluded for systematic bullying and harassment, some of which had involved a series of offensive phone calls to another pupil. Part of T's case was that one of the members of the governors' discipline committee which upheld the exclusion was a teacher governor who had had dealings with T in her capacity as a teacher, including forming some judgment as to T's participation in bullying of the victim by phone. The court considered her participation to be just on the right side of the line between fairness and unfairness (bias).

The official guidance envisages an exclusion appeal case being subjected to a three-stage process of assessment by the appeal panel.[144] First, the panel must decide whether, on the balance of probabilities, the pupil is responsible for the conduct that led to the exclusion. Secondly, the panel should consider the basis for the head teacher's decision, having regard to the school's published policy on equal opportunities, special educational needs and behaviour and to whether the official guidance was followed by the head teacher. Thirdly, the panel should decide whether permanent exclusion is the right response to the behaviour. So far as the first element is concerned, a relevant factor in cases of bullying is that where exclusion is for violent or sexual conduct a higher degree of probability is needed. Several judgments have adopted the test that it has to have been 'distinctly more probable than not' that the claimant was involved.[145] One case involved a 13 year old boy who was excluded following the alleged sexual harassment of a female pupil involving leg touching and interference with her bra strap.[146] Richards J said that the seriousness of the conduct alleged was a matter to be taken into account in deciding as to the standard of proof. He said that the panel had not applied the 'distinctly more probable' approach although on the facts he did not think they would have reached a different conclusion even if they had.[147] However, in a recent case in the Court of Appeal,[148] an even higher standard of proof was alluded to in cases where criminal conduct might be involved. Laws LJ said that 'in dealing with a disciplinary matter where the accusation amounts to a crime under the general law, the head teacher and

---

143 Ibid, at para [48].

144 Above n 133, part 5 paras 120-122.

145 *The Queen on the application of B v Head Teacher of Alperton Community School and Others; The Queen v Head teacher of Wembley High School and Others ex p T; The Queen v Governing Body of Cardinal Newman High School and Others ex p C* [2001] ELR 359, Newman J. See also *R v Headteacher and Independent Appeal Committee of Dunraven School ex p B* [2000] ELR 156, per Brooke LJ.

146 *The Queen on the application of S v Head Teacher of C High School and Others* [2002] ELR 73 (per Richards J).

147 Ibid, at para 20.

148 *The Queen on the application of S v Governing Body of YP School* [2003] EWCA Civ 1306.

governors must be sure that the child has done what he has been accused of.'[149] It is assumed that this standard would also apply to IAPs deciding such cases.

A problem can arise in exclusion cases where the pupil has been reported to the police and the question of criminal prosecution is still under consideration or the case has yet to be tried. In one case,[150] where a sexual assault was alleged, the matter had been reported to the police and a prosecution was pending, the IAP had decided to apply the presumption of innocence so that in order to refuse the appeal it would need to be satisfied that, inter alia, the pupil was responsible for the misconduct alleged. The panel did not find the matter proven and decided to reinstate the pupil. The alleged victim was upset that the alleged perpetrator would remain at her school and on the advice of her parents ceased attendance. Moses J held that the best approach would be for the appeal panel to accept that it could not investigate the truth or otherwise of the charge and to consider a free-standing separate issue, namely whether it was in the best interests of the school, all the pupils, the alleged victim and of course the pupil who was charged, for the exclusion to stand, bearing in mind that the truth or otherwise of the accusation could not be determined until the criminal proceedings were resolved. He said that the panel would be making all sorts of difficulties for itself in attempting to decide the issue of guilt or innocence with its hands tied behind its back.

This approach is now reflected in the regulations and in the official guidance, which advises that an exclusion decision need not be postponed by the possibility of criminal proceedings and that in deciding whether to exclude consideration should be given to the seriousness of any allegation made against the pupil by the victim and to the effect that the continuing presence of the alleged perpetrator at school might have on the complainant and the promotion of order and discipline at the school.[151] This is consistent with the appeal panel's general duty to 'balance the interests of the excluded pupil against the interests of all the other members of the school community,'[152] but obviously means that account will be taken of a suspicion rather than proof of criminality, which could be unjust. The problem is compounded if the criminal justice process is subsequently influenced by the pupil's exclusion from school. The guidance acknowledges that if the exclusion decision comes before an appeal panel, an adjournment pending the outcome of the police investigation or criminal proceedings might be desirable but should not be automatic.[153]

Irrespective of whether criminal proceedings are possible, the guidance envisages a situation where exclusion was unreasonable but reinstatement 'is not a practical way forward in the best interests of all concerned.'[154] This mirrors the

---

149 Ibid, at para 5.

150 *R v Independent Appeal Panel of Sheffield City Council ex p N* [2000] ELR 700.

151 Above n 133, part 6, para 124.

152 Ibid, part 5, para 123.

153 Ibid, part 6, para 127.

154 Ibid, para 129.

approach taken by the Court of Appeal in a 1996 judgment[155] where the governing body's discipline committee decided to reinstate two pupils responsible for firing an air pistol in the schoolyard, striking another pupil. Kennedy LJ said: 'where, as here, there was a child victim the overall case did require some serious investigation of the effect that the proposed setting aside of the head's decision would have on the injured boy.'[156] While accepting that the panel had found that the injury was caused inadvertently, the court held that the committee had not properly considered the impact of the reinstatement of the two pupils on the victim and thus on the school as a whole. This decision was cited by the Court of Appeal in a recent case[157] where a male pupil was excluded followed an investigation into a complaint by a female pupil that she had been raped by a group of five boys in a classroom during lunchtime. The male pupil had dissociated himself from the incident by leaving the room before the rape actually occurred, but he had touched the girl's bottom and after leaving the room had not alerted anyone to the continuing attack upon the girl. Simon Brown LJ said:

> A fellow pupil was raped and the appellant was one of a group of five boys who, with obvious ill-intent, had shut her alone with them in a darkened classroom where the attack took place... When... he left he took no steps to alert anyone to the continuing attack upon the girl. He simply left her to her fate... In my judgment the decision taken by the majority of the [IAP]... was entirely reasonable, a "permissible option"... K and her parents would surely have been devastated had she been required to face these boys for the remainder of her schooldays.[158]

As noted above, in cases involving this kind of behaviour or where there is persistent and defiant misbehaviour including bullying, governing bodies and appeal panels are in any event now advised against reinstatement. As also noted, panels may in appropriate cases refuse to reinstate even where the exclusion itself was unjustifiable because, for example, the probability test is not fully satisfied. This and the fact that panels are advised to take into account the school's anti-bullying policy when reaching their decision[159] means that reinstatement in bullying cases, even where the bullying itself is not fully proven, is going to become far less likely. Changes to the composition of appeal panels in January 2003 to include more people with teaching experience[160] are likely to reduce still further the prospects of an appeal succeeding.

---

155 *R v London Borough of Camden and the Governors of Hampstead School ex parte H* [1996] E.L.R. 360.

156 At 378B.

157 *R (DR) v Head Teacher and Governing Body of S School* [2003] ELR 104, CA.

158 At paras 49-51.

159 Above n 133, para 121(b).

160 The Education (Pupil Exclusions and Appeals) (Maintained Schools) (England) Regulations 2002 (SI 2002/3178).

A further point to note is that head teachers are advised, when considering whether to exclude a pupil, to consider whether the pupil's behaviour might have been provoked by bullying, including homophobic bullying, or racial or sexual harassment.[161] Once again, therefore, the effect of bullying on the mind of the victim is acknowledged, although the issue is not fully explored by the guidance.

Conclusion

Pupil bullying is part of a culture of oppressive behaviour and violence in schools that appears to be endemic internationally.[162] In remains a particularly significant problem in schools in England despite a decade of initiatives, a statutory framework of duties and a policy of encouraging tougher action against it and other forms of violent or anti-social behaviour among pupils. Schools in England are at least starting to make genuine attempts to get to grips with the problem, as the latest annual report from the Chief Inspector of Schools in England indicates.[163] However, there is evidence that some pupils continue to feel vulnerable and to believe that some teachers are not doing enough to tackle bullying,[164] and not all that much comfort can be found in the statistics.

One the most important aspects of this effort is an increasing engagement with the principle of pupil participation, of involving pupils in the development, implementation and monitoring of school policies on pupil behaviour and anti-bullying. It supports the idea that misbehaviour and bullying are as much a threat to the rights and interests of the generality of children as they are to the good order and educational effectiveness of the school. It is often believed that pathological problems such as bullying can only be tackled from within. Creating an environment hostile to bullying and harnessing the school's own resources, especially its pupils and staff, to fight systemic bullying are seen as the most effective ways to support this process. Ofsted has concluded that 'practical action founded on clear moral principles and the active involvement of pupils and parents can combat bullying and challenge a culture that accepts it as inevitable.'[165] Outside support will also be needed, from specialist professionals to help with individual cases and from the LEA in organising staff training.

---

161 Above n 133, part 2 para 17(d).

162 C. Harber, above n 4.

163 'In four out of five schools, the approaches used to counter or eliminate instances of oppressive behaviour, including harassment or bullying, are good or better... Schools take bullying seriously and, in the main, pupils and parents report that incidents are dealt with effectively': Chief Inspector of Schools in England, *Standards and Quality 2002-03. Annual Report of Her Majesty's Chief Inspector of Schools* (London: The Stationery Office, 2004), paras 160 and 161.

164 See A. Osler and K. Vincent, *Girls and Exclusion* (London: Routledge Falmer, 2003), p 96.

165 Above n 94, p 2.

Clearly the law has a role to play in establishing a framework for preventive and responsive action and for accountability. Recent clear acknowledgement in the courts in England that schools' duty of care extends to victims of bullying in school and that there is a possibility of negligence liability is important in recognising that bullying is not merely a social problem, but a cause of serious long term mental health problems and consequent disadvantage in later life. It is also likely to engender a more proactive engagement with the problem by schools and education authorities, especially when fears of liability are reinforced by reports of significant awards in other jurisdictions, for example, Japan.[166] The extension of statutory duties on schools in the independent (private) sector is also important in conveying the message of 'zero-tolerance' and that there should be no safe territory for bullies.

Just a final note of caution is needed, however. The law has greatly strengthened the hand of head teachers to exclude those believed to be engaged in bullying. It is important that this does not result in complete abandonment of the perpetrators of bullying who, as we have seen, often have mental health or behavioural problems themselves. A holistic response to bullying demands an effort to limit re-offending and to prevent the adverse short and long term consequences of bullying for both bullies and their victims.

---

166 See M. Fitzpatrick, 'Parents of bullied boy win record payment,' *Times Educational Supplement*, 2 February 2001, reporting an award of the equivalent of £232,000 to the parents of a boy who committed suicide as a result of bullying which the school had failed to prevent.

Chapter 3

Drug Policy in English Schools: An Analysis

Charlotte Walsh

Introduction

The British government's ongoing ten year strategy for dealing with drug usage, *Tackling Drugs to Build a Better Britain*, was published in 1998.[1] In his foreword to this document, the Prime Minister, Tony Blair, stated that the overall aim of the new strategy was to: 'break once and for all the vicious cycle of drugs and crime which wrecks lives and threatens communities.'[2] In an attempt to achieve this, one of the strategy's four stated key objectives was 'to help young people resist drug misuse in order to achieve their full potential in society.'[3] An *Updated Drug Strategy* was published in 2002.[4] In his foreword to this document, the Home Secretary, David Blunkett, stressed that:

> Young people are our highest priority. They need good quality drug education, information and advice based on a credible assessment of the damage drugs do, within a framework which makes clear that all controlled drugs are harmful and will remain illegal.[5]

In relation to young people, the government's aim is to discourage them from using drugs in the first place. Education in schools is one of the key methods by which they aim to achieve this: firstly, by expanding the provision and improving the quality of drug education so that, by March 2004, all primary and secondary schools have drug education policies; and secondly, it is hoped that, by March 2006, the quality of drug education lessons will have improved to the extent that

---

1 Home Office, *Tackling Drugs to Build a Better Britain. The Government's Ten-Year Strategy for Tackling Drug Misuse*, Cm 3945 (London: The Stationery Office, 1998). http://www.archive.official-documents.co.uk/document/cm39/3945/3945.htm

2 Ibid.

3 Ibid.

4 Home Office, *Updated Drug Strategy 2002* (London: Home Office, 2002).

5 Ibid, p 3.

none of them are described as 'poor' by the Office for Standards in Education (Ofsted).[6]

With a view to meeting these aims, the government has recently published updated drug policy guidance for schools.[7] Following an evaluation of the success of schools in tackling the social problem of drug taking to date, this chapter charts progressions in drug education policy, assisted by a comparison of the earlier guidance with its replacement. The increasing focus on educating young people about drugs—as opposed to a narrow focus on abstention—is welcomed, as it reflects important research findings in this area. In stark contrast, however, the move towards drug testing as part of drug management in schools is decried. Comparative analysis of similar developments in the USA is also presented. Importantly, drug testing regimes there are more restrictively applied than has been proposed in the UK: yet, this had not prevented repeated challenges to their constitutionality. Questions have also been raised as regards the efficacy of drug testing. Parallel concerns apply in this country, and are explored from, inter alia, a human rights based perspective. The tension inherent in adopting such contradictory responses to drugs in schools is highlighted, set against the background of discrepancies in drug policy more generally.

The Role of Schools in Tackling the Social Problem of Drug-Taking

The classroom is viewed as crucial in the government's drug strategy: it is seen as the place where young people's perceptions of drugs are most likely to be influenced. The Education Act, section 78(1), requires every school to provide a balanced curriculum that:

> (a) promotes the spiritual, moral, cultural, mental and physical development of pupils at the school and of society; and
> (b) prepares pupils at the school for the opportunities, responsibilities and experiences of later life.

Drug education is part of this curriculum. There is a requirement for drug education in the National Curriculum Science Order:[8] this represents the statutory minimum. Ideally, it is viewed as being best delivered through well-planned Personal, Social and Health Education and Citizenship provision; a whole-school

---

6 Ibid, p 7.

7 Department for Education and Skills, *Drugs: Guidance for Schools* (London: Department for Education and Skills, 2004).

8 SI 2000/1600.

approach is advocated.[9] Further guidance is produced by the Qualifications and Curriculum Authority.[10]

Since the implementation of the government's ten-year drug strategy in 1998, universal programmes of education and information have been expanded and are considered to have improved.[11] Ofsted carries out school inspections and special exercises in schools, and thus has evidence of the drug education provided. For instance, in 2002, Ofsted carried out a postal survey of drug education programmes in 1,200 schools: the main findings were that pupils achieved adequate (or better) levels of appropriate knowledge of drugs and their effects in most lessons in primary school and in 80 per cent of lessons in secondary school. However, follow-up teaching was not always found to do enough to help pupils develop their values, attitudes, and the personal skills they need to make informed choices.[12]

The delivery of drug education in practice is affected by the question of priorities: teachers are under an enormous amount of pressure to deliver all the statutory elements of the National Curriculum and constraints of time will obviously affect the proportion of class time that can be given over to drug education. In lessons where pupils' knowledge was weak, this was usually attributable to poor teacher awareness of drugs and their effects, or to lessons being too short or insufficiently planned. That said, the report found that the proportion of schools with a drug education policy was ever increasing, and that the quality of drug education continued to improve.[13] However, what is more difficult to ascertain is whether this translates into changes in attitudes and behaviour.

The difficulties with evaluating the effects of these programmes are highlighted by the Health Development Agency, who are currently involved in collating and assessing reviews of the evidence base for drug education and prevention, particularly in relation to reducing health inequalities. They have commented on the fact that the evidence base in England and Wales does not meet established quality standards for scientific evidence. Further, most initiatives in this field are not evidence-based, nor are they subjected to systematic evaluation: 'In other words, there are very few peer-reviewed journal articles, which employ a rigorous methodology to compare different types of drug education and prevention interventions and their outcomes.'[14]

---

9 Above n 7, p 20.

10 For example, QCA, *Drug, Alcohol and Tobacco Education: curriculum guidance for schools at key stages 1-4*, Teachers' Booklet (London: QCA, 2003).

11 Office for Standards in Education, *Drug Education in Schools: an update* (London: Ofsted, 2002). http://www.ofsted.gov.uk.

12 Ibid.

13 Ibid.

14 Home Affairs Select Committee, *The Government's Drug Policy: is it working?*, Memorandum 30 (London: House of Commons, 2002).

With these limitations in mind, an attempt will be made to evaluate the success of schools in tackling the social problem of drug-taking by looking at: the available statistics; a review of the literature; the views of young people; and recent policy shifts in this area.

Statistics

A (rather crude) method of assessing whether drug education works, is to look at the statistics on drug use. Information to monitor drug use for those under 16 years and for those of 16 years and over is available from two separate sources. Concentrating firstly on the under-16s, the most recent published statistics come from a survey carried out by the National Centre for Social Research and the National Foundation for Educational Research in 2002.[15] This is the latest in a series established in 1982, studying the smoking, drinking and drug use of young people aged 11-15. Whilst this chapter focuses on use of illegal drugs, it is important to note that smoking, drinking and drug use are all highly interrelated behaviours: all of the surveys have consistently found that those pupils who either smoke or drink are more likely to take illegal drugs. Eighteen per cent of those surveyed had taken drugs in the last year, which represented a marginal decrease from 20 per cent in 2001.[16] As would be anticipated, the survey found that cannabis was by far the most widely used drug, with 13 per cent of the group having taken it: however, amongst 11 and 12 year olds, misuse of volatile substances was more common than smoking cannabis.[17] In total, four per cent reported using any Class A drug in the past year:[18] Class A is a category created by the Misuse of Drugs Act 1971 and includes those drugs perceived to be the most dangerous to the user and to society, such as cocaine, heroin and Ecstasy.

The main source of information in relation to the older age group, those aged 16 to 24 years, is the British Crime Survey, which has included a self-report component on drug use since 1994. The latest published results on drug use derived from this source estimated that 28 per cent of young people had used at least one illicit drug in the last year, with around 8 per cent of these having used a Class A drug.[19] There have been changes in the use of specific Class A drugs among young people: use of amphetamines, LSD and ecstasy have decreased; cocaine is the only such drug whose usage has increased.[20]

---

15 NatCen / NFER, *Smoking, Drinking and Drug Use Among Young People in England in 2002* (London: The Stationery Office, 2003).

16 Ibid, p 100.

17 Ibid, p 102.

18 Ibid.

19 J. Condon and N. Smith, *Prevalence of Drug Use: key findings from the 2002/2003 British Crime Survey*, Findings 229 (London: Home Office, 2003), p 1.

20 Ibid.

However, gauging the success of drug education programmes is more complex than simply measuring whether or not levels of drug taking amongst young people have dropped: clearly factors other than drug education, such as drug availability, will impact upon the statistics. It is generally accepted that young people in this country have increasing access to illegal drugs,[21] so it is feasible that the number of young people refusing drugs could increase and yet levels of drug-taking remain the same (or even increase). Alternative research sources to these statistics have to be used.

Literature Reviews

Many evaluations of drug prevention initiatives have been published in recent years, particularly in the United States. Dorn and Murji carried out a comprehensive review of these evaluations in the early 1990s: they concluded that drug education does not stop drug-taking; however, they felt that it could be instrumental in restraining post-initiation escalation of use and felt that it should, therefore, focus on harm reduction.[22] A more recent review of drug education programmes and their potential to prevent or to reduce the use of illicit substances was published in *Addiction* in 1998.[23] Focusing predominantly on initiatives in the USA, the researchers reported that the impact of evaluated interventions was small, with dissipation of programme gains over time: 'Sixty-two evaluations were included in this review, 18 produced evidence of programme effectiveness on drug using behaviour, but in only two cases was hard evidence produced to demonstrate an impact on drug use.'[24]

Life Skills Training (LST) was one of the programmes demonstrated as having some continuing success five years after the end of the programme.[25] LST was developed in the USA by Botvin of Cornell University and has been implemented there for many years. Its impact has been evaluated across a number of research studies and it has been promoted as one of the few effective drug education programmes.[26] LST is a highly successful commercial concern that focuses on developing skills in drug resistance and self-management, alongside more general social skills; attempts are also made to tackle underlying factors in the origins of drug use. The programme's website makes great claims as regards

---

21 J. D. Wright and L. Pearl, 'Knowledge and Experience of Young People Regarding Drug Misuse, 1969-1994' (1995) *British Medical Journal*, 309, 20-23.

22 N. Dorn and K. Murji, *Drug Prevention: a review of the English language literature* (London: ISDD, 1992).

23 D. White and M. Pitts, 'Educating Young People About Drugs: a systematic review' (1998) *Addiction,* 93(10), 1475-1487.

24 Ibid, p 1484.

25 Ibid, p 1482.

26 G. Botvin, 'Substance Abuse Prevention: Theory, Practice, and Effectiveness', in M. Tonry and J. Q. Wilson (eds.), *Drugs and Crime* (Chicago, IL: University of Chicago Press, 1990).

its effectiveness, asserting that it can reduce tobacco, alcohol and illicit drug use by as much as 87 per cent.[27] Researchers White and Pitts found that there were too few studies carried out in Britain to determine whether programmes such as LST succeeded over here; however, it was noted that drug prevention programmes in Britain were generally less intensive than in the USA, which may have a negative impact on what is already a fairly low impact rate: 'One way of expressing an effect of this size is that exposure to school based drugs education accounts for 0.14 per cent of the variance in drug use. This statistic suggests that drugs education has such a trivial impact on behaviour that in its present form it is of no practical relevance.'[28]

Exploring this issue further, the Scottish Executive carried out a recent review of LST.[29] The reviewers noted that, whilst such programmes *can* have statistically significant effects on substance use onset rates, the size of these effects is consistently small: they warned that LST promotional material overstates the programme's effectiveness. In line with White and Pitts, this led to them questioning whether the costs and resources required for LST training and implementation are justified, given the limited impact it delivers.[30] Even the propensity to produce minimal effects is questioned by Stothard, an independent consultant in health education, specialising in drug education and prevention, who makes the valid point that: 'There is ... still no proven causal link between LST programmes and processes and the measured outcomes. To test this, the study would need to have control groups that devote the same amount of time delivering other, possibly basic drugs awareness, interventions.'[31] In a more generalized research review of school based drug prevention programmes, published by the Scottish Executive, the authors commented: 'It is clear from these studies that certain aspects of these programmes are more beneficial. These include skills development, self-esteem and confidence building, targeting high risk groups, using health professionals and peers, booster sessions, and involving parents.'[32] However, it is important to note that this review of the literature also reported that some studies have discovered negative effects of school interventions, such as an increase in cannabis use amongst those exposed to a life skills programme in the USA.[33] Recognition of all of these factors has informed good practice in this area.

27 http://www.lifeskillstraining.com.

28 D. White and M. Pitts, above n 23, p 1484.

29 N. Coggans (et al), *The Life Skills Drug Education Programme: a review of research* (Edinburgh: Scottish Executive Effective Interventions Unit, 2003).

30 Ibid, p 5.

31 B. Stothard, 'Lies, Damned Lies and Research: does lifeskills training work?' (2003) *DrugLink,* May/June, p 18.

32 S. Burniston et al, *Drug Treatment Services for Young People: a research review* (Edinburgh: Scottish Executive Effective Interventions Unit, 2002), p 27.

33 Ibid.

The Views of Young People

The 2001 statistical publication on smoking, drinking and drug use among young people included a qualitative evaluation of their views on drug education.[34] It reported that lessons about drugs were remembered by approximately 64 per cent of pupils.[35] The survey considered two opposing views on the impact of drug education: on the one hand, the view that talking about drug issues encourages experimentation; on the other, that ignorance leads to greater experimentation due to a lack of understanding of the consequences of drug use. On this matter, it concluded: 'This survey found no evidence that having lessons on smoking, drinking and drugs either encouraged or discouraged experimentation or use.'[36]

In his submission to the Home Affairs Select Committee's 2001 review of government drug policy, researcher Neil Hunt, drawing on a qualitative study he had previously conducted involving 235 young people and their views on drugs education, highlighted the cynicism felt by many of them towards drug education programmes. This appeared to stem from what were considered to be flaws with drug policy in general, such as the irreconcilable way in which alcohol and cannabis are treated so differently from one another: this lack of coherence seemed to have the effect of undermining the perceived legitimacy of efforts to provide health information and advice. Hunt also noted that drug education is largely irrelevant to the many young people who have no intention of trying drugs, and to those who find the 'prohibition' agenda to be patronising.[37]

Drug Education Policy in Schools

However, there has recently been a shift in policy as regards the most effective approach to take with drug education, with the focus on prohibition being lessened: the previous reliance on shock tactics has largely been abandoned in favour of a more pragmatic approach. This change in stance is particularly welcome given that those drug education programmes that are most vocal in their anti-drugs message have been found to glamorise drug use and, potentially, to increase usage.[38] The abandonment of shock tactics will be welcomed by researchers such as Cohen, who made the following comment on the old approach to drug education:

---

34 R. Boreham and A. Shaw (eds), *Smoking, Drinking and Drug Use Among Young People in England in 2000* (London: Department of Health, 2001).

35 Ibid, p 17.

36 Ibid.

37 Home Affairs Select Committee 2002, above n 10, Memorandum 31.

38 M. Plant and M. Plant, *Risk Takers: alcohol, drugs, sex and youth* (London: Routledge, 1992).

> Many of the school programmes have been more in the realm of propaganda than education. Simplistic messages and sloganeering have been prominent and the dangers of drug use have often been exaggerated to the exclusion of all else in an attempt to put young people off drugs... Such an approach is fundamentally flawed. When young people eventually find out that they have been lied to (as they invariably do, through their own experience or that of their friends) they will cease to trust adult sources of drug information... At a time when more young people are using more types of drugs it is important to pursue approaches to drug education that are based on firm educational principles rather than propaganda.[39]

Cohen argues that many flawed assumptions have previously been made by drug educators: that shock tactics will discourage young people from using drugs; that people who know the 'facts' will not take drugs; that people with a sense of personal responsibility and 'morality' will abstain; that people only take drugs because of peer pressure and so, once coached in resistance skills, will be able to refrain; that drug taking is never the result of a fully informed rational choice; and that people who take drugs have low self-esteem. He argues that it is misleading to characterise all those who take drugs as 'immoral,' irrational or lacking in self-esteem, just as it would be wrong to pigeonhole the majority of the population who drink alcohol in the same way. As a result, drug education has tended not to work, being that it is based on fundamental misinterpretations of the reasons why people take drugs in the first place, ignoring both the pleasurable aspects of drug-taking and the acceptance of risk by adolescents.[40]

Thus, it follows that good drug education programmes should attempt to identify correctly the motivations behind drug taking. A qualitative study by Boys et al, involving in-depth interviews with 50 16-21-year-olds, looked into the range of factors that are influential in young people's decision on whether or not to use drugs in an attempt to see if drug education programmes were rationally targeted.[41] This research made the important point that it is not just those factors that influence a young person's initial decision to use drugs that need to be identified, but also those factors that influence later decisions to continue or discontinue drug-taking; influences upon levels of drug-taking were also felt to be worthy of investigation, as many drug users had established certain boundaries for themselves that they would not cross.[42]

The reasons and motivations cited for taking drugs were seen to range from quite broad statements, such as that drug-taking made you feel better, to specific functions, like increased self-confidence, with different drugs being used to

---

39 J. Cohen, 'Drugs in the Classroom: politics, propaganda and censorship' (1996) *DrugLink,* March/April 12-14, p 12.

40 Ibid.

41 A. Boys et al, 'What Influences Young People's Use of Drugs? A Qualitative Study of Decision-Making' (1999) *Drugs: Education, Prevention and Policy,* 6(3), 373-387.

42 Ibid, p 374.

perform different functions.[43] It was recommended that drug education programmes should take greater note of the various uses to which drugs are put, including for dieting, staying awake and increasing motivation, rather than focusing almost exclusively on the recreational and sociable aspects of drug taking.[44] The point was also made that, despite the prioritisation given to teaching life skills aimed at helping young people to resist peer pressure to take drugs, the prevailing opinion of the interviewees was that drug use was engaged in through choice, not as a result of social pressures: in reality, like-minded individuals tend to gravitate towards one another.[45]

Another developing element of good practice is that it has increasingly been recognised as important that fanciful aims are not set for drug education programmes, lest they be doomed to fail. This is recognised in previous Department for Education and Employment guidance, which stated: 'We do not wish to raise unrealistic expectations of what drug education can achieve. A pragmatic and realistic approach is needed by all—acknowledging that no conceivable approach will stamp out drug-taking altogether.'[46] In his submission to the Select Committee, researcher Neil Hunt also communicated his views on the foolishness of expecting too much from drug education:

> Unlike other forms of education, for the most part 'drug education' is poorly done and not based on informing and enabling people to make up their own minds. Instead, the conclusion that young people should reach is predetermined and, with few exceptions, the content of drug education is skewed to try to achieve this. That is not to say that reducing drug-related harm and developing informed citizens regarding this area of public policy is not an important objective. However, grounding this in a 'primary prevention' framework drives people towards an unattainable outcome, is inconsistent with the general principles of education and disenchants pupils and teachers alike.[47]

It is because of this that Cohen recommends that, in most cases, it is more realistic for schools to focus on *educational*, rather than *behavioural* aims:

> If drug education can't stop young people using drugs, some may say, why bother? On the positive side, research evaluations indicate that drug education can increase knowledge and understanding, clarify attitudes and values and help develop personal and social decision-making skills. In other words drug education can have important *educational* outcomes.[48]

---

43 Ibid.

44 Ibid, p 385.

45 Ibid, p 383.

46 Department for Education and Employment, *Protecting Young People*, (London: Department for Education and Employment, 1998), p 2.

47 Home Affairs Select Committee 2002, above n 21.

48 J. Cohen, 'Just Say—Oh No, Not Again' (2002) *DrugLink,* July/August 13-14, p 13.

The logic is that a choice is only genuine if it is informed. The difficulty with this approach is that drug taking is illegal and strongly disapproved of by many members of society. Whilst their attitude to illegal drugs is often hypocritical and inconsistent with their views on legal drugs, such as alcohol, the prevalence of such opinions will inevitably affect drug education which, as with sex education, is expected to take a certain 'moralistic' stance. Unfortunately, such a stance may have adverse effects on harm reduction, making young people less likely to approach adults openly about drug issues: 'in the case of drugs, where experimentation is likely to be covert and potentially dangerous, there is a strong case in favour of sound knowledge, especially in terms of harm reduction.'[49] Harm reduction is especially important, given that Britain has the highest proportion of drug related deaths in relation to its population in Europe.[50] The difficulty here is in trying to strike the balance between simply condemning drug usage—which has been seen to be ineffective—and giving a credible message on drugs, without being seen to encourage drug taking. The extent to which these principles of good practice inform drug education policy in schools, with a focus on recent developments, will now be considered.

In their evidence to the Select Committee drug policy review, the Drug Education Forum cited anecdotal evidence gathered from discussions with teachers and other practitioners, indicating that there was a lack of consensus about the purpose of drug education and that this was confusing and overburdening them.[51] Following their large-scale survey of teachers, the NUT were enormously concerned that many teachers had remarked that they did not receive adequate support from management or from headteachers in delivering drug education and in developing drug prevention strategies in schools: this, in spite of the support offered by local Drug Action Teams, LEA Advisers and other external agencies.[52] In response to such concerns, a revision and consolidation of earlier guidance contained within documents such as the Department for Education and Skills Circular 4/95[53] and within *Protecting Young People*[54] was instigated, including an incorporation of the key messages contained within a range of DrugScope publications,[55] and recommendations made both as

49 A. Rogers, 'Drugs and Drugs Education in the Inner City: the views of 12-year-olds and their parents' (1999) *Drugs: Education: Prevention and Policy*, 6(1), p 58.

50 http://www.drugscope.org.uk.

51 Home Affairs Select Committee 2002, above n 10, Memorandum 19.

52 Ibid, Memorandum 47.

53 Department for Education and Employment, *Drug Prevention in Schools*, DfEE Circular 4/95 (London: Department for Education and Employment, 1995).

54 Department for Education and Skills, above n 46.

55 DrugScope, *The Right Choice: guidance on selecting drug education materials for schools* (London: DrugScope, 1998); DrugScope, *The Right Approach: quality standards in drug education* (London: DrugScope, 1999); DrugScope, *The Right Responses: managing and making policy for drug-related incidents in schools*

part of the National Healthy School Standard[56] and by Ofsted.[57] To this end, a consultation on the draft revision of guidance took place in 2003,[58] resulting in *Drugs: Guidance for Schools* being published in February 2004.[59]

The most striking difference between the original 1995 drug guidance for schools and its replacement is the length, with the new version being roughly 100 pages longer than its sparse 20 page predecessor: this can be seen as evidence of the increased knowledge base in this area, alongside an increase in its prioritization. Another notable change is the fact that, in the updated guidance, the terms 'drugs' and 'drug education' are taken to refer to both illegal and legal drugs:[60] in the earlier circular, cigarette smoking and alcohol were dealt with as separate issues.[61] In the list provided of drugs of particular significance, it is of symbolic importance that alcohol and tobacco are at the top.[62] This is in recognition of the fact that the distinctions made in policy between illegal and legal drugs are largely arbitrary. It is worth noting that this will not prevent many pupils finding the punitive legislative consequences attached to the use of illegal drugs, yet not to that of legal drugs, hard to reconcile. In contrast to the 1995 Circular, the aim of drug education is clearly stated in the 2004 document, as being: 'to provide opportunities for pupils to develop their knowledge, skills, attitudes and understanding about drugs and appreciate the benefits of a healthy lifestyle, relating this to their own and others' actions.'[63] The fact that this has been made explicit is to be welcomed. It is telling that the second part of this stated aim, as included in the earlier draft of the updated guidance that went out to consultation, has been omitted. It read: 'Drug education cannot be value free. Schools need to set realistic aims for their drug education programmes which are consistent with the moral values and framework of the school and with the laws of our society.'[64]

The subsequent deletion of any reference to morals or values, and the content of the aim of drug education that remains, represents a significant shift away from the traditional 'war on drugs' to a more pragmatic approach. This shift is

(London: DrugScope, 1999); DrugScope/Alcohol Concern, *Opportunities for Drug and Alcohol Education in the School Curriculum* (London: DrugScope, 2001).

56 Department for Education and Skills, *National Healthy School Standard: guidance* (London: DfES, 1999); see further, Health Development Agency, *National Healthy School Standard: drug education (including alcohol and tobacco)* (London: HDA, 2003).

57 Ofsted 2002, above n 11.

58 Department for Education and Skills, *Drugs: Guidance for Schools*, Consultation Paper (London: Department for Education and Skills, 2003).

59 Department for Education and Skills, above n 7.

60 Ibid, p 13.

61 Department for Education and Employment 1995, op cit, n 53, part III.

62 Department for Education and Skills above n 7, p 23.

63 Ibid, p 18.

64 Department for Education and Skills, above n 58, p 12.

further evidenced by the fact that the aim does not incorporate any direct reference to trying to achieve a *reduction* in levels of drug usage. This recognition that schools need to have realistic aims for their drug education contrasts with the earlier guidance where it was stated that students 'should be encouraged to reject drugs.'[65] The new approach is reflective of the updated circular drawing from the evidence base for drug education. It states:

> Research shows that certain models of drug education can achieve modest reductions in the consumption of cannabis, alcohol and tobacco and delay the onset of their use. There are also indications that drug education has a role in reducing the risks associated with drug use, reducing the amount of drugs used and helping people to stop.[66]

This clearly demonstrates that the government is under no illusions as regards the rather minimal primary preventative effects that can be expected from drug education. In terms of delivery, the ensuing focus on, inter alia, drug education for primary school children, the use of peer education, and parental involvement, all find their roots in contemporary good practice in this area.[67] Worthy of further analysis is the increasing policy recognition of the special drug education needs of vulnerable young people.

The Select Committee review highlighted the importance of targeting drug prevention and education programmes towards particularly vulnerable groups of young people, such as truants, those excluded from school and children in care;[68] this is reflected in the new guidance.[69] Such prioritization takes account of a recognised hurdle in this field: namely, that those most vulnerable to drug problems are often not in school for drug education sessions.[70] An earlier report, published in 2000, examined the provision of drug education for excluded young people.[71] The report stressed the critical importance of drug education in this area:

---

65 Department for Education and Emplyment, above n 53, para 16.

66 Department for Education and Skills , above n 7, p 19.

67 See further, C. Lloyd (et al), 'The Effectiveness of Primary School Drug Education' (2000) *Drugs: Education, Prevention and Policy*, 7(2), pp 109-126; M. Shiner, *Doing It for Themselves: an evaluation of peer approaches to drug prevention*, DPAS Briefing Paper 6 (London: Home Office, 2000); R. Velleman, W. Mistral and L. Sanderling, *Taking the Message Home: involving parents in drugs prevention*, DPAS Briefing Paper 5 (London: Home Office, 2000).

68 Home Affairs Select Committee, above n 14, para 213.

69 Department for Education and Skills, above n 7, pp 51-54.

70 See further, B. Powis and P. Griffiths, *Working at the Margins: an evaluation of a drugs-prevention programme for young people who have been excluded from school*, DPAS Briefing Paper 15 (London: Home Office, 2001).

71 DrugScope, *Drug Education for School Excludees: a study of six local authorities' provision of drug education for young people not in school* (London: DrugScope, 2000).

> On an anecdotal level, it has long been believed that young people excluded from school are also likely to be excluded in other ways, to have less access to services than non-excluded young people, and are more likely to engage in potentially harmful activities including those relating to drug use ... The reverse of this is that successful drug education has the potential to be a factor in tackling exclusion—assisting a young person's return to mainstream schooling as well as addressing wider issues of exclusion and healthier choices.[72]

It is important to recognise that many of the children who are excluded from school have been excluded *for* involvement in drug offences. How such offences are dealt with in schools is of crucial importance and it is to this issue that this chapter now turns.

Dealing with Drug Offences in Schools

In their submission to the Home Affairs Select Committee, DrugScope pointed out: 'There is still some evidence that schools use exclusion for minor drug offences as a first response and that looked-after children remain particularly vulnerable to drug misuse.'[73] The issue of how schools should deal with drug-related incidents was the subject of a 1999 advisory publication.[74] The report advised that it was inappropriate for schools to take disciplinary action harsher than that which would be imposed by the law.[75] It also stressed that the aim of all interventions should be to promote pupils' understanding and minimise harm, and noted that over-reacting to incidents, especially labelling pupils as drug misusers, can actually lead to an escalation in drug use.[76] On the question of exclusion, the report suggested that constructive strategies that helped pupils re-invest in their own education were to be preferred; primacy was placed on the welfare of students.[77] These issues are addressed in the guidance, which recommends:

> Any response should balance the needs of the individual with those of the wider school community, and aim to provide pupils with the opportunity to learn from their mistakes and develop as individuals... Schools should develop a range of responses in line with local protocols and consider all the factors... before determining their response.[78]

---

72 Ibid, p 7.

73 Home Affairs Select Committee 2002, above n 14, Memorandum 20.

74 DrugScope, *The Right Approach* (Etc), above n 55.

75 Ibid, p ix.

76 Ibid, p x; see also Addaction, *Collecting the Evidence: clients' views on drug services* (London: Addaction, 2004).

77 Ibid.

78 Department for Education and Skills, above n 7, p 67.

Alongside the more progressive responses that are suggested, such as referral, counselling and the drawing up of behaviour support plans, one of the options available is exclusion, be that fixed-period or permanent.[79] The guidance states that:

> Permanent exclusion should usually be the final step in the process for dealing with disciplinary offences after a wide range of other strategies have been tried without success. Supplying an illegal drug is a serious breach of school rules and it may be one of the exceptional circumstances where the headteacher judges that it is appropriate to permanently exclude a pupil, even for a one-off or first-time offence.[80]

Whilst on the face of it this (arguably) does not seem overly problematic, it is important to appreciate that, as is made explicit earlier in the document, the term 'supply' is drawn very broadly and includes instances of pupils sharing drugs or a group of friends taking it in turns to bring drugs in for their own use, as well as habitual organised supply for profit.[81] This definition of supply, whilst being, it is submitted, overly inclusive, is consistent with the government's broader refusal to distinguish between social and commercial supply.[82]

Whilst, legally, schools have no obligation to report an incident involving drugs to the police,[83] this is clearly a further option that is available. It is interesting that the following proviso from the 1995 Circular has no equivalent in its successor, with the result that there seems to be unspoken encouragement for schools to use their discretion to deal with incidents 'in-house': 'Although there is no statutory requirement to do so, the Secretary of State would expect the police to be informed when illegal drugs are found on a pupil or school premises.'[84] Traditionally the police have supported schools in a variety of ways, including in the area of drug education: they have specific expertise in relation to law and procedures and the criminal consequences of drug offending. However, one of the difficulties with police involvement in drug education is that their role as enforcers can conflict with their role as educators. A report that looked at the involvement of the Metropolitan Police Service in this area noted this tension:

> Police managers see the opportunities for intelligence gathering around drugs and other crimes presented by school visits. However, there is a lack of clarity on

---

79 Ibid, p 68.

80 Ibid, p 73.

81 Ibid, p 66.

82 Home Office, *The Government's Drug Policy: is it working? The Government Reply to the Third Report from the Home Affairs Committee Session 2001-2002 HC 318* (London: Home Office, 2002), p 11.

83 Above n 7, p 59.

84 Department for Education and Employment, above n 53, para 49.

> whether School Involvement Officers should have an enforcement role on school premises… Police practitioners hold ambivalent feelings on their new mixed role.[85]

The DrugScope website highlights these tensions in its Drug News.[86] For example, in January 2002 four boys were arrested after a police sniffer dog found cannabis during an anti-drugs talk at a school in Devon; a year later a school near Sollihull announced its plans to deploy sniffer dogs to randomly search pupils as part of its drug education programme. The new guidance aims to ensure that such incidents will not occur in the future, by clearly stating that demonstrations and educational visits should never be used surreptitiously as a detection exercise.[87] However, that is not to say that sniffer dogs cannot be legitimately used as a tool of detection: this is dealt with, for the first time, in the new guidance:

> Some schools have adopted further strategies such as urine-testing or requesting police handlers or private companies with sniffer dogs to enter the school in order to detect illegal possession or use. Headteachers are entitled to use such strategies and they are best placed to make decisions on whether such approaches are appropriate.[88]

It is notable that, since its reclassification, if cannabis is the drug that is sniffed out or otherwise detected, it is only young people who run the risk of being arrested: an adult committing the same offence would simply have their drugs confiscated and receive a warning.[89] Thus, the separate treatment of young people under the youth justice system, instigated to deal with them more leniently in recognition of their lesser level of responsibility, actually results in a more intrusive response.

The use of sniffer dogs and urine testing came in for severe criticism during the consultation period, with many respondents considering it to be highly inappropriate, representing a fundamental breach of trust between the school and its pupils.[90] In response to such concerns, before utilising either of the above strategies, schools are required to follow the guidance in an attached appendix.[91] This appendix states that either tactic can be adopted where a school believes that

---

85 L. O'Connor, N. Coggans and S. McKellar, *From Policy to Practice—The New Metropolitan Police Service Strategy for School Drug Education and Support: an evaluation of implementation and impact across five pilot sites* (London: MPS, 2001), p 5.

86 http://www.drugscope.org.uk/news

87 Above n 7, p 63.

88 Ibid.

89 Misuse of Drugs Act 1971 (Modification) (No 2) Order 2003; ACPO, *Cannabis Enforcement Guidance* (London: ACPO, 2003).

90 Department for Education and Skills, *Revision of DfES Guidance to Schools on Drugs* (London: Department for Education and Skills, 2003), Q9.

91 Department for Education and Skills, above n 7, Appendix 10. NB. This appendix is unclear as regards which aspects of it apply to sniffer dogs and which to urine testing, though it shall be taken as applying throughout to both.

there is reasonable evidence of drug-related incidents occurring. Whilst it is strongly recommended that the police are involved, the guidance does not rule out the possibility of schools using private companies to carry out these functions. Schools are advised to make sure that their intention to use one or both of these measures is made transparent in their drug policy. Moreover, thought should be given in advance to the response that will be triggered by drugs being detected. This should be in line with the pastoral responsibility of the school to create a sensitive environment and the need to be culturally sensitive.[92]

Tony Blair announced plans for drug testing in state schools to the media prior to the new guidance being distributed, giving it far greater weight than was apparent from the document itself: 'We cannot force them to do it, but if heads believe they have a problem in their school, then they should be able to use random drug testing.'[93] His comments were followed by a rash of media reports, echoing many of the concerns voiced in the consultation process. For example, *The Mirror* warned of the numbers of pupils who will fail drug tests, or else play truant in order to avoid them: the prospect of legal challenges over such tests was also raised, as it is questionable whether they are compliant with the European Convention on Human Rights (ECHR).[94]

Drug Testing: ECHR Compliability?

The provisions of the ECHR with which drug testing in schools may be seen to conflict include Articles 5 and 8. Article 5 states that everyone has the right to liberty and security of person: whilst this can be derogated from in certain specified circumstances,[95] none of them appear to validate such tests. Under Article 8, everyone has the right to respect for their private and family life. Again interference with this right by a public authority is only allowed in certain circumstances, most notably, 'for the prevention of disorder or crime [or] for the protection of health or morals.'[96] The key issue is whether drug testing is a proportionate response to the perceived problem of drug taking in schools: if not, Article 8 will have been transgressed.

Whilst no test cases have been brought as yet in relation to the compatibility of school drug testing with the ECHR, analogous situations have arisen in the fields of penology and employment law. In *R v Secretary of State for the Home Department ex parte Tremayne*,[97] the applicant argued that the random element of mandatory drug testing in prisons infringed both Article 8 and Article 6 of the Convention, the latter on the basis that it was tantamount to self-incrimination.

---

92 Ibid.

93 'Blair: I Won't Quit,' *News of the World*, 22 February 2004.

94 B. Roberts, 'PM Warned Over School Drug Tests,' *The Mirror,* 23 February 2004.

95 ECHR, Art 5(1).

96 Art 8(2).

97 [1996] CLY 4583.

The court denied that this was so, and asserted that Article 8 was not infringed as random drug testing was in the interests of all prisoners generally.

In *O'Flynn v Airlinks the Airport Coach Company Limited*[98] the applicant was dismissed after testing positive for cannabis in a random drugs test. The tribunal did not believe that the fact that O'Flynn was expected to report for duty without drugs in her system interfered with her private life; in any event, it believed that, even if it did, the intrusion was justified under Article 8(2) for public safety reasons, as she was expected to serve hot coffee. In the Privy Council case of *Whitefield v General Medical Council*,[99] the view was taken that it was not a transgression of Article 8 for the General Medical Council to require a GP to be tested to ensure that he was abstaining completely from drinking alcohol as a condition of his registration; again, even if it did, it was felt that this was justified under Article 8(2) for public safety reasons. This is a somewhat surprising decision, given that alcohol is not even a controlled drug. Commenting on these cases, Delaney notes the rather conservative view that has emerged in relation to testing and Article 8 compatibility.[100]

However, case law has also seen tentative development of the idea that Article 8 should be construed more broadly, to protect against 'lifestyle' discrimination, namely, the right to live as oneself.[101] Discussing these developments, McColgan notes that it is clear from the jurisprudence of the ECHR that compulsory urine tests amount to an 'interference' under Article 8; however, she also points out that it is important not to lose sight of the limitations of the Convention in its application to the workplace.[102] It remains to be seen whether the differences in role between school pupils and employees affect the scope of these limitations, and in which direction.

In light of this lack of clarity and unresolved fears of litigation, John Dunford, General Secretary of the Secondary Heads Association, has commented: 'The reaction of any reasonable headteacher to this guidance would be not to touch random drugs testing with a bargepole.'[103] Parallel concerns about the constitutional legitimacy of school drug testing have arisen in the United States, from where this idea was transported. The use of such tests there will now be considered in detail, with a view to ascertaining whether any lessons can be learned from their experience.

---

98 [2002] Emp LR 1217.

99 [2003] IRLR 39.

100 A. Delaney, 'Employee Privacy—Grasping the Nettle' (2003) *Employment Law Bulletin*, 56 (Aug), 4-6.

101 *Lustig-Prean v United Kingdom (No 1)* (2000) 29 EHRR 523 (ECHR); *Smith v United Kingdom (No 1)* [1999] IRLR 734 (ECHR).

102 A. McColgan, 'Do Privacy Rights Disappear in the Workplace?' (2003) *European Human Rights Law Review* (Special Issue, Priv.), 120-140.

103 As quoted in T. Miles and B. Leapman, 'Drug Test Plan in Disarray' *Evening Standard*, 23 February 2004.

Drug Testing in Schools in the United States: Constitutional Compatibility?

In the US, a minority of schools carry out drug testing: questions have been raised as regards whether this transgresses their students' constitutional rights.[104] In particular, the Fourth Amendment provides that 'the right of people to be secure in their persons, houses, papers, and effects, against unreasonable searches and seizures, shall not be violated.'[105] State compelled drug testing is treated as a 'search' for the purposes of the Fourth Amendment. A search must ordinarily be based upon individualised reasonable suspicion that a violation of the law has occurred; the need to search must be balanced against the invasion that the search entails.[106] The aim is to check unfettered government intrusion into the lives of citizens.[107] The Supreme Court has developed a number of exceptions to these Fourth Amendment rights. Of most relevance, a 'Special Needs' Doctrine has grown up as a significant subset of the broader 'administrative search' exception: it comes into play where individualised reasonable suspicion is incompatible with law enforcement needs.[108]

The 1995 case of *Vernonia*[109] is crucial in understanding the development of the perceived relationship between the Fourth Amendment and drug testing of school children. In *Vernonia*, drug testing was targeted at student athletes who, as a group, were considered to have a recreational drug problem. In determining the constitutionality of the school's policy of drug testing these athletes, the Supreme Court held that the Fourth Amendment does not contain an irreducible requirement of individualised suspicion. Instead, the court applied a balancing test, weighing three factors: (1) the nature of the privacy interest at issue; (2) the character of the intrusion; and (3) the nature and immediacy of the governmental concern and the efficacy of the means employed to address that concern. Of great significance to the court in their decision to approve the school's testing policy was the fact that there was a proven drug problem amongst their athletes. That athletes have a lower expectation of privacy than students do generally, due to the fact that they have pre-season examinations and utilise communal changing areas, was also considered crucial.

---

104 Some schools reward their students for a clean drug test result. Somewhat bizarrely, those who test negative in the Auatauga County School System, Alabama, receive discounts and other perks at more than 55 participating restaurants and stores: see further, Office of National Drug Control Policy, *What You Need to Know About Drug Testing in Schools* (Washington: ONDCP, 2003).

105 US Constitution.

106 *T.L.O.* (1985) 469 U.S. at 340-42.

107 *Camara v Municipal Court* (1967) 387 U.S. 523 at 528.

108 *Griffin v Wisconsin* (1987) 483 U.S. 868 at 881.

109 *Vernonia School District v Acton* (1995) 515 US 646.

However, neither of these factors was present for those students subjected to drug testing in the 2002 case of *Earls*,[110] where the Supreme Court once again looked at the constitutionality of school drug testing and expanded the principles laid down in *Vernonia*. In this instance, school policy required that all middle and high school students consent to random drug testing in order to participate in *any* extra-curricular activity, not just athletic activities. This targeting of those engaged in extra-curricular activities seems misguided: it is suggested that students who join clubs such as Future Homemakers of America are some of the least likely candidates for drug use. Indeed, these students were not deemed to have a particular drug problem, and for the majority of them there seemed to be no reason why they should expect a lower level of privacy than any other student. The balancing test adopted by the court in *Earls* differed from that used in *Vernonia*: the court simply weighed the intrusion upon the young people's Fourth Amendment rights against the promotion of a legitimate interest. In a 5-4 decision, the Supreme Court held that the policy was a reasonable means of furthering the school district's important interest in preventing and deterring drug use amongst its schoolchildren, and therefore did not violate the Fourth Amendment. This can be viewed as a dilution of the rights previously protected under this provision. As a result of this decision:

> School districts today educate America's children on the virtues of the Constitution while simultaneously disregarding their right to be free from unreasonable searches and seizures... That they are educating the young for citizenship is reason for scrupulous protection of Constitutional freedoms of the individual if we are not to strangle the free mind at its source and teach youth to discount important principles of our government as mere platitudes.[111]

Lessons to be Learned

As can be gleaned from the above quote, the sanctioning of drug testing in schools has come in for a great deal of criticism from certain quarters. The most vociferous reaction to this development has come from the American Civil Liberties Union (ACLU),[112] a group particularly concerned with defending the Bill of Rights. Following the failure to have drug testing declared unconstitutional under Federal Law by the Supreme Court in *Earls*, the ACLU has shifted its attention to supporting challenges to school drug testing at state level, where certain state constitutions can offer greater protection of individual rights. Whilst an important case was lost in front of the highest state court in New Jersey,[113]

---

110 *Board of Education of Independent School District No 92 of Pottawatomie County v Earls* (2002) 122 S Ct 2559.

111 G. Thomas, 'Random Suspicionless Drug Testing: are students no longer afforded Fourth Amendment protections?' (2002/03) *New York Law School Review*, 46, 821.

112 http://www.aclu.org.

113 *Joye v Hunterdon Central Bd of Education* (2003) 826 A 2d 624 NJ.

more recently, a significant victory was won when the Supreme Court of Pennsylvania deemed the Delaware School Valley District's drug testing policy to be unconstitutional, on the basis that it 'authorizes a direct invasion of student privacy, with no suspicion at all that the students targeted are involved with alcohol or drugs, or even that they are more likely to be involved than the students who are exempted from the policy.'[114]

The ACLU are also involved in publishing and distributing an information booklet on drug testing.[115] This booklet draws attention to the groundswell of opposition to random drug testing among school officials, experts, parents, and state legislatures.[116] In spite of its promotion at the highest level,[117] lack of general support for drug testing is evidenced by the fact that most schools do not carry out such tests: 95 per cent of schools do not randomly drug test student athletes and no public school district randomly drug tests all of its students.[118] The booklet summarises the main objections to student drug testing as follows:

> Drug testing is not effective in deterring drug use among young people; drug testing is expensive, taking away scarce dollars from other, more effective programs that keep young people out of trouble with drugs; drug testing can be legally risky, exposing schools to potentially costly litigation; drug testing may drive students away from extracurricular activities, which are a proven means of helping students stay out of trouble with drugs; drug testing can undermine relationships of trust between students and teachers and between parents and their children;[119] drug testing can result in false positives, leading to the punishment of innocent students;[120] drug testing does not effectively identify students who have serious problems with drugs; and drug testing may lead to unintended consequences, such as students using drugs that are

---

114 *Theodore* v *The Delaware Valley School District* 836 A.2d 76.

115 F. Gunja (et al), *Making Sense of Student Drug Testing: why educators are saying no* (ACLU/Drug Policy Alliance, 2004).

116 Ibid, p 7.

117 As part of his 2004-05 budget submission to Congress, President George Bush has included an additional $23 million for increased drug testing in schools, up from the $8 million in the previous year. In addition, US Congressman John Peterson has sponsored legislation that would expand drug testing in schools to include the random testing of all students in grades 8-12 (Bush, *State of the Union Address 2004-05* http://www.issues.2000.org).

118 Gunja, above n 115, p 7.

119 The negative impact of drug testing on the teacher-pupil relationship should not be under-estimated: 'trust is jeopardized if teachers act as confidants in some circumstances but as police in others' (Gunja, above n 115, p 8). In my view, testing for drugs as part of a drug education programme is the equivalent of checking for virginity as part of a sex education programme.

120 Over the counter decongestants may produce positive results for amphetamine; codeine can produce a positive result for heroin; the consumption of food products with poppy seeds can produce a positive result for opiates (Gunja, above n 115, p 13).

more dangerous but less detectable by a drug test, and learning the wrong lessons about their constitutional rights.[121]

A number of these concerns warrant exploration in greater depth, as they contain pertinent lessons for English policy-makers. The issue of the effectiveness of drug testing is of crucial importance. For some (though not the author), concerns regarding human rights may well diminish were it to be proven that adopting a policy of drug testing in schools had a reductive impact on the drug taking habits of students. Rather than relying on anecdotal evidence, the first scientific comprehensive study of schools operating a drug testing policy was published in 2003: the researchers reported that there was no evidence of an association, be that positive or negative, between drug testing by schools and levels of reported drug use by students.[122] In view of this lack of proven positive results in the US, spending scant school resources on such a programme in English schools would seem perverse: further, it completely contradicts the 'What Works' approach supposedly advocated by the current government.

In relation to the ACLU's point about possible unintended consequences from drug testing, it needs to be recognised that, in practice, the scheme would become a test for cannabis usage: harder drugs are processed through the human body much more quickly and inhalants are not picked up by drug tests. Thus, the extraordinary situation arises whereby a drug that has recently been reclassified to reflect the lesser harms associated with it will become the subject of expensive and time-consuming testing. Further, as a result, cannabis smokers *may* switch to harder, synthetic drugs to avoid testing positive: a drug such as Ecstasy can be taken on Friday night and will be undetectable by Monday.[123] Whilst the likelihood of switching to harder drugs should not be exaggerated—with young people's drug taking habits being moderated by perceptions of harmfulness[124]—switching to untested, legal (but potentially harmful) drugs, such as alcohol and tobacco, seems a predictable development. The fact that alcohol and tobacco are seen as distinct from the controlled drugs, and not tested for, is a by-product of our arbitrary and illogical drug policy and fits uneasily with the all-inclusive definition of drugs adopted in the new guidance.

There are also a number of procedural issues raised by drug testing. In order for students to be tested, they need to be separated out from the main student

---

121 Gunja, above n 115, p 2.

122 R. Yamaguchi, L. Johnston and P. O'Malley, 'Relationship Between Student Illicit Drug Use and School Drug-Testing Policies' (2003) *Journal of School Health* 73(4), 159.

123 There is some evidence that 'switching' has occurred in English prisons following the introduction of drug testing in these institutions: see further, M. Ramsay (ed), *Prisoners' Drug Use and Treatment: seven research studies*, HORS 267 (London: Home Office, 2003).

124 See further, M. Shiner, 'Out of Harm's Way? Illicit Drug Use, Medicalisation and the Law' (2003) *Brit J Criminology*, 43, 772-796.

body: it is unlikely that this potentially stigmatising process will go unnoticed. In *Earls* the announcement that certain students were to be tested was greeted by the other students with 'giggles and snickers.'[125] Further, as a response to the problem of a trade in clean urine developing in schools in the US, *Earls* describes how teachers there now listen outside stalls (or stand next to urinals) whilst samples are produced: a private act is essentially being performed in public. Urine samples are then tested for temperature and held up to the light to look for any evidence of tampering immediately upon being handed over. These features of the testing procedure, presumably to be replicated in this country out of necessity, are exceptionally intrusive and have the potential to cause a severe degree of embarrassment. Adolescents are vulnerable to sensitivity over bodily functions due to their being in a state of development.

The students' privacy is compromised still further by the fact that, in order to avoid false positives in the test results, they will have to list the prescription medications that they have recently used, thus inadvertently being forced to disclose information about potentially sensitive medical conditions (or even addictions). Urine samples can also reveal private information, such as whether or not a student is pregnant. These possibilities will not only cause anxiety in the young person, but there is also a real risk that the information will leak out beyond the immediate parties concerned. As an illustration, a case in the US involved a choir teacher leaving a list of the prescription drugs used by students, obtained as a precursor to drug testing, on a chair where all the other pupils could see them.[126]

When considering proposals to test school children for drugs in English schools, it should be remembered that the many criticisms of this procedure in the US have been put forward *despite* the fact that the tests are limited to those who participate in sports and other extra-curricular activities. Most importantly, repercussions for a positive drug test in the US are limited to suspension from the said activity: they categorically do not appear on the student's academic record and the information will not be passed on to the criminal authorities in the absence of a valid subpoena. As the Office of National Drug Control Policy makes clear: 'For those who worry about the "Big Brother" dimension of drug testing, it is worth pointing out that test results are generally required by law to remain confidential, and in no case are they turned over to the police.'[127] In contrast, in England, the school's governing body decides on its behaviour policy and the headteacher has discretion to exclude pupils in response to serious breaches of this policy.[128] Unlike in the US, there is nothing to stop English headteachers passing information gleaned from a drug test on to the police. There

125 (2002) 115 F Supp 2d at 1291 n 38.

126 Brief of Respondents at 3, *Earls* (2002) 536 US 822.

127 ONDCP 2003, above n 104, p 16.

128 Education Act 1996, s 156; Education Act 2002, s 52.

is no doubt that the proposals for drug testing in England would be in breach of the Fourth Amendment.

Conclusion

In their recommendations on drug policy, the Select Committee stressed the importance of the government conducting rigorous analysis into drug education and prevention work, to ensure that money was only spent on what works.[129] Thus, the on-going shift towards evidence based practice in drug education, an area previously riddled with propagandising, is to be welcomed. With a view to gaining a clearer picture as regards what *does* work, the £6 million Blueprint Research Programme has been developed. This ground-breaking initiative draws its methods from the global evidence base which supports the view that open communication between parents, teachers and children is the key to postponing or preventing drug-taking.[130] The focus is on giving credible information and developing life skills so that young people are equipped to make and follow through informed decisions. The two year programme for selected pupils will run from September 2003 to June 2005, followed, crucially, by an assessment of the knowledge, attitudes and behaviour of young people that will be reported upon in 2007. A group of six comparison schools will continue with their traditional drug education programmes to act as a control group for the purposes of the evaluation. This scheme represents the biggest evaluation of drug education in this country ever.[131]

It is a shame that, in the midst of all these positive developments, drug testing has been encouraged: it is ill-fitting, in the context of wider drug education policy, to force young people to undergo medical procedures such as these. Drug testing seems more suited to the unsuccessful—and allegedly abandoned—'War on Drugs' approach of previous decades. The manner in which Tony Blair announced these proposals to the media at the same time as announcing his attention to stand for a third term smacked of a populist pre-election vote-winning tactic: parallels can be drawn with George Bush's promotion of this issue in his pre-election State of the Union address.[132]

As a final note, it needs to be remembered that one of the major obstacles to having an effective drug campaign in schools lies in our ill-conceived drug legislation. Whilst drug education is moving towards a pragmatic response to drug taking, criminal justice policy lags behind somewhat. There is a real danger that the absence of a punitive or moralising tone in drug education lessons, whilst

---

129 Home Affairs Select Committee 2002, above n 14, para 211.

130 ODCCP, *Lessons Learned in Drug Abuse Prevention: a global review* (New York: United Nations, 2002).

131 Home Office, *Press Release 245/2003* (London: Home Office, 2003).

132 See above n 117.

welcome, may create false expectations in young people that those in authority will be sympathetic should they be found to be involved with drugs. As has been shown, the response to drugs being found in young people's possession in schools is often highly accusatory and condemnatory, which may be seen as inconsistent with the drive towards open communication in drug education lessons. Tony Blair's proposal to introduce random drug tests in schools only exacerbates this conflict. At best, young people will be confused by these mixed messages; at worst, they may find themselves in a dire predicament, either legally or in terms of their ongoing education.

PART III
SEX EDUCATION

Chapter 4

Enlightenment and Trust: The Debate Over Sex Education in the United States

Charles Glenn

Introduction

It is often forgotten that instruction about our sexuality began, at least in the United States, at university level; only since the Second World War has it generally been an aspect of the school curriculum, and indeed earlier and earlier in that curriculum with the passing years. Boston University may lay claim to have offered the first elective course on marriage and sexual relations, in 1926, in response to a petition by a group of male students in their final year of undergraduate study. Over the following years, more and more American colleges provided such courses.[1]

Today, it seems likely that few higher education institutions believe that they need to offer courses about sex, except to those who plan to specialise in the field. The subject has, however, become well-established in the secondary and even in the elementary school curriculum in many countries. This has led to much political and legal conflict, and has been a precipitating factor in the withdrawal of many children from public schools. It is the significance of such conflicts that will be discussed in this chapter. I will be suggesting that there are fundamentally two sources of these difficulties. The first is the way that the definition of the purposes and methods of sex education, perhaps more than any other aspect of the school curriculum, was for decades a monopoly of specialists whose 'progressive' views were in conflict with the views of the general public, and especially of parents. To use a medical analogy, this has been a sort of continuing infection which has prevented sex education from becoming a broadly-accepted aspect of the curriculum. The second is the periodic eruption of conflict over this issue between public schools and groups of parents who hold views on the subject at sharp variance from those conveyed by the general culture. I will also be suggesting how each of these could become at least a less serious problem for the effective implementation of sex education programmes.

---

1 J. Moran, *Teaching Sex: The Shaping of Adolescence in the 20th Century* (Cambridge, MA: Harvard University Press, 2000), p 126.

The Role of Schools

That a state system of schooling may sometimes serve as an instrument of conformity and manipulation of the most vulnerable members of the population to serve political ends would surely not be doubted. We have seen how this has occurred—to limit ourselves to European examples—in the Soviet Union and its satellites,[2] in Mussolini's Italy,[3] in Hitler's Germany,[4] in Franco's Spain,[5] and in Vichy France.[6] On the other hand, advocates for state systems of schooling have often (and not unjustly) claimed for them the mission of bringing light into the darkness of local habits and assumptions, and introducing children to a wider world where they were exposed to what claimed to be universal—and were at least 'national'—principles. Whether turning 'peasants into Frenchmen,' or 'making Italians,' or 'knitting the [Dutch] nation together,' or 'making immigrants into Americans,' state schools served a political function which—though perhaps at times high-handed—could not fairly be called totalitarian. For example, in the 1920s the Irish government 'focused almost exclusively on transforming the schools into key agents of the revival of Irish and Gaelic culture generally,' as an essential aspect of the revival 'of the ancient life of Ireland as a Gaelic State, Gaelic in language and Christian in its ideals.'[7] By all accounts, the steam has gone out of efforts to make the Irish language the primary medium of communication in Ireland, while civic education has been carried out with less and less conviction in most Western nations. Patriotism of the sort that we find in school texts of a hundred years ago would be hard to find in schools today, and the obligations of the republican citizen are less evidently present than are the rights of individuals and of minority groups of all sorts, including the most recently-arrived.

As state schools have—by all indications—lost confidence in their ability to form citizens, they have been able, not unjustly, to claim to be more concerned with enlightenment than with political mobilisation. No longer seeking to form republican citizens, they are (some critics argue) engaged in forming the sort of

---

2 C. Glenn, *Educational Freedom in Eastern Europe* (Washington, DC: Cato Institute, 1995).

3 J. Charnitzky, *Facismo e Scuola: La Politica Scolastica del Regime (1922-1943)* (Florence: La Nuova Italia, 1996).

4 W. Keim, *Erziehung unter der Nazi-Diktatur*, Band I (Darmstadt: Wissenschaftliche Buchgesellschaft, 1995); G. Knopp, *Hitlers Kinder* (Munich: Goldmann, 2000); E. Mann, *Zehn Millionen Kinder: Die Erziehung der Jugend im Dritten Reich, 1938* (Hamburg: Rowohlt, 2001); H. Scholz, *Erziehung und Unterricht unterm Hakenkreuz* (Göttingen: Vandenhoeck, 1985).

5 R. Navarro Sandalinas, *La Enseñanza Primaria Durante el Franquismo (1936-1975)*, (Barcelona: PPU, 1990).

6 P. Giollitto, *Histoire de la Jeunesse sous Vichy* (Paris: Perrin, 1991).

7 S. Farren, *The Politics of Irish Education, 1920-65* (Belfast: Institute of Irish Studies, The Queen's University, 1995), p 57.

democratic men and women described by Plato in Book 8 of *The Republic*: 'There is neither order nor necessity in his life,' with the result that 'too much freedom seems to change into nothing but too much slavery.' That is, the democratic man or woman is enslaved to impulses which are constantly stimulated by the entertainment and commercial cultures.

Although state schools have abandoned the effort to promote particular convictions and civic virtues, however, they have not abandoned their old mission of relativising, or 'unveiling,' alternative versions of settled dispositions and conviction. In the past, this effort to provide 'enlightenment' was often considered integral to their mission, on the assumption that the Catholic Church or Calvinism, or some other competing source of strong accounts of what matters, would make it impossible to convey the messages for which the state school was intended. It is in sex education that this continuing agenda of weakening strongly-held convictions is most evident.

What has changed is that now state schools, having generally lost their nerve about promoting civic agendas, have little to put in the place of what they are encouraging their pupils to abandon. As William Kirk Kilpatrick has pointed out:

> For students, it has meant wholesale confusion about moral values: learning to question values they have scarcely acquired, unlearning values taught at home, and concluding that questions of right and wrong are always merely subjective.

State schools have lost their nerve about promoting any particular moral framework for living because 'for some reason we have come to believe that one can be a good person without any training in goodness.'[8]

The agenda of state schools—this is another change—is no longer set by government acting upon political or nation-building motives, but by 'leading elements' of the education profession. This is a process which John Dewey and others had advocated in the 1930s, whereby educators 'dare to build a new social order' through their direct influence on children and youth, with parents and elected officials kept at arm's length whenever possible:

> The schools will surely, as a matter of fact and not of ideal, share in the building of the social order of the future according as they ally themselves with this or that movement of existing social forces. This fact is inevitable...according as teachers and administrators align themselves with the older so-called "individualistic" ideals—which in fact are fatal to individuality for the many—or with the newer forces making for social control of economic forces.[9]

---

8 W. K. Kilpatrick, *Why Johnny Can't Tell Right from Wrong* (New York: Simon & Schuster, 1992), p 25.

9 J. Dewey, 'Can Education Share in Social Reconstruction?' in *Later Works, 9: 1933-1934* (Carbondale: Southern Illinois University Press, 1986), p 207.

It is notable that, despite Dewey's frequent invocation of 'democratic education' (the title of one of his most influential books), he has very little to say about how democratic processes such as elections might give direction to how and toward what ends schools and teachers should work.

The subject of sex education, perhaps more than any other aspect of the curriculum, brings us to the central issue in educational law and policy: does the school educate children on behalf of the family, or of the wider society? Most professionals in the field, it seems clear, have shared Dewey's belief that schools have a special mission on behalf of society and of their pupils, even if parents and indeed society at large—that is, real people, acting through the political process—do not understand or support that mission. As asserted by Dr Helen C. Putnam, an early leader in the social hygiene cause, in 1909:

> "Parenthood" rarely confers the ability to train twentieth-century citizens... The parents' problem was not merely their scientific ignorance but also their sexual attitudes. According to reformers, parents were handicapped by generations of prudery.[10]

A study by the Alan Guttmacher Institute (self-described as seeking 'to protect the reproductive choices of all women and men in the United States and throughout the world') reported that 'teachers regard pressure from parents, the community or school administration as the major problem they face in providing sexuality education.'[11] This raises the interesting question: from what source do these teachers believe that they should receive their marching orders, if it is from neither parents, nor the community, nor the administrators who employ them? It seems likely, from their response to this survey, that they share Dewey's belief that educators possess a mission derived entirely from their own self-understanding as emancipators of the young.

For at least the last half-century, indeed, teachers have been encouraged to believe that, because of their 'professional' training (though for most until the last several decades this has been limited, and often is of little rigour still), they were more competent than parents to decide what was in the interest of children and youth:

> As part of their drive toward professionalism, teachers were already claiming that they possessed esoteric, "expert" knowledge that prepared them to take over many functions performed by parents and other child-rearing agents.[12]

This was especially the case among the growing sub-profession of 'experts' on social adjustment, family life, sex education, and related specialties. Van Loon

---

10 In Moran, op cit, n 1, p 33.

11 A. McKay, *Sexual Ideology and Schooling* (Albany: State University of New York Press, 1999), p 2.

12 Moran, op cit, n 1, p 38.

observes that, in the Netherlands as in England—and we could add the United States:

> sexual health expertise... emerged from the same cultural roots of the 1960s and had similar associations with the promotion of women's rights, including abortion rights, and homosexual rights. Its normative basis is equally derived from liberal individualism.[13]

In the decades after the Second World War, 'sex education was one major expression of the new experts' claim that they possessed the right to pass on society's moral code to the next generation,'[14] and indeed to decide what that code should be. In England, in fact, the government guidelines adopted in 1986 allowed school governing bodies to decide whether to dispense sex education, but specified that when taught it must promote moral values.[15]

Not that all of those concerned with sexual behaviour were satisfied with this emphasis upon moral codes—however updated they might be—as an aspect of sex education in schools. Alfred Kinsey complained as long ago as 1941 that:

> the sex instruction which is gradually creeping into our science classrooms is animated by a desire to impose particular systems of morality, and as such does not belong in our science teaching.[16]

Schools should simply present the facts about the range of possible sexual behaviours (and he sought to convince the public that this range was very wide indeed), without offering judgments about them.

In 1948, in his enormously influential book *Sexual Behavior in the Human Male*, Kinsey wrote that, by the time they reached adolescence, children had been turned by their parents into 'conforming machines which rarely fail to perpetuate the mores of the community,'[17] an outcome which he deplored. One of Kinsey's long-time colleagues suggested that Kinsey 'had led such a wretchedly, sexually inhibited life himself as a young man that he was determined that he was going to promulgate a more rational approach to sex so that people would be happier.' His studies of sexual behaviour, using research methods which are now widely considered invalid, claimed to document that 'Americans were awash in sexual activity, only a small fraction of which was confined to behaviour sanctioned by society.' The book was in fact a plea for the abandonment of all sexual inhibitions and norms: 'For example, when he discussed young boys who had

13 J. Van Loon, *Deconstructing the Dutch Utopia* (London: Family Education Trust, 2003), p 52.

14 Moran, op cit, n 1, pp 38 and 42.

15 Van Loon, op cit, n 13, p 18.

16 In Moran, op cit, n 1, p 96.

17 In J.H. Jones, *Alfred C. Kinsey: A Public/Private Life* (New York: W. W. Norton, 1997), p 96.

somehow found the courage to defy the sexual morality of their parents, Kinsey spoke . . . of children who "triumph over their parents."'[18]

Unfortunately, sex education has become something of an obvious lightning rod for those who have concerns about the ways in which state schooling may have contributed to the general weakening of moral norms in contemporary society. 'Opponents,' it has been pointed out, have 'worked up a faith in sex education's ability to do harm that outstripped even its most fervent supporters' faith in its ability to do good.'[19]

In fact, local control of schools, as in the United States and in the Netherlands (and, to a much-reduced degree recently in England), allows the concerns of parents to be taken into account in how—and at what ages—schools address these sensitive issues. Van Loon comments that, in the Netherlands, the residual nature of local autonomy of teachers and parents, whose views on sexual morality are accused of being too conservative, is a source of great concern for the sexual health experts, and shows that for them the sexual reformation is far from complete. The possibility that the apparent resilient nature of traditional parenting may have contributed to low teenage conception rates is completely overlooked. Instead, the sexual health experts seem more interested in unhinging sexual morality in favour of increased openness and experimentation.[20]

Even when local majorities are supportive of or indifferent to the sex education methods used, it is a reality which educational policy must always take into account that, in our time especially, but indeed at all times, many families do not accept the values prevalent among their fellow citizens. A free society, as de Tocqueville and Mill and others have reminded us, must avoid the 'tyranny of the majority': we rely upon the courts to protect individuals from the effects of legislation supported by a majority which denies their rights. In the United States, it is ultimately the federal Constitution which articulates the general principles on the basis of which individuals may appeal against the temporary will of the majority, while in Europe there is a substantial body of both national and international law which provides similar protections.

Kjeldsen and its Implications

One of the most important cases in this European jurisprudence involving education is *Kjeldsen, Busk Madsen and Pedersen v Denmark,*[21] decided by the European Court of Human Rights in November 1976. The case was brought by three Danish couples with children of school age who objected to the integrated, and thus in effect compulsory, sex education introduced into state primary

---

18 Jones, above n 17, pp 519-520.

19 Moran, above n 1, p 187.

20 Van Loon, above n 13, p 20.

21 (1976) 1 EHRR 711.

schools in Denmark by a law adopted in 1970. This legislation had directed that, in state primary schools, 'road safety, library organisation and sex education shall form an integral part of teaching in the manner specified by the Minister of Education.' Parents had the option of choosing state-funded private schools,[22] which were required to teach their pupils about the biological aspects of sexuality but not about sexual practices, but the claimants alleged that there were none within reasonable distance or with space available for their children.

The Danish government had issued guidelines for the integrated sex education which should occur at all levels of schooling, starting in the third grade. According to the *Kjeldsen* ruling:

> [t]he Guide advocates an instruction method centered on informal talks between teachers and children on the basis of the latter's questions. It emphasises that "the instruction must be so tactful as not to offend or frighten the child" and that it "must respect each child's right to adhere to conceptions it has developed itself." To the extent that the discussion bears on ethical and moral problems of sexual life, the Guide recommends teachers to adopt an objective attitude; it specifies: "The teacher should not identify himself with or dissociate himself from the conceptions dealt with." However, it does not necessarily prevent the teacher from showing his personal view. The demand for objectivity is amplified by the fact that the school accepts children from all social classes. It must be possible for all parents to reckon safely on their children not being influenced in a unilateral direction which may deviate from the opinion of the home. It must be possible for the parents to trust that the ethical basic points of view will be presented objectively and soberly.[23]

The claimants in this case alleged that their children had been exposed to vulgar pictures and other undesirable information through this compulsory sex education. They claimed that this programme violated their rights under Article 2 of the First Protocol to the ECHR, which provides that 'in the exercise of any functions which it assumes in relation to education and teaching, the State shall respect the right of parents to ensure such education and teaching in conformity with their own religious and philosophical convictions.'

The Danish government pointed out that it provided extensive subsidies to private schools, which were not required to follow the guidelines for sex education, and thus it 'does not force parents to entrust their children to the State schools; it allows parents to educate their children, or to have them educated, at home and, above all, to send them to private institutions.' The Court found, however, that Article 2 of the First Protocol 'applies to each of the State's functions in relation to education and to teaching [and thus] does not permit a distinction to be drawn between religious instruction and other subjects. It enjoins the State to respect parents' convictions, be they religious or philosophical,

---

22 See C. Glenn and J. De Groof, *Finding the Right Balance: Freedom, Autonomy, and Accountability in Education* (Utrecht: Lemma, 2002), volume 1, pp 185-203.

23 Para 29.

throughout the entire State education programme.'[24] The existence of a private alternative, even publicly-subsidised, did not exempt the government from ensuring that its own schools respect the rights of parents. The Court concluded, however, that:

> the second sentence of Article 2 of the Protocol does not prevent States from imparting through teaching or education information or knowledge of a directly or indirectly religious or philosophical kind. It does not even permit parents to object to the integration of such teaching or education in the school curriculum, for otherwise all institutionalised teaching would run the risk of proving impracticable. In fact, it seems very difficult for many subjects taught at school not to have, to a greater or lesser extent, some philosophical complexion or implications. The same is true of religious affinities if one remembers the existence of religions forming a very broad dogmatic and moral entity which has or may have answers to every question of a philosophical, cosmological or moral nature. The second sentence of Article 2 implies on the other hand that the State, in fulfilling the functions assumed by it in regard to education and teaching, must take care that information or knowledge included in the curriculum is conveyed in an objective, critical and pluralistic manner. The State is forbidden to pursue an aim of indoctrination that might be considered as not respecting parents' religious and philosophical convictions. That is the limit that must not be exceeded.[25]

The Court noted that the Danish public authorities wished to enable pupils, when the time came, 'to take care of themselves and show consideration for others in that respect,' 'not … [to] land themselves or others in difficulties solely on account of lack of knowledge'[26] The Court concluded that:

> These considerations are indeed of a moral order, but they are very general in character and do not entail overstepping the bounds of what a democratic State may regard as the public interest. Examination of the legislation in dispute establishes in fact that it in no way amounts to an attempt at indoctrination aimed at advocating a specific kind of sexual behaviour. It does not make a point of exalting sex or inciting pupils to indulge precociously in practices that are dangerous for their stability, health or future or that many parents consider reprehensible. Further, it does not affect the right of parents to enlighten and advise their children, to exercise with regard to their children natural parental functions as educators, or to guide their children on a path in line with the parents' own religious or philosophical convictions.
>
> Certainly, abuses can occur as to the manner in which the provisions in force are applied by a given school or teacher and the competent authorities have a duty to take the utmost care to see to it that parents' religious and philosophical convictions are not disregarded at this level by carelessness, lack of judgment or misplaced proselytism.[27]

---

24 Para 51.

25 Para 53.

26 Para 54, quoting from Executive Order of 15 June 1972, s 1.

27 Para 54.

The Danish government's policy, and the judgment upon it by the European Court of Human Rights, make good sense, and my own observations in Danish schools incline me to believe that most of their excellent teachers exercise appropriate tact and objectivity in dealing with sexuality. American policymakers could benefit greatly from reflecting on the principles which the Court has laid down in this regard. A similar position is taken by German federal and state laws, which stipulate that schools may not seek to indoctrinate pupils to adopt or to reject a particular sexual behaviour, and that they must take into account the religious or philosophical convictions of parents. Thus 'a one-sided sex education, such as an emancipatory, repressions-free approach, would overstep the limits set by the Constitution,' which is explicitly concerned to protect marriage and the family.[28]

Sex Education, Morality and Educational Freedom

Unfortunately, however, the matter is not as simple as these fine words suggest. As a recent study of sex education points out, 'our society's disagreements related to sexuality are not trivial differences of opinion but rather represent a clash of opposing systems of belief about the nature of the world and humankind.' The question imposes itself, 'is it really possible to arrive at a genuinely authentic or definitively objective conclusion regarding the true nature and purpose of human sexuality?'[29]

A good case can be made that the goal of 'objectivity' in teaching children and youth about their sexuality is a comfortable myth that can seldom be realised in practice. After all, as Van Loon has argued:

> ultimately the message that young people must be set free to explore their own sexuality is an extreme form of relativism. Regardless of nationality, teachers (especially those who have children of their own) who work with young people on a daily basis know that moral relativism is detrimental to education.[30]

An historical study of sex education in the United States points out that, in the 1960s and 1970s, 'ironically, as it turned out, sex educators conceived of moral neutrality primarily as a way of sidestepping moral and religious controversy,' only to find themselves continually enmeshed in such controversy. After all, 'moral neutrality seemed an attempt to label religious considerations irrelevant' and 'as a practical matter, when teachers urged young people to make their own

28 H. Avenarius and H. Heckel, *Schulrechtskunde*, 7th ed (Kriftel: Luchterhand, 2000), p 528.

29 McKay, above n 11, pp 7-8.

30 Van Loon, above n 13, p 51.

moral decisions, they were implicitly suggesting that adolescents need not accept their parents' authority.' As a result, 'at a time when many Americans believed that the nation's youth had discarded all codes of sexual morality, the sex educators' "surrender" [of the claim to offer moral prescriptions] seemed to exemplify the moral bankruptcy of the elite establishment.'[31]

A study of sex education in the Netherlands suggests that this moral neutrality is especially problematical to teachers working in schools with high proportions of lower-class children, who are especially prone to risky sexual behaviours. As commented by Van Loon:

> What is most striking in these cases is the difficulty of addressing moral questions regarding sexual issues, because the liberal ethos within which sex education is being delivered erodes the ability of teachers to provide a consistent and non-ambivalent normative framework within which they can be handled.[32]

As a result:

> in the absence of adults taking responsibility for the moral development of young people, the pressures and risks are shifted downwards to individuals [that is, the youth themselves], who at the same time are not equipped with the necessary tools to make proper judgements.[33]

It is in this aspect of the curriculum, then, that one can see with particular clarity what could be called the paradox of educational freedom. Is the mission of schools and of teachers to set pupils free from inherited norms, so that they will be able to choose freely among competing systems of values and life-styles, all of which the school pronounces equally valid? If so, is that not a denial of the freedom of parents to guide the development of their children? As John Coons pointed out in an important law review article nearly twenty years ago:

> [t]he right to form families and to determine the scope of their children's practical liberty is for most men and women the primary occasion for choice and responsibility. One does not have to be rich or well placed to experience the family. The opportunity over a span of fifteen or twenty years to attempt the transmission of one's deepest values to a beloved child provides a unique arena for the creative impulse. Here is the communication of ideas in its most elemental mode. Parental expression, for all its invisibility to the media, is an activity with profound First Amendment implications [for freedom of conscience].[34]

---

31 Moran, above n 1, pp 192-193.

32 Van Loon, above n 13, p 45.

33 Ibid.

34 J. E. Coons, 'Intellectual Liberty and the Schools' (1985) *Journal of Law, Ethics & Public Policy,* 1, p 511.

This is precisely the concern of the First Protocol to the ECHR, addressed by the European Court of Human Rights in the *Kjeldsen* case. The problem is not with the state of the law, but with what one could call the culture prevalent among an elite of educators and transmitted by their influence to countless classrooms.

The emancipatory self-image of educators is nowhere more clearly manifested than in sex education, one of the recurrent battlegrounds between the progressive elites in public education and the stubborn but rarely successful rearguard of those who hold to more traditional views. That rearguard won a rare victory in May 2000, when the Massachusetts Commissioner of Education felt compelled to dismiss two state employees who had provided graphic and favourable accounts of 'fisting' and other unconventional sexual practices to high school students at a conference sponsored by a homosexual organisation. While they had apparently been holding similar sessions for some time, on this occasion a secret tape was made and its distribution caused a public outcry. Predictably, however, the disciplinary action evoked immediate protests, and the press was more hostile to the one who taped than to those who were taped.

What would inspire educators to consider providing 'how-to-do-it' information on unusual sexual practices a commendable professional activity? While there are some adults who enjoy talking to children and youth about sexual practices, there is no reason to believe that this is the primary motivation in such cases. Difficult as it may be for non-educators to believe, there are those who believe that, by breaking down the (already fragile) inhibitions of their pupils, teachers can help to create a better world. They share the conviction of Wilhelm Reich 'that by encouraging freedom in pre-adolescent sex play, and free adolescent intercourse, a unique generation would be trained, one politically enabled by a general capacity for freedom.'[35]

Sex educators have apparently always seen themselves as crusaders for a better and freer society. One of the giants in the field, Mary Calderone, founding director of SIECUS (Sex Information and Education Council of the US), wrote in 1968 that the goals of a sex education programme were no longer 'the relatively limited aims of reducing unwed pregnancies or venereal disease rates,' but had evolved to 'the much more comprehensive goal of providing the kind of knowledge and opportunity for learning and discussion that will develop the ability of young people to make rational and responsible decisions in their personal lives.' She was not referring to dating practices or how to use condoms alone for, as she added:

---

35 P. Rieff, *The Triumph of the Therapeutic: Uses of Faith after Freud* (New York: Harper Torchbooks, 1968), p 160.

> If man as he is, is obsolescent, then what kind do we want to produce in his place and how do we design the production line? In essence, that is the real question facing those who are concerned with sex education.[36]

Calderone was appointed by the National Council of [Protestant] Churches to serve as a member of its Commission on Family Life, suggesting how deeply into mainstream thinking had penetrated the idea that public schools could, through 'comprehensive sexuality education,' legitimately seek to remake humanity in a more acceptable form.

But it is, after all, a fundamental principle of free societies that individuals have a right not to be interfered with 'for their own good,' except for the most pressing reasons; of course, judging when those reasons are sufficiently pressing is a central problem of every society with a commitment to individual freedoms. As Isaiah Berlin wrote:

> if the essence of men is that they are autonomous beings, authors of values, of ends in themselves, the ultimate authority of which consists precisely in the fact that they are willed freely—then nothing is worse than to treat them as if they were not autonomous, but natural objects, played on by causal influences... (T)o manipulate men, to propel them towards goals which you—the social reformer—see, but they may not, is to deny their human essence, to treat them as objects without wills of their own, and therefore to degrade them.[37]

Where did Mary Calderone get the bizarre idea that 'man as he is, is obsolescent,' and that educators are somehow authorised to remake human nature? She could easily have found it in Rousseau ('force them to be free') and, though more cautiously stated, in John Dewey. In his enormously influential *My Pedagogic Creed* in 1897, Dewey had written that 'education is the fundamental method of social progress and reform.'

The implication of this programme for reform—what Dewey liked to call 'reconstruction'—was that 'the teacher is engaged, not simply in the training of individuals, but in the formation of the proper social life,' and 'in this way the teacher always is the prophet of the true God and the usherer in of the true kingdom of God.'[38]

Reich, Dewey, and other prophets of emancipatory education argued that social reform would not be achieved simply by developing new skills and attitudes; it required also a direct challenge to those retrograde norms and that passive obedience to them that prevented the new world from being born. The

---

36 M. S. Calderone, 'Sex Education and the Roles of School and Church,' (1968) *Annals of the American Academy of Political and Social Sciences,* 376, pp 53-60.

37 I. Berlin, 'Two Concepts of Liberty,' in *Four Essays on Liberty* (Oxford: Oxford University Press, 1969), pp 136-137.

38 J. Dewey, 'My Pegagogic Creed,' in *The Early Works, 1882-1898, 5: 1895-1898* (Carbondale: Southern Illinois University Press, 1972), p 95.

targets were various: traditional religion, the expressions of high culture, even the family. After all, as Rieff points out (critically):

> the chief institutional instrument of repressive authority is the family. As political revolution must overthrow the power of the state, moral revolution must overthrow the power of the family—all families. Reich makes a standard point: the family, being the training ground of morality, is authoritarian by definition.[39]

As a result, 'sex education becomes the main weapon in an ideological war against the family; its aim is to divest the parents of their moral authority.'[40]

While Dewey, typically, is more discrete, it is significant that parents and families are almost never mentioned in his voluminous works and, when they are, they appear as barriers to the appropriate development of their children: 'parents, priests, chiefs, social censors have supplied aims, aims which were foreign to those upon whom they were imposed, to the young, laymen, ordinary folk.'[41] The role of schools is to liberate pupils to seek their own ends, while ensuring that those aims are rationally arrived at and thus, by definition, socially constructive.

There is a vast naïveté about human nature and about what makes a society and a culture work lurking behind this programme. As one of Dewey's contemporary critics pointed out:

> initiative and originality imply freedom, but the kind of initiative that is worth while is the kind that builds on the gains that the past has made, and the kind of freedom that is worth while is the kind that has been achieved through discipline and sacrifice. ...(O)ne who asserts or implies that American children are so dangerously addicted to blind obedience as to imperil their originality is attempting to demolish a man of straw.[42]

Even less today than in 1915 was American public education dedicated to inculcating blind obedience; we may be reminded of E. D. Hirsch's sardonic comment that education reformers continue to assume that classrooms are saturated with facts and rote learning, though in fact these have long since been largely abandoned in American public schools: 'the anti-rote-learning reforms being advocated are already firmly in place.'[43]

---

39 Rieff, above n 35, p 156.

40 Ibid, p 160.

41 J. Dewey, *Human Nature and Conduct*: *Middle Works, 14: 1922*, (Carbondale: Southern Illinois University Press, 1988), p 5.

42 W. C. Bagley, 'Editorial' from (1915) *School and Home Education*, 35 in J. Dewey, *The Middle Works, 8: Essays on Education and Politics 1915* (Carbondale: Southern Illinois University Press, 1979), p 468.

43 E. D. Hirsch, Jr., *The Schools We Need... and Why We Don't Have Them* (New York: Doubleday, 1996), p 45.

For Dewey and other theorists, then, education is primarily about liberating the minds and the personalities of youth as a means of refashioning humanity. Sex education, like multicultural education and Afro-centric education, is a privileged sphere for this beneficent activity, and many of its practitioners seem to see themselves as successors to the great heroes of free thinking.

In this complacent self-understanding, the sex educators have much in common with Alfred Kinsey, who provided the (increasingly challenged) scientific basis for their assumptions about human sexuality. Kinsey's 'conception of history,' we are told, 'was appallingly simpleminded, although it was not without its Voltairian charms. He viewed the historical process as a great moral drama, in which the forces of science competed with those of superstition.' The implication was that 'all sexual regulation...reflected only human folly and willfulness.' The prime enemy of a sane approach to sexual behaviour was religion, which he considered 'a powerful and repressive force in American sexual life.'[44]

What is evident in the sex education movement—which should be distinguished carefully from more modest and information-based approaches to this necessary subject—is a crusading zeal to upset all conventional barriers to full sexual expression. In the 1960s, 'SIECUS leaders denied that one uniform moral code could apply; rather, sex educators would respect young people's right to choose themselves from what was becoming...a buffet of competing moral systems.'[45] By placing a primary stress upon 'safe sex,' the message is conveyed that it is all right to do anything, provided that one employs the right techniques.

I am reminded of the anti-AIDS brochure that my 12-year-old daughter brought home from her public school in Boston, with a series of admonitions to be careful in a variety of activities which I doubt she had considered engaging in. 'When you shoot drugs,' she was advised, as though it was inevitable that she would, 'always use a clean needle.' 'When you have oral sex with someone's anus, always use a latex shield.' My protest to the school that such ideas should not be introduced without normative as well as mechanical guidance was turned away with the suggestion that I was naive, since children could be expected to do such things and needed to be told how to protect themselves.

If it is a good thing to reduce risks, as of course it is, then presumably the best way to do that is to reduce the likelihood of risky behaviour. Research published by Dr David Paton in the *Journal of Health Economics* last year challenges the assumption that the availability of contraception reduces teenage conception rates.[46] 'On the one hand,' he writes, 'teenagers who will engage in sexual activity in any case face a reduced risk of pregnancy. On the other hand, family planning raises the likelihood of engaging in sexual activity in the first

---

44 P. Robinson, *The Modernization of Sex* (New York: Harper & Row, 1975), pp 83-6.

45 Moran, above n 1, p 162.

46 D. Paton, 'The Economics of Family Planning and Underage Conception' (2002) *Journal of Health Economics*, 21(2), 207-225.

place.' After all, most 'teenagers who experienced unwanted pregnancies were using contraceptives at the time.' This is consistent with the fact that 'at least since 1990, unobstructed availability of and access to contraceptives, especially the pill, does not correlate with reductions in conception rates among teenagers in the Netherlands.'[47] Similarly, a study by the Alan Guttmacher Institute found that teen pregnancy rates in the United States 'increased an alarming 23 per cent from 1972 to 1990—the period during which "comprehensive sex education" (read: contraceptive education) began and became widespread.'[48]

What is true of contraceptives seems also to be true of sex education. Another research review by Di Censo and others, also last year, in the *British Medical Journal*,[49] 'concludes that sex education has very little effect on reducing sexual risk behaviour among teenagers, and find that, in some cases, it may even have made a significant contribution to increased sexual activity among girls.' To cite the Dutch experience again, 'the official introduction of sex education into the primary and secondary school curricula...has not corresponded with further reductions in teenage conception rates, abortions or incidence of STIs; and that—instead—these have all slowly but steadily increased.'[50]

As the historian and former assistant secretary in the US Department of Education, Diane Ravitch has pointed out, 'It would be difficult to see how teenagers could spend a semester reading how to do it right, how good it feels when you do it, and how meaningful the experience is, without wanting to try it as soon as possible.'[51]

All this is not to say that sex education should be banished from schools, but that it is time for those of us who believe that schools should include the massive reality of our sexuality in their curriculum, both because it is an important part of human experience and also because the great majority of parents want it to be included, to reject the fuzzy thinking which suggests that moral norms are an entirely individual project. 'Emancipation' from inherited or societal norms is not to be confused with freedom. Freedom is among the goals of all education worthy of the name—the freedom to think, to imagine, to criticise, to explore. It is not the same as aimless drifting.

Emancipation can of course help to prepare the way for the exercise of freedom by removing barriers, but it does not of itself make a man or woman free. To be truly free requires self-mastery, a settled disposition to judge rightly and act accordingly rather than to be swept about by impulse and influence. The free man or woman has an inner consistency which expresses itself externally. A

---

47 Van Loon, above n 13, pp 21, 29 and 47.

48 K. Napier, 'Chastity Programs Shatter Sex-Ed Myths' (1997) *Policy Review*, May/June, pp 12-15.

49 'Interventions to Reduce Unintended Pregnancies Among Adolescents,' (2002) *British Medical Journal*, 324, 1426.

50 Van Loon, above n 13, pp 21 and 46.

51 Moran, above n 1, p 204.

Canadian educator has warned that 'we must be careful not to put too much value on autonomy, recognizing that there are other equally important values such as dependence, love, goodwill, benevolence, and harmony.' He goes on to point out that 'children must be initiated into a particular home, a particular language, a particular culture, a particular set of beliefs before they can begin to expand their horizons beyond the present and the particular.'[52]

The study of sex education in the Netherlands, much cited above, argues that the relatively low rate of teenage conceptions in that country compared with England or the United States should be attributed to aspects of the social structure of each country rather than to their approaches to sex education, which the author finds largely similar. Significant factors include the more-intact family life in the Netherlands and the greater responsiveness of schools to parents as a result of the country's long-standing policy of basing schooling upon parental demand.[53] The close alignment of families and schools helps to form the 'seedbeds of civic virtue' of which Mary Ann Glendon of Harvard Law School has written:

> Neglect of the social dimension of personhood has made it extremely difficult for us to develop an adequate conceptual apparatus for taking into account the sorts of groups within which human character, competence, and capacity for citizenship are formed. In a society where the seedbeds of civic virtue—families, neighborhoods, religious associations, and other communities—can no longer be taken for granted, this is no trifling matter.[54]

Real education, then, is induction into a culture, not as a straightjacket but as the context of meanings and restraints that make the exercise of real freedom possible. As Philip Rieff notes:

> a culture must communicate ideals, setting as internalities those distinctions between right actions and wrong that unite men and permit them the fundamental pleasure of agreement. Culture is another name for a design of motives directing the self outward, toward those communal purposes in which alone the self can be realized and satisfied.[55]

The most prominent recent development in relation to sex education in the United States is a strong emphasis, in some states and school districts, upon sexual abstinence outside of marriage: 'by 1999, fully a third of public school districts were using abstinence-only curricula in their classrooms. Of a nationwide sample of sex-ed instructors, ...41 per cent cited abstinence as the

---

52 E. J. Thiessen, *Teaching for Commitment: Liberal Education, Indoctrination, and Christian Nurture* (Montreal: McGill-Queen's University Press, 1993), p 220.

53 Van Loon, above n 13, pp 44-57.

54 M. A. Glendon, *Rights Talk: The Impoverishment of Political Discourse* (New York: Free Press, 1991), p 109.

55 Rieff, above n 35, p 4.

most important message they wanted to convey to their students, compared with 25 per cent in 1988.'[56] As described by one of its advocates, abstinence education denies the possibility of the sort of neutrality invoked by the European Court of Human Rights and many policymakers:

> there is no neutral position. To simply say that it is okay to abstain conveys the idea that is okay not to abstain. Directive abstinence [education] teaches that the only right, good, and healthy activity is to abstain from sexual intercourse until marriage.[57]

It appears that this strategy may have had some limited success in postponing the onset of adolescent sexual activity—we will not try to assess the research over which there is much conflict—but probably more important are slow cultural changes that seem to be occurring in society at large, and among youth, away from excesses of the recent past. To the extent that the abstinence message is fear-based, it is likely to have only a short-term effect—all of us, and especially teenagers, engage in risky behaviours frequently, and sometimes precisely because they *are* risky.

No, the only sound approach is a positive one, to emphasise the role of our sexuality in building and sustaining committed marriage relationships. Public schools in the United States, at least, have been sadly neglectful of the importance of marriage to human fulfilment and to the flourishing of children as well as of society. Twenty years ago a government-commissioned study of forty social studies texts for the primary grades found that

> there is not one text reference to marriage as the foundation of the family. Indeed, not even the word marriage or wedding occurs once in the forty books [in an American context]... neither the word husband nor wife occurs once in any of these books. ...Public school officials may constantly bemoan teenage pregnancy and the frequency of illegitimate children, but their own textbooks begin fostering the notion of family without marriage in grades 1 to 4.[58]

Conclusion

I suggested at the start of this chapter that there are fundamentally two sources of the present conflict over sex education. The first is specialists on sex education whose 'progressive' views have been in conflict with the views of the general public and especially of most parents. The second is groups of parents who hold views on the subject at sharp variance from those conveyed by the general culture

---

56 J. Levine, *Harmful to Minors: The Perils of Protecting Children from Sex* (Minneapolis: University of Minnesota Press, 2002), p 92.

57 McKay, above n 11, p 70.

58 P. Vitz, *Censorship: Evidence of Bias in Our Children's Textbooks* (Ann Arbor: Servant Publications, 1986).

and who are unlikely to be satisfied with any attempt by public schools to provide comprehensive sex education which goes beyond limited biological information.

Much is at stake in this conflict: not simply the adequacy of education about one of the central dimensions of human life, but also the credibility of public education itself. Schools are a culture-conveying institution. They can also sometimes be culture-weakening institutions, and many parents and others have come to fear that, after a century and more in which state schools contributed enormously to raising the general level of culture and to bringing the broad masses into the mainstream of society, they are now helping to undermine the civic and personal virtues upon which a free society depends. Whether the charge is fair or not cannot concern us here; that it is widely believed, both among the broad public and in some intellectual circles as well, cannot be doubted, as both surveys and thoughtful books in a number of countries demonstrate. The old concern that public schools are insufficiently effective or insufficiently equitable has been joined by a concern that they may be culturally toxic.

Sex education, as it is commonly provided, is a focal point of such concerns. There are a number of policy measures that could be taken to reduce the conflict and go some way toward restoring confidence in the public schools.

The first recommendation is a greater degree of autonomy on the part of individual schools and of choice among schools on the part of parents. As the study of sex education in the Netherlands shows, conflict is greatly reduced when those in each school know their clientele and adapt curriculum and instruction accordingly. Despite constant prediction in the United States, by opponents of diversity and choice in education, that it will produce social conflict, it is obvious from the example of other countries that it actually reduces conflict over sensitive issues such as sex education.

Secondly, it is useful to distinguish between instruction about the biological aspects of intercourse, conception, risk avoidance, and so forth, and what the Dutch call *vorming*, the shaping of attitudes toward sexuality and the choices which individuals may be called upon to make. The former may well be made mandatory in rather specific ways, but the latter—as the unfortunate American experience with 'Outcome-based Education' teaches us—should not be specified by government. Van Loon points out that the Dutch curriculum 'targets' for secondary schooling are quite explicit about biological aspects of sexuality, but then include a rather general objective that pupils be able to 'articulate different functions of sexuality and opinions thereof.' This is so stated, he notes, 'to enable schools of different denominations to control the content of the curriculum.'[59] Similarly, in the Republic of Ireland, where—as in the Netherlands—most schools are denominational, the government 'has left a high degree of autonomy in this matter [sex education] to individual boards of management,' which may adapt the state guidelines to reflect the ethos of the school.[60]

59 Van Loon, above n 13, p 19.

60 D. Glendenning, *Education and the Law* (Dublin: Butterworths, 1999), p 274.

Thirdly, parents should be kept informed about *what* is going to be discussed and *when*, and encouraged to review these topics with their children from the perspective of their own religious or other convictions about the particular topic, as is legally required in Germany.[61] This is not to say, however, that schools should be expected to offer a cafeteria of topics from which parents may choose; the curriculum should be coherent. In Northern Ireland, education authorities, while recognising that many parents believe that certain topics—such as homosexuality and abortion—should not be taught about in schools, have nevertheless advised that 'schools and colleges cannot ignore consideration of sexual practices which run counter to the moral standards of society in Northern Ireland.'[62]

Fourthly, to the extent that public schools do offer sex education in a form which seeks to shape behaviour, or—alternatively—which seeks to persuade youth that they should decide autonomously about their behaviour on the basis of their own 'values,' it should be voluntary with a clear right of excusal, just as most countries that provide religious education in public schools allow pupils to opt out. As the *Kjeldsen* decision recognised, issues of conscience do not appear only in religious education classes. One should note that German law does not make provision for such excusal,[63] just as it does not allow for 'home schooling.' This places all the greater burden on the school to avoid what could seem like advocacy for 'value neutrality' which amounts to no more than moral relativism.

Fifthly, this points to the central dilemma of sex education: almost everyone believes that it should involve more than mere biological information, but how can we reach agreement on what? We have seen how leaders of the sex education movement promised that it should reshape values and emancipate youth from inherited norms. By contrast, leaders of the 'character education' movement insist that, in Thomas Lickona's words, 'sexual behavior is determined by values, not mere knowledge. Consequently, sex education must educate young people about the moral dimensions of sexual conduct.'[64] But on what possible basis, if there is no consensus about a normative morality? This suggests, again, the importance of offering choices among schools that take very different approaches to *vorming*, with very clear explanations to parents before they make their choices among schools. Moral consensus may not exist in the society at large, but it can exist in an individual school that is freely chosen by teachers and by

---

61 Avenarius and Heckel, above n 28, p 528.

62 Department for Education in Northern Ireland, Circular 1987/45, quoted by L. Lundy, *Education Law, Policy and Practice in Northern Ireland* (Belfast: SLS Legal Publications, 2000), p 141.

63 Avenarius and Heckel, above n 28, p 528.

64 T. Lickona, *Educating for Character: How Our Schools Can Teach Respect and Responsibility* (New York: Bantam Books, 1991), p 348; see also K. Ryan and K. E. Bohlin, *Building Character in Schools: Practical Ways to Bring Moral Instruction to Life* (New York: Jossey-Bass, 1998).

parents, and shaped by a coherent ethos.

Finally, there should be an abandonment of all utopian schemes to reshape humanity by means of the school. The approach to sex education urged by the progressive specialists in the generation after the Second World War should certainly be available in those schools whose parents wish their children encouraged to take a vigorously experimental and open-minded approach to their own sexuality, but it should not be a programme of social and cultural change imposed on the unaware or the unwilling. Full disclosure of goals and methods should be the minimal requirement of candour with parents and their children.

Chapter 5

Some Shortcomings in the Provision of Sex Education in England

Paul Meredith

Introduction

The provision of sex education in maintained schools raises some of the most acute and intractable problems in relation to the realisation of parental and children's rights in the sphere of education, not least because it is an area in respect of which very strongly held views are frequently expressed, often based on deep moral, cultural and religious convictions. It is also an area which has been the subject of significant reform in England—both legal and administrative—in recent years through the promulgation of new and in some cases highly controversial statutory provisions, and new 'guidance' issued by the government to local education authorities (LEAs), school governing bodies and head teachers. The provision of sex education has also been the subject of some criticism as well as constructive proposals for reform in the recent past in the form of a number of influential reports by key bodies, including the Social Exclusion Unit (SEU) (a unit within the Cabinet Office), the Office for Standards in Education (Ofsted), and by the House of Commons Select Committee on Health.

It seems appropriate in a volume devoted to consideration of issues relating to children, health and education to focus on some aspects of the provision of sex education and on some of the shortcomings that have been identified in this field. We will, however, begin by briefly considering some aspects of the nature of rights in this context, in particular, the extremely weak basis of their legal underpinning, and—in so far as they can be said to exist at all—their location in parents rather than in children. We will then go on to consider some of the shortcomings identified in the provision of sex education in English schools, before examining in more detail the legal framework within which sex education is provided and the realisation of rights within that legal framework.

The Limited Notion of Rights in Relation to Sex Education

Although the volume of statutory regulation of the provision of education in England is nowadays enormous, there is very little positive statutory underpinning of individual rights of a substantive nature in respect of education. Such rights as do exist tend to be procedural rather than substantive in nature, and even then may well be qualified by a range of limitations or exceptions, in some cases rendering them of little procedural value.[1]

Not only are individual rights in relation to the provision of education highly limited and qualified in practice, but there has in general been virtually no attempt within the statutory framework to make provision for the articulation—let alone the realisation—of the interests or wishes of children themselves independently of their parents or guardians.[2] This is clear from a symbolically significant—even if in practice otherwise largely redundant—provision of the Education Act 1996, requiring the Secretary of State and LEAs to 'have regard to the general principle' that pupils should be educated in accordance with their parents' wishes, so far as this is compatible with the provision of efficient instruction and training and the avoidance of unreasonable public expenditure.[3] It has been generally assumed in the development of both statute law and case law that the claims and interests of parents and children simply coincide.[4]

The very important medical law case of *Gillick v West Norfolk and Wisbech Area Health Authority*,[5] in which the House of Lords recognised a degree of independent autonomy in adolescents under the age of 16 years—the minimum age for lawful sexual intercourse in England—has not been directly paralleled in

---

1 The best example of this is perhaps to be found in s 86, School Standards and Framework Act 1998, conferring on parents a right to express a reasoned choice as to the placing of their child in a particular school. The duty on the part of the LEA or governing body to comply with the parental preference is highly qualified, in particular by s 86(3)(a) which states that the duty of compliance is lifted if this would prejudice the provision of efficient education or the efficient use of resources.

2 See P. Meredith, 'Children's Rights and Education,' in J. Fionda (ed), *Legal Concepts of Childhood* (Oxford: Hart Publishing, 2001), pp 203-222, at pp 203-207.

3 Education Act 1996, s 9.

4 But see s 1(1) and 1(3) (a), Children Act 1989, requiring the court in certain family proceedings to have particular regard to the ascertainable wishes and feelings of the child, considered in the light of their age and understanding. See also s 176, Education Act 2002, requiring LEAs and school governing bodies to have regard to guidance given from time to time by the Secretary of State about consultation with pupils in connection with the taking of decisions affecting them. This is a weak provision, requiring the LEA or governing body only to 'have regard to' the Secretary of State's guidance. S 176(2) provides, further, that any such guidance must provide for a pupil's views to be considered in the light of the child's age and understanding.

5 [1986] AC 112.

the context of education law. In *Gillick*, the House of Lords endorsed in certain circumstances the giving of advice by medical practitioners to girls under the age of 16 without the knowledge or consent of their parents. The courts have not, however, as yet applied a principle of developing autonomy or capacity for self-determination on the part of older adolescents in respect of crucial educational decisions, for instance in relation to choice of school or withdrawal from religious education or sex education. The predominant approach in the educational context has been paternalistic in nature. The children's liberation movement has had little impact in England on educational provision for minor children.[6] The approach in the educational field, rather, has followed the view expressed by the influential Victorian philosopher, J S Mill, that children lack the capacity for personal autonomy enjoyed by adults:

> It is, perhaps, hardly necessary, to say that this doctrine (of personal autonomy) is meant to apply only to human beings in the maturity of their faculties. We are not speaking of children, or of young persons below the age which the law may fix as that of manhood or womanhood. Those who are still in a state to require being taken care of by others, must be protected against their own actions as well as against external injury.[7]

This has been the predominant view despite the potential for conflict between the interests of parents and their children, which may sometimes arise in a particularly acute way in respect of families from minority ethnic, religious or cultural backgrounds, in some cases of a fundamentalist persuasion. Such parents may in all sincerity wish to shelter their children from what in their opinion may be harmful educative influences prevalent in mainstream schools, preferring the view that their particular moral, cultural or religious preferences and traditions are best safeguarded by segregated arrangements or education in the home under parental control and influence.[8] There is, indeed, a deep and fundamental tension here between opposing views held by those on the one hand who believe that the best interests of children are served by exposing them to the enriching experience of diverse cultural, religious, social and educational influences, leaving the children themselves to draw upon a multiplicity of influences in the development of their personality and outlook; and those on the other who consider that parents have a profound moral right—or even a duty—to mould the development of their children's personality, preferences and moral and cultural outlook in accordance with their own convictions and traditions. This is, indeed, such a fundamental

---

6 See J. Fortin, *Children's Rights and the Developing Law,* 2nd. ed (London: Butterworths, 2002), ch 1.

7 J.S. Mill, *On Liberty* (1869), quoted from M. Warnock (ed), *Utilitarianism,* (London: Fontana Press, 1962), p 135.

8 For more detailed discussion, see P. Meredith, op cit, n 2 above. See also S. Poulter, *Ethnicity, Law and Human Rights: The English Experience* (Oxford: Clarendon Press, 1998), especially ch 1.

divide that there may be little common ground between the opposing positions, but the children themselves may well be caught in the middle of profoundly conflicting views as to the appropriate educational approach. This paper cannot offer a solution to these differences, but it must recognise them, and recognise their very real relevance to the discussion of the deeply controversial topic of sex education.

The Government's Policy of Diversity and Sensitivity - Distancing Itself from the Front Line of Curricular Content

In the light of these acute differences, it perhaps comes as no surprise that one of the defining characteristics of the approach taken by the educational system in England towards sex education has been a marked reluctance to adopt a prescriptive approach from the central department towards the nature, content or delivery of sex education (or the counselling of pupils with regard to sexuality) in maintained schools. It is an area of educational provision in which—despite its arguably crucial importance for the development of children's personality, cultural and moral outlook as well as for their physical and mental well-being—the government is noticeably reluctant to intervene in a positive and unambiguous way. This is in marked contrast to other areas of the curriculum where—with the exception in large part of religious education—the government's approach since the incremental introduction of the national curriculum following the Education Reform Act 1988 has been one of direct and extensive prescription and control. Although the level of prescription in recent years has lessened, the national curriculum in England remains in general one of the most highly centralised in Europe, LEAs, school governors and the teaching profession having a relatively weak consultative role in its formulation. Sex education is in sharp contrast to this, remaining—as we will see below in the discussion of the legal framework—strictly outside the national curriculum.

The government's reluctance to prescribe from the centre over sex education is attributable in large part to its fear of causing offence and treading on delicate ethnic, religious and cultural sensitivities. The government is also no doubt mindful of its obligations under the ECHR to respect parents' religious and philosophical convictions in the provision of education by virtue of Article 2 of Protocol 1 to the ECHR, and that a prescriptive approach to the formulation of the sex education curriculum might render it liable to challenge by parents under the Human Rights Act 1998, alleging a breach of their Convention right. Such challenges might possibly be based also on Articles 8 and 9, concerning the right to respect for private and family life, and religious and cultural convictions. More detailed consideration will be given below to possible challenge under Article 2 of the Protocol 1 to the ECHR by parents and, conceivably, by children: suffice it here to say that it is by no means certain, particularly in the light of the well-known case of *Kjeldsen, Busk Madsen and Pedersen v*

Denmark,[9] that any such challenge would be successful, but it is fair to assume that the possibility of such a challenge is a consideration which to an extent conditions the government's approach to the promulgation of legislation and administrative guidance in this area.

These considerations go far to explain the government's underlying policy of decentralising the formulation of the sex education curriculum to the lowest viable level, subject, as we will see below, to the promulgation of central departmental 'guidance' which is required merely to be 'taken into account' in the drawing up by school governors of statutory sex education policies, and at the level of delivery. This is qualified by certain very broad statutory provisions of a highly moralistic nature which may be of significant symbolic value and which may well inform policy formulation, but which would be unlikely to be enforceable in a legal sense. The government's core policy in this area is, in effect, to distance itself from the policy making and curricular formulation process so far as it possibly can, thereby deflecting criticism and possible challenge to lower levels, and to present by way of justification for this the merits of diversity of provision and sensitivity to local wishes and the ethnic, religious and cultural complexion of the area concerned. No doubt there is much to commend this approach, but the practical consequence of this diversity of approach is that the nature, content and quality of the provision of sex education vary considerably from one area to another, and from one school to another. While all secondary school pupils will receive at least some sex education (subject to the parental right of withdrawal), this may not be the case at primary level where the governing body of the school may determine as a matter of policy that sex education will not be provided, even though such a policy runs counter to the central departmental guidance. And the substantive content of the provision, particularly in relation to such controversial topics as contraception, abortion and homosexuality, may vary considerably. These considerations may in part explain some of the findings in the reports discussed in the following section with regard to inconsistent and patchy provision of sex education, high levels of ignorance even as to basic facts with regard to sexuality, and high levels of teenage pregnancy and sexually transmitted infections.

Recent Reports of Relevance to Sexual Health and Sex Education

Three recent reports are of direct relevance to the issues addressed in this chapter by focusing attention on some significant shortcomings in the provision of sex education in schools, and putting forward recommendations for reform. The first is the report by the Social Exclusion Unit (SEU) on *Teenage Pregnancy* issued in 1999.[10] One of the recommendations in the *Teenage Pregnancy* report was that

9 [1976] 1 EHRR 711.

10 Cm 4342.

Ofsted should carry out a survey of sex and relationships education (SRE) and produce a guide to good practice: this led directly to the issuing by Ofsted of its report in 2002 on *Sex and Relationships*.[11] More recently this has been followed by a report from the House of Commons Health Select Committee in June 2003 on *Sexual Health*:[12] this was a more wide-ranging inquiry going beyond issues relating to education and schools, but the report contains important findings and recommendations relating to sex education. It is not intended in this chapter to provide an extended discussion of the findings contained in these reports, but some of the key findings form an important background to the discussion that follows of law, policy and individual rights in relation to sex education in schools.

The findings of the SEU report on *Teenage Pregnancy*[13] were stark, indicating that the UK had the highest rate of teenage births in Western Europe, with a rate twice as high as in Germany, three times as high as in France, and six times as high as in the Netherlands. The rate for England was nearly 90,000 conceptions a year to teenagers, including some 7,700 to girls aged under 16 and some 2,200 to girls aged 14 or under.[14] These figures reflected a worsening in the UK's position relative to other Western European countries since the 1970s, at which time the rates were broadly comparable. The rate in other European countries has since then significantly fallen, but a similar decline has not occurred in the UK. Two particularly important explanations for this were suggested by the SEU: one was the low expectations of many teenagers from disadvantaged backgrounds and with poor employment prospects. Many such teenagers saw little reason not to become pregnant. The second—of direct relevance to the question of sex education—was widespread ignorance about contraception, sexually transmitted infections, what to expect in relationships, and what it meant to be a parent. Many had little understanding of the reality of single parenthood. The SEU found that only about half of under 16 year olds and two thirds of those aged 16-19 used contraception when they started to have sexual intercourse, in comparison to some 80 per cent in the Netherlands, Denmark and the USA.[15] Ignorance deriving from lack of effective sex education was a core factor underpinning the high incidence of teenage pregnancy.[16] The SEU found that good, comprehensive sex and relationships education did not make young people more likely to start engaging in sexual activity at an earlier age; indeed, it found that it was likely to help them to delay sexual activity, and make them more likely to use contraceptives when they did so.[17] Although the SEU found that

---

11 HMI 433.

12 Third Report from the Health Committee, 2002-03, HC 69.

13 For a more extended discussion, see chapter 6, below.

14 *Teenage Pregnancy*, p 6, para 1.

15 Ibid, p 7, para 6.

16 Ibid, p 36, para 5.1.

17 Ibid.

there was much evidence of good practice in SRE, in some schools it was under-resourced as a subject, allocated an excessively limited amount of time, inadequately supported by training, and not connected with wider local strategies to combat teenage pregnancy and improve sexual health.[18] Furthermore, the weaknesses in the provision of SRE in schools adversely affected not only the minority who became pregnant in their teens. The adverse consequences were significantly more far-reaching. The SEU commented that:

> The universal message the Unit received from young people during its consultation is that the sex and relationships education they receive falls far short of what they would like to equip them for managing relationships as they grow in to adulthood.[19]

Against this background, the SEU set out two primary goals: firstly, a reduction in the rate of teenage pregnancy by 50 per cent among under 18 year olds by 2010; and, secondly, ensuring that more teenage parents came back into education, training or employment, with a view to reducing the risk of their long-term social exclusion.[20] It set out an action plan including as one of its core elements the promotion of better education both in and out of school, and it proposed as a specific measure in this context the promulgation of new guidance to be issued by the government to LEAs and schools on SRE, replacing the existing guidance contained in the Department for Education's Circular 5/94.[21] It also proposed improvements in the context of teacher training, and it proposed that all Ofsted inspections be extended to cover the establishment, implementation and monitoring of SRE policies.

The *Teenage Pregnancy* report in 1999 acted as a catalyst for further action, and its proposals were taken up by Ofsted through the conduct of a survey of SRE policy and practice, based upon a wide range of evidence, including inspection by Her Majesty's Inspectorate of 140 primary, secondary and special schools, an analysis of Ofsted inspections of primary, secondary and special schools during 2000-2001, discussions with some 650 young people during these inspections, and a postal survey of some 1,000 primary, secondary and special schools in 20 LEA areas. This Ofsted survey was also informed by the Department for Education's most recent guidance to LEAs and schools, *Sex and Relationship Education Guidance* (*SRE Guidance*), issued in July 2000,[22] and operated as an early review of the new *SRE Guidance* in action. Key findings of the Ofsted survey were that most of the primary and secondary schools covered in the survey taught about sex and relationships conscientiously and, for the most

18 Ibid, p 36, para 5.2.

19 Ibid, p 37, para 5.6.

20 Ibid, p 8, para 12.

21 Ibid, p 93, para 11.9. See Annex 4 for detailed principles informing the proposals for new guidance.

22 Department for Education and Employment, 0116/2000, July 2000.

part, effectively, although there were deficiencies in the development in pupils of values, attitudes and personal skills; in one tenth of all schools surveyed, the SRE policy adopted by the governing body was poor; education about HIV/AIDS was receiving less attention than in the past, despite its continuing importance as a health problem; education about parenthood did not feature in all secondary school programmes; and the monitoring and evaluation of SRE programmes were weak in most schools surveyed.[23] Particular weaknesses were found at Key Stage 3 in pupils' knowledge and understanding of relationships and sexual health, some 20 per cent of pupils' achievement here being judged unsatisfactory or poor.[24] Common problems identified in the survey in relation to teaching included unclear expectations as to what pupils should learn in terms of knowledge and understanding, values and attitudes, and personal skills; and inadequate assessment of pupils' knowledge and progress.[25] In relation to assessment, the Ofsted survey found that one third of primary schools did not make regular assessments of pupils' knowledge and understanding; in one fifth of secondary schools, there were no assessments of pupils in relation to SRE; and in three fifths of secondary schools, assessment practices were described as weak.[26] Ofsted's view was that clearly defined learning outcomes for each Key Stage should be adopted,[27] and assessment procedures linked to these learning outcomes should be developed and implemented. To this end, Ofsted included in Annex 1 to the report an illustrative set of learning outcomes for SRE throughout the Key Stages for consideration by governing bodies.[28] A further major problem identified in the Ofsted survey was the lack of specialist teachers of SRE, and the widespread practice of involving form tutors with no specialist knowledge of the subject in the teaching of SRE.

The Ofsted survey thus revealed a far from satisfactory picture of the provision of SRE: its findings indicated patchy and inconsistent provision in terms of its extent, scope and quality. Of key importance was the fact that, with the exception of certain specific aspects of sex education which fall within the Science national curriculum programmes of study, SRE fell outside the prescriptive framework of the national curriculum and was not subject to formal assessment arrangements as required for national curriculum subjects. While Ofsted did not recommend bringing SRE within the national curriculum, it was nonetheless sharply critical of the inadequacies of many schools' assessment practices in this context. In many respects, this factor, coupled with the absence of clearly defined learning outcomes, lay at the heart of Ofsted's findings.

---

23 Ofsted, *Sex and Relationships*, p 5.
24 Ibid, p 9, para 16, Table 1.
25 Ibid, p 21-2, para 59.
26 Ibid, p 25, para 71.
27 Ibid, para 72.
28 Ibid, p 35-41.

The third report of relevance to this discussion is the House of Commons Health Committee's report on *Sexual Health* issued in June 2003. The Health Committee warned that:

> the evidence we have taken from teachers, educationalists and, most importantly of all, from young people, has identified serious shortcomings in this area.[29]

The Committee went on to state that:

> Our evidence from young people...suggests that even basic factual knowledge about sex and sexual health cannot be assumed, and we believe that providing young people with accurate and appropriate information through school relationships and sex education programmes is an essential building block for securing improved sexual health for this and for future generations.[30]

A number of key shortcomings were identified by the Health Committee, including the lack of experienced and specialist teachers in the area;[31] the fact that SRE was not included within the initial teacher training programme;[32] and the Committee commented that they had seen little evidence that the government's *SRE Guidance* was being consistently implemented, especially in relation to crucial areas including sexual orientation and HIV/AIDS.[33]

A core factor for the Health Committee, echoing some of the concerns expressed earlier in the Ofsted report, was the position of SRE outside the national curriculum, and in particular the tendency for SRE to be treated as essentially peripheral by virtue of its status and by virtue in particular of the absence of formal assessment arrangements, in contrast to national curriculum subjects:

> We have heard strong evidence that sex education in schools is frequently starved of time and resources in order to accommodate subjects which are accorded a higher priority because of their National Curriculum status.[34]

The Committee strongly recommended that SRE be incorporated within the national curriculum,[35] in that respect going significantly further than either the SEU or Ofsted. The Health Committee took the view that the exclusion of SRE from the national curriculum represented a key structural faultline, undermining the effectiveness of its teaching. Many, on the other hand, would strenuously

---

29 *Sexual Health*, para 253.
30 Ibid, para 267.
31 Ibid, para 292.
32 Ibid.
33 Ibid, para 303.
34 Ibid, para 282.
35 Ibid, para 286.

argue that SRE should be left to the discretion of the governing bodies of individual schools, in order appropriately to reflect local wishes and cultural and religious preferences, particularly in the case of faith schools. Inclusion of SRE within the national curriculum would inevitably present considerable problems in terms of the formulation of the contents of the statutory programmes of study. Mr Stephen Twigg, the Minister in the Department for Education and Skills with responsibility for the school curriculum, stated in his evidence to the Health Committee that his Department was 'very sceptical' about extending national curriculum status to SRE, as

> the whole direction of policy in terms of the national curriculum...is away from compulsory elements...[36]

Whether this is the primary reason for the government's reticence here is open to question: arguably the true reason is the government's wish to distance itself from curricular formulation in this most contentious of subject areas. It is clear, however, that the position of SRE outside the national curriculum is a central feature of the legal framework for the provision of SRE in schools, and it is to that legal framework that we will now turn.

The Legal Framework for the Provision of Sex and Relationship Education

At the most general level, education legislation in England provides that the curriculum in maintained primary and secondary schools shall be balanced and broadly based, and that it shall promote the spiritual, moral cultural, mental and physical development of the pupils and of society.[37] It is also required to prepare pupils for the opportunities, responsibilities and experiences of later life.[38] These provisions are perhaps little more than aspirational in nature and are in effect unenforceable in any legal sense, but nonetheless provide a background for a range of more specific statutory requirements. In the case of secondary schools, sex education is included as a compulsory element in the basic curriculum (not the national curriculum) for all registered pupils—not only for those of compulsory school age,[39] although this is subject to an unqualified parental right of withdrawal,[40] discussed below. In the case of primary schools, sex education is not a compulsory part of the basic curriculum, and it is open to the governing body to decide not to provide sex education, although the Department for Education's *SRE Guidance* strongly recommends that it should be provided. All

---

36 Ibid, para 285.

37 Education Act 2002, s 78(1)(a).

38 Ibid, s 78(1)(b).

39 Ibid, s 80(1)(c).

40 Education Act 1996, s 405.

maintained school governing bodies are required to formulate and keep up to date a policy on sex education,[41] although in the case of primary school governors that policy may be not to provide any.

The Secretary of State for Education and Skills is required to issue guidance to LEAs and schools on SRE. In formulating this guidance, the Secretary of State is required to bear in mind certain statutory constraints which were imposed by the Learning and Skills Act 2000.[42] These constraints require the Secretary of State to secure that the guidance is designed to ensure that, when sex education is given to pupils at maintained schools,

> (a) they learn the nature of marriage and its importance for family life and the bringing up of children; and
> (b) they are protected from teaching and materials which are inappropriate having regard to the age and the religious and cultural background of the pupils concerned.[43]

These constraints are reflected in a number of provisions in the statutory guidance issued by the Secretary of State to LEAs and schools in July 2000, the *SRE Guidance*.[44] LEAs, school governors and head teachers are statutorily obliged to 'have regard to' this guidance,[45] though this does not require them to follow it to the letter. Indeed, they may argue that they enjoy a considerable element of discretion in the matter, and this is particularly evident in the case of governors of primary schools, and is arguably reflected in some of the critical comments in the reports referred to above. Whatever view they may take of the contents of the *SRE Guidance*, however, governing bodies and head teachers are statutorily required, wherever sex education is given in their school, to

> take such steps as are reasonably practicable to secure that...it is given in such a manner as to encourage...pupils to have due regard to moral considerations and the value of family life.[46]

That, very briefly, is the legal basis for the promulgation of the *SRE Guidance*, and the highly qualified obligation on the part of LEAs, school governors and head teachers to follow it. In addition to this loosely framed provision for SRE, the more specifically biological aspects of human sexuality are included within the statutory programmes of study in Science laid down as part of the national curriculum. From this there is no right of parental withdrawal. Under the Education Act 1996, it was formerly provided that the

---

41 Education Act 1996, s 404.

42 Learning and Skills Act 2000, s 148, inserting new s 1A, 1B, 1C and 1D into s 403, Education Act 1996.

43 Education Act 1996, s 403 (1A).

44 Op cit, n 22 above.

45 Education Act 1996, s 403(1A) and (1B).

46 Education Act 1996, s 403(1).

national curriculum Science orders must exclude the topics of HIV and AIDS, other sexually transmitted diseases, and non-biological aspects of human behaviour.[47] Thus children whose parents had exercised their right to withdraw them from SRE would strictly receive no formal school education in relation to these crucial issues. This exclusion has, however, now been dropped by the Education Act 2002, thus creating some further element of curricular discretion in this context.

The *SRE Guidance* provides a wide range of recommendations by the central department to governing bodies as to the formulation of their policies on SRE.[48] The government firmly emphasises in the guidance that SRE should not be delivered in isolation but should be 'firmly rooted' within the broader framework of personal, social and health education. The moral overtones of the few formal statutory provisions constraining SRE mentioned above are strongly reflected in the *SRE Guidance*, which stresses that

> pupils should be taught about the nature and importance of marriage for family life and bringing up children.[49]

This is a direct reflection of section 403 of the Education Act 1996, and arguably adds little. In a later passage it stresses that SRE should reflect

> understanding of the importance of marriage for family life, stable and loving relationships, respect, love and care.[50]

These moralistic strictures are, however, to an extent softened in an attempt by the government to promote a more inclusive and pluralistic approach, by the statement that

> there are strong and mutually supportive relationships outside marriage... Care needs to be taken to ensure that there is no stigmatisation of children based on their home circumstances.[51]

This represents a significant modification of the earlier guidance contained in Department for Education Circular 5/94,[52] in which the government, having indicated that teachers needed to acknowledge that many children did not come from stable married family backgrounds, made the arguably highly insensitive and patronising comment that

---

47 Education Act 1996, s 356(9).

48 See D. Monk, 'New Guidance/Old Problems: Recent Developments in Sex Education' (2001) *Journal of Social Welfare and Family Law*, 23, 271-291.

49 *SRE Guidance*, p 4, para 4.

50 Ibid, p 5, para 9.

51 Ibid, p 4, para 4.

52 *Education Act 1993: Sex Education in Schools.*

> sensitivity is therefore needed to avoid causing hurt and offence to them and their families; and to allow such children to feel a sense of worth. But teachers should also help pupils, whatever their circumstances, to *raise their sights*. [53]

The omission of this patronising statement from the 2000 *SRE Guidance* is to be welcomed, although the overall tenor of the guidance remains striking in the strength of its promotion of traditional moral and traditional family values.

It is not intended here to explore specific areas covered by the *SRE Guidance* in detail, but it is important to stress some points of particular concern. The guidance emphasises that knowledge of the different types of contraception, and of access to and availability of contraception, is a major part of the government's strategy for reduction of teenage pregnancy. Accordingly it explicitly endorses the provision of education about contraception in secondary schools.[54] The guidance goes significantly further in this context, however, suggesting that trained staff (who may be health professionals rather than teachers) should be able to give secondary school pupils full information about different types of contraception, including emergency contraception, and their effectiveness. And teachers may also give pupils—individually or in class—additional information and guidance as to where and how to obtain confidential advice, counselling and, where necessary, treatment.[55] The guidance indicates that this should be made clear in the school's SRE policy.[56]

On the question of abortion, the *SRE Guidance* is more equivocal in its position. It states that 38 per cent of teenage pregnancies ended in abortion in 1998 - some 39,000 abortions. It then merely goes on to emphasise that:

> There are strongly held views and religious beliefs about abortion and some schools will apply a particular religious ethos through their sex and relationship education policy to the issue which will enable pupils to consider the moral and personal dilemmas involved. The religious convictions of pupils and their parents should be respected.[57]

The key task for schools according to the guidance is, however, through appropriate information and effective advice on contraception and on delaying sexual activity, to reduce the incidence of unwanted pregnancies.[58]

The guidance is quite clear that information and knowledge about safer sex, HIV/AIDS and other sexually transmitted diseases should be included within SRE

---

53 Ibid, para 8. Emphasis added.
54 *SRE Guidance*, para 2.9.
55 Ibid, para 2.10.
56 Ibid, para 2.12.
57 Ibid, para 2.14.
58 Ibid, para 2.16.

at secondary level.[59] The guidance drew upon a National Opinion Poll survey in 1996 indicating that young adults were becoming increasingly complacent about the importance of safer sex, thereby increasing their risk of infection and unwanted pregnancy or paternity.[60] Accordingly the guidance specifically recommends that SRE policies recognise that information about HIV/AIDS is vital, that young people need to understand the nature of risk in this context, and that young people have specific information about condom use and safer sex in general.[61]

On the question of sexual orientation and homosexuality, the *SRE Guidance* says relatively little, which may not be surprising given the particularly emotive nature of the subject. It does, however, make at least some attempt to be inclusive, commenting that:

> Young people, whatever their developing sexuality, need to feel that sex and relationship education is relevant to them and sensitive to their needs. The Secretary of State...is clear that teachers should be able to deal honestly and sensitively with sexual orientation, answer appropriate questions, and offer support.[62]

A further very important attempt at inclusivity is evident from a new provision in the *SRE Guidance* drawing attention to the need for schools to be able to deal with homophobic bullying: it refers to the unacceptability of and emotional stress caused by bullying in whatever form, whether racial, as a result of a pupil's appearance, related to sexual orientation or whatever other reason.[63]

While the 2000 *SRE Guidance* undoubtedly goes considerably further towards an inclusive approach in the context of sexual orientation than its predecessors,[64] it remains—perhaps not surprisingly—extremely cautious in its handling of the issue. The government treads extremely carefully in this context, for fear in particular of causing offence to minority ethnic and religious groups, suggesting somewhat timidly that:

---

59 Ibid, paras 2.17-2.22 and 3.5.

60 Ibid, para 2.18.

61 Ibid, para 2.19.

62 Ibid, para 1.30.

63 Ibid, para 1.32. See ch 2 above by Neville Harris for a more extended discussion of bullying.

64 See in particular Department of Education and Science Circular 11/87, *Sex Education at School*, para 22: 'There is no place in any school in any circumstances for teaching which advocates homosexual behaviour, which presents it as the "norm", or which encourages homosexual experimentation by pupils. Indeed, encouraging or procuring homosexual acts by pupils who are under the age of consent is a criminal offence. It must also be recognised that for many people, including members of various religious faiths, homosexual practice is not morally acceptable, and deep offence may be caused to them if the subject is not handled with sensitivity by teachers if discussed in the classroom.'

Sexual orientation and what is taught in schools is an area of concern for some parents. Schools that liaise closely with parents when developing their sex and relationship education policy and programme should be able to reassure parents of the content of the programme and the context in which it will be presented.[65]

The limited coverage of the topic of homosexuality and sexual orientation in the *SRE Guidance* may have been attributable in part to the pervasive influence of one of the best known but most widely misunderstood provisions relating to English education law—section 28 of the Local Government Act 1988.[66] This section prohibited local authorities—including local education authorities—from intentionally promoting homosexuality or publishing material with that effect, and from promoting the teaching in any maintained school of the acceptability of homosexuality as a 'pretended family relationship.' This provision was proposed as a new clause in the Local Government Bill 1988 by a Conservative backbench MP, Mr David Wilshire, but was enthusiastically adopted by the then Conservative government as part of a broader campaign to underpin traditional family values in education. Despite the immense controversy attracted by the new clause, it was duly enacted in the Local Government Act 1988, and it remained on the statute book until its final repeal following a bitter and prolonged Parliamentary battle in the Local Government Act 2003.[67]

The drafting of section 28 was obscure in the extreme, and arguably the section was directed at the wrong target:[68] it applied strictly to local authorities and not to the governing bodies of individual schools, let alone to head teachers and teachers. Given that the legal responsibility for formulating SRE policies and delivery of the SRE curriculum and the counselling of pupils in relation to sexuality are all matters which fall outside the scope of responsibility of LEAs as such, the provision was arguably misdirected. Furthermore, the phraseology of the section was obscure in the extreme: it was virtually impossible to say with any certainty what element of positive portrayal of homosexuality would be needed to constitute its 'promotion.' The mere mention of the subject would clearly not constitute promotion, but it was extremely difficult for teachers to know with confidence how far they could safely go in discussion of alternative lifestyles without being in danger of falling foul of the prohibition.[69] Of no less importance, teachers were left in much uncertainty with regard to the counselling of individual pupils. Not only was the concept of 'promotion' fraught with difficulty, but the phrase 'pretended family relationship' was also somewhat

---

65 Ibid, para 1.31.

66 Which inserted a new s 2A into the Local Government Act 1986.

67 S 122.

68 See P. Meredith, *Government, Schools and the Law* (London: Routledge, 1992), at pp 73-77.

69 S 28(2) did, however, expressly provide that nothing in the section should be taken to prohibit the doing of anything for the purpose of treating or preventing the spread of disease.

bizarre: arguably, what section 28 actually intended to strike at was the promotion of homosexual relationships as *genuine* rather than as *pretended* family relationships. Furthermore, it was difficult to envisage how the section could be practically enforced in legal terms. Judicial review of a school governing body's SRE policy would not be appropriate, given that the section did not apply to governing bodies; and LEAs would be able to deflect judicial review by arguing that they did not carry direct responsibility for SRE policies. Nonetheless, governing bodies and teachers felt a significant degree of unease and vulnerability by virtue of section 28.

In practice, the section had a significant chilling effect on school governors in formulating their SRE policies and on teachers in delivering them in the classroom and in counselling pupils. Indeed, this chilling effect on discussion and debate over matters of human sexuality could be argued to have constituted a breach of the ECHR, in particular of the right to freedom of speech under Article 10, and it is possible that section 28 might have been subject to challenge under the Human Rights Act 1998.[70] Following the section's repeal, this possibility is now of largely academic interest, but the impact of the section on teachers was and remains very real: teachers in particular were fearful of potential disciplinary proceedings resulting from parental complaints that they had contravened the section. Despite the repeal of section 28, it is very likely that this chilling effect will remain as a pervasive influence for a considerable time.

How far section 28 in fact conditioned the department's thinking when drafting the 2000 *SRE Guidance* is difficult to estimate. The department may well have been more concerned over possible offence to minority groups than over a legislative provision which they knew was effectively unenforceable in legal terms, although of considerable symbolic importance. Nonetheless it is arguable that the spirit of section 28 is discernible in a somewhat obscure message in the *SRE Guidance* to the effect that 'there should be no direct promotion of sexual orientation.'[71] This statement seems inconsistent with the overwhelming tenor of the *SRE Guidance* which does exactly that—it directly promotes the virtues of marriage and the traditional family unit as one of the key building blocks of society, thereby promoting heterosexual orientation. To suggest that the *SRE Guidance* seeks to promote a neutral stance through the avoidance of any direct promotion of any sexual orientation is arguably mistaken.

---

70 See M. Bell and P. Cumper, 'Section 28 and the Human Rights Act' (2003) *Journal of Social Welfare and Family Law*, 25(3), 215-228.

71 *SRE Guidance*, para 1.30.

Possible Areas of Conflict

Few areas of education could be of deeper concern than sex education and the wider pastoral care and counselling of children in relation to sexuality. Acute issues of personal conscience and moral, cultural and religious convictions may be raised. Not surprisingly it is an area in which acute issues of conflict may arise.[72] Parents—or, indeed, pupils—may take issue with the content or mode of delivery of sex education as provided in a particular school, in respect of which the parental right to withdraw their child may be viewed as only a very partial and perhaps unsatisfactory solution. It is also possible to envisage challenge by children to the exercise by their parents of the parental right of withdrawal.

It would, however, be extremely difficult for parents or children to launch any form of legal challenge to the policy statement on SRE adopted by a school's governing body, or to the delivery of sex education classes in a school, beyond the mere submission of a complaint at local level in the hope of an informal resolution.[73] Given the breadth of the governing body's discretionary power over the formulation of their SRE policy, judicial review would seem a remote prospect. This in effect is an aspect of discretionary decision-making beyond effective legal challenge, despite the fundamentality of its importance to the individual parent or child. In the case of parents, it could be argued that their claim could be met, at least in part, by the fact of parental representation on the school's governing body.[74] Arguably their claim could further be met through exercise of the parents' absolute right to withdraw the child—for some or all of the time—from sex education classes by virtue of section 405 of the Education Act 1996. Neither, however, could be said to provide full satisfaction: while the inclusion of parental representatives on the governing body is of crucial importance—and may indirectly offer an outlet for the interests of the children themselves—that representation is limited numerically and also, arguably, in terms of the extent of influence exerted by parents in relation to curricular policy-making when faced with the educational expertise of other members of the governing body, in particular the teacher representatives. Furthermore, the capacity of parents to withdraw their child from sex education classes affords, arguably, a highly undesirable remedy of last resort whose exercise could be

---

72 See P. Meredith, 'Children's Rights and Education,' in J. Fionda (ed), *Legal Concepts of Childhood* (Oxford: Hart Publishing, 2001), pp 205-222.

73 LEAs are required under s 409(1), Education Act 1996 to make arrangements for dealing with curricular complaints. These complaints mechanisms were originally introduced under s 23, Education Reform Act 1988: see N. Harris, 'Local Complaints Procedures under the Education Reform Act 1988' (1993) *Journal of Social Welfare and Family Law,* 19-39, at pp 32-33. Once the LEA complaints mechanism has been exhausted, it would be possible to complain further to the Secretary of State under s 496 or s 497, Education Act 1996, although intervention by the Secretary of State would be most unlikely.

74 See Education Act 2002, ss 19-21.

seriously damaging to the child's interests, given the crucial importance that children should receive balanced, coherent and sensitively delivered education on sex and sexuality. Parents may thus be highly reluctant to exercise their right of withdrawal,[75] despite having considerable misgivings about the content or presentation of SRE in the school concerned.

In considering the possibility of parental challenge to a school's SRE policy or the delivery of SRE in the classroom, a key question would clearly be whether the second sentence of Article 2 of the Protocol 1 to the ECHR would provide a sufficient foundation on which to base a legal action. Article 2 provides that signatory states, in exercising their functions in relation to education and teaching, shall respect the right of parents to ensure such education and teaching in conformity with their religious and philosophical convictions. This Article was acceded to by the UK government subject to its compatibility with the provision of efficient instruction and training and the avoidance of unreasonable public expenditure, a reservation expressly preserved by the UK government in the Human Rights Act 1998, incorporating most of the Articles of the ECHR into domestic UK law.[76] This reservation is extremely important and may well provide a practical mechanism for the government to avoid liability on the basis, for instance, that the provision of specially adapted sex education for a minority of pupils would be educationally impractical or that it would be unduly expensive. The central question, however, is how far the second sentence of Article 2 of Protocol 1 truly restricts the discretion of state authorities—including the governing bodies of maintained schools—in the formulation of their policies.

The key authority in this context is *Kjeldsen, Busk Madsen and Pedersen v. Denmark*:[77] in this case, parents of children attending state primary schools in Denmark challenged before the European Court of Human Rights the imposition of compulsory sex education integrated into the teaching of other subjects in the school curriculum under an Act of the Danish Parliament of 1970. The parents objected to the nature and content of the sex education, and to the fact that it would be integrated into the teaching of other subjects in such a way that it would be impracticable to withdraw their children from the sex education elements alone. Although it would have been possible to have their children educated in private schools, to which the statute did not apply, or to educate the children in the home, neither possibility was practical. In its judgment, the European Court of Human Rights stressed that Article 2 did not prohibit schools from imparting in schools 'information or knowledge of a directly or indirectly religious or philosophical kind.'[78] Indeed, it took the view that it would be very difficult for many aspects of subjects taught at school not to have, to a greater or less extent,

---

75 The incidence of withdrawal was estimated by Ofsted in its report at four in every 10,000 pupils (0.04 per cent): see Ofsted, *Sex and Relationships*, op cit, n 23, p 6.

76 See Human Rights Act 1998, s 15.

77 (1976) 1 EHRR 711.

78 Ibid, p 733.

'some philosophical complexion or implications.'[79] The Article did, however, require that the state must ensure that information or knowledge included in the curriculum was conveyed in an 'objective, critical and pluralistic manner,'[80] and that the state must avoid anything which could be regarded as constituting indoctrination.

The Court found as a matter of fact that the statute in question was intended to ensure that the children were given better factual information about sexual matters rather than permitting the information to be conveyed in such a manner as to further support for any particular opinion as to moral attitudes or behaviour. The Court regarded this as being of central importance, although it recognised that 'appraisals of fact easily lead on to value judgments.'[81] The Court found that:

> the Danish State, by providing children in good time with explanations it considers useful, is attempting to warn them against phenomena it views as disturbing, for example, the excessive frequency of births out of wedlock, induced abortions and venereal diseases...
>
> These considerations are indeed of a moral order, but they are very general in character and do not entail overstepping the bounds of what a democratic state may regard as the public interest. Examination of the legislation in dispute establishes in fact that it in no way amounts to an attempt at indoctrination aimed at advocating a specific kind of sexual behaviour. It does not make a point of exalting sex or inciting pupils to indulge precociously in practices that are dangerous for their stability, health or future or that many parents consider reprehensible. Further, it does not affect the right of parents to enlighten and advise their children, to exercise with regard to their children natural parental functions as educators, or to guide their children on a path in line with the parents' own religious and philosophical convictions.[82]

The *Kjeldsen* case is clearly permissive in the sense of granting state authorities a wide element of discretion as to the contents of the sex education curriculum, provided that it is formulated and delivered in an 'objective, critical and pluralistic' manner, and that it does not seek to indoctrinate the pupils with any particular moral or ethical view as to human sexuality. Furthermore, although in *Kjeldsen* the children concerned could have been educated in private schools with state funding, it was not practical for them to be educated in these schools for a variety of reasons, including geographical location. Hence the parents did not have a practical option of withdrawing their children from the sex education provided, given its integrated nature within the curriculum. Hence the *Kjeldsen* case indicates that it is not necessary for the state to provide an opportunity for parents to withdraw their children. Thus a state which does provide such an opportunity would be even less likely to be successfully

---

79 Ibid.

80 Ibid, p 731.

81 Ibid.

82 Ibid, p 731-732.

challenged under Article 2 on the basis of parental dissatisfaction with a school's SRE policy or its delivery.

One final and largely academic point arising out of the *Kjeldsen* decision relates to the requirement formulated by the Court that, in order to comply with Article 2 of Protocol 1, sex education should be objective, critical and *pluralistic* in its content and delivery. Does the requirement that it be *pluralistic* raise a potential ground of challenge in relation to SRE policies adopted by school governors based on the 2000 *SRE Guidance*? The argument here would be that the *SRE Guidance* is reflective of a narrow and highly moralistic sector of society, that it fails adequately to reflect the reality of life for very large numbers of children and their parents, and it is therefore excessively narrowly focused and insufficiently *pluralistic* in its approach. It fails adequately to acknowledge the legitimacy of alternative lifestyles and thus tends to stigmatise the many children from family backgrounds which do not fit within the government's perceived ideal model. Such an argument would in practice be almost bound to fail: while it is true that the overwhelming tone of the *SRE Guidance* is indeed highly moralistic and supportive of traditional notions of marriage and family values, it does nonetheless expressly recognise that 'there are strong and mutually supportive relationships outside marriage,' and that 'teaching in this area needs to be sensitive so as not to stigmatise children on the basis of their home circumstances.'[83] While the earlier versions of the *SRE Guidance* were more stridently moralistic in tone and perhaps more susceptible to challenge on this ground, it is thought highly unlikely that SRE policies adopted by school governing bodies modelled upon the 2000 *SRE Guidance* could be successfully challenged by virtue of failing to meet the *Kjeldsen* requirement of pluralism.

Most of the discussion thus far in respect of challenges to the content or presentation of sex education has focused on parental challenges, based on the assumption that the parents' and the children's interests coincide. This, however, may be a fallacious assumption in relation to some aspects of educational provision, and the fallacy is very clearly illustrated by sex education, and in particular by the absolute right of parental withdrawal. While the parental interest may well be satisfied, at least in part, by withdrawal of the child, the exercise of the parental right may serve to damage the child's interest: this is perhaps most graphically illustrated by the fact that such a child may receive no formal education at school relating to matters of sex and sexuality beyond the biological aspects contained within the Science national curriculum, yet if aged 16 years or over may lawfully marry or engage in consensual intercourse. Children in such circumstances could potentially be placed in a life-threatening situation by virtue of a legal structure which in this, as in so many other areas, accords a significantly higher priority to the realisation of the interests of parents than those of their children. Indeed, it is arguable that the provision by statute of an unqualified right on the part of parents to withdraw their children from any or all

83 *SRE Guidance*, para 1.21.

sex education in maintained schools is seriously misconceived. Not only is the parental right of withdrawal absolute, but there is no obligation on parents to express any reasons for their decision to withdraw their child, nor to make any alternative satisfactory provision. The *SRE Guidance* 2000 exhorts schools to make alternative arrangements for children withdrawn from sex education classes, and offers schools a standard pack of information for parents who withdraw their children.[84] Nonetheless it remains open to the parents to refuse all forms of support from the school. Whether parents may lawfully refuse to make any form of alternative provision for their children's education, whether at home or otherwise, is an open question: it has been suggested[85] that parents of compulsory school age children who fail to do so could conceivably be in breach of their duty to ensure their children's 'efficient full-time education' suitable in the light of their age, ability and aptitude.[86] Though many may sympathise with that view, it is thought unlikely that this would constitute a breach, given the wide diversity of opinion as to what constitutes appropriate sex education and the sensitivity of the issues in the light of individual conscience and convictions.

Children denied sex education through school against their wishes by virtue of their parents' decision to withdraw them are afforded no remedy under domestic education legislation; nor do they even have a procedural right to be heard as part of the process of parental exercise of the statutory right of withdrawal. There simply are no mechanisms under education law in England for giving vent to the child's view in this context, let alone for the child's view to prevail. This important omission from education law exists despite Article 12 of the UN Convention on the Rights of the Child, which requires that children should be heard in relation to all matters affecting them, due weight being given to their views in the light of their age and understanding.[87] This omission is not thought to have been remedied by the enactment of section 176 of the Education Act 2002, which now provides for the first time in education legislation in England for the consultation of pupils by LEAs and school governing bodies 'in connection with the taking of decisions affecting them.'[88] Section 176 imposes a duty on LEAs and governing bodies to have regard to any guidance issued by the Secretary of State about the carrying out of such consultation. It is thought that this provision will apply primarily in the context of the exclusion of pupils from school, and that it will probably have little or no application in the context of the exercise of the parental right of withdrawal from sex education, since the

---

84 *SRE Guidance*, para 5.7.

85 See N. Harris, 'The Regulation and Control of Sex Education,' in N. Harris (ed), *Children, Sex Education and the Law* (London: National Children's Bureau, 1996), p 14.

86 Education Act 1996, s 7.

87 See *Concluding Observations of the Committee on the Rights of the Child: United Kingdom of Great Britain and Northern Ireland* (1995) CRC/C/15/Add.34, para 14.

88 See n 4 above.

unqualified nature of the parental right leaves no room for any decision to be taken on the part of the LEA or the school.

Domestic education law would thus appear largely to fail children here, and it is very doubtful, furthermore, whether the ECHR would provide an alternative avenue of redress. As discussed above, the second sentence of Article 2 of Protocol 1 focuses on the *parents'* religious or philosophical convictions. The first sentence, requiring that no person shall be denied the right to education, might, however, appear to offer greater potential in terms of supporting the child's interest: the ECHR, however, nowhere defines the substantive content of the education which may not be denied, and the European Court of Human Rights has held in the *Belgian Linguistics Case*[89] that the first sentence imposes no obligation on public authorities to provide education of any particular type or at any particular level. Furthermore, the negative formulation of the first sentence may have the effect in practice of limiting its enforceability, and was perhaps adopted deliberately with that significance in mind in order to allay the fears of some states that the imposition of a positive obligation might impose on them obligations which they would find it impossible to meet. It is therefore thought unlikely that the first sentence of Article 2 would be of significant value to an individual child seeking to challenge the exercise by his or her parents of their right of withdrawal.

Conclusion: An Exercise in Compromise?

The reports discussed in the earlier part of this chapter point with some consistency towards a number of key shortcomings in the provision of sex education in English maintained schools, in particular a widespread ignorance on the part of children even as to basic factual information; inconsistency of provision between schools; in many cases, a seriously inadequate or non-existent assessment of pupils' knowledge and attainment in relation to SRE; inadequate provision of specialist teachers of SRE; and the widespread perception of SRE as a peripheral subject hidden within a broader personal, social and health education curriculum with inadequate resources and low status, largely squeezed out by an overwhelming focus on subjects within the national curriculum on which pupils are subjected to formal assessment arrangements, the results of which are so crucial for schools' standing in comparative performance league tables. The consequences which flow from these shortcomings for the sexual health and broader physical and mental well-being of young people may in many cases be extremely serious, as seen in particular in the findings of the SEU report on *Teenage Pregnancy*. These shortcomings and their implications for the health and well-being of young people raise fundamental questions of policy for the government. It is clear that, in determining its policy, the government is faced

89 (1968) Series A, No 6.

with an intractable problem in striking a balance between very powerful arguments pulling in radically different directions—a problem whose solution is very likely to take the form of a compromise. On the one hand are those who see it as the responsibility of state schools to adopt an activist and interventionist approach, making extensive provision for SRE for all children, possibly without permitting a parental right of withdrawal, to accord it a high status within the curriculum, and to devise and implement effective mechanisms for the assessment of pupils' knowledge and achievement. On the other hand are those who would profoundly question the legitimacy of state interference in this delicate area, who see it as an unwarranted incursion into the role of the parent and the family to provide for the moral upbringing and the education of the child in relation to human sexuality, and who would adamantly insist on a parental right of withdrawal.

The approach the government has in the event taken could fairly be described as a compromise, as seen perhaps most clearly in the tenor of the *SRE Guidance*. This stresses the centrality of married family life and stable relationships as key building blocks of community and society, but it makes a significantly greater effort to be inclusive in its approach than either of its predecessors, issued as Departmental Circulars respectively in 1987 and 1994. The 2000 *SRE Guidance*, furthermore, goes out of its way to emphasise the vital importance of taking full account of the ethnic, religious and cultural complexion of the area concerned. The *SRE Guidance* without doubt provides constructive and welcome advice to be taken into account by LEAs and school governing bodies on a wealth of key issues within sex and relationship education, and this could be viewed as a constructive and fairly balanced accommodation of divergent views, although it is undoubtedly anodyne in nature, but perhaps inevitably so.

The key problem, however, is one of structural responsibility: at what institutional level should SRE policy and the SRE curriculum be formulated, and where should the responsibility for these lie? The approach taken by the government has been to devolve responsibility to the level of the individual school governing body. This approach can be readily justified on the basis that it is essential that the views of parents and the local community should be conscientiously taken into account in the light of local preferences. The consequence, however, as reflected in the findings of the reports discussed earlier, is that the provision of sex and relationship education in schools across and within LEAs is inconsistent in nature, content and quality. Patchy and inconsistent provision of SRE in schools is not the sole cause of high rates of teenage pregnancy, sexually transmitted infections and wider problems of social exclusion, but it is one of the core contributory factors underlying these phenomena. The government does not, however, appear to be prepared to alter the essential structural responsibilities for policy formulation and action in this field. While the government has ambitious targets for improvement—for example, in terms of a significant reduction in teenage pregnancy rates—it continues to distance itself from the structural responsibility for policy formulation, beyond the promulgation of largely anodyne guidance to LEAs and governing bodies. Furthermore, recommendations—as, for example, by the Select Committee on Health—for incorporation of SRE within the national curriculum, are consistently rejected on the basis that this would go against the fundamental principle of devolved decision-making in this sensitive area, and in recognition of the immensely problematic task of formulating programmes of study that would be culturally acceptable. The danger, however, is that we will continue to have a highly variable and in some cases highly unsatisfactory level of provision, with the potential for extremely damaging consequences for young people's health.

Chapter 6

Calculating the Risk of Teenage Pregnancy: Sex Education, Public Health, the Individual and the Law*

Ann Blair

Introduction

The current law of sex and relationship education (SRE) was introduced by the Education Act 1993. The legislation is now contained in the Education Act 1996 (as amended), but the framework created in 1993 remains broadly intact. Since its introduction, many writers have commented on the contradictory nature of this legal framework.[1] In this chapter the aim is not to concentrate exclusively on parental and children's rights issues which have been at the centre of much of this discussion, but to look at this as a question of public health. The central theme is the question of whether the concept of risk can shed any light on the contradictions in sex education law in England and Wales.

---

* I am very grateful to Daniel Monk for his very helpful comments on a draft of this chapter. Any mistakes are the author's own.

1 A. Blair and C. Furniss, 'Sex, Lies and DfE Circular 5/94: the Legal Limits of Sex Education' (1995) *Education and the Law*, 7(4), 197-202; J. Bridgman, 'Don't Tell the Children: the Department's Guidance on the Provision of Information About Contraception to Individual Pupils,' in N. Harris (ed), *Children, Sex Education and the Law* (London: Sex Education Forum, National Children's Bureau, 1996), 45-64; C. Furniss and A Blair, 'Sex Wars: Conflict in, and Reform of, Sex Education in Maintained Secondary Schools' (1997) *Journal of Social Welfare and Family Law*, 19(2), 189-202; N. Harris (ed), *Children, Sex Education and the Law* (London: Sex Education Forum, National Children's Bureau, 1996); P. Meredith, 'Children's Rights and Education,' in Julia Fionda (ed), *Legal Concepts of Childhood* (Oxford: Hart Publishing, 2001), 203-222; D. Monk, 'New Guidance/Old Problems: Recent Developments in Sex Education' (2001) *Journal of Social Welfare and Family Law*, 23(3), 271-291.

The United Nations Population Fund (UNFPA) Report, *State of World Population 2003*,[2] graphically highlights sex education as both a human rights and a public health issue. The report examines the impact of premature sexual experience, lack of education, lack of sex education and sexual health services and poverty on both the global community and on vulnerable individuals—particularly adolescents.[3] These are not discrete factors; one of the key drivers of what are deemed unacceptable rates of pregnancy, early marriage and incidence of sexually transmitted infections (STIs) is lack of education, and in particular the low priority some communities attach to the education of girls. Ensuring that girls have good access to education is seen as crucial to addressing these problems as a whole. The report dramatically describes the impact of early pregnancy in both health and social terms and highlights the abuse of young women that often goes hand in hand with this early sexual experience. Although the report concentrates on Third World issues, the underlying theme of the report is 'investing in adolescents' health and rights,' and this forms a useful backdrop to the issues raised here.

Law and Guidance

Paul Meredith's contribution to this volume contains a more detailed account of the law of sex education in England[4] than there is space for here, but for the sake of completeness it is necessary to highlight some of the main elements of the law here. The governing bodies of all schools must have a policy on sex education, and all secondary schools must provide sex education as part of the basic curriculum.[5] Some sex education forms part of the national curriculum in science and is, therefore, effectively compulsory for all pupils.[6] SRE that falls outside the

---

2 New York: United Nations Publications 2003, available on line at http://www.unfpa.org/swp/swpmain.htm.

3 Ibid, chapter 1; http://www.unfpa.org/swp/2003/english/ch1/.

4 See chapter 5, above.

5 S 80, Education Act 2002 and Schedule 19, School Standards and Framework Act 1998.

6 As originally legislated, the only binding provision on the content of the Science curriculum was that the Secretary of State should by order ensure that the subject of Science did not include certain matters. These were HIV/AIDS, any other sexually transmitted disease, or aspects of human sexual behaviour, other than biological aspects: s 356(9), Education Act 1996. Other than this, the content is at the discretion of the Secretary of State. At present relevant content ranges from the fact that humans and animals reproduce, and offspring grow into adults (at key stage 1), to the way in which hormonal control occurs, including the effects of sex hormones, and some medical uses of hormones, including the control and promotion of fertility (at key stage 4): Education (National Curriculum) (Attainment Targets and Programmes of Study in Science in respect of the First, Second Third and Fourth Key Stages)

national curriculum is provided in accordance with the policy of the school's governing body. Sex education must be 'given in such a manner as to encourage...pupils to have due regard to moral considerations and the value of family life.'[7] In addition, pupils must learn 'the nature of marriage and its importance for family life and the bringing up of children,' and pupils should be 'protected from teaching and materials which are inappropriate having regard to the[ir] age and religious and cultural background.'[8] A parent has an unconditional right to withdraw their child from all or any part of SRE, except that which forms part of the national curriculum.[9]

In exercising functions in relation to sex education, governing bodies and headteachers must have regard to the Secretary of State's guidance.[10] A related legal issue that has been included in this departmental guidance on SRE is the role of teachers in advising individual pupils, especially where sexual activity, actual or proposed, that is disclosed might involve criminal behaviour because the pupil is too young to consent to it. This is discussed below.

Some of the inherent problems that the 1993 Act was criticised for have been addressed by subsequent reforms. Provisions that kept teaching of anything other than the 'biological basics' out of the national curriculum in Science were quietly dropped when the national curriculum was re-legislated in 2002.[11] Also, importantly, the notorious section 28 of the Local Government Act 1988, which prohibited local authorities from intentionally promoting the acceptability of homosexuality as a 'pretended family relationship,' was repealed by section 122

(England) (No 2) Order 2004, SI 2004/1800. Detail of the content of the curriculum can be found at http://www.nc.uk.net/index.html.

7 S 403, Education Act 1996.

8 S 403(1A), Education Act 1996, inserted by s 148, Learning and Skills Act 2000.

9 S 405, Education Act 1996.

10 S 404(1B), Education Act 1996, as inserted by s 148, Learning and Skills Act 2000. Guidance first appeared in the form of DfE Circular 5/94, which was issued as the provisions of the Education Act 1993 came into force. This was replaced in 2000 by *Sex and Relationship Education Guidance,* Department for Education and Employment, 116/2000, to update and account for legislative reform.

11 This was the result of an amendment introduced by Baroness Walmsley and accepted by the government in the House of Lords: HL Debs 26 June 2002, col 1433. Somewhat confusingly, sex education is still defined as including education about AIDS/HIV and any other STIs: s 579(1), Education Act 1996. The government indicated at the time that they did not intend to revise the Science Orders to include such matters. This method of amending the law may have created the potential for a worrying lack of internal coherence. It has always seemed to the present author that the only logical interpretation of the definition of sex education is that it outlines the scope of the parental right of withdrawal: see A. Blair and C. Furniss, above n 1. If this is correct, and HIV/AIDS were to become part of the compulsory national curriculum, s 205 would contradict itself. Parents could not opt a child out of the study of this part of sex education without opting them out of part of the national curriculum, which is not permissible.

of the Local Government Act 2003. Equally, the tone of the guidance on advice to individual pupils published in 1994, which contained veiled threats of potential criminal liability if underage pupils were given contraceptive advice, has also been moderated. More recent guidance now makes it very clear that teachers can give contraceptive advice in classroom discussion and to individual pupils.[12] Although an improvement, this did not altogether settle fears that there might be criminal liability for aiding and abetting unlawful sexual intercourse by advising pupils below the age of consent about the use of contraceptives. Fortunately, the potential for this liability through the principles of aiding, abetting or inciting unlawful sexual intercourse (as discussed in *Gillick*[13]) was finally put to rest by section 73 of the Sexual Offences Act 2003. This provides that a person is not guilty of aiding, abetting or counselling the commission against a child of an offence if he acts for the purpose of:

- protecting the child from sexually transmitted infection,
- protecting the physical safety of the child,
- preventing the child from becoming pregnant, or
- promoting the child's emotional well-being by the giving of advice, and not
- for the purpose of obtaining sexual gratification or for the purpose of causing or encouraging the activity constituting the offence or the child's participation in it.

Sadly this very welcome reform, which should allay teachers' fears about advising pupils in good faith, is coupled with the introduction of a whole range of new criminal offences, which bring a vast range of young people's sexual activity within the scope of the criminal law. Section 13 of the Act makes new offences of young people's sexual activity by applying adult liability for sexual offences against children to the same acts if committed by children. Unfortunately this is not confined to relationships between young people that have the scope for abuse. Although it is not expected that prosecution discretion would be used to criminalise two 12 year olds for kissing (an extreme example), this is a possibility as the law is now drafted.[14] A more likely problem is that this possibility could

---

12 Prescription of contraceptives and abortion services to underage pupils seeking individual advice would necessarily require medical intervention. A teacher who referred a pupil to a relevant medical practitioner, who might be a school nurse, is also clearly advised that this is an acceptable course of action. See Department for Education and Employment, 116/2000, above n 10, at p 15. See also A. Blair, and C. Furniss, above n 1.

13 *Gillick v West Norfolk and Wisbech Health Authority* [1986] AC 112.

14 This is particularly problematic as the offence of sexual assault includes 'sexual touching' by virtue of s 3, Sexual Offences Act 2003. This could include consensual petting or even kissing between two young people if one of them is under 13 and thus unable to consent. Touching is sexual if a reasonable person would consider that (a)

leave some young people unwilling to seek adult advice because they fear the possibility of prosecution. Although the problem of sexual abuse by young people should not be minimised, the idea that it is normal and acceptable for children and young people to learn about sex, at least in part, through displays of physical affection towards one another seems to have been lost along the way.[15]

Other than this potential criminalisation of perfectly normal sexual activity between young people, all of the changes outlined here have in one way or another improved young people's access to the information they will need as they grow older and their sexual identity begins to develop. This chapter as a whole, however, is concerned principally with remaining issues of young people's access to information about sex and relationships. Thus the parental opt-out, as set out in section 405 of the Education Act 1996, is of critical importance. Government policy is based on the assumption that the best way of deferring the age of first sexual activity and of increasing the probability that safe sex practices and effective contraceptive methods will be adopted from the start, is to provide effective SRE.[16] This has been at the centre of government initiatives following the government's Social Exclusion Unit's (SEU) influential 1999 report on

---

whatever its circumstances or any person's purpose in relation to it, it is because of its nature sexual, or (b) because of its nature it may be sexual and because of its circumstances or the purpose of any person in relation to it (or both) it is sexual. And touching includes touching- (a) with any part of the body, (b) with anything else, (c) through anything: ss 78 and 79, Sexual Offences Act 2002. As B. Fitzpatrick has commented, 'The Act criminalises certain sexual conduct between minors, even where such conduct is consensual. It may be that, in certain such circumstances, the Act represents an excessive widening of the net of criminal law. The minimalist approach to prosecution in such instances countenanced in the policy documents preceding the Act appears not to be translated into a clear statement of legislative purpose in the Act itself. Moreover, it is not acceptable that such significant decision-making powers are vested, beyond public scrutiny, in prosecutors': B. Fitzpatrick, 'Reformulating Sex Offences: Some Fundamental Problems in Criminal Law,' seminar, University of Leeds, School of Law, 20 April 2004. See also J.R. Spencer, 'The Sexual Offences Act 2003: (2) Child and Family Offences' (2004) *Crim. L.R.*, May, 347-360.

15 See Furedi quotation at n 39 below.

16 Department for Education and Employment, above n 10, at p 4. But compare D. Wight et al, 'Limits of Teacher Delivered Sex Education: Interim Behavioural Outcomes From a Randomised Trial' (2002) *British Medical Journal,* 324(7351), 1430-33, which showed that within the first two years of delivery of the SHARE programme in Scotland there was no effect on behavioural outcomes. Note also that presumptions that have been made about the causes of the high birth rate and the validity of comparisons with other Western European countries are challenged in L. Arai, 'British Comparisons on Teenage Pregnancy and Childbearing: the Limitations of Comparisons with other European Countries' (2003) *Critical Social Policy,* 23(3), 89-102.

Teenage Pregnancy.[17] It has led to the setting up of the Teenage Pregnancy Unit (TPU) (now within the Department for Education and Skills), the establishment of ambitious targets to reduce teenage conceptions by 15 per cent by 2004 and by 50 per cent by 2010, and the dropping of the prohibition on including various matters within the compulsory Science curriculum. However, what the reforms have not done is ensure that all pupils are entitled to the sort of sex education that is promoted by the government and other agencies as most effective in helping young people to make choices that will protect their health and life chances. Parents cannot withhold information about the biological basics from their children. However, the unconditional legal right of the parent to withdraw their child from SRE means that parents can withhold the part of SRE that will aim to give pupils the skills necessary to avoid abuse, coercion or exploitation, or to negotiate safer sex. This remains the case even though SRE is subject to the statutory obligation to set it in a strong moral framework.

The Independent Advisory Group on Teenage Pregnancy (IAG), a group that advises the TPU on policy issues, pointed out in their second Annual Report:

> SRE is lifelong learning about sex, sexuality, emotions, relationships, and sexual health. Undertaking SRE presents young people with a valuable opportunity to acquire information, to develop skills and form positive beliefs, attitudes and values. Effective SRE, firmly rooted in good Personal, Social and Health Education (PSHE), empowers young people and equips them with skills to make informed decisions, and take responsibility for their health and well-being. The importance of SRE alongside the provision of good quality advice and sexual health services for young people, cannot be underestimated as a key to achieving the aims of the strategy.[18]

If this is the aim and value of SRE, it seems in principle wrong to allow parents to withhold this from their children. Departmental guidance on SRE suggests ways of encouraging parents not to exercise their rights of withdrawal, but the rights remain.[19]

When sex education is so much at the heart of the ability of the government to deliver its target on social exclusion, why has the right of withdrawal been allowed to stand? Clearly there is no objection on human rights grounds to pluralistic programmes of SRE, as is demonstrated by the important challenge in the case of *Kjeldsen*[20] in the European Court of Human Rights. This established that the right enshrined in Article 2 of Protocol 1 of the European Convention on

---

17 Social Exclusion Unit, *Teenage Pregnancy*, Cm 4342 (London: The Stationery Office, 1999).

18 Independent Advisory Group on Teenage Pregnancy, *Second Annual Report,* (London: Department of Health, 2003), p 18.

19 Department for Education and Employment, op cit, n 10.

20 *Kjeldsen, Busk Madsen and Pedersen v Denmark* (1976) 1 EHRR 711.

Human Rights[21] did not prevent compulsory provision of SRE in state schools. The IAG have recommended that all PSHE should be part of the national curriculum: it remains to be seen if this plea will be heeded. Certainly the addition of citizenship as part of PSHE to the national curriculum at key stages 3 and 4 has raised its status, and a similar strategy could work for SRE. The effect of this would be that the parental right of withdrawal, at least in its unconditional form—which was established only in 1993—would be removed. That other official reports such as the SEU's report on *Teenage Pregnancy* and the Office for Standards in Education's (Ofsted's) report on *Sex and Relationships* have failed to call for this is disappointing.[22] A factor in this may be data showing that few parents have to date exercised the right of withdrawal. Ofsted's report showed only 0.04 per cent of pupils as having been withdrawn from sex education lessons.[23] The issue of whether the 0.04 per cent figure accurately represents the proportion of pupils who do not benefit from SRE is also open to doubt, as formal withdrawal from this part of the school curriculum is not the only means of avoiding such lessons, and some implications of this are discussed below. Needless to say, however, even a rate of 0.04 per cent represents a considerable number of pupils, and gives ample cause for concern in terms of the impact on the individuals involved, if not on the community as a whole.

Calculating the Risks of Sex Education Policy

This section examines some general points on the nature of risk and on the question of how government assesses risk. 'Risk' has become a multi-faceted concept.[24] It is a mathematical and statistical construct. It is also a principal ingredient of the basis of legal liability for harm that results from an individual's activities.[25] As a consequence of this, risk has become a fact of everyday existence that should be assessed carefully before decisions affecting business or individuals are taken. Perhaps related to this is the view that risk is a feature of everyday life that has taken on an inflated and destructive importance as individuals become obsessively averse to taking even small risks. Academic

---

21 That the State shall respect the right of parents to ensure such education and teaching in conformity with their own religious and philosophical convictions.

22 Ofsted, *Sex and Relationships* (London: Ofsted, 2002).

23 Ibid, p 6.

24 For a discussion of some of the complexity see E. Fisher, 'The Rise of the Risk Commonwealth and the Challenge for Administrative Law' [2003] *Public Law,* 455-478.

25 A defendant to a personal injury claim or a claim for property damage will only be liable generally if they have failed to take reasonable steps to prevent harm that could be reasonably foreseen. In determining what is reasonable the factors that will be considered are the probability of occurrence and the magnitude of the threat, weighed against the cost of precautions and the benefits of the activity.

discourse has identified questions of risk as the key to understanding the whole nature of late industrial society, as people's lives become ever more dominated by the need to assess and respond to real and imagined risks.

The government has identified teenage pregnancy as one of the key contributing factors to problems of social exclusion, and as such sees it as something that is almost necessarily best avoided. Although this is open to doubt, an obvious question in relation to the field of sexual relations is why it is that young people will risk unprotected sex and the possible consequences of pregnancy and STIs.[26] This is a question that has had primary importance for both policy-makers and educators, as a cursory glance at documents such as the SEU report, the latest version of government guidance,[27] and any number of documents from the TPU and the IAG among others show. How do young people weigh these sorts of risks? What are the patterns of risky behaviour? Is this behaviour based on inadequate information or on faulty calculation of the benefits/disadvantages of sexual activity, or are the underlying reasons for risky behaviour more complex than this?[28] These are not questions that this chapter will provide answers to, but they are central to the planning of programmes of education, advice and support and to the provision of sexual health services for young people.[29]

A second question is how government weighs the risks that it seeks to address, including the risk that its own actions in determining law and government policy in this area might make things worse rather than better. This is the question that sits at the heart of this chapter. The risks of not acting, both domestically and globally, are daunting. The cost of early pregnancy has been acknowledged in the SEU *Teenage Pregnancy* report and in most work that has stemmed from interventions based on the report. This is reflected in the global analysis provided by the UNFPA report, which identified significant costs flowing from early childbirth. These included private costs such as lower lifetime earnings of the mother—reflecting earlier school dropout, childcare demands affecting education and employment and reduced job experience. They also included, among others, public costs such as lower tax revenues, child support costs, higher health care costs and social exclusion costs.

---

26 Sex of course has always been a risky business: see the quotation from Shucksmith at n 65.

27 Above n 10.

28 See E. Bullen, J. Kenway, and V. Hey, 'New Labour, Social Exclusion and Educational Risk Management: the Case of the 'Gymslip' Mums' (2001) *British Educational Research Journal,* 26(4), 441-56.

29 Considered by A. Blair and N. Stanley in 'Taking Risks with Sex Education,' a paper given in the Education Law and Policy stream of the Socio-Legal Studies Annual Conference, Glasgow, April 2004. See also E. Burtney and M. Duffy (eds), *Young People and Sexual Health: Individual, Social and Policy Contexts* (London: Palgrave MacMillan, 2004).

Further, the World Health Organisation recently identified HIV/AIDS as the fourth biggest cause of mortality in the world and identified unsafe sex as the second greatest risk to health after malnourishment.[30] In the light of these effects, governments are under a strong imperative to do something to protect health: it is not an option to sit back and do nothing. The difficulty is that in trying to balance conflicting interests and rights, such as the right to have children educated in accordance with their parents' religious and philosophical convictions,[31] policies and law may have unintended effects. As Buckingham and Bragg observe in their recent research on young people, sex and the media, parents held 'different views about what children did or did not "need to know" and about the balance between preserving their "innocence" and preparing them for the realities of adult life.'[32] The danger is that policy might fail to address important risks, or indeed it might create risks that were not present before. In doing so, policy might inadequately protect children's rights and the public interest in reducing the social costs of STIs and the effects of social exclusion that are said to result from teenage pregnancy.

Theorising Risk in Late Industrial Society

Can recent highly influential theories of risk cast any light on the risk concerns of government or the risk-related behaviour of individuals? Perhaps most influential is Beck who, in his theory of 'Risk Society,' considers how 'risks' (or harms) are distributed in late industrial society. As part of this theory, Beck and his commentators have had much to say about how this has impacted on relationships between men and women and the family, however there has been much less comment on how individuals manage the risks of sexual activity. In spite of this there is much that has been said about health in a 'risk society' that may give us some insights.

According to Beck, the poorest members of society suffer the most harms, have the poorest access to knowledge about these harms and are, as a consequence, least able to avoid them. This risk is unquantifiable, nevertheless, in 'risk society' individuals are given choices and made accountable for them, even though it is impossible to predict the outcome of these decisions.[33] Beck's

---

30 World Health Organisation, *The World Health Report 2002,* http://www.who.int/whr/.

31 See Art. 2, Protocol 1, ECHR,discussed above at n 21.

32 D. Buckingham and S. Bragg, *Young People, Sex and the Media: The Facts of Life?* (Basingstoke: Palgrave MacMillan, 2004), p 234.

33 U. Beck (Translated M. Ritter), *Risk Society* (London: Sage, 1992). Obviously this carries the possibility that the response will be one of negative fatalism—one might as well do nothing—but perhaps a better response is to consider carefully what the intended benefits of the decision are and where the harm is most likely to fall, and to

theory is concerned primarily with 'manufactured' risks (of which environmental risk is the archetypal example). Although this theory is not applied directly to the 'natural' risks of sexual activity, this theory is clearly relevant to issues relating to sexuality, sexual health and SRE.

According to Beck and Beck-Gernsheim, health has a particular significance in a competitive labour market, as it is necessary for the individual to be fit and healthy to survive.[34] A particular concern is the pre-eminence of health as a value; the fear being that this emphasis on the importance of health has tended to displace other values. The fear is that this can outweigh important ethical and moral concerns.[35] Present government concerns use notions of social exclusion in a way that is wholly consistent with this conceptualisation. However, SRE may provide a poorer fit with this theory than it appears at first sight. In reality many of the risks SRE seeks to address can be reduced simplistically to information about activities and potential consequences. The causal connection between unprotected sex and pregnancy or STIs is not difficult to explain or understand. What seems to be necessary here is to factor in more complex issues such as questions of risk to reputation and cultural questions that mean that young people will persist in taking chances that many concerned adults would prefer they did not.[36] Burtney and Duffy note that:

> [young people's] assessment of risk and appraisal of outcomes is shaped by broader aspects of the social and cultural environment, as is (sic) their patterns of behaviour with regard to sex and relationships. [37]

A rather different approach to the impact of concepts of risk on society is adopted by Frank Furedi. His book, *The Culture of Fear,* directly addresses issues arising out of SRE. Furedi's primary concern is that society has become paralysed by fears such that it rejects any activity that carries even remote risks. Furedi condemns the prominence that has been achieved by the 'precautionary principle': this is the idea that, where doubt exists as to the extent of any risk, the

---

carry on making decisions but to pay close attention to the outcomes and be prepared to adjust accordingly.

34 U. Beck and E. Beck-Gernsheim, *Individualization: Institutionalized Individualism and its Social and Political Consequences*. (London: Sage, 2002), p 140.

35 E. Beck-Gernsheim, 'Health and Responsibility' in B. Adam, U. Beck, and J. Van Loon (eds), *The Risk Society and Beyond: Critical Issues for Social Theory* (London: Sage, 2002), pp 122-135.

36 '...(Y)oung people still feel that this particular transition to adulthood is a risk worth the taking, and, despite the welter of health promotion advice on the topic, often do little to diminish the risk to themselves': E. Shucksmith, '"A risk worth the taking": Sex and selfhood in adolescence' in E. Burtney and M. Duffy (eds), op cit, n 29 at p 6.

37 Above n 29, at p 3.

assumption should be to avoid the activity in order to avoid the risk. According to Furedi:

> Although the precautionary principle is usually discussed in relation to environmental management, it now provides a guide to life in other spheres—health, sexuality, personal safety or reproductive technology.[38]

This fear has deprived parents of the power of their status and experience, especially the field of sexuality:

> Sex education is now declared to be mandatory—the only responsible way of socialising the new generation—but practical information is obscured by excessive moralising. The adult supervision of childhood acquires its most grotesque formulations in the smug assumptions about the virtues of moral-based sex education. The idea that children should find out about sex on their own, and without professional guidance, is dismissed as hopelessly outdated by the new experts of sexual health.[39]

Furedi sees this obsession with risk as the mirror image of the decline in the certainty of shared moral values (a concern reflecting those raised by Beck and Beck-Gernsheim). This is curious in the light of his expressed feelings about the contexts of sex education and the fact the stated ethos of most SRE is in fact the notion of equipping young people with the skills they need to make 'good' choices.[40] However, he goes on to posit that, a 'new etiquette' has arisen to fill this vacuum in which medicalised concerns about safer sex disguise a new, but no less intrusive, moral agenda: 'Whereas young women were once told that good girls did not go all the way, today they are made aware that responsible girls exercise caution.'[41]

These are two highly distinctive approaches to questions of risk in present day society. Both raise concerns about the impact on disadvantaged groups and ordinary citizens; Beck because of the unequal sharing of risk that impacts more highly on such groups; Furedi because of the culture of fear that arises by virtue of policymakers and commentators holding such a low opinion of the capacity of ordinary actors and the impact that this has had on individuals' self esteem and ability to take actions based on their own judgment. The aim of the remainder of this chapter is to consider whether the policy approaches embedded in current law and guidance on SRE exemplify or address the concerns raised by such theory. In

---

38 F. Furedi, *The Culture of Fear: Risk Taking and the Morality of Low Expectation* (London: Continuum, 1992), at p 10.

39 Ibid, at pp 134-137.

40 It seems evident from the policy framework that a young person who makes a positive decision to have a baby at the age of 17 or 18 is nevertheless making a choice that should be discouraged.

41 Above n 38, at p 151.

doing this I hope also to consider whether practice suggests that these concerns are in any way unfounded in this policy area. First I want to concentrate on some of the particular issues that arise in the context of sex education and the implications for individual and public health.

Why Does the Public Health Agenda Not Require All Pupils to Have Effective Sex and Relationships Education?

Despite Furedi's concerns, accepted techniques of effective risk management do not require that all risks be eliminated or addressed whatever the cost. For example, health and safety at work is managed through a process of risk assessment and uses a system of classification which seeks to prioritise risks and eliminate them where possible.[42] However, it is not expected that all possible effort should be made to eliminate or avoid risk. If the risk is low it might not be addressed as a matter of urgency. Even for matters that do merit attention, there is no expectation that all possible steps must be taken whatever the cost, the primary aim being to reduce the likelihood of the risk occurring. It is also acknowledged that providing palliatives might be acceptable rather than addressing the hazard directly. Even in the field of environmental protection, business is not prevented from risk taking by Furedi's bête noir, the precautionary principle discussed earlier. Rather, where there is an environmental risk this should be addressed by the 'best available techniques *not entailing excessive cost*.'[43] Clearly the rhetoric of the precautionary principle may have led to a culture of fear, but there is little in the way that risks are actually regulated that should stop people taking measured and proportionate risks.

In public health, which is of course one element of the concerns addressed by SRE, further factors influence the calculation of what action is required to address risks. The discussion of this rests on two basic propositions that need to be tested. The first hypothesis is that to deliver an effective public health programme it is not necessary to address the needs of 100 per cent of the 'at risk' population. Because of this, decisions will be made about the level at which the impact on the community of rare or isolated cases is outweighed by the financial or social costs of addressing the final few 'hard to reach' instances.

The starting point for research into this question of risk and the parental right of withdrawal was an analogy with programmes of vaccination. Certain infectious diseases have highly significant implications not only for the individual, but also for public health. In the case of many diseases there is the possibility of addressing this through a programme of vaccination. In these cases the

---

42 See, for example, Heath and Safety Executive, *Five Steps to Risk Assessment* (Sudbury: HSE Books, 1999).

43 Environmental Protection Act 1990, ss 7, 109, 112, 119 and Schedule 2A, paragraph 2; emphasis added.

effectiveness of the vaccine and the rate of take up of the vaccination do not have to be 100 per cent for the programme to be considered effective. What is required is sufficient 'herd immunity,' so that the chances of an unprotected individual coming into contact with a person who is contagious are reduced to a level where the disease cannot spread easily. Hence, the pockets of infection that arise from time to time will die out quickly and will not lead to infection on a scale greater than society can cope with effectively. Individuals are asked to take the supposed individual benefits of vaccination (though this will not be guaranteed for any individual) and also to accept the risks of any side effects. What is seldom acknowledged to the public is that vaccination is as much, or more, about protecting one's neighbours as it is about protecting oneself and one's family.[44] However, there is no need for coercion to protect the health of the public unless take-up rates drop below the level at which protection of the population as a whole is effective. Even then persuasion is likely to be in the form of an attempt to minimise fears about side effects and raising fears about individual effects rather than by drawing attention to the social consequences of refusal.[45]

It should be remembered that vaccination is not generally compulsory in the UK, or effectively compulsory, as seems to be the case in the US, because it is a prerequisite of access to various important services.[46] Bradley argues that, in the context of the generally high levels of immunisation that apply in the UK and the consequent high levels of population immunity, a policy of compulsory vaccination is not necessary and cannot be justified.[47] Do these ideas apply, by analogy, to levels of parental withdrawal from SRE? If most pupils and young people do have the benefit of SRE, can intervention to compel be justified where the risk to public health is small?

The second hypothesis is that it is easier to achieve a 50 per cent reduction in total by targeting action where there is a great prevalence of the problem at issue than to do so in areas where the problem is sporadic or rare.[48] This raises the

---

44 P. Bradley, 'Should Childhood Immunisation be Compulsory?' (2002) *Journal of Medical Ethics,* 25(4), 330-334; E. Vermeersch, 'Individual Rights Versus Societal Duties' (1999) *Vaccine,* 17 (suppl. 3), S14-S17.

45 Major concerns about the impact of the MMR scare continued to be raised in the media during the period that this chapter was in preparation, e.g. J. Meikle, 'Lancet Regrets MMR Report' (2004) *The Guardian,* 21 February, and S. Boseley, 'Doctors Turn on Each Other as MMR Debate Rages Again' (2003) *The Guardian,* 1 November.

46 J.P. Baker, 'The Pertussis Vaccine Controversy in Great Britain 1974-1986' (2003) *Vaccine*, 21(25), 4003-4010.

47 Above n 44.

48 I am grateful to Daniel Monk for providing me with the 'Sure Start' programme as a highly relevant example of this. Not only is social exclusion tackled by targeting childcare resources on what is perceived to be the most vulnerable section of the community, 'Sure Start Plus' identifies pregnant teenagers and parents under the age

position of groups who are vulnerable to a particular risk but who might be hard to reach.

It is seen as crucial to the success of the target for 50 per cent reduction in teenage pregnancies that effective sex education reaches certain target groups who might otherwise escape the message.[49] Within 'hard to reach' groups there will be some who are vulnerable because they are likely to have poor school attendance and hence more likely to miss out on the SRE that is provided at school. Young offenders are also likely to miss out on vital aspects of their education, and pregnant young offenders may find themselves outside the scope of statutory support agencies. Some young people are just more subject to all of the high risk factors: looked after children[50] and care leavers are high on this list. Some are vulnerable because they are less able to benefit from SRE due to slower educational development and as such are more vulnerable to exploitation. Some are male, hardly a minority, but this concern reflects the tradition of seeing SRE as connected solely with the risks of teenage pregnancy, and this as a girls' problem not a shared problem, even though males are 'half the solution.'[51]

Of particular interest are those from those faith communities and minority ethnic groups that oppose young people's autonomy in decision making in matters of sexual relations. Research on the specific needs of those from minority ethnic groups has been commissioned by TPU, and guidance has been issued by the TPU[52] for the development of services to such groups. However, the term Black and Minority Ethnic (BME) hides obvious and significant variation between the communities that fall within its categorisation. This is important because needs and issues relating to one group are likely to be vastly different from the needs of other groups because of extreme variation in cultural backgrounds. This is acknowledged in the guidance, but the guidance avoids the issue, saying it

> does not offer specific information or advice about particular constituencies within BME Communities. It is expected that local Teenage Pregnancy Partnerships will develop specific responses for the BME young people in their area.[53]

The guidance notes that young people from Bangladeshi, African Caribbean and Pakistani communities are substantially more likely to be teenage parents

---

of 18 as key targets for delivering advice (including advice on contraception) and support: see http://www.dfes.gov.uk/teenagepregnancy/dsp_content.cfm?pageid=74.

49 Independent Advisory Group, op cit, n 18 at p 15. Note that 'juvenile secure estate' refers to young offenders who are detained in secure accommodation.

50 That is, in the care of the local authority.

51 Of course those young people whose sexual orientation is lesbian, gay or bisexual also need to be ensured of high quality SRE, whatever their circumstances.

52 Teenage Pregnancy Unit, *Guidance for Developing Contraception and Sexual Health Advice Services to Reach Black and Minority Ethnic (BME) Young People* (London: TPU, 2001): Http://www.teenagepregnancyunit.gov.uk.

53 Ibid.

than the national average. The guidance goes on to claim that the link between disadvantage and early parenthood impacts disproportionately on a range of BME young people. These young people live in deprived areas, experience the social and economic inequalities that affect these areas and are vulnerable to racial discrimination and language and cultural barriers to accessing information and services. As a result, BME young people are disproportionately represented among groups at risk of teenage conception, early parenthood, STIs, school exclusion, being in care, being in Youth Offender Institutions or being within the mental health system. The guidance also notes that there may be reluctance to discuss the poor sexual health of these groups in order to avoid further stigma.

It is a credit to the approaches that are being developed that this guidance explicitly addresses the need to reduce poverty, social deprivation and racial discrimination to improve sexual health: it does not lay the issues solely at the door of cultural difference and poor SRE. However, it still seems open to two criticisms. First, it links all BME young people together in a way that seems unjustified and seems to minimise the extent to which these factors will be significant in relation to some groups and not in relation to others. Second, while it acknowledges that some may have missed out on SRE at school, it notes that, 'for a very small minority,' parents and carers may have requested withdrawal from SRE, it does not recommend reform necessary to address this. Thus the guidance observes that '[t]his may result from some parents and carers perceiving that sex and relationships education is culturally and religiously inappropriate within the school.'[54]

The consequence of this, that chronological age may not be a good guide to levels of knowledge and understanding, and that this might result in requests for late abortions as individuals from some groups may not seek advice early due to fear of ostracism, is also acknowledged. However the guidance makes no judgment on whether this is something that could or should be addressed through legal reform.

The Sex Education Forum notes that 49 per cent of Muslim, 78 per cent of Hindu and 75 per cent of Sikh parents support idea of sex education at school.[55] However note that this means that 51 per cent of Muslim and 22 per cent of Hindu and Sikh parents respectively do not support the idea of sex education in schools. Where these parents are unable to place their child in a faith school that will deliver SRE in what they consider to be a culturally appropriate context, they will be particularly prone to exercising the right of withdrawal. Clearly, it is not that the government, national agencies and the voluntary sector do not see SRE for BME groups as a serious issue, or that the existence of these perspectives is not understood or is ignored. In fact the position seems to be quite the reverse.

---

54 Ibid, p 12.

55 Sex Education Forum, *Forum Factsheet 10: Developing Partnerships in Sex Education: a Multicultural Approach* (London: National Children's Bureau, 1996), quoting research from 1994.

The Sex Education Forum's advice on faith and values in SRE notes that many educators shy away from including religious perspectives on issues such as marriage, homosexuality and contraception in case they frighten or exclude young people. Nevertheless they insist that it is important to include a range of both religious and secular perspectives, but that they must ensure that children and young people know about their legal rights. So for example a lesson on contraception may include a variety of religious perspectives, including the Catholic belief that forbids contraception. Nevertheless, young people also need to know that they are legally able to access contraception services and advice even if they are under sixteen and even if they come from a Roman Catholic background. Equally, despite general disapproval from orthodox religious perspectives, 'lesson[s] covering this issue will need to ensure that young people know that homosexuality is legal, and that the school upholds positive beliefs about diversity, and that discrimination and prejudice is not acceptable.'[56]

For pupils who have been withdrawn from sex education, the presentation of such perspectives, in a pluralistic way that affirms diversity and respects cultural difference but treats pupils as individuals with rights, is not an option.[57] As is well known from the important *Kjeldsen*[58] case, a distinction is drawn between information presented in a pluralistic fashion, which does not infringe the parental right to ensure that such education and teaching are in conformity with their own religious and philosophical convictions, and education which seeks to indoctrinate. In spite of this safeguard, the right is denied to the child who has been withdrawn. Why have the needs of these individuals been ignored?

It seems that the public health agenda has not concerned itself sufficiently with the needs of children and young people from communities that have strong cultural prohibitions on extra-marital sexual activity. This may be because there is an implicit assumption that the prevalence of early sexual activity, particularly that involving pre-marital intercourse and promiscuity, will be very low where community values that prohibit sexual activity outside marriage are strong. If this is the case it could easily be felt that this does not form a sufficient risk to the health of the population as a whole to merit intervention. What evidence can be drawn in support of this submission? Of course it would be useful if there were good empirical data on teenage conception rates and sexual activity broken down by ethnicity. Unfortunately at present this data does not exist. In the absence of such evidence one can only surmise that policy making is based on the sorts of

---

56 Sex Education Forum, *Forum Factsheet—Faith, Values and Sex and Relationships Education* (London: National Children's Bureau, 2002), p 3. See also SEU, *Teenage Pregnancy*, Cm 4342, above n 17 at p 19, and N. Low, *Briefing Paper on Sexual Health of Young People from Black and Minority Ethnic Groups* (London: TPU, undated).

57 It is the opinion of the present author that it is possible to square this particular circle. See A. Blair, 'Negotiating Conflicting Values: the Role of Law in Educating for Values in England and Wales' (2002) *Education and the Law*, 14, 39-56.

58 Above n 20.

cultural stereotypes that are present elsewhere in society and which the present author is as apt to make as anyone else. Indeed it may have been unfair to criticise policy makers earlier for not making distinctions between groups. It may be that this is an implicit acknowledgement that they cannot offer advice targeted at the needs of different groups because they do not have sufficient objective information to base such advice on. However, if policy has been shaped by a view that those from communities who are most likely to exercise the right of withdrawal are at least risk, the decision not to amend the law to guarantee SRE is easy to justify on the normal principles for managing health risks. By way of the analogy with immunisation, public health is unlikely to be affected significantly by these groups not benefiting from SRE. If it is assumed that those withdrawing their children will come from communities where there are strong cultural prohibitions on early sexual activity, they are not part of the 'at risk' population. This presumes that the choices that are made by members of such communities will be choices that government would want all parents and children to make.

Another risk perspective that perhaps ought to be acknowledged here is the parental perception of risk that leads them to decide that their child should not have, or does not need, sex education. According to the UNFPA report, it is a common misconception among parents and community leaders that providing sex education will lead young people to become sexually active at an early age.[59] However, despite the fact that parental oversight of adolescent relationships is common, the report suggests that significant numbers of young adolescents engage in sexual relationships without parental knowledge. The report notes that where there is an insistence on premarital abstinence, there is a greater tendency to withhold information about sexual and reproductive health from youth and from policy discussion.[60] However lack of parental knowledge about their children's sexual activity raises the question of whether parents do have sufficient information on which to base their decisions. This forms a useful point of reference back to Beck's theory, and hence questions the validity of an unconditional right. It might be that it is impossible for parents to predict the outcomes of their decisions, but it does not alter the fact that decisions are better made on the basis of a wide picture of the situation rather than a narrow set of assumptions. Obviously Furedi's response would be somewhat different because he feels that parents do know better than experts, and that children should be able to find out about sex for themselves.

A more important point in practical terms is whether this evidence of parental misunderstandings about the impact of sex education also throws into confusion the whole question of whether young people from some communities conform to the stereotype that early sexual activity is not prevalent because of the

---

59 UNFPA, *State of World Population 2003*, ch 4: available at http://www.unfpa.org/swp/2003/english/ch4.

60 Ibid, ch 2. Available at http://www.unfpa.org/swp/2003/english/ch2/.

control provided by cultural norms and structures. Until data becomes available it is impossible to know the extent to which such stereotypes are true in the UK. However one thing is certain: the stereotype is not universally true. Anecdotal evidence suggests that some young Asian women, for instance, are subject to pressures that are widespread outside the boundaries of their communities.

In a press report in late 2003, Hai noted that, although in one Asian community parents strove officiously to police their daughters' sexual behaviour, and hence the family's honour, nevertheless the subjects of the interview had become adept at avoiding their parents' scrutiny. For this group of young Asian women, one-night stands were unacceptable, but having sex with a long-term boyfriend was considered normal. They reported that their participation in sex was often the result of pressure from boys, and that girls in their culture are

> too prone to listening to men. [W]hen we meet a boy and they promise us love, we naively hang on their every word. If they ask us to have sex, and we know it's sort of acceptable, we just say yes.... There are so many Asian pregnancies because the boys don't want to use contraception.[61]

Reproductive Rights as Human Rights

The introduction to the UNFPU report identifies reproductive health as a human right in the clearest terms. It finds these in the aims of the 1994 International Conference on Population and Development (ICPD) and its associated 'Programme of Action,' the 1999 Special Session of the General Assembly (ICPD+5). It also finds these rights in Article 24 of the UN Convention on the Rights of the Child and the UN Monitoring Committee report of June 2003. Finally, they are identified in the 1979 UN Convention on the Elimination of All Forms of Discrimination against Women. Individually and collectively these support the right of adolescents to information and services necessary to protect sexual and reproductive health. The approaches advocated by the report to address the public health implications of its findings are however, in contrast with the approach of the Department for Education and Skills, heavily based on principles of the child's human rights and on principles of youth participation.

The UNFPA insists on the need for a rights oriented foundation, holding that '[f]or adolescents, this implies progressive measures to remove barriers to the realization of their reproductive health and rights, to prevent and punish rights violations, and to take concrete measures to achieve rights.'[62] To achieve this, the report recommends mainstreaming human rights education in educational policies and the mobilising of public and political commitment to policies that address reproductive rights issues, including rights to sexual and reproductive health

---

61 Y. Hai, 'Sex is part of our culture now' (2003) *The Guardian*, 17 October.

62 Op cit, chapter 7: available at http://www.unfpa.org/swp/2003/english/ch7/.

information and services. It calls for the establishment of national and local youth policies, and programmes that emphasise gender equality and the rights of young people to sexual and reproductive health, and specifies measures for the allocation of funds to fulfil them. A final recommendation is to ensure young people's participation in these efforts.

From this perspective, SRE is not simply a matter of competing values but a matter of binding fundamental rights.[63] It cannot be right to call for these initiatives to protect the most vulnerable parts of the global population and global health, and not acknowledge that the most vulnerable groups in our own communities deserve and demand the same levels of protection. To do otherwise is to perpetuate the distribution of risk to the most vulnerable sections of society, or, to put it in the language of the present government, to perpetuate the cycles of social exclusion that result from a great many teenage pregnancies.

Conclusion

It has been said that in late industrial risk society 'one cannot argue against health.'[64] Of course, this is only true if it is accepted that major ethical, moral and religious beliefs have ceased to have significant impact, though the parameters of the definition of 'risk society' seem to assume that this is indeed the case. What is argued here is that this need not be the case. It is not inevitable that late industrial society need be value free and that health will necessarily become pre-eminent. The values that legislation and departmental guidance embed in the SRE curriculum are strong, if not uncontested. Health is certainly an important value, but it is not necessarily the only value that is recognised and granted importance. The key conclusion of this paper, however, is that health has not only an individualised existence but it also has a public dimension. Importantly, human rights, which provide their own framework of law and values, give much support to the notion that health, as an individual responsibility, also remains, and is perhaps increasingly to be seen as, both an individual and a community right.

Ideas of risk can help us to make sense of the issues and the urgency with which they need to be addressed. As Shucksmith observes: '[s]exual activity has always carried risk: risk of unwanted pregnancy, risk of transmission of infections and, of course, risk to reputation.'[65] Nevertheless, mathematical

---

63 See also L. Lundy, chapter 1, above. That is not to say that these rights will meet the approval of all groups. Clearly they are antithetical to the strongly held values perspectives of groups such as the Catholic Church.

64 Beck-Gernsheim, above n 35, at p 127.

65 E. Shucksmith, ' "A Risk Worth the Taking": Sex and Selfhood in Adolescence,' in E. Burtney and M. Duffy (eds), above n 29. Furedi is dismissive of this, however: 'there is a contemporary equation between sex and risk. Positive views about

models can look at the probability of unprotected sex resulting in pregnancy or STIs, or the mathematical expression of the effectiveness of different forms of contraception. Sex and risk appear in theories about the nature of changing societies, as women, because of their biological functions, have been seen particularly affected by such developments. A further, possibly contradictory, agenda is posed by the extent to which people have been (rightly or wrongly) encouraged to desist in sexual practices because of the 'risks' and/or handed over their discretion in such matters to 'experts.' This can be seen as part of what Furedi has called the 'culture of fear.' Whether one agrees with his main arguments in this regard or not, the precautionary principle has resulted in some individuals becoming unwilling to accept even unquantifiably small risks—to their own detriment and to that of social life as a whole. Meanwhile young people, perhaps partly through ignorance, or partly through pressure or lack of confidence, continue to take risks that the majority of concerned adults would rather they did not—for their own benefit and for the assumed benefits to society as a whole.[66] However, if we accept the human rights agenda, the right to reproductive health at some point ceases to be that of the parent and becomes that of the child. If the right includes not only access to services but also access to information and education, then the parental opt-out in its current form cannot be justified.

Monk has attempted to explain the contradictions inherent in this area of law by suggesting that it is 'the role of schools and education law to construct ideal children, it is the function of the rest of the law to deal with the children who fail to conform to this ideal.'[67] Thus the ideal child is non-sexual, and health law is left to deal with young people who do not conform to this ideal by giving them access to services such as contraception advice. What this chapter suggests is that it is time for education law to reflect the needs of all young people, ideal or otherwise, who come within its scope as a matter of both their rights and the interests of everyone else. Prevention is certainly better than cure, and in this case education seems to be, at least for the moment, the best vaccine we have. Calculations about what 'failure rate' can be acceptable at a societal level should not affect our judgment when it comes to the need to protect and promote the individual rights of young people.

---

definition a risk. Why this elementary form of human activity should be interpreted through the prism of risk will not be clarified by an investigation of the physical act' (above n 38, at p 59).

66 These are taken to be those sought by government: the addressing of social exclusion resulting from high teenage pregnancy rates and the costs of STIs and so forth.

67 D. Monk, 'Children's Rights in Education – Making Sense of Contradictions' (2002) *Child and Family Law Quarterly*, 14(1), 45-56.

Chapter 7

Education and Sexual Health in the Russian Federation

Gracienne Lauwers

Introduction

In the 1990s, educational reform programmes were introduced in the Russian Federation aimed at overhauling the Soviet-era pedagogical philosophy and substantially revising curricula. In this chapter, the author discusses the introduction of health and sex education in Russian curricula,[1] thereby focusing on the legal issues and the conflict between traditional societal attitudes towards sexuality and the international human rights obligations of the country.[2] She also traces the legacy of the schools' additional ideological function under communism that has proved difficult for educators, parents and policy makers to overcome in the post-Soviet system.

Particular Health Challenges Facing the Russian Federation

The contrast in health, particularly in the area of reproductive health, between the EU countries and the Russian Federation is striking.[3] Indicators for Russia have shown relatively high maternal and infant mortality rates, a high and rising incidence of sexually transmitted infections (STIs) and high abortion rates in contrast to the low prevalence of contraceptive use. Within this disproportionate burden of ill health, adolescents are at particular risk through the increase in

---

1 The Russian education system consists of 9 years of basic education, followed by secondary education—either general or vocational/technical—lasting between 2-5 years. Higher education consists of 4-6 years for the first degree, in academies, institutes or universities. The enrollment ratio is nearly 100 per cent for basic education, 90 per cent for secondary and about 20 per cent for higher education.

2 A. Rotkirch, *The Man Question: Loves and Lives in Late 20th Century Russia* (Helsinki: University of Helsinki—Department of Social Policy, Research Reports 1/2000, 2000).

3 World Health Organisation, *Regional Strategy on Sexual and Reproductive Health* (Copenhagen: WHO Reproductive Health/Pregnancy Programme, November 2001).

abortions,[4] in STIs, in relation to the health problems faced by sex workers, and in the emerging epidemic of HIV/AIDS.[5]

The incidence of syphilis in particular, which is fairly well documented, is now extremely high, with 262 per 100,000 inhabitants in the Russian Federation in 1997. Numerous sex-workers have appeared in all the major cities, many of whom are involved in sex tourism and contribute to the spread of STIs and AIDS over national borders. Public opinion demonstrates a growing tolerance towards prostitutes. In a 1997 national poll, 47.4 per cent supported the legalisation of prostitution.[6] Meanwhile, prostitution is one of the main channels of dissemination of STIs. STIs are a particularly serious problem among adolescents, where infection rates tend to be higher than in the general population. Observations have raised questions about the impact of STIs and post-abortion complications, both of which increased in the 1990s, on the current magnitude and nature of infertility in Russia. In 1996, the Committee on Economic, Social and Cultural Rights (CESCR Committee)[7] urged Russia to address the eightfold increase in HIV-infection as a health question of the utmost importance. It recommended that an information campaign explaining the nature of the disease and modes of transmission, including sexual modes of transmission, and prevention techniques, be undertaken in the mass media. It also recommended that Russia should adopt laws and take all necessary measures to prevent discrimination against persons who are HIV-positive, so that they may live normal lives.[8]

Russia has been identified as one of the five countries[9] of strategic importance that have large populations at risk of HIV infection.[10] While the

---

4 A. Murcott and A. Feltham, 'Beliefs about Reproductive Health,' in H. Pilkington (ed), *Gender, Generation and Identity in Contemporary Russia* (London: Routledge, 1996), pp 152-153 and 162-163.

5 See M. Wines, 'The Rise of HIV in Russia is Quickening, Official Says' (2003) *New York Times*, 22 May, reporting that: 'At least a half-million Russians now are infected with HIV and the true number could range as high as 1 per cent of the overall population. Foreign experts now say that 1 in every 25 Russians could be infected in as few as five years, according to a report by Vadim V. Pokrovsky of the Russian Center for AIDS Prevention and Treatment.'

6 Y.A. Levada, 'Homo Soveticus Five Years Later: 1989-1994 (Preliminary results of comparative research)' (1995) *Informational Bulletin of Monitoring*, January-February, p 10.

7 The Committee on Economic, Social and Cultural Rights is a United Nations human rights monitoring body. It is composed of 18 members elected for a term of four years by the Economic and Social Council. The Committee meets annually for a period of up to three weeks, taking into account the number of reports to be examined. The Committee submits an annual report which contains the concluding observations of the Committee relating to each State Party's report.

8 CESCR, *Russian Federation*, E/1987/28, p 126.

9 Russia, India, China, Nigeria and Ethiopia.

10 D.F. Gordon, 'The Next Wave of HIV/AIDS: Nigeria, Ethiopia, Russia, India, and

epidemic in these five so-called 'next wave countries' is still in its early-to-middle stages, they are led by governments that have not yet given the issue the sustained priority and attention that has been key to successfully controlling the epidemic elsewhere. In order to keep the scale of the epidemic at a manageable level, active high-level leadership focused on increasing awareness, eliminating HIV-related stigma and providing treatment (all of which help to change the behaviour that leads to the spread of HIV) is required.[11]

The serious health deterioration of Russia, including the spread of AIDS, poses unusually severe threats to this country because of its skewed demographics. Russia's population is inexorably falling, and the country will be likely to face a labour shortage in future decades due to already high mortality rates among working-age men. This shortage should accelerate as young Russian men and women, who predominate among HIV cases, drop out of the work force due to maturation into AIDS.

Policy Options and Legislation

A range of national and international instruments are relevant to the promotion and protection of health by the education system in Russia.

General

The 1993 Constitution of the Russian Federation explicitly states: 'In the Russian Federation no laws shall be adopted cancelling or derogating human rights and freedoms.'[12] General issues of upbringing, education, and coordination of issues of health care are a joint jurisdiction of the Russian Federation and the 'subjects' (that is, the regions) of the Russian Federation.[13] However, it is the duty of the government of the Russian Federation to ensure the implementation in the Russian Federation of a single state policy in the sphere of education and health protection.[14] According to Article 15.4 of the Russian Constitution:

> the universally-recognized norms of international law and international treaties and agreements of the Russian Federation shall be a component part of its legal system. If an international treaty or agreement of the Russian Federation fixes other rules than those envisaged by law, the rules of the international agreement shall be applied.

China' (2002) ICA, 2002-04 D, September 2002, downloaded from the National Intelligence Council public website at www.odci.gov/nic.

11 R. Van de Braak and D. Veazey, 'The AIDS Epidemic: can it be contained?' (2003) *Moscow Times*, 20 November, p 8.

12 Russian Constitution, Art 55.

13 Ibid, Art 72.

14 Ibid, Art 114.

The Obligation of the State to Protect, Enhance and Strengthen Health

The UN Convention on the Rights of the Child[15] obliges States Parties to protect the child from all forms of physical or mental violence, injury or abuse, neglect or negligent treatment, maltreatment or exploitation, including sexual abuse, while in the care of parent(s), legal guardian(s) or any other person who has the care of the child.[16] According to the CIS Convention,[17] every minor child shall have the right to such special protective measures as their particular situation requires on the part of the family, society and the state.[18]

The Russian Constitution provides that federal programmes for protecting and strengthening the health of the population shall be financed by the State.[19] The labour and health of the people shall be protected and state support ensured to the family, maternity, paternity and childhood.[20] The Federal Law on Education[21] requires educational institutions to create the conditions that guarantee the protection and enhancement of the health of students and pupils. The health authorities are responsible for medical services for students and pupils within an educational institution.[22] The competence of the Russian Federation in the field of education entails the determination of federal requirements for educational institutions with respect to building norms and regulations, sanitary norms, and the protection of the health of students and pupils.[23] The role of the Russian Federation in education includes the determination of additional requirements to those imposed at the federal level to educational institutions concerning these matters.[24] The procedure for the formation and regulation of the activities of an educational institution is to determine whether the conditions necessary for the

---

15 UN Convention on the Rights of the Child, adopted and opened for signature, ratification and accession by General Assembly resolution 44/25 of 20 November 1989, entry into force 2 September 1990.

16 Ibid, Art 19.1.

17 Commonwealth of Independent States (CIS), Convention On Human Rights and Fundamental Freedom, Minsk, 26 May, 1995, (1995) *Human Rights Law Journal*, 17(3-6), 159-164. See n 31 below.

18 Ibid, Art 17.

19 Russian Constitution, Art 41.

20 Ibid, Art 7.

21 In the version of the Federal Law of January 13, 1996 N 12-FZ, with amendments and additions introduced by the Federal Laws of November 16, 1997 N 114-FZ, of July 20, 2000 N 102-FZ, of August 7, 2000 N 122-FZ, of February 13, 2002 N 20-FZ, of March 21, 2002 N 31-FZ, of June 25, 2002 N 71-FZ, of July 25, 2002 N112-FZ, of January 10, 2003 N 11-FZ, with the amendments introduced by the decision of the Constitutional Court of the Russian Federation of October 24, 2000 N 13-P, of the Federal Laws of December 12, 2000 N 150-FZ, of December 30, 2001 N 194-FZ, of December 24, 2002 N176-FZ.

22 Ibid, Art 51.

23 Ibid, Art 28.

24 Ibid, Art 29.

realisation of the educational process proposed by the educational institution are in conformity with the state and local requirements with respect to building standards and norms, sanitary and hygienic norms and the protection of the health of students, pupils and staff.[25]

The federal and ministerial agencies of educational administration are not entitled independently to deal with problems that, under the present law, are within the competence of the agencies of educational administration of the regions (so-called 'subjects') of the Russian Federation and the local agencies of educational administration, except for certain cases that are provided for by legislation of the Russian Federation relating to health care.[26] The educational institution has responsibility concerning the life and health of the students, pupils and employees of the educational institution during the educational process.[27]

The Obligation of the State to Promote Health

The UN Convention on the Rights of the Child obliges States Parties to ensure that parents and children are informed, have access to education and are supported in the use of basic knowledge of child health and nutrition; and to develop preventive health care, guidance for parents and family planning education and services.[28] The Convention on the Elimination of all Forms of Discrimination against Women[29] urges States Parties to provide access to specific educational information to help to ensure the health and well-being of families, including information and advice on family planning.[30] Furthermore, the CIS Convention[31] states that in order to guarantee that the right to health protection may be effectively exercised, the Contracting Parties shall provide advisory services and an instructional scheme for the fortification of health and the encouragement of personal responsibility in health matters.[32]

The Russian Constitution provides that measures shall be adopted to develop

---

25 Ibid, Art 33.

26 Ibid, Art 30.

27 Ibid, Art 32.

28 UN Convention on the Rights of the Child, Art 24.2(e) and (f).

29 The Convention on the Elimination of All Forms of Discrimination against Women (CEDAW), adopted in 1979 by the UN General Assembly.

30 CEDAW, Art 10(h).

31 Minsk, 26 May, 1995. For translation see: (1995) *Human Rights Law Journal*, 17(3-6), 159-164. The Convention on Human Rights and Fundamental Freedoms of the Commonwealth of Independent States (CIS Convention on Human Rights) was opened for signature in Minsk on 26 May 1995, and signed by seven of the eleven CIS member states on that day (Armenia, Belarus, Georgia, Kyrgyzstan, Moldova, Russia, Tajikistan). It has since been ratified by the Russian Federation, Tajikistan and Belarus, and entered into force on 11 August 1998, the day the third instrument of ratification was deposited by Belarus.

32 CIS Convention, Art 15.

state, municipal and private health services, and that activities shall be promoted which facilitate the strengthening of health,[33] while the National Doctrine of Education of the Russian Federation obliges the State to provide in the sphere of education overall concern for health and physical training and development of pupils and students. The Federal Law on Education states that 'educational institutions can independently elaborate health-improving measures.'[34] A network of pre-primary institutions exists to assist the family in the education of children of pre-primary age and for the protection and strengthening of their physical and mental health.[35] The State has in place a mechanism of social protection of children and minors, and elaborates and carries out goal-oriented programmes for the protection of rights, life and health of children.[36]

The Obligation of the State to Provide Health Education in Schools

Few of the international Covenants make explicit reference to a person's right to health education.[37] However, the right to health education can be inferred from broader statements about the goals of education. Against the background of preventing the spread of HIV/AIDS[38] and the state's obligation under the International Covenant on Economic, Social and Cultural Rights to take measures for the 'prevention, treatment and control of epidemic, endemic, occupational and other diseases,'[39] the significance of education in tackling the HIV/AIDS crisis has been emphasised. The Russian Federation has been urged several times to improve the primary health care system regarding health education, including sex education,[40] and information about contraception and STIs. It has also been urged to improve and promote adolescent health by strengthening reproductive health, family planning and counselling services, and to prevent and combat HIV/AIDS, STIs and teenage pregnancy and abortions.[41] Russia has also been urged by

---

33 Russian Constitution, Art 41.

34 Federal Law on Education, Art 42.

35 Ibid, Art 18.

36 Ibid, Art 50.

37 The key exceptions are: the African Charter on the Rights and Welfare of the Child, which requires State Parties under Art 14(20)(f) to 'develop preventative health care and family life education'; and the Convention on the Elimination of all Forms of Discrimination against Women, which under Art 10(h) requires State Parties to ensure 'access to specific educational information to ensure the health and well being of families...'

38 The United Nations High Commissioner for Human Rights identified this as one of the most pressing global concerns for public health and human rights: Message on World AIDS Day, 1 December 1999.

39 International Covenant on Economic, Social and Cultural Rights, Art 12(c); Art 11(3) of the revised European Social Charter (1966) contains a similar provision.

40 Russian Federation, CRC, CRC/C/16 (1993) 21 at para 88.

41 Russian Federation, CRC, CRC/C/90 (1999) 18 at para 110.

various committees to strengthen family planning programmes and provide affordable access to contraceptive measures for all women in all regions and to include sex education in the school curriculum.[42]

The European Court of Human Rights has considered the question of sex education programmes for schools in *Kjeldsen, Busk Madsen and Pedersen v Denmark*.[43] The Court maintained that the second sentence of Article 2 of Protocol 1 implies that the setting and planning of the curriculum fall in principle within the competence of the contracting States. However, the Court proceeded to set some boundaries to the State's role in this regard. It held that the State must ensure that information or knowledge contained in the curriculum is conveyed in an objective, critical and pluralistic manner. The State was forbidden to pursue an aim of indoctrination that might be considered as not respecting parents' religious and philosophical convictions. It follows that, if the State is to discharge its duties in respect of the above provisions, it must draft and implement a programme of basic sex education in schools. However, this programme may not pursue an 'aim of indoctrination.' Parents or pupils in public educational institutions do not have a right to opt out because of religious or philosophical convictions. Once the State has devised and presented this programme for the schools, however, the denominational school authorities have a right to adjust that programme.

The CIS Convention, which is very similar to the European Convention on Human Rights (ECHR), states that no person shall be denied the right to education.[44] States are obliged in relation to education and teaching to respect the right of parents to ensure for their children such education and teaching as corresponds with their own convictions and national traditions.[45] The Council of Europe has always felt concern about the legal implications for states ratifying both the ECHR and the CIS Convention. In particular, concerns were expressed about the possibility that the CIS Convention might jeopardise the effective use of the right to submit individual applications to the European Court of Human Rights. The CIS Convention offers less protection than the ECHR, both with regard to the scope of its contents and with regard to the body (the CIS Commission) charged with enforcing it. According to the Parliamentary Assembly of the Council of Europe, no regional human rights mechanism, such as the CIS Convention, should be allowed to weaken the unique unified system of human rights protection offered by the ECHR and the European Court of Human Rights. The ECHR and the European Court of Human Rights have primacy and supremacy for all member states of the Council of Europe. The Parliamentary Assembly recommended to the Russian Federation that it should issue a legally

---

42 Recommendation on education for health and drug misuse in the member states of the Council of Europe and the European Community, Recommendation 1169 (1991).

43 (1976) 1 EHRR 711.

44 CIS Convention, Art 27.

45 Ibid.

binding declaration confirming that the procedure set out in the ECHR shall not be in any way replaced or weakened through recourse to the procedure set out in the CIS Convention on Human Rights.[46]

The Russian Constitution, furthermore, guarantees everyone the right to education. According to Article 43, the Russian Federation shall establish federal state educational standards and support various forms of education and self-education.[47]

The State's Obligation to Guarantee Access to Education, and Inclusion, for Children with Health-related Problems

Article 23 of the UN Convention on the Rights of the Child states that assistance should be provided to ensure that the child has effective access to and receives education 'in a manner conducive to the child's achieving the fullest possible social integration and individual development.' Notwithstanding the National Doctrine,[48] which states that the Russian system of education must provide public and free specialised education for people with limited health abilities, and which guarantees that citizens of the Russian Federation shall be educated independently of health, discrimination against children with HIV/AIDS is clearly evident through the denial of their access to education in Russia. HIV/AIDS discrimination in access to education is prohibited by Article 14 of the ECHR, taken in conjunction with the right to education in Article 2 of Protocol 1. The Federal Law on Education guarantees to citizens of the Russian Federation the opportunity to receive education regardless of their state of health. Furthermore, restrictions on citizens' right to vocational education on the basis of state of health may only be established by a law.[49] In their alternative commentary on behalf of Russian Non-Governmental Organisations on Russia's formal State Reply to the Committee on the Rights of the Child (CRC), Boris Altshuler and Lyubov Kushnir state that:

> It is also necessary to comment on the tragic fate of children who are born with HIV and are subsequently abandoned in the hospital by their mothers. We are aware of cases in which newborn infants, having been refused by their mothers, stay in the hospital for months.

---

46 Text adopted by the Standing Committee, acting on behalf of the Assembly, on 23 May 2001.

47 Russian Constitution, Art 43.

48 The 'National Doctrine of Education of Russian Federation' is the basic national document approved by the Federal Law (4 October 2000). It sets up priority of education in national politics, determines its strategy and the main directions of its development.

49 Federal Law on Education, Art 5.

In its report, the government cites the Federal Law on the prevention of diseases caused by HIV from February 24, 1995 which

> stipulates social welfare of HIV infected minors... forbidding any limitation of the rights of those infected with HIV, not allowing them to be refused acceptance into educational institutions...

In practice, however, this law functions poorly, and families with children infected with HIV or with AIDS find themselves in an extremely difficult situation as a result of the absence of a system of special social and psychological support for such families. [50]

Implementation Strategies and Contrasting Societal Attitudes

The biggest gap is that between what it is that policymakers are under a duty to do by virtue of legislative obligation, and current societal attitudes which foster or impede action and implementation of the legal provisions.[51] There are major differences between Russian society and Western Europe in engaging in open debate on health and sex education. Russia did not experience the sexual revolution of the 1960s, with the introduction of the contraceptive pill; neither was it exposed to the explosion of injecting drug use and sex tourism in the 1970s, nor did it face new ideas about health promotion, embodied, for example, in the Ottawa Charter[52] in the 1980s—all factors which prepared the West for broader perspectives and open debates on sexual relations and greater openness concerning sex and drugs. Changes in sexual behaviour which had taken place over 20 years in most Western countries, were in Russia compressed into only two years[53] at the beginning of the 1990s, when sex and human sexuality became the subject of marketisation and politicisation. Despite the compressed sexual

---

50 CRC/C/Q/RUS.2

51 See World Health Organisation, *WHO Regional Strategy on Sexual and Reproductive Health*, Copenhagen: World Health Organisation, November 2001.

52 *Ottawa Charter for Health Promotion*, presented at the first International Conference on Health Promotion, meeting in Ottawa on 21 November 1986.

53 V. Chervyakov, 'Early Sex and Risk Taking Behaviour of Teenagers,' in *Abstracts*, The 4th Biennial of the European Association for Research on Adolescence, May 28-June 1, 1994, Stockholm; V. Chervyakov, 'Survey Supports Arguments to Start Sexuality Education in Russia,' in SIECUS Report, December 1996; V. Chervyakov and I. Kon, 'Adolescent Sexuality in Russia,' in *Aids in Europe: New Challenges for Social and Behavioural Sciences*, 2nd European Conference on the Methods of Social and Behavioural Research on Aids, Working papers for synthesis sessions (Paris: January 12-15, 1998); V. Chervyakov and I. Kon, 'Sexual Revolution in Russia and the Tasks of Sex Education,' in T. Sandford (et al) (eds), *AIDS in Europe: New Challenges for Social Sciences* (London: Routledge, 2000), 119 -134.

revolution and the liberation of sexuality in the course of the current process of social transformation, the developing debate on sexuality and sex education in Russia remains a controversial topic.

Sexuality is now part of the politicisation of every possible issue by different political forces, including the moralising discussions of conservatives. Policymakers discuss sexual relations, prostitution, homosexuality, drug use and AIDS as a pragmatic strategy for social and economic survival. Conservative proponents of 'good citizenship' claim the legitimacy of traditional values. This contrasts with the proponents of 'healthy citizenship,' who promote health rationality, aiming at the creation of responsible citizens, communities and even policy-makers, adhering to a coherent set of principles and practices in line with the Ottawa Charter concerning public health. The school is being considered as an institution which should deal with the sexual enlightenment of the younger generation. They consider that education on sexuality and reproduction should be included in all secondary school curricula. The school should inform and educate adolescents on all aspects of sexuality and reproduction and assist them in developing the life skills needed to deal with these issues in a satisfactory and responsible manner, with the aim of reducing the levels of unwanted pregnancies, induced abortions and STIs among young people.

These two distinct directions on sex education, which can be discerned in Russian society, are also reflected in abortion legislation. As Elena Sargeant has pointed out:

> During the seventy years of Soviet power, women were not liberated, but mobilized as a workforce for the construction of communism, and obligated to carry a double burden of duties.[54]

The Soviet Union legalised abortion on request by a joint decree of the Commissariats of Health and Justice on 18 November 1920. According to Andrej Popov, legalised induced abortions were selected in Russia at the beginning of this century as an instrument for destruction of the traditional basis of the state:

> Legalization of abortion seemed the most rapid way to create changes in traditional family relations and in women's social position. The family became an important object of attention for the new Soviet authorities. Traditional family life and religion were the most basic bearers of the old culture. They were the most serious targets of destruction in the attempt to achieve the principal aims of the new Soviet authorities: "the construction of a New Society" and "the creation of a New Soviet Man." Thus abortion policy was an instrument in the purposeful destruction of the pre-revolutionary Russian family and Russian culture.[55]

---

54 E. Sargeant, 'The 'Woman Question and Problems of Maternity in Post-communist Russia,' in R. Marsh (ed), *Women in Russia and Ukraine* (New York: Cambridge University Press, 1996), p 269.

55 A. Popov, 'The USSR,' in A. Rolston and B. Eggert (eds), *Abortion in the New*

During Stalin's pro-natalist restrictive period, a repressive mobilisation of sexuality started with the prohibition of abortion in 1936 (but there existed authorised abortion for women with large families and for eugenic reasons). This coincided with the period of the policy of mobilisation of people in general against the background of forced industrialisation and urbanisation.[56] Sex was not discussed in the mass media as a separate issue. Sex became officially limited to reproduction, whereby reproduction (for biological reasons) was held to be the duty of female Soviet citizens and to be exploited by the state.[57] Both work and maternity for fertile females were considered as social duties. Sex education was a non-issue in education policy.

The next period started with the liberalisation of Soviet society at the end of the 1950s,[58] and can be traced to the new abortion law that was adopted in 1955 when abortion ceased to be illegal. This period can be characterised by the discrepancy between liberal legislation on sexuality and repressive provisions of this legislation, the under-development of industrial production of contraceptive products, and the absence of sex education. In general, the whole service sector of the economy connected with the comfort of the human body was purposefully under-developed. On the other hand, abortions were made available free of charge in state gynaecological clinics. As a result, abortions became a universal birth-control technique. However, although it had been legalised, the practice of abortion was painful both physically and emotionally for women. Soviet women were punished by the state medical facilities for the decision not to give birth to another Soviet citizen, and for the decision to separate sex from reproduction.[59] In the late 1950s, the Department of Ethical and Aesthetic Problems in Sex Education was set up in the USSR Academy of Pedagogical Sciences. At first, sex education was presented as a form of moral education. In 1973 the first Consulting Office on Issues of Marriage and Family was established, and in 1983 a two-part course on preparation for marriage and family life was formally introduced in Russian schools. However, the introduction of this subject in the secondary school curriculum was not matched by appropriate training for schoolteachers. In the late 1980s, the USSR State Committee on Education

Europe (Westport: Greenwood, 1994), p 274; I. Boutenko, 'Norms of Conduct,' in I. Boutenko and K. Razlogov (eds), *Recent Social Trends in Russia, 1960-65* (Montreal: McGill-Queen's Univ. Press, 1997), pp 124-27; P. J. Flood, 'Life after Communism: Democracy and Abortion in Eastern Europe and Russia,' UFL, volume 10 (http://www.uffl.org/vol10/flood10.pdf).

56 The onset of the mobilisation of the person started in 1932 when restrictive passport and residency permit systems were introduced. See also V. Volkov, 'The Concept of Kul'turnost: Notes on the Stalinist Civilizing Process,' in S. Fitzpatrick (ed.), *Stalinism: New Perspectives* (London: Routledge, 1998).

57 A. Dallin, 'Conclusions,' in D. Atkinson, A. Dallin and G. Lapidus (eds), *Women in Russia* (Stanford: Stanford University Press, 1977), p 390.

58 I. Kon, *The Sexual Revolution in Russia* (New York: Free Press, 1995).

59 I. Voznesenskaia, *Zhenskii Dekameron* (Tallin: Tomas, 1991).

announced that the course, which was deemed to have been a complete failure, would be replaced.

During the Yeltsin period, a decree was issued, and became effective in January 1993, on sustaining the lives of infants weighing 500 grams or more, and the registration of all newborn infants in accordance with the criteria of the World Health Organisation. In a related development, the government increased allowances and payments to families with children, and the President issued a decree with the intention of expanding support for large families who were facing growing problems in the deteriorating economy. Implementation of this decree, however, quickly ran into practical difficulties.

In 1996 the Russian Ministry of Education applied to the United Nations Foundation of Population and UNESCO for financial help for three years' support in developing a curriculum for a 30-hour course for the seventh to ninth grades (12 to 15 year old pupils) of 16 pilot Russian secondary schools. The Russian Association for Family Planning coordinated the project. It has more than 200 regional offices all over Russia. New establishments were also set up, including medical pedagogical centres and youth centres. Although the programme was not adopted, the research and trials that were conducted caused a discussion on this topic to take place in the mass media at the end of the 1990s. The issue was also debated in the State Duma, which led the Ministry of Education to cancel the project on 'Sexual Education of Russian School Children' in April 1997. It was strongly opposed by a section of the pedagogical elite and by many parents, as well as church authorities.[60] The Orthodox Church opposed the programme on the grounds that it was incompatible with Russian culture and had a destructive effect on morality. In May 1998, in a significant interview, Patriarch Aleksii II of Moscow and All Russia called for the abolition of the death penalty, which he said was tantamount to murder, and followed this with a denunciation of abortion, which he said was also murder.[61]

Until early 2001, the law remained unchanged from the Soviet era. Abortion was de facto available on request and tax-funded. In August 2003, Russia approved a new law limiting abortions performed after the first 12 weeks of pregnancy. After 12 weeks, women considering abortions can only cite four reasons that allow them to have an abortion: rape, imprisonment, the death or severe disability of the husband, or a court ruling stripping a woman of her

---

60 I. Medvedeva and T. Chikhova, opponents of the experiment on sex education, published a paper that had been presented to the Duma Committee on Security in (1997) *Rossiiskaia Gazeta,* 15 March. Academician Baranov of the Research Centre for the Health Security of Children and Teenagers in Moscow believed that sex education programmes would not prevent 'sexual dissolution (raspushennost), which is a threat for the nation's health': Baranov (1997) *Rossiiskaia Gazeta*, 22 March.

61 (1998) *RFE/RL NewsLine*, May 13. See also N. Babasyan, 'Freedom or "Life": Secular and Russian Orthodox Organizations Unite in a Struggle against Reproductive Freedom for Women' (1999) *Izvestia*, February 26, excerpted in (1999) *Current Digest of the Russian Press*, 51:14, no. 12, April 21.

parental rights. As before, abortions can still be legal if the baby has severe physical deformities or if the pregnancy endangers the mother's life. In this way, access to low-cost, safe abortions—a primary method of birth control for almost five generations of Russian women—was drastically curtailed. This risks driving women to unsafe back-street clinics. Where once women enjoyed free and practically unlimited access to abortion, legal services became restricted beyond the first trimester of pregnancy. While the adolescent pregnancy rate tends to be between 12 and 25 per 1000 aged between 15 and 19 in most western European countries, the reported rate in the Russian Federation is 102 per 1000. Adolescents tend to become sexually active at an earlier age, but proper sex education and sexual health services are largely lacking. In its comments on the Russian Federation, the Committee on the Elimination of Discrimination Against Women expressed its concern as to:

> the deterioration in the lot of women and children (e.g. in their health, life expectancy, employment opportunities, and educational opportunities), which seemed to be profound, despite recognition of women's political, economic and social rights.

The Committee strongly recommended that:

> in the light of the serious consequences of the current economic restructuring during the period of transition the government should implement, as a matter of priority, emergency economic measures to alleviate the acute suffering of Russian women.[62]

Conclusion

International conventions can be used by Russian educational policy makers to inform the content of new laws and the substance of sex education programmes, while the standards can be harnessed by non-governmental organisations to highlight gaps.[63] At present, notwithstanding adherence by the Russian Federation to international obligations and the political will,[64] Russia has not yet elaborated a clear response to its general health deterioration and AIDS. The control of the AIDS epidemic has not been taken as seriously as it should, especially due to the lack of success of prevention policies, particularly among young people. However, health goes to the very heart of the economic and human development

62 *Report of the Committee on the Elimination of Discrimination Against Women* (Fourteenth Session), General Assembly, Official Records, Fiftieth Session, Supplement No. 38 (A/50/38), 1995, sections 542 and 549, CEDAW meeting of 26 January 1995 (CEDAW/C/SR. 3 and 4).

63 Such as Memorial Human Rights Group.

64 The emerging HIV/AIDS epidemic in Russia was a topic on the agenda of the summit between Presidents George W. Bush and Vladimir Putin in Washington in the autumn of 2003.

of Russia. Deterioration in health, and especially the spread of AIDS—which is becoming the fastest-growing epidemic in Russia—is causing serious problems for social and economic development, as well as profound demographic shifts ripping the very fabric of Russian society. Health deterioration and the spread of HIV/AIDS will accelerate Russia's population decline. A contracting work force and exploding healthcare costs will be serious counterweights to energy-driven economic growth. The high cost of treatment of HIV/AIDS could drive out other claims on health systems, leading to a steeper decline in already declining general health than caused by HIV/AIDS alone. Considerable resources are required to expand and reform the healthcare infrastructure. Economic problems are likely to fuel social and political tensions over spending priorities. Devoting more money to combating HIV/AIDS probably would just leave that much less for other pressing health problems.[65]

After enlargement, the EU will share borders with Russia, Belarus and Ukraine. According to the Russia Country Strategy,[66] 'the EU has an interest and a capacity to contribute to the solution of Russia's serious social challenges, e.g. in health, education and social welfare, as an accompanying measure for the consolidation of a market economy and democracy.'[67]

Leadership is of the first importance. No money can replace courageous leadership at all levels. This is not a major priority for Russia alone, but should also be a leading priority of international institutions, such as the EU. Europe can take a stand in mobilising the political will to make health and HIV/AIDS a top

---

65 See D. Gordon, above n 11.

66 EU/EC relations with the Russian Federation are based on the Partnership and Co-operation Agreement (PCA), which provides for trade liberalisation and closer relations, as well as on an EU Common Strategy on Russia which dates from June 1999 and will remain until June 2004. It came as the first of a series of such Strategies in response to the recognition that more coherence was needed between the EU and the Member States' policies *vis-à-vis* certain partner countries. It provides for an overall policy framework in the priority areas of: consolidation of democracy, rule of law and public institutions, integration of Russia into a common European economic and social space, stability and security in Europe and beyond, common challenges on the European continent (including environment, crime and illegal immigration). The Russia Country Strategy Paper (CSP) was adopted by the European Commission on 27 December 2001 and provides the strategic framework within which EC assistance will be provided for the period 2002-2006. The CSP constitutes the Indicative Programme as described in Art 3.2 and 3.3 of Council Regulation (EC, Euratom) No 99/2000 of 29 December 1999). The CSP sets out EC co-operation objectives, policy response and priority fields of co-operation based on a thorough assessment of policy agenda and the political and socio-economic situation in Russia.

67 The Russia CSP was adopted by the Commission on 27 December 2001 and provides the strategic framework within which EC assistance will be provided for the period 2002-2006 (downloaded from the EU public website at http://europa.eu.int/comm/external_relations/russia/csp/).

priority in this region. Europe can bring in valuable expertise in creating a constructive attitude toward such sensitive topics as sex education, and promote advocacy, awareness-raising and training projects in all the subjects of the Federation. The significance of education in tackling the HIV/AIDS crisis is repeatedly emphasised.[68] As has been aptly commented, 'nothing spreads HIV faster than silence.'[69] To find the country's own language for addressing these realities is the duty of the leadership in Russia as well as in Europe.

---

68 Address by the Secretary General of the United Nations at the World Education Forum on 26 April 2000.

69 P. Piot and J. Wolfensohn, 'Act Now or Pay Later' (2003) *Moscow Times*, November 28, p 8.

PART IV
INCLUSION AND HEALTH

Chapter 8

HIV/AIDS, Inclusion and the Law in American Public Schools

Charles J Russo

Introduction[1]

News reports from throughout the world, whether in Africa following the Fourteenth International AIDS Conference[2] or the United States,[3] reflect the extent to which Acquired Immune Deficiency Syndrome (AIDS) and Human Immunodeficiency Virus (HIV) have developed into an international health crisis.[4] HIV/AIDS was first recognized in 1979 and was classified as a separate disease in 1981.[5] There is no known vaccine or cure for AIDS, a disease which results in severe and irreversible damage to the body's immune system, thereby causing one to become vulnerable to a variety of uncommon infections, most of which would have been repelled had an individual's immune system been operating properly.[6]

---

1 This chapter is an expanded version of an article that was published as 'Recent Developments in the United States: HIV/AIDS in Schools,' (2003) *Education and the Law,* 15(2-3), 171-181.

2 See, for example, Thomas H. Maugh II, 'The World Bleak AIDS Conference Reports Deliver a Global Reality Check Disease: The Meeting Closes with Daunting Projections on the Epidemic's Spread and the Efficacy and Cost of New Treatments', *Los Angeles Times*, 5 August 2002 (no page number available), (2002) WL 2490080.

3 See Will Lester, 'Public Worries About AIDS Threat to Kids,' *Dayton Daily News*, 26 July 2004, A2 (noting that more than half of Americans fear that their children might become infected with the virus that causes AIDS).

4 See, for example, AIDS Conference: More Money, Determination Needed to Halt the March of AIDS, Campaigners Say, *AIDS Weekly*, 5 August 2002, (2002) WL 9287992; South Africa: AIDS Drug Roll Out 'Hangs in the Balance,' *Sunday Times* web site, Johannesburg, 4 August 2002, (2002) WL 25158412.

5 See Centers for Disease Control, Kaposi's Sarcoma and Pneumocystis Pneumonia Among Homosexual Men—New York City and California, (1981) *Morbidity and Mortality Wkly. Rep.* 30, 305; M.D. Victor Gong and Norman Rudnick (eds), *AIDS, Facts and Issues 3* (1986).

6 Scientific American Medicine, *Acquired Immunodeficiency Syndrome*, 7: XI: 1-24 at 1 (Edward Rubenstein & Daniel D. Federman, eds, 1994).

Notwithstanding the spread of HIV/AIDS among high-risk groups, it is the case that since the earliest days following the discovery of the disease there have been no known cases where it has been transmitted through casual contact.[7] Even so, a recent poll reveals that parents and the general public continue to worry about the risk of AIDS to school-aged children.[8] Medical experts believe that the virus is not air-borne like colds, transmitted through fecal contamination of food such as hepatitis A, or carried by insects as with malaria; rather, they believe that it is transmitted through the blood like hepatitis B. Consequently, blood or contaminated semen must be passed directly into another person's blood system if the virus is to be transmitted. The AIDS virus is also present in other body fluids such as saliva, but is in an attenuated condition and apparently is not transmissible in that state.[9]

As reflected by the relatively brief, yet contentious period during which the rights of students with HIV/AIDS were litigated in American courts roughly during the latter part of the 1980s, and the absence of litigation but for one case involving a teacher during that time, it is well settled in American law that students and teachers who have HIV/AIDS have a right to attend and to work in public schools. Even though the issue is well settled, while controversy raged in school communities in the United States, the litigation generated a host of legal issues and questions. In the light of issues surrounding HIV/AIDS and school personnel, this chapter is divided into three major sections. The first part provides a brief overview of American laws on disability dealing with the rights of individuals with HIV/AIDS. The second section, which focuses on litigation involving educational personnel, is divided into two parts: the first discusses the only case hitherto involving a school employee, while the second examines disputes over the rights of students. The third section of the chapter offers recommendations for educational practice that should be of relevance to educators throughout the world.

---

7 See, for example, Surgeon General, (1986) JAMA, 256, 2785-68.

8 Will Lester, 'Public Worries about AIDS threat to kids,' *Dayton Daily News*, 24 July 2004 at A 3. (reporting that 'more than half of Americans fear that their children might become infected with the virus that causes AIDS, even though fewer people believe the overall threat is very serious').

9 The AIDS virus also has been discovered in the saliva of victims, yet appears not to be very infectious in that state. Researchers speculate that antibodies deactivate the virus in the saliva, so that it does not infect others. In support of this claim is the fact that there are no reported cases to date where either kissing or lesbian sex have resulted in transmission. Scientific American Medicine, *Acquired Immunodeficiency Syndrome*, 7:XI: 1-24 (Edward Rubenstein and Daniel D. Federman, eds. 1994).

An Overview of American Disability Law

The two federal statutes that are most likely to come into play in relation to school personnel with AIDS are section 504 of the Rehabilitation Act of 1973[10] (section 504) and the Individuals with Disabilities Education Act[11] (IDEA).[12] A third statute, the Americans with Disabilities Act (ADA) (1990), is designed to provide 'a comprehensive national mandate for the elimination of discrimination against individuals with disabilities.'[13] Similar to section 504, in that it requires reasonable accommodations for otherwise qualified individuals, but for one case,[14] the ADA is largely beyond the scope of this chapter since it has, for the most part, not come into play in litigation arising in school settings even though Congress clearly intended for it to protect individuals with HIV/AIDS.[15] Rather than engage in a lengthy discussion of section 504 and the IDEA, this part of the chapter provides a very brief thumbnail sketch of their main features.

Section 504 has occupied a much more significant role involving school personnel with HIV/AIDS since the standard for qualifying is not as stringent as under the IDEA. According to section 504:

> [n]o otherwise qualified individual with a disability in the United States... shall, solely by reason of her or his disability, be excluded from the participation in, be denied the benefits of, or be subjected to discrimination under any program or activity receiving [f]ederal financial assistance...[16]

Section 504 defines an individual with a disability as one

---

[10] 29 U.S.C. § 794(a).

[11] 20 U.S.C. §§ 1400 *et seq.*

[12] Although first known as the Education for All Handicapped Children's Act, for the sake of consistency, the author refers to the statute under its current title, the Individuals with Disabilities Education Act (1975, amended 1997).

[13] 42 U.S.C. § 12101(b)(2).

[14] See note 57 below and accompanying text for a case that arose under the ADA.

[15] 42 U.S.C. §§ 12101 et seq. The ADA's legislative history reflected Congressional desire to protect people with HIV/AIDS from discrimination. See, e.g., S. Rep. No. 116, 101st Cong., 1st Sess. 22 (1989); H.R. Rep. No. 485, 101st Cong., 2d Sess., pt. 3, at 28 (1990); 135 Cong. Rec. S10722 (daily ed. Sept. 7, 1989) (statement of Sen. Cranston); ibid, at S10768 (statement of Sen. Helms); ibid, at S10718, S10789 (statement of Sen. Kennedy); 136 Cong. Rec. H2422 (1990) (statement of Rep. Dannemeyer); ibid at H2442-43 (statement of Rep. Weiss); ibid at H2481 (statement of Rep. Dymally); ibid, at H2625 (statement of Rep. McDermott); ibid, at S7444 (statement of Sen. Harkin quoting Pres. Bush).

[16] 29 U.S.C. § 794(a).

who (i) has a physical or mental impairment which substantially limits one or more of such person's major life activities, (ii) has a record of such an impairment, or (iii) is regarded as having such an impairment,[17]

a much broader approach than discussed below under the IDEA.

In order to have a record of impairment under Section 504, an individual must have a history of, or have been identified as having, a mental or physical impairment that substantially limits one or more major life activities,[18] including work.[19] Once an individual is identified as having a disability, the next step is to determine whether he or she is 'otherwise qualified.'[20] An individual who is 'otherwise qualified,' meaning that he or she is eligible to participate in a programme or activity despite the existence of an impairment, must be permitted to participate in it as long as it is possible to do so by means of a 'reasonable accommodation.'[21]

The IDEA's voluminous requirements with regard to special education mark it as the most comprehensive federal statute safeguarding the rights of children with disabilities. The IDEA ensures that each young person between the ages of three and twenty-one[22] with specifically identifiable disabilities,[23] but,

---

17 29 U.S.C. § 706(7)(B).

18 An individual who is regarded as having an impairment has:
(A) a physical or mental impairment that does not substantially limit major life activities but that is treated by a recipient as constituting such a limitation; (B) a physical or mental impairment that substantially limits major life activities only as a result of the attitudes of others toward such impairment; or (C) none of the impairments... but is treated by a recipient as having such an impairment. 45 C.F.R. § 84.3(j)(2)(iv), 34 C.F.R. § 104.3(j)(2)(iv).

19 According to the regulations, '"Major life activities" means functions such as caring for one's self, performing manual tasks, walking, seeing, hearing, speaking, breathing, learning, and working.' 45 C.F.R. § 84.3(j)(2)(I).

20 See *Southeastern Community College v Davis*, 442 U.S. 397 (1979) (holding that an otherwise qualified person is one who meets a programme's requirements in spite of, rather than except for, the disability). In *School Bd. of Nassau County Florida v Arline*, 480 U.S. 273 (1987) the Court applied section 504 to a teacher with the infectious disease of tuberculosis. The Court enunciated a four-part test to determine whether an individual with a contagious disease is otherwise qualified. The test must be grounded in 'reasonable medical judgments... about (a) the nature of the risk (e.g. how the disease is transmitted), (b) the duration of the risk (how long is the carrier infectious), (c) the severity of the risk (what is the potential harm to third parties), and (d) the probabilities the disease will be transmitted and will cause varying degrees of harm': ibid, at 284-289. The test is cited in this form in the Syllabus, ibid, at 274.

21 34 C.F.R. § 104.39.

22 20 U.S.C. § 1412(a)(1)(B)(i)(ii).

23 20 U.S.C. § 1401 (A)(3). The IDEA's definition of a child with a disability is much more stringent than section 504:
'3) Child with a disability--
(A) In general

importantly, not naming HIV/AIDS, is entitled to a free appropriate public education,[24] in the least restrictive environment,[25] directed by the contents of an Individualized Education Program[26] (IEP). In addition to instructional matters, an IEP must include a list of all related services that a child is entitled to receive.[27] The IDEA also affords students with disabilities, and their parents, extensive procedural due process rights which, as noted in the litigation discussed below, ordinarily requires an aggrieved party to submit a dispute to due process hearings before proceeding to court.[28]

As comprehensive as these statutes are in protecting the rights of individuals with disabilities, neither section 504 nor the IDEA directly addresses HIV or AIDS. Rather, HIV is included under a regulation enacted pursuant to section 504 which reads that: 'The populations served may include, but are not limited to, the following: (a) Individuals with chronic and progressive diseases that may become more disabling, such as multiple sclerosis, progressive visual disabilities, or HIV...'[29] Moreover, as reflected in litigation discussed later in this paper, insofar as children, in particular, with HIV/AIDS are not protected by the IDEA unless their physical condition is such that it adversely affects their educational performance, then the primary vehicle safeguarding the rights of students and school employees is section 504.[30]

School Students and Employees with HIV/AIDS

Employees

School employees who are infected with HIV/AIDS are primarily protected by section 504. To date, the only case directly involving the rights of a teacher with

---

The term "child with a disability" means a child—

(i) with mental retardation, hearing impairments (including deafness), speech or language impairments, visual impairments (including blindness), serious emotional disturbance (hereinafter referred to as 'emotional disturbance'), orthopedic impairments, autism, traumatic brain injury, other health impairments, or specific learning disabilities; and

(ii) who, by reason thereof, needs special education and related services.'

24 20 U.S.C. § 1401 (8).

25 20 U.S.C. § 1412(5)(A).

26 20 U.S.C. §§ 1401 (11), 1414 (d).

27 20 U.S.C. § 1401 (3)(A) (ii).

28 20 U.S.C. § 1415.

29 34 C.F.R. § 373.4

30 In addition to cases cited herein, see also *Glanz v Vernick*, 756 F. Supp. 632 (Mass. 1991) (holding that HIV-positive status is a disability the meaning of Section 504).

HIV/AIDS and his right to continue in the classroom[31] is *Chalk v United States District Court, Central District of California*.[32] When a teacher of children with hearing impairments was diagnosed as having the infection, officials at the Orange County (California) Department of Education reassigned him to an administrative position preparing grant proposals. Administrators changed the teacher's job even though his physician and the Director, Epidemiology and Disease Control, examined him and concluded that there was little risk of transmission to his students or colleagues. After a federal trial court denied the teacher's request for an order reinstating him to his job, on the ground that the risk of harm to his students and co-workers outweighed any harm to him, he sought further review. The Ninth Circuit reversed in favour of the teacher on the basis that the Department of Education had violated his rights under section 504. The court relied on the four-part test enunciated by the Supreme Court for use in cases involving contagious diseases; these elements consider the nature of the risk, its duration, its severity, and the probabilities that the disease will be transmitted and will cause varying degrees of harm.[33] It concluded that there was inadequate medical evidence that the teacher would pass the disease on to his students or co-workers and that the public fear of AIDS was insufficient ground to deny the injunction. In ordering the teacher's reinstatement, the court expressed its belief that he would have suffered irreparable harm if he continued to be barred from the classroom, and that by excluding him from the classroom pending a trial, productive time would be irretrievably lost both to him and his students.[34]

Students

Medical evidence makes it clear that children with HIV/AIDS do not pose a significant health risk to peers. Yet, parents have had to resort to litigation to protect the rights of their children with HIV/AIDS to attend school, primarily under section 504. Perhaps the most publicised case was that of Ryan White, a

---

31 For a more recent case involving a teacher and HIV, see *Velez Cajigas v Order of St. Benedict*, 115 F. Supp. 246 (D. Puerto Rico 2000) (dismissing the case of a teacher with HIV, who filed suit under the ADA claiming that his contract was not renewed because of his condition, where school officials relied on legitimate non-discriminatory grounds that he was frequently late for work and was unable to control students).

32 832 F.2d 1158 (9th Cir. 1987) (reversing and remanding the trial court's denial of the teacher's request for a preliminary injunction); 840 F.2d 701 (9th Cir. 1988) (decision on the merits).

33 See *Arline*, above n 20.

34 The teacher died not long after being reinstated. Kevin Johnson, 'AIDS-Stricken Teacher Remembered as a Hero Memorial: Students, Family, and Friends Pay Tribute to Vincent L. Chalk Who Fought to Stay in the Classroom,' *Los Angeles Times*, 5 October 1990 (pagination not available), (1990) WL 2328460.

teenager in Indiana with haemophilia who contracted HIV/AIDS through a blood transfusion. When school officials refused to admit him because of his medical condition, they developed a homebound programme, which included audio and video communications[35] as well as a tutor, in order to prevent him from attending classes, based on their fear that the risk of transmission to other students was too great. When the youth's mother challenged the board's action under section 504, the IDEA, and equal protection,[36] a federal trial court dismissed her claim for failure to exhaust administrative remedies. Exhaustion of remedies is a term of art indicating that a party must ordinarily complete administrative review, unless it is otherwise futile to do so, in the form of a due process hearing at which a hearing officer can order a range of placement options including leaving a child in a current placement, modifying an existing IEP, or calling for new placement procedures before filing suit.[37] Although a hearing officer agreed that the homebound placement was inappropriate, when parents of other children filed suit, a state trial court ordered his exclusion before the end of his first day of classes; the court relied on a state statute that prohibited a person with custody of a child with a communicable disease from attending school.[38] After a local health officer gave Ryan White permission to attend classes, the court relied on legislative intent that the statute did not apply to persons with custody of children with a communicable disease, if such an official gives written permission for a child to attend school, in ordering his reinstatement.[39]

Following the *White* case,[40] all but one of the suits involving children with HIV/AIDS were based on section 504, and were resolved in favour of having them placed in regular public school settings.[41] The following cases are categorised by issue and are in chronological order within category.

---

35 See 'AIDS Victim Starts School Over Telephone,' *New York Times*, 27 August, 1985, at A19.

36 Section 1 of the Fourteenth Amendment to the United States Constitution guarantees that 'No State shall... deny to any person within its jurisdiction the equal protection of the laws.' In effect, this means that if any state opens public schools, and all have, then all children may attend.

37 *White v Western School Corp.*, IP85-1192-C, slip op. (S.D. Ind. 1985).

38 *Bogart v White*, No. 86-144 (Clinton Cir. Ct., 21 Feb. 1986) (granting temporary restraining order); the court relied on Ind. Code § 16-1-9-7 (1983).

39 *Bogart v White*, No. 86-144 (Clinton Cir. Ct. 10 April 1986) (dissolving temporary restraining order). Even so, Ryan was assigned a separate bathroom and was to be given disposable utensils to use in the cafeteria: *New York Times*, 26 August 1986, at B3, col. 2.

40 Ryan White died at the age of 18 in April 1990. See '1,500 Attend Funeral of Courageous AIDS Fighter,' *New York Times*, 11 April 1990, at B12.

41 In 1990 the Ryan White Comprehensive AIDS Resources Emergency Act of 1990, Pub. L. No. 101-381, 104 Stat. 576 (1990) (codified at 42 U.S.C. §§ 201, 300ff to 300ff-90 (2002), was enacted to provide emergency assistance to localities disproportionately affected by HIV and to offer financial assistance available to States

State and local policies The first of two cases under this heading arose in New York City after officials promulgated a policy concerning the admission of children with HIV/AIDS to public schools. The policy stated that rather than automatically exclude children with HIV/AIDS, each of their cases would be reviewed on an individual basis to evaluate whether their health and development permitted them to attend school in an unrestricted setting. The policy also called for the creation of a four-member panel to review the cases of school-aged children reported to have HIV/AIDS.

One of the panel's initial reviews involved a seven-year-old child who was diagnosed as having the infection. When the panel recommended that the child be allowed to remain in a regular school setting, two local community school boards unsuccessfully sought to prohibit officials from admitting any child with HIV/AIDS to any public school in the City if it was attended by students who did not have the infection and the school was not designed to accommodate the needs of such children. In refusing to enjoin the policy, the court held that a blanket exclusion of students with the infection would have violated section 504 since they were otherwise qualified to attend public schools.[42] The court also decided that such an exclusion of students with HIV/AIDS but not those with AIDS-related complex or asymptomatic carriers who represented an equal risk of transmission, would have violated equal protection. At the same time, the court maintained that students with HIV/AIDS or related illnesses were not covered by the IDEA because of their impairments but would be eligible under the statute if their conditions deteriorated.[43]

At about the time the case arose in New York City, a similar dispute was going to court in neighboring New Jersey. At issue in this action was a challenge to policy guidelines promulgated by the State Commissioner of Education dealing with the admission of students with AIDS and related illnesses such as AIDS Related Complex and Human T-Lymphotropic Virus, Type III (HLTV-III, referring to HIV). The policy guidelines called for a Medical Advisory Panel to review the actions of two local school boards which excluded kindergarten aged children with AIDS. Rather than reach the merits of the case, an appellate court found that the regulations and an order of admittance for the students were null and void since the Commissioner failed to afford the local boards procedural due process when directing them to admit the children. The court 'believe[d] that

---

and other public or private nonprofit entities to deliver essential services to individuals and families living with HIV).

42 *District 27 Community Sch. Bd. v Board of Educ. of N.Y.*, 502 N.Y.S.2d 325 (Sup. Ct. 1986).

43 See Frederick A.O. Schwarz, Jr. and Frederick P. Schaffer, 'AIDS in the Classroom,' (1985) *Hofstra L. Rev* 14, 163 (written by the attorneys who defended the board policy).

there has been a sufficient showing of a potential risk of exposure to contagious disease to warrant hearings prior to the admission of...' the two children.[44]

On further review, the Supreme Court of New Jersey held that the exclusion issue was moot since one of the children was admitted to a class for the neurologically impaired while the other moved out of the district.[45] Even so, the court was satisfied that the policy guidelines, which provided adequate due process protection for individuals and the public at large, were valid as modified. The court reasoned that the amended regulations satisfied due process since they allowed for a fair hearing at which the parties have the right to present evidence, to provide witnesses, and to cross examine witnesses. In addition, the court viewed the State Commissioner as having the authority to override the power of local boards of education which sought to exclude students from public schools due to health reasons.

Exhaustion of remedies As indicated by the cases in this section, both of which arose in Illinois, exhaustion of remedies, discussed above, was an issue in disputes involving children who had HIV/AIDS. When a six-year-old haemophiliac with the infection was denied admission to the first grade, his parents challenged the school board's action in a federal trial court claiming that school officials had violated section 504. The court rejected the board's contention that the case should have been dismissed for failure to exhaust administrative remedies under the IDEA. The court ruled that the IDEA's exhaustion of remedies provisions did not apply because since the child's physical condition did not adversely affect his ability to learn, he could not be classified as 'other health impaired.'[46] Even if the IDEA did apply, the court reasoned, exhaustion still would have been unnecessary since further administrative appeals would have been futile. The court added that further appeals would have been useless since school officials had failed to comply with guidelines promulgated by the State Department of Public Health and that they had already informed the parents that their only avenue of redress was a local board policy.

A seven-year-old with haemophilia was assigned to a modular classroom, meaning that he was placed in a specialised separate room built specially for him, after he was diagnosed as having an AIDS-related complex. When his mother discovered that he was the only student in the modular classroom, she requested that he be returned to a regular first grade class with other students. After school officials denied the mother's requests, a federal trial court decided that since the child's learning and behavioural problems were not a result of his health

---

44 *Board of Educ. of Plainfield v Cooperman*, 507 A.2d 253, 277 (N.J. Super. Ct. App. Div 1986).

45 *Board of Educ. of Plainfield v Cooperman*, 523 A.2d 655 (N.J. 1987).

46 *Doe v Belleville Pub. Sch. Dist. No. 118*, 672 F. Supp. 342 (S.D. Ill. 1987).

condition, he was not covered under the IDEA.[47] As such, the court pointed out that the mother was not required to exhaust administrative remedies. In adding that the child was otherwise qualified under section 504, the court ordered school officials to return the child to a regular classroom setting. In its analysis, the court observed that it could imagine nothing more traumatic than for a child to go to school and then be 'placed in a classroom by himself, not being allowed to play with other children, [or]... to eat with his classmates.'[48]

AIDS and the IDEA The one AIDS-related case that was resolved under the IDEA originated in Wagoner, Oklahoma. Acting in response to the parents of other children who sought to bar him from classes on the basis of a state law regarding contagious diseases, a local board refused to place an HIV-positive haemophiliac child with an emotional disorder in a special education classroom. When the child's parents challenged the board's decision, a federal trial court held that the since the child had an identifiable mental disability under the IDEA, he was entitled to its protections.[49] The court also decreed that school officials could not rely on the state statute to exclude the child from school because by accepting federal funding, they had no choice but to comply with federal law when it came into conflict with the state law.

General exclusion/homebound placement The courts are unwilling to accept homebound placements as a means of removing children with HIV/AIDS from the general school population. Where three elementary aged school children with haemophilia from a single family tested positive for HIV and were identified as carriers of the antibodies for AIDS, their parents challenged their removal from regular classroom settings and placements in homebound instruction. The parents filed suit under section 504, seeking to enjoin the school system from excluding their children from regular classroom settings. In granting the parents' request for an injunction that would permit their children to attend school, a federal trial court in Florida acknowledged 'the concern and fear which is flowing from this small community, particularly from parents of school age children,' but refused to 'be guided by such community fear, parental pressure, and the possibility of lawsuits,'[50] because doing so would have violated the rights of the children. As such, the court ordered school officials to admit the children 'unless and until' they could prove that their presence represented a 'real and valid' threat to others in the school. The court also directed school officials to create an educational programme to better inform parents about AIDS and its transmissibility.

---

47 *Robertson v Granite City Community Unit Sch. Dist.* No. 9, 684 F. Supp. 1002 (S.D. Ill. 1988).

48 Ibid, at 1005.

49 Parents of Child, Code No. 870901, *W v Coker*, 676 F. Supp. 1072 (E.D. Okla. 1987).

50 *Ray v School Dist. of De Soto County*, 666 F. Supp. 1524, 1535 (M.D. Fla. 1987).

A state case from California concerned an eleven-year-old with haemophilia who was exposed to the virus. School officials refused to admit the child and provided him with a home tutor on the basis that the board was in the process of formulating an AIDS policy. On further review of an injunction ordering school officials to admit the child, an appellate court affirmed, subject to periodic re-evaluation of his medical condition.[51] The court was of the opinion that since the student had been attending school regularly without incident, there was no reason why he should have been excluded.

When school officials in Illinois excluded a twelve-year-old who apparently contracted HIV/AIDS from blood transfusions while undergoing open-heart surgery from regular classrooms and extracurricular activities on the basis of his illness, his parents filed suit under section 504, seeking his reinstatement. A federal trial court in Illinois, relying on testimony from the school superintendent, ruled that the homebound instruction that the board offered was inferior to what students received in the regular classroom setting.[52] As such, the court asserted that since the child was otherwise qualified to attend school based on section 504, and that he did not pose a significant risk of infecting others, he was entitled to curricular and extracurricular activities with the exception of contact sports due to the risk of transmission.

Children who may present risks of harm to others When an infected child bit a classmate shortly after being admitted to kindergarten but failed to break the skin, the school board relied on a psychologist's report that he would probably continue his aggressive behaviour. Based on this concern, school officials removed the child from a regular classroom setting and provided him with home instruction. In response to a suit by the child's parents, a federal trial court in California acknowledged that there were 'no reported cases of the transmission of the AIDS virus in a school setting' and the 'overwhelming weight of medical evidence [was] that the AIDS virus is not transmitted by human bites, even bites that break the skin.'[53] The court directed officials to return the child to a regular classroom since he was 'otherwise qualified' to attend regular kindergarten under section 504 insofar as there was no evidence that he posed a significant risk to others.

A case from Florida dealt with a trainable mentally handicapped (TMH) kindergarten child with the infection who was incontinent, often had blood in her saliva, and sucked her fingers. After school officials excluded the child from a class for children who were TMH, her mother filed suit. Relying in part on guidelines from the Centers for Disease Control, which stated that children who lack control of body secretions may need a more restricted learning environment,

---

51 *Phipps v Saddleback Valley Unified Sch. Dist.*, 251 Cal. Rptr. 720 (Cal. Ct. App. 1988).

52 *Doe v Dolton Elementary Sch. Dist. No. 148*, 694 F. Supp. 440 (N.D. Ill. 1988).

53 *Thomas v Atascadero Unified Sch. Dist.*, 662 F. Supp. 376, 380 (C.D. Cal. 1987).

a federal trial court in Florida found that since the child's presence in school represented a specific potential harm to others that clearly outweighed her interests in a more integrated placement, she could not be admitted to a regular classroom. However, rather than exclude the child from school entirely, the judge ordered school officials to create a separate classroom for the child that afforded her a full view of her peers. The child's mother refused to permit her daughter to attend under such conditions.[54] On further review, the Eleventh Circuit vacated and remanded on the basis that the child was otherwise qualified to attend regular classes for children who were TMH.[55] On remand, in light of the low overall risk of her transmitting HIV/AIDS, the trial court ordered the board to admit her to a regular TMH classroom and to have a school nurse available to consult should there be a question as to the advisability of the child being in the classroom on a given day.[56]

After school activity In apparently the only case involving an after school activity, when parents in Virginia enrolled their twelve year-old son who had AIDS in a private karate school, they did not disclose his condition for fear that he would not be admitted. After an anonymous caller informed the school's proprietor/ instructor about the child's condition, and the parents admitted that he had AIDS, he told them that the boy could not take classes. The owner explained to the parents that he could not admit the child due to the risk of transmission of HIV/AIDS insofar as karate involved physical contact and frequent injuries involving bleeding. Although the owner offered to provide the child with private lessons, his parents refused because their son wished to be with his friends. The parents unsuccessfully filed suit in a federal trial court under the ADA, claiming that its prohibitions of discrimination on the basis of disability in places of public accommodation meant that the school had to admit their son.

On further review of a judgment in favour of the owner, the Fourth Circuit affirmed that even though the karate school was a place of public accommodation, the proprietor did not have to admit the child.[57] The court agreed that since the child's condition posed a direct threat to the health and safety of others, he was beyond the coverage of the ADA. The court added that since neither 'softening' the teaching styles of karate nor enhancing safety precautions amounted to reasonable modifications that might have been suggested under the ADA, the owner was not required to take such steps.

---

54 For an in-depth case study of this case, see Monte L. Betz, *The Kindergartner with AIDS and the Glassroom Barrier* (Horsham: PA LRP Publishing, 1992).

55 *Martinez v School Bd. of Hillsborough County, Fla.*, 675 F. Supp. 1574 (M.D. Fla. 1987), *vacated and remanded*, 861 F.2d 1502 (11th Cir 1988), *on remand*, 711 F. Supp. 1066 (M.D. Fla. 1989). See also *Martinez v School Bd. of Hillsborough County, Fla.*, 692 F. Supp. 1293 (M.D. Fla. 1988) for a related case.

56 *On remand*, 711 F. Supp. 1066 (M.D. Fla. 1989).

57 *Montalvo v Radcliffe*, 167 F.3d 873 (4th Cir. 1999).

Implications for Practice

As litigious as Americans are, generally, as well as in matters to relating education,[58] there has been virtually no litigation involving children (or school employees) with HIV/AIDS, after an initial flurry of disputes in the late 1980s and early 1990s. The dearth of litigation is based on two related facts. First, federal and state laws prohibit discrimination against school personnel with HIV/AIDS. Second, federal and state case law has also made it clear that, in the absence of exigent circumstances, employees and/or students with HIV/AIDS cannot be prohibited from working in or attending public schools. Thus, educational leaders must take the necessary steps to devise and implement policies[59] ensuring the rights of all members of school communities. Accordingly, school officials would be wise to consider the following in developing policies on HIV/AIDS awareness and prevention.

First, educational leaders should develop teams to review existing policies to ensure that they, and ongoing sex-education programs, conform to current law and up-to-date research on HIV/AIDS awareness and prevention. Teams should include parents, students (as age-appropriate), educators (including, but not limited to, teachers, counselors, school nurses), an attorney who practises education law, people who are living with HIV/AIDS since their experiential knowledge can be most informative, representatives of social services and other public health-type agencies, and a broad range of community representatives, including clergy as well as leaders of ethnic minority groups. By ensuring a broad representation of community members in working with HIV/AIDS awareness policies, school officials may be able to head off the inevitable litigation filed by opponents.[60]

Second, policies should lead to the development and implementation of age-appropriate, culturally-relevant educational programs. These programs should provide practical guidance to all school personnel, including faculty and staff to students, on how to address specific issues (ranging from dealing with school children with HIV infection to following universal precautions) to avoid

58 *See* Perry A. Zirkel & Anastasia D'Angelo (2002) 'Special Education Case Law: An Empirical Trends Analysis,' *Educ. L. Rep.* 161, 731 (reporting on the growth of litigation in special education); Perry Zirkel, 'The 'Explosion' in Education Litigation: An Update,' (1997) *Educ. L. Rep.* 114, 341.

59 For a discussion of policies in this area, see Matthew, J. Welker and Sarah J. Pell, *The Formulation of AIDS Policies: Legal Considerations For Schools* (Topeka: KS, National Organization on Legal Problems of Education, 1992).

60 For cases on challenges to instruction about AIDS, see for example *Ware v Valley Stream High Sch. Dist.*, 551 N.Y.S.2d 167 (N.Y. 1989) (upholding the constitutionality of the State Commissioner of Education's AIDS Education Program); *Fink v Board of Educ. of Tully Cent. Schs.*, 542 N.Y.S.2d 918 (N.Y. Sup. Ct. 1989) (unsuccessfully challenging a board's implementation of a state regulation regarding AIDS instruction).

contracting the disease. As an important feature, programmes would be wise to do more than discuss 'safe sex' and should consider including consideration of abstinence from high risk activity, whether involving sex or intravenous drug use, in order to present a more balanced approach. Yet, since abstinence programmes have generated controversy as opponents argue that it is not only religion-based but also an insufficient basis on which to fight the spread of HIV/AIDS, educational leaders should help opponents to realise that all will benefit from such a multi-faceted approach to fighting this disease.[61]

Third, appropriate HIV/AIDS programs for children must be incorporated throughout the curriculum rather than focusing on the topic on an occasional basis. To this end, it is important to present HIV/AIDS education at every grade level in the hope that students' knowledge and attitudes about the disease will translate into avoidance of high-risk practices, whether involving sexual activities or intravenous drug use. Even so, educational leaders should take community values and sensitivities into consideration and should avoid sponsoring highly explicit, and arguably age inappropriate programs such as the ones that have led to litigation in the United States since they detract from the otherwise important lessons that they seek to impart.[62]

Fourth, policies must safeguard the legal rights of employees and students with HIV/AIDS by maintaining the confidentiality of their records. Moreover, educational leaders would be wise to consider the parameters of the Family Educational Rights and Privacy Act,[63] a far-reaching American statute designed to grant eligible students and their parents access to their educational records while limiting the access of outsiders to these records. A policy that is consistent with this well thought out law, but which applies to all members of a school community, not just students, will make it clear that the names of all who may have HIV/AIDS cannot be released without first checking with the individual who will be affected by such a disclosure. A policy should also explain that violations of policies and/or laws governing the confidentiality of employee and student

---

61 Thomas J. Coates, 'Danger when science serves theology—Administration is wrong to rely so heavily on abstinence education to prevent AIDS,' *Newark Star-Ledger*, 14 September 2004, at p 25; Angie Brunkow, 'Schools Rethink AIDS Ed Telling students about condom use goes against a state policy of teaching abstinence only,' *Omaha World-Herald*, 2 March 2001, at p 1.

62 *See, e.g.*, *Brown v Hot, Sexy and Safer Productions*, 68 F.3d 525 (1st Cir. 1996), cert. denied, 516 U.S. 1159 (1996) (upholding the authority of school officials to permit a sexually explicit AIDS awareness programme); *Akshar v Mills*, 671 N.Y.S.2d 856 (N.Y. App. Div 1998) (affirming that a parent was not entitled to either a hearing before the state commissioner of education or a trial on the merits of her opposition to a sexually explicit AIDS peer education programme).

63 For a discussion of this statute, *see* Charles J. Russo (2002). 'The Family Education Rights and Privacy Act: An Update.' *School Business Affairs*. Vol. 68, No. 10, 40-43.

records can lead to liability for defamation, invasion of privacy, and the intentional infliction of emotional distress.[64]

Finally, policies should include anti-discrimination provisions relating to employees and children. Such language is essential because, in an approach consistent with American law, there is the presumption that individuals with HIV/AIDS are qualified to work in a school or attend classes in the absence of verified evidence establishing that they pose a significant risk to others.

Conclusion

The United States has probably seen more education and health litigation in the context of HIV/AIDS than elsewhere, offering insights into the difficulties involved in trying to balance judicially the interests of all interested parties, but also highlighting the risks posed by ignorance and prejudice. The cases could be seen as guideposts for the development of policies based on the needs of all who are affected by this disease and the formulation of appropriate legal responses to safeguard the rights of students and educators who suffer from HIV/AIDS, promoting their equal inclusion in education.

Fortunately, beyond the litigation discussed herein, HIV/AIDS has shown virtually no signs of entering American public schools in recent years, no doubt, in part, because school officials have adopted pro-active educational programmes to help stem the tide of the disease in school. At the same time, insofar as the schools play a major, but by no means the only, role in the development of children, educators must continue to be vigilant in the effort to fight the spread of the disease. Moreover, in addition to not excluding staff and students who have HIV/AIDS, all school personnel must receive instruction about the disease in order to help prevent its further spread. As such, educators must remain informed about the many dimensions of HIV/AIDS and be willing to spearhead a drive to inculcate prevention education, because only in doing so can they help to preserve and foster the well-being of current and future generations.

---

64 For an early discussion of the need for confidentiality, *see* Ralph D. Mawdsley, 'Privacy Rights of AIDS Victims,' (1986) *Educ. L. Rep.* 31, 697.

Chapter 9

HIV/AIDS Policy in South African Schools

Christa Van Wyk

This chapter gives an overview of the work of the South African Law Reform Commission culminating in the adoption of an HIV/AIDS policy for South African schools in 1999. The ambit of the policy is set out, including the four pillars on which it rests: the principle of inclusivity and non-discrimination; the application of universal precautions for a safe school environment; the development of curricula to include HIV/AIDS issues; and the development of structures for the implementation of the policy. The successes to date with the implementation of the policy and challenges for the future are also discussed.

The HIV Epidemic in South Africa

South Africa is considered to have one of the highest HIV prevalence rates in the world. The first two known AIDS-related deaths in South Africa occurred in 1982. Since then HIV infection has increased dramatically. We know this, despite the fact that HIV/AIDS is not a notifiable condition in terms of South African health legislation. Information on infection rates is gathered by making use of anonymous and voluntary national HIV antenatal sero-prevalence surveys on pregnant women, which are carried out on a yearly basis by the Department of Health at clinics of the public health services. The information gained from these surveys is then extrapolated to the wider population. By 1992, the annual survey showed that the HIV prevalence rate among pregnant women (aged between 15 and 49) who attend public health antenatal clinics was 2.2 per cent. Ten years later, by 2002, the prevalence rate had increased to a massive 26.5 per cent.[1] This led to estimates that almost three million South African women between the ages of 15 and 49 were infected with HIV by the end of 2002.[2] When these figures are extrapolated, the national HIV prevalence rate among the almost 46

1 Department of Health, *National HIV and Syphilis Antenatal Sero-Prevalence Survey in South Africa: 2002* (Pretoria: Department of Health, 2003), p 6.

2 Ibid, p 11.

million South Africans is currently estimated to be around 12 per cent. This means that one in eight South Africans of all ages (and one in four sexually active adult South Africans) is infected.[3] Put differently, this means that between five and six million South Africans are infected. It is further estimated that 800 to 1,000 South Africans die of AIDS per day, which brings the total to approximately 300,000 people per year.[4]

The Impact of HIV on Education

It is estimated that without antiretroviral treatment, about 30 per cent of babies born to infected mothers are themselves infected,[5] and that by the end of 2002 more than 90,000 babies had been born HIV-positive.[6] Many of these children will—with better medical care—reach school going age and attend primary schools. Early sexual activity among adolescents further means that increasing numbers of learners attending secondary schools might be infected. (In this respect it has been said that the 'window of opportunity' for educating children in Africa about HIV presents itself by the time they turn nine.[7]) Studies carried out by the Department of Health reveal that 24 per cent of learners at primary schools are already sexually active and that only a quarter of these use condoms.[8] In addition, sexual abuse and rape are rife in South Africa, and are often based

3 Ibid, p 12; R.E. Dorrington, D. Bradshaw and D. Budlender, 'HIV/AIDS profile in the provinces of South Africa: Indicators for 2002' (Cape Town: The Centre for Actuarial Research, University of Cape Town, Medical Research Council and the Actuarial Society of South Africa, 2002), pp 4-5.

4 R.E.Dorrington, D. Bradshaw and D. Budlender, above n 3, p 28.

5 When antiretroviral therapy such as nevirapine is administered to the mother during labour and to the infant within 72 hours after birth, the transmission from mother to child can be reduced by 50 per cent. This was one of the arguments in *Treatment Action Campaign v Minister of Health* 2002(4) BCLR 356 (T), which dealt with the constitutional right of access to health care services, specifically in the context of HIV/AIDS. The issue was a government policy decision not to provide nevirapine to pregnant HIV-positive women to prevent or reduce mother-to-child transmission. The court was asked to declare this policy unreasonable, and to order government to develop a specific treatment programme. The Pretoria High Court not only found the policy unreasonable, but also ordered government to make nevirapine available. On appeal against this judgment, the Constitutional Court in *Minister of Health v Treatment Action Campaign(No 2)* 2002(5) SA 721 (CC) in essence confirmed this judgment.

6 Above n 1, p 11.

7 South African Law Reform Commission, *Third Interim Report on Aspects of the Law Relating to AIDS: HIV/AIDS and Discrimination in Schools* (Project 85) (Pretoria: South African Law Reform Commission, 1998), p 60.

8 Department of Health, *School Health Policy and Implementation Guidelines* (Pretoria: Department of Health, 2003), p 7.

on the mistaken belief that a man may cure his infection by having sexual intercourse with a virgin.

It should be accepted, therefore, that children *infected* with HIV will increasingly form part of the school population. Thousands of children will also be *affected* by HIV/AIDS. It is estimated that by July 2002 there were over 885,000 orphans in South Africa, 38 per cent of these being orphaned as a result of AIDS.[9] The number of street children will increase, and many will turn to crime and prostitution for survival. In the school context, learners may have to take time off to look after young ones at home or to carry out household tasks. The Children's Bill, which is currently before Parliament and which will replace the Child Care Act,[10] for example, makes provision for child-headed households in circumstances where parents suffer from or have died of AIDS.[11]

AIDS will also further weaken the already fragile management and financial situation in the South African education system. Rising AIDS mortality and morbidity rates will increase attrition in the ranks of educators, and replacing them is going to be costly. A multi-faceted study on HIV/AIDS among educators in South Africa is currently being conducted by the South African Human Sciences Research Council, in collaboration with, among others, the national and provincial Departments of Education. This study aims to determine the impact of HIV/AIDS on educators and on their morale, workload and job satisfaction. It will study their perceptions regarding the spread and prevention of infection, and the possible role of curriculum and classroom instruction on the prevention of HIV. The prevalence of HIV infection and mortality rates amongst educators will be assessed through anonymous and unlinked, voluntary HIV testing.[12] From this information educator demand and supply projections will be made, which will facilitate future planning in education.

---

9 R.E. Dorrington, D. Bradshaw and D. Budlender, above n 3, p 7. An orphan is defined as a person under the age of 18 whose mother has died.

10 74 of 1983.

11 Clause 234 of the Children's Bill.

12 See n 21 below on the provisions of the Employment Equity Act 55 of 1998. South African Labour Courts have held that the voluntary and anonymous HIV testing of workers does not fall within the ambit of s 7(2) of Act, and that employees do not require the the permission of the Labour Court for their employees to be tested. See *Irvin & Johnson Ltd v Trawler & Line Fishing Union* (2003) 24 *ILJ* 565 (LC) and *PFG Building Glass (Pty) Ltd v Chemical Engineering Pulp Paper Wood & Allied Workers Union* (2003) 24 *ILJ* 974 (LC). Surveys of varying nature are increasingly being carried out in the workforce, since testing would enable employers to assess the number of infected employees in various age and health categories in their workforce and to plan for the potential impact of HIV infection on their companies.

The Legal Response to the Epidemic

From its inception, the AIDS epidemic posed a major challenge to South Africa's legal system and values. As in many other countries, tension soon arose between public health and human rights. Calls were made for the restriction of human rights, supposedly based on public health considerations. For example, some demanded the compulsory testing of large parts of the population and the quarantine or isolation of people with HIV.[13] Fortunately, it was accepted early on that the human rights of people with HIV and the preservation of the common good, need not be antithetical. Consequently, the legal response has not yielded to public fear and panic, nor to the desire for the law to use extreme measures. Instead a legislative framework was created to secure people's rights and to protect them from unfair discrimination. The premise was accepted that no public health rationale justifies discriminatory and coercive measures based *solely* on HIV infection—which approach is in line with that of the United Nations *International Guidelines on HIV/AIDS and Human Rights* (1996). Coercive measures not only infringe people's rights and result in severe social discrimination, but are often counterproductive and alienating, doing nothing to advance understanding of the HIV epidemic or to slow its spread.[14] Measures which are aimed at combating HIV/AIDS, and which invade rights, should therefore always be tested as to whether they actually do combat the spread of HIV, and if they do, whether they are the least restrictive way possible of attaining this objective.

In contrast, non-coercive measures *do* harmonise and improve both human rights and public health. They value autonomy, education, cooperation, consent, and the empowerment of vulnerable people to protect themselves. This non-coercive approach was made possible by the adoption of a liberal Constitution in South Africa[15] which is based on the values of human dignity, equality and human rights,[16] and the introduction of a Bill of Rights.[17] Furthermore, this approach was informed by South Africa's international obligations in terms of the United Nations Convention on the Rights of the Child (1989).[18]

---

13 See E. Cameron 'Human rights, racism and AIDS: the new discrimination' (1993) *South African Journal on Human Rights* 22-29; M. Kirby 'AIDS and the law' (1993) *South African Journal on Human Rights* 1-21.

14 E. Cameron and E. Swanson 'Public health and human rights—the AIDS crisis in South Africa' (1992) *South African Journal on Human Rights* 200-233.

15 An interim Constitution was adopted in 1993 (Act 200 of 1993), followed by the final Constitution (the Constitution of the Republic of South Africa, Act 108 of 1996).

16 S 1 (a) of the Constitution.

17 Contained in ch 2 of the Constitution.

18 South Africa ratified this convention on 16 June 1995. S 39(1) of the Constitution provides that when interpreting the Bill of Rights, a court, tribunal or forum *must* consider international law (own emphasis).

A non-coercive approach was also advocated by the South African Law Reform Commission, which started investigating reform of the law relating to HIV and AIDS in 1993. The Commission published a discussion document in 1995, giving effect to the then interim South African Constitution of 1993.[19] This report contained preliminary recommendations addressing unfair discrimination on the basis of HIV infection and proposed AIDS-specific anti-discrimination legislation. This initial work, together with public responses to it, formed a basis for the discussion papers and interim reports, addressing various legal problems, which followed after 1996, when the final South African Constitution was adopted. The underlying general aim of the Commission's work throughout was to find solutions to HIV-related legal problems which would serve to protect the rights of persons with HIV while at the same time accommodating the common good. The five interim reports which resulted from the investigation by the Commission included, *inter alia*, a proposal that pre-employment testing for HIV—except in certain defined circumstances—should be prohibited.[20] These recommendations were embodied in the Employment Equity Act of 1998.[21]

The *Third Interim Report*, also published in 1998, covered the issue of HIV/AIDS and discrimination in schools. It followed upon the well-publicised crisis caused by the application in early 1997 by Nkosi Johnson, an eight-year-old boy with AIDS (who has since died) to be admitted to a public school in Johannesburg. Following the alarmed reaction of some members of the public, the Ministers of Education and Health issued a joint statement in which it was

---

19 South African Law Reform Commission, *Aspects of the Law Relating to AIDS* (Project 85) Working Paper 58 (Pretoria: South African Law Reform Commission,1995).

20 South African Law Reform Commission, *Second Interim Report on Aspects of the Law Relating to AIDS: Pre-employment HIV Testing* (Project 85) (Pretoria: South African Law Reform Commission, 1998). Other reports dealt with, inter alia, specific health-related issues, the compulsory testing of people arrested on sexual offence charges and the possible criminalisation of harmful consensual sexual activity by persons with HIV.

21 55 of 1998. See ss 6, 7 and 50 of the Act. The Act prohibits medical testing of employees or applicants for employment, unless legislation permits or requires testing, or it is justifiable in the light of medical facts, employment conditions, social policy, the fair distribution of employee benefits or the inherent requirements of a job. 'Medical testing' includes any test, question, inquiry or other means designed to ascertain, or which has the effect of enabling an employer to ascertain, whether an employee has any medical condition. Where medical testing amounts to HIV testing, such testing is prohibited unless it is determined to be justifiable by the Labour Court. *Hoffmann v South African Airways* 2001(1) SA 1 (CC) dealt with the HIV testing of and refusal to employ and HIV positive man as cabin crew. This case was decided in terms of the constitutional right to equality, and not the Employment Equity Act (which came into force only after the inception of the case). The Constitutional Court found that the discrimination had been unfair, that it had impaired Hoffmann's dignity and that he had to be instated in the position he had applied for.

categorically stated that no governing body has the right to deny a child access to a public school. After this, Nkosi was duly admitted. This was despite the fact that two important education laws were passed in 1996,[22] which gave effect to both the spirit and letter of the 1996 Constitution by protecting learners from unfair discrimination and guaranteeing them their rights to a basic education and to equal access to public schools. The reaction of some members of the public and the apparent absence of a national education policy on this issue, underscored the need for intervention.

After a process of joint consultation had been followed between the Department of Education and the project committee of the Law Reform Commission, the Commission recommended that the Minister of Education, under the National Education Policy Act of 1996, should determine national policy on HIV/AIDS in schools. A clearly targeted policy would create legal certainty and help prevent injustice to learners with HIV. Furthermore, a clear national policy on a core curriculum on HIV/AIDS education and on universal precautions to prevent infection in the school environment, including contact sport, would bring about much needed guidance on these issues. A draft national policy on HIV/AIDS in public schools was included in the Commission Report and recommendations. The national Department of Education not only adopted the Commission's recommendations, but also extended these to cover educators, as well as students in further education institutions (excluding universities). It promulgated the *National Policy on HIV/AIDS for Learners and Educators in Public Schools, and Students and Educators in Further Education and Training Institutions* in August 1999 (hereafter called the National Schools Policy).[23] In this policy the Ministry of Education acknowledged the increasing prevalence of HIV infection in schools, and the need for each school to have a planned strategy to cope with the epidemic. It further emphasised its commitment to minimise the social, economic and developmental consequences of HIV/AIDS on the education system and to provide leadership in this regard.

The National Schools Policy is based on a number of premises, including the following: that persons with HIV/AIDS should be accommodated in society to the extent that their infection does not expose others to significant risks that cannot be eliminated by ordinary measures or reasonable adaptations;[24] that children with HIV do not expose others to significant risks within the school environment; that they should lead as full a life as possible and should not be denied the opportunity to receive an education to the maximum of their ability; that no unfair discrimination should be practised against them; that learners have a right to be educated on HIV/AIDS, sexuality and healthy lifestyles in order to protect

22 The South African Schools Act 84 of 1996 and the National Education Policy Act 27 of 1996.

23 General Notice 1926 in *Government Gazette* 20372 of 10 August 1999. The policy does not apply to private or independent schools.

24 For example by the use of universal precautions.

themselves; and that universal precautions should be applied regardless of the known or unknown HIV status of the individuals concerned. However, if it ascertained that an infected learner poses a 'medically recognised significant health risk' to others, appropriate measure may be taken.

Some of the most important fundamental rights that were taken into consideration when the policy was being drawn up are: the right to equality (which includes the right not to be unfairly discriminated against either by the state or its organs, or by other individuals and juristic persons);[25] the right to dignity;[26] the right to privacy;[27] the right of access to information;[28] the right of access to health care services;[29] the right to freedom of association;[30] the right to life,[31] bodily integrity[32] and an environment that is not harmful to health or well-being;[33] the right to freedom of conscience, religion, thought, belief and opinion;[34] and the right to a basic education.[35] The state has to respect, protect, promote and fulfil all these rights.[36] The Constitution further provides that the best interests of children are of paramount importance in every matter concerning the child (that is, a person under the age of 18).[37]

The National Policy on HIV/AIDS in Public Schools

The National Schools Policy applies to public schools which enrol learners in one or more grades between grade zero (now called reception grade) and grade 12. It also applies to school hostels. It does not apply to independent (private) schools or to nursery schools. It was, for instance cautioned that toddlers would be inclined to assist indiscriminately another child who bleeds rather than adhere to precautionary guidelines.

---

25 S 9 of the Constitution.
26 S 10 of the Constitution.
27 S 14 of the Constitution.
28 S 32 of the Constitution.
29 S 27 of the Constitution. The *Treatment Action Campaign* cases (*Treatment Action Campaign v Minister of Health* 2002(4) BCLR 356 (T) and *Minister of Health v Treatment Action Campaign(No 2)* 2002(5) SA 721 (CC)) dealt with this socio-economic right which has to be progressively realised by the state.
30 S 18 of the Constitution.
31 S 11 of the Constitution.
32 S 12(2) of the Constitution.
33 S 24 of the Constitution.
34 S 15 of the Constitution.
35 S 29(1)(a) of the Constitution. This right has no internal qualifier (as does the right of access to health care services contained in s 27, which the state must progressively realise within its available resources).
36 S 7(2) of the Constitution.
37 S 28(2) and (3) of the Constitution.

The National Schools Policy rests on four pillars: inclusivity and no unfair discrimination; the need to take universal precautions; curricular development and the training of educators; and the development of structures within the school system to implement the policy. As pointed out below, this policy is a legal document which has to be implemented.

Inclusivity and No Unfair Discrimination

The National Schools Policy prohibits the testing for HIV/AIDS for attendance at schools. The governing body of a public school may not administer any test (including an HIV test) related to the admission of a learner to a public school.[38]

Children with HIV have the right to attend any public school and their needs should, as far as is reasonably practicable, be accommodated in the school. Learners of compulsory school age (between ages seven and 15 or up to the ninth grade)[39] who are unable to benefit from attendance at school may be educated at home, or granted exemption from attendance.[40] Learners aged under 18 who are severely incapacitated due to chronic illness, such as AIDS, can also be accommodated in special needs schools where they can develop to their full potential. However, placement at these schools may not be used as an excuse to remove HIV-positive learners from mainstream schools.[41] Special needs education is learner-centred, has flexible curricula and offers support and trained staff, but will only become fully operational some time in the future.

Under the National Schools Policy no unfair discrimination will be tolerated and any special measures in respect of a learner or educator with HIV should be fair and justifiable in the light of medical facts, established legal rules and principles, ethical guidelines and the best interests of those with HIV as well as other learners and educators.[42] There could, for example, be justification for withdrawing a learner with HIV from school or reasonably accommodating him or her elsewhere (such as allowing him or her to receive education at home) in cases where he or she poses a medically recognised significant health risk to others which cannot be excluded by ordinary precautionary measures. A significant health risk would, for example, be present where a learner has a serious secondary infection (such as multidrug resistant tuberculosis) which

38 s 5(2) of the South African Schools Act and paragraph 4 of the National schools policy.

39 S 3 of the South African Schools Act requires that every parent must cause every learner for whom he or she is responsible to attend a school from the first school day of the year in which such learner reaches the age of seven years until the last school day of the year in which such learner reaches the age of 15 years or the ninth grade, whichever occurs first.

40 National Schools Policy, para 5.

41 Department of Education (2001) White Paper on Special Needs Education and paragraph 5 of the National Schools Policy.

42 National schools policy, para 3.

cannot be treated and could be transmitted to other persons in the course of day-to-day contact, or where the learner behaves in an aggressive manner (sexually or otherwise). In instances like these, discrimination would probably be fair and rational.[43]

Learners' or educators' HIV/AIDS status need not be disclosed to school authorities, although voluntary disclosure to a member of the staff, such as the principal, is encouraged.[44] It may generally be in the best interests of the learner with HIV if a member of staff directly involved with the learner's care is informed of his or her condition either by his or her parents or guardians (in the case of learners under the age of 14) or by the learner him or herself (if the learner is above the age of 14 years).[45] Awareness of a learner's infection would facilitate informed decisions regarding his or her management. An effective policy of confidentiality, as well as an enabling and caring environment, needs to be created for such disclosures. Any person to whom this information is divulged must keep it confidential. Unauthorised disclosure could give rise to legal liability.[46] Other parents or learners who wish to rely on their fundamental right of access to information in order to gain access to such information held by the school, would have to show that such disclosure is needed to protect their right(s) and that it would not involve the unreasonable disclosure of personal information about a third party.[47]

Universal Precautions and a Safe School Environment

Under the National Schools Policy, all schools must implement universal precautions to eliminate the risk of transmission of blood-borne diseases, including HIV. In situations of potential exposure to HIV, all persons are

---

43 The limitations clause of the Constitution (s 36) may justify discrimination if certain conditions are met. For a discussion of the staged approach followed by South African courts in this respect, see, for example, *Harksen v Lane NO* 1998(1) SA 300 (CC).

44 National Schools Policy, para 6.

45 According to s 39(4)(b) of the Child Care Act 74 of 1983 (soon to be replaced by a new Children's Act), a child over the age of 14 years is competent to consent, without the assistance of his or her parent or guardian, to the performance of any medical treatment on himself or herself or his or her child. The implication of this provision is that a person who is competent to consent to an HIV test, would also be competent to consent to the disclosure of such test result.

46 *Jansen van Vuuren NNO v Kruger* 1993(4) SA 842 (A) dealt with the infringement of the privacy in the context of HIV. A medical practitioner disclosed his patient's HIV infection to another general practitioner and dentist who, the court found, had no right to this information since they were not involved in his immediate care and were not exposed to any risk.

47 See the Promotion of Access to Information Act 2 of 2000, which was promulgated to give effect to, and co-exists with, the constitutional right of access to information.

assumed to be potentially infected and treated as such. All blood and open skin lesions, as well as all body fluids and excretions which could be stained with blood are treated as potentially infectious. Specific guidelines in this respect have to be followed, such as that such skin lesions should at all times be covered completely with a non-porous or waterproof plaster, and that all persons attending to such lesions should wear protective latex gloves or plastic bags (as a cheaper alternative) over their hands to eliminate the risk of HIV transmission.[48]

All schools should train learners and educators in first aid, and have available at least two first aid kits, which should be accessible at all times—even on outings and tours—and checked regularly so that expired or depleted items may be replaced. The kits should contain, inter alia, disposable latex gloves, household rubber gloves for handling blood-soaked material in specific instances, protective eye wear and a protective face mask to cover nose and mouth. Less sophisticated and cheaper barriers (for example plastic bags, spectacles and scarves) may be used in resource-poor communities. Learners, especially those in primary schools, should be instructed never to touch blood or open wounds but should call for the assistance of an educator or staff member. All staff, including cleaners, and learners should be informed about the universal precautions that will be adhered to at a school, and a copy of the policy must be displayed at each school.

Although the risk of HIV transmission during contact play and sport is insignificant, no learner or educator may participate in such sport with an open wound or skin lesion.[49] If bleeding occurs during play, the injured player must leave the field immediately and be treated appropriately. The player may only resume play if the wound is completely and securely covered. Blood stained clothes must be changed. A fully-equipped first-aid kit must be available wherever contact sport takes place.

The duties of learners, sport participants, educators, coaches and parents are also emphasised. Players and coaches, for example, should seek medical counselling in order to assess their own health as well as the risk of transmission before participating in sport.[50] Managers and coaches must ensure adherence to universal precautions and should encourage players to seek medical counselling where appropriate. Parents should consult medical opinion to assess whether their child, owing to his or her condition or conduct, poses a medically recognised significant health risk to others. If such risk is established, the principal of the school should be informed. The principal must then refer the matter to the health advisory committee of the school[51] so that the necessary steps may be taken to ensure the health of other learners and educators. Parents are ultimately responsible for the behaviour of their children at school and their adherence to

---

48 National Schools Policy, para 7.

49 Ibid, para 8.

50 Ibid, para 8.4.

51 Discussed below.

the Code of Conduct, which must be adopted by every school.[52] Parents must encourage their children to observe all rules aimed at preventing behaviour which may create a risk of HIV transmission.

Curricular Development

The National Schools Policy provides that continuing life-skills and HIV/AIDS orientation programmes must be implemented at all schools.[53] Age-appropriate education on HIV/AIDS must form part of the curriculum and should include information on HIV/AIDS and other sexually-transmitted diseases (STDs), first-aid principles, the role of drugs, sexual abuse and violence. Life skills necessary for the prevention of transmission should be developed and learners should be empowered to deal with difficult situations. They should be given information on prevention measures, including abstinence from sexual intercourse, the use of condoms, and faithfulness to one's partner. They should also know that they should obtain prompt medical treatment for STDs and tuberculosis, avoid contact with blood, and apply universal precautions. Information must be given in an accurate and scientific manner and in understandable language. As pointed out below, these provision have to a large extent been implemented by the National Curriculum 2002.

Learners should be encouraged to make use of health care, counselling and support services offered in the community. If learners are infected with HIV, they should be informed that they can still lead normal, healthy lives for many years by taking care of their health.

Structures for Implementation

The National Schools Policy recommends that each school should establish its own health advisory committee as a committee of the governing body.[54] This committee should use the assistance of community health workers. Other members could include educators, representatives of the parents and learners at the school, and representatives from the medical or health care professions. The committee advises the governing body on all health matters, including HIV/AIDS, and is jointly responsible with the governing body for developing and promoting a school plan of implementation on HIV/AIDS. It also reviews the plan from time to time, especially as new scientific knowledge becomes available. It is further involved in the development of a Code of Conduct to prevent HIV transmission in the school environment.

---

52 S 8 of the South African Schools Act deals with the aims and adoption of codes of conduct.

53 National Schools Policy, para 9.

54 Ibid, para 13.

The need for parent and community involvement is also recognised in order to ensure that sexuality education will take into account the community ethos and values. For example, parents have to be informed about all life-skills and HIV/AIDS education offered at school, the learning content and methods used, as well as values that are imparted.[55] In general, they are invited to participate in parental guidance sessions and are made aware of their role as educators and role models at home. They are encouraged to take an active interest in acquiring information on HIV supplied by the school and to attend meetings convened for them by the governing body of the school.[56] Parents are informed and educated on the necessity of the information that is imparted to their children. Complaints of parents, for example that the nature of the learning material is not suitable for a specific age group, are investigated.

The National Schools Policy provides that the governing body of a school, on which parents are represented, may develop and adopt its own implementation plan on HIV/AIDS to give effect to the national policy.[57] Other major role players in the community and the health advisory committee should be involved in developing an implementation plan for the school. This implementation plan should adhere to the basic principles laid down in the national policy, but should take into account the needs and values of the specific school and community. Consultation could address and resolve complex questions, such as whether condoms need to be made available at school, and if so, under what circumstances.

The national and provincial Departments of Education are responsible for the implementation of the National Schools Policy. Every education department designates an HIV/AIDS programme manager and a working group to communicate the policy to staff, and to implement, monitor and evaluate the programme, to advise management on programme implementation and progress, and to create a supportive and non-discriminatory environment. The principal is responsible for practical implementation at school level, and for maintaining an adequate standard of safety. Disciplinary action may be taken in terms of the Employment of Educators Act[58] if educators are unfit to carry out their jobs or fail to carry out the policy.[59]

Codes of Conduct are further important structures for implementation of the National Schools Policy. Codes must be adopted by the governing bodies of all schools to establish disciplined and safe school environments and outline the

---

55 Ibid, para 9.4.

56 Ibid, para 10.3.

57 Ibid, para 12.

58 76 of 1998.

59 Sections 16, 17 and 18 of the Employment of Educators Act deal with incapacity and misconduct on the part of educators.

duties of learners.[60] They should contain provisions regarding the unacceptability of behaviour which may create a risk of HIV transmission (for example, aggressive sexual behaviour), as well as disciplinary measures and procedures, categories of offences and sanctions to be imposed. Learners may be temporarily suspended and expelled in case of serious offences. However, if a learner is subject to compulsory school attendance and is expelled from school, an alternative arrangement must be made for his or her placement at another public school. This may include a gender-specific school.[61]

Successes to Date of the National Policy on HIV/AIDS in Public Schools

The National Schools Policy is an ambitious policy, if one considers the limited resources available in South Africa, and it would be a pity if the policy should fail because of poor or incomplete implementation. Nevertheless, according to officials in the national Department of Education, the implementation of the National Schools Policy has thus far been running smoothly. This is despite misgivings that the National Schools Policy was inappropriate, impracticable and unrealistic and would 'not be able to make the transition from the drawing board to the school grounds.'[62] Parents and the public have accepted the policy, as well as the principles of inclusivity and non-discrimination. The fact that the National Schools Policy may be adapted to suit local requirements (provided that its implementation adheres to the guidelines set by the policy) has contributed to its success. Universal precautionary measures are reported to be in place, despite initial fears that these would prove to be too costly for many South African schools. Unfortunately, however, no independent evaluations of the policy are as yet available.

The National Curriculum 2002 of the Department of Education, with its emphasis on curricular development, has to a large extent implemented the national HIV/AIDS schools policy. The curriculum includes, as one of eight learning areas, 'life orientation.' Life orientation consists of five subdivisions, including health promotion and personal development. The National Curriculum lays down the required outcomes that must be attained, but provinces and local

---

60 An undertaking by a learner and his or her parents to abide by the Code of Conduct, however, does not amount to an enforceable contract.

61 Sections 9 and 12 of the South African Schools Act 84 of 1996.

62 See P.J. Visser and J.L. Beckmann, 'Some comments on the discussion paper by the South African Law Commission: "Aspects of the Law Relating to AIDS: HIV/AIDS and Discrimination in Schools"' (1998) *Journal of Contemporary Roman Dutch Law* 127, at p 132. See also C. van Wyk 'A reply to: "Some comments on the discussion paper by the SA Law Commission: Aspects of the law relating to HIV/AIDS and discrimination in schools 1998 (61) THRHR p 127"' (1998) *Journal of Contemporary Roman Dutch Law* 677.

communities may choose *how* to achieve the prescribed outcomes. Local communities therefore have a measure of discretion regarding the content of the learning material and the methods to be used in classrooms. In the area of health promotion, issues such as HIV/AIDS and STDs, violence, abuse, sexuality and safety are discussed. Values, attitudes, skills and knowledge are imparted. Life orientation, which includes sexuality education, forms part of the prescribed curriculum on which learners are assessed. The desired outcomes are that learners will be able to make informed decisions regarding personal health. These issues are addressed from the foundation phase, through the intermediate phase, to senior level, and study material is adapted to learners' level of understanding. During the foundation phase, learners are told about diseases including HIV/AIDS, abuse and safety measures to avoid contracting diseases. During the intermediate phase (grades four to six) sexuality is discussed in a sensitive and caring manner and substance abuse and associated risks are also addressed. During the senior phase (grades seven to nine) learners learn about risky situations and acquire the skills to make informed lifestyle choices, including those relating to sexuality. Since 'life orientation' forms part of the prescribed curriculum and learners are examined on the contents of these courses, parents may not withdraw their children from these classes.

Educators are being trained to implement universal precautions and to meet the curriculum requirements. As indicated above, if they fail to carry out their professional duties, they may face disciplinary hearings in terms of the Employment of Educators Act.

The structures to implement the policy are being put in place. The School Health Policy and Implementation Guidelines (2003) developed by the national Departments of Education, Health and Social Development jointly, make provision for the establishment of health advisory committees for each school. A school health nurse, attached to a local clinic, forms part of this committee. Community based clinics also cooperate with schools in that they identify 'at risk' children who may need special education. This integrated national strategy and the cooperation between the various state departments, each primarily responsible for its own area of expertise, must be seen as a positive development.

Conclusion: Challenges for the Future

As was indicated above, the National Schools Policy does not apply to universities, independent schools or nursery schools. It could, however, constitute a broad model on which, for example, nursery schools could base policies more suitable for situations where very young children are cared for. In a recent case which came before the Johannesburg High Court, a mother launched a civil action against a Johannesburg nursery school that refused entry to her toddler with HIV.[63] The court ruled that the nursery school had acted reasonably when it deferred admission. The nursery school claimed that it was not adequately prepared, and wanted to postpone admission for at least six months until the child was 'past the biting stage.' This ruling is to be challenged on appeal.

Tertiary education also has no consistent approach or national policy. The Law Reform Commission's recommendations have nevertheless led to individual universities addressing the position of students and teachers with HIV/AIDS in tertiary education institutions.

The Ministry of Education has made the national policy also applicable to *educators* in public schools and in further education and training institutions. The main principles applicable to them are broadly that of no unfair discrimination; no pre-employment testing; confidentiality of HIV status; and no unfair dismissal. However, it must be borne in mind that the Department of Labour requires that each workplace, including the education sector, develop a policy to deal with HIV/AIDS which ensures that employees affected by HIV/AIDS are not unfairly discriminated against. This is required by the *Code of Good Practice* (2000) which was adopted under the terms of the Employment Equity Act of 1998. Such policy must include the organisation's position on HIV/AIDS; an outline of the HIV/AIDS programme; details of employment policies (for example the position regarding testing, employee benefits and performance management); standards of behaviour expected of employers and employees; means of communication within the organisation on HIV/AIDS issues; details of employee assistance available to persons affected by HIV/AIDS; and details of implementation, monitoring and evaluation mechanisms. The current HIV/AIDS policy will have to be assessed in terms of the above requirements, and if it does not meet the requirements, it will have to be amended.

The question remains whether HIV education has indeed brought about a decline in or stabilisation of infection rates. Have young people grasped the basic facts about how HIV is transmitted, and has this knowledge changed their sexual behaviour? Has an enabling environment in fact been created where people can take responsibility for their own health? A glimmer of hope may be found in indications that the prevalence rate of HIV infection among women under the age of 20 may be decreasing. According to statistics the rate has fallen from 16.5 per cent in 1999 to 14.8 per cent in 2002.[64]

Another pressing problem is that of the ever-growing number of street children. Even though they may have a legal obligation (and a fundamental right) to attend school, there is often nobody who enforces this. In terms of the South African Schools Act, parents have the duty to make sure that their children attend

63 *Perreira v Buccleuch Montesorri School* case no 4300/02 (WLD).

64 *Full Report of the Joint Health and Treasury Task Team Charged with Examining Treatment Options to Supplement Comprehensive Care for HIV/AIDS in the Public Health Sector*, (Pretoria: 2003), p 8.

school. Where a learner fails to attend school, the provincial authorities may investigate the circumstances of the learner's absence and take appropriate measures to remedy the situation. The authorities may issue a written notice to the parent of the learner requiring compliance. It is clear that neither present legislation nor the National Schools Policy deals in a satisfactory manner with the problem of street children who have no parents.

The current version of the Children's Bill[65] makes provision in respect of children in especially difficult circumstances, including children affected by HIV/AIDS, those living or working on the streets, or those in child-headed households. It provides that the Minister responsible for the protection of children must prepare a national policy framework in which a comprehensive national strategy is included, aimed at the following: identifying, assisting and promoting the best interests of children in difficult circumstances; identifying child-headed households; assisting children with chronic illnesses to have access to educational services; and integrating street children into the education system. The Bill further provides that municipalities must monitor the location and socio-economic conditions of street children in its area, and make needs analysis for the provision of services to them.[66] The Bill provides that schools must identify children who are frequently absent from school and take steps to assist them in returning to school.[67] It is hoped that the envisaged legislation, coupled with the necessary political will, will ameliorate the current situation.

---

65 Ch 16.

66 Clause 235 of the Children's Bill.

67 Clause 236.

Chapter 10

Disability and School Education: Law and Policy in the UK and Australia

Marcia Conroy and Jim Jackson

Introduction

The historic nature of rights in relation to education for disabled children has only in the past 20 years been seriously considered. In the past, their rights to inclusive education have been ignored through law and this has meant that they have not had the same school experiences as their non-disabled peer group. The establishment of disability discriminatory law has started to encourage disabled children to be socially included within their community schools and this now means that they have the same basic right of access to life opportunities.

In this chapter we will briefly examine models of disability, compare disability legislation in Australia and the UK as it applies to school education, and examine cases that have arisen in regard to a series of matters, including enrolment, physical access, behavioural, communication and attitudinal issues. A major theme is that disabled children should have a significant voice in their experiences. A second theme, demonstrated in a number of cases examined, is that many of the difficulties which disabled children continue to face in schools are based on attitude or ignorance on the part of educators.

This chapter is based on a social model of disability and incorporates the holistic nature of education. It therefore considers disabled children's health needs; their needs for academic opportunity, to develop relationships, and to take part in the same activities as their peer group; and, most fundamentally, their right not to be discriminated against.

Models of Disability

Throughout the history of disabled people, there is evidence to show that disability has been perceived as varying from something which is 'wrong' to something that is evil or dangerous. There is evidence that disabled people have also experienced hatred as a result of their impairment.

The concept of disability as representing evil can be traced to biblical times. Millington notes:

> Leviticus 21: 16-20 cites God himself as being guilty of discrimination when he tells Moses: none of your descendants throughout their generations shall draw near, a blind or lame man, or he that hath a mutilated face or a limb too long, or man that has an injured foot or an injured hand, or a hunchback or dwarf or that hath a blemish in his eye, or be with scurvy, or scabbed.[1]

Such ignorance contributed to society's understanding of disability as one based upon fear, pity and shame. The disability was something to be 'got rid of.' This gave rise to the medical model of disability, which centred on the inabilities of an individual and implied that barriers are a result of something the person is unable to do. The classic example of this is in relation to physical access to buildings. The medical model would assert that if a wheelchair user were unable to access a building—for example, because it has steps—it would be the disability that would be preventing the person from doing so.

The medical, sometimes called the individual, model has a deep-rooted history within the medical profession. Doctors aim to cure, to heal, to take away that which is causing pain. In the case of disability, the disabled person almost becomes two separate people, the 'person' and the 'disability.' The disability is perceived as something 'bad' which needs to be removed; the 'person' is that which remains. One of the clearest examples of aspects of the medical model in use today is in the definition of disability appearing in s 17(11) of the Children Act 1989, which incorporates a philosophy of separating the child from his/her impairment and ignores the experiences of the child. Furthermore the Children Act focuses on need, the medical model approach.

In the last 30 years this model has been overtaken by the social model, in which the impairment and experiences of the disabled child are seen as a fundamental part of the child. This was because disabled people and sympathetic commentators started rejecting the medical model, replacing it with the societal model, which reclassified the 'problem' as one of society failing in its obligation to make allowance for difference. Within this model we should also examine the word 'disabled.' The social model asserts that the term is in reference to how society disables a person from accessing services, or being discriminated against, for example, within an education context by not allowing a child to attend a mainstream school. On a macro level the model asserts that disabled people are marginalised and have more restricted opportunities than other groups of people.

To take the above example of the inaccessible building, under the social model, it is the *building*, not the disability that is creating the barrier to access. Responsibility is placed on society to fix the offending building and not to fix,

---

1 P.A. Millington, *History of Disability and Disabled People* 2003, http://www.bgfl.org/dhistory/index.cfm

hide or remove some 'offending' disabled individual. Perhaps the word 'disabled' should be replaced by 'dis-enabled.'

The Voice of the Disabled Child

Disabled children's experiences are often different from those of adults. To be a disabled child incorporates many experiences that shape the way that they both perceive themselves and how others perceive them. Laura Middleton suggests that 'the birth of a child is usually cause for celebration and its parents are to be congratulated.'[2] However, when a disabled baby is born 'the birth is a tragedy, the parents to be commiserated with.'[3] Often the baby is 'treated' in hospital, doctors attempting to minimise or cure the disability, the medical input continuing for many years.

Historically, specialist education was provided as the child got older, often through 'special schools' where disabled children were isolated from their non-disabled peer group. Special education is one part of isolation, ensuring that disabled children feel 'different.' The media, other adults, legislation and society as a whole have an impact on disabled children's lives. Difference is still seen as negative for many disabled children. Oliver states that 'if children are brought up to believe, through experiencing a range of medical and paramedical interventions, that they are ill, we cannot be surprised if they passively accept the sick role.'[4] Thus disabled children may be left with feelings of disempowerment, isolation, vulnerability and having little power to control their lives. Hutchinson and Tennyson reinforce this view by their observation that disabled children often 'appear to have been conditioned into accepting a devalued role as sick, pitiful, a burden of charity.'[5] Ultimately this will have an effect on the disabled child's self image and self-esteem. However, some parents choose to assert their child's rights to be included within the systems that non disabled children are involved in, for example, mainstream education. These families recognise the strengths of the child and, as Lukes states, parents understand the need of their child 'to be treated and to live in a social order which treats them as possessing dignity, as capable of exercising and increasing their autonomy, of engaging in valued activities within a private space and of developing their several potentialities.'[6]

---

2 L. Middleton, *Making a Difference: Social Work with Disabled Children*, (Birmingham: Venture Press, 1995), at p 61.

3 Ibid.

4 M. Oliver, *The Politics of Disablement* (London, Macmillan Press Limited, 1990), at p 2.

5 D. Hutchinson, and C. Tennyson, *Transition to Adulthood* (London, Further Education Unit, 1986), at p 33.

6 S. Lukes, *Individualism* (Oxford: Basil Blackwell, 1973), at p 153.

Article 23(1) of the United Nations Convention on the Rights of the Child states that:

> States Parties recognize that a mentally or physically disabled child should enjoy a full and decent life, in conditions which ensure dignity, promote self-reliance and facilitate the child's active participation in the community.

The article seeks to ensure that the disabled child has the same opportunities as her/his non-disabled peers. Of particular importance is the establishment by the United Nations in Articles 12 and 13 of the Convention of an active role for the child, including a right to participate in legal proceedings, contained in Article 12(2). This right is further recognised and applied in the UK in the Department for Education and Skills' *Special Educational Needs Code of Practice*, requiring the views of the child to be sought and taken into account.[7] The (albeit limited) right of the disabled child to participate in appeal proceedings is contained in regulation 30(2) of the Special Educational Needs and Disability Tribunal (General Provisions and Disability Claims Procedure) Regulations 2002 (SI 2002/1985). Not as strong, but at least moving in the right direction, is the Australian draft *Disability Standards for Education 2004*, which require consultation with the student, or an associate of the student, in regard to reasonable adjustments.[8]

Lindsay notes:

> In the vast majority of disability discrimination in education complaints it is the parent who initiates action with the Anti-Discrimination Board or the Human Rights and Equal Opportunity Commission. However it is the student/pupil who has been the recipient of alleged discriminatory treatment. The human rights in question are those of the student and not the parent. This cannot be forgotten, especially in circumstances where the student with the disability has difficulty in articulating his/her wishes or is not able to present a first hand account of his/her experiences.[9]

Agreeing with Lindsay, we assert that not only is it for the parents to seek to achieve levels of equality for their children, the child too should have a forceful voice in his/her future.[10] Many parents will be passionate in their quest for a better education for their disabled child. The school will operate within a legal

---

7 (London: Department for Education and Skills, 2001), at para. 1.5 and Part 3, providing significant detail on pupil participation rights, allowing, *inter alia,* participation in decision making processes affecting their education.

8 cl.3.5.

9 K. Lindsay, 'Discrimination Law & Special Education' in *School Law-1997 National Seminar Papers* (Sydney: Legal & Accounting Seminars Pty Ltd, 1997), paper 4, 1 – 12 at p 5.

10 See B. Badham 'Participation—for a Change: Disabled Young People Lead the Way' (2004) *Children and Society*, 18, 143–154.

environment, often tempered by genuinely felt concerns that they may face discrimination law action if they do not follow a certain cause of action, or with health, safety and negligence concerns if they do. An example might be a teacher allowing or not allowing a disabled child to participate in a sporting event, or the presence or absence of a teacher's aide for the child. In this tussle there is every likelihood that passion and concern on the one hand and excessive legalism on the other could leave the child voiceless.

One cannot automatically assume that the child's view will coincide with the parents'; non-disabled children often voice their disagreement. The disabled child may be quite at odds with the parent and/or the teacher, and wish to reject an accommodation such as a teacher's aide, fought for by the parent and eventually provided in good faith by the school, because their presence is embarrassing for the child in front of other children, promoting difference where the child wishes to 'blend in.' Furthermore, the child may not want or believe he or she needs the additional assistance. In such instances, the well meaning actions of a parent in seeking accommodations for the child or a school insisting on providing these for occupational health and safety or disability law reasons may exacerbate the unhappiness of the disabled child, and not work for better education.

To the extent that we are concentrating on the human rights of the child this should also include the right of the child to reject accommodations, but in a way which protects the school from subsequent legal action. The difficulties are twofold: first, the child may not be of legal age and not legally capable of offering a valid release. Secondly, the child may be at odds with their parents who may have sided with the school on the matter. Where the child rejects and is at odds with both parents and school, the school would be well advised to maintain a clear evidentiary record of accommodations offered and refused.

On occasion the judiciary will give a voice to the child. In an Australian case which will be discussed in detail later, *Finney v Hills Grammar School*,[11] Commissioner Innes took evidence from a six year old child, Scarlett Finney, who was denied admission to a school in Sydney. The Commissioner explains how and why he did this:

> The Complainants' representative made an application that Scarlett, who was aged six at the time of the hearing, should give evidence relating to her feelings when she was told of the school's decision. The Respondent challenged her competence to give evidence. After asking her several questions relating to her disability, and the limitations it placed on her in the playing of sports and games, I was satisfied that she was able to understand such issues and was competent to give evidence.
>
> Scarlett stated that 'I felt a bit disappointed that I could not go to that school—I wanted to go to that school. They wrote in a book that they do take people with

---

11 HREOC decision No. H98/60 20 July 1999.

disabilities.' She further said 'it (the school) had lots of things that I'd like to go on.'[12]

Later the Commissioner said:

> The opinion of the person with the disability should not be accepted without question because this could place respondents in very invidious positions. But the person's views should be given weight, alongside the views of experts in the field who have had a chance to assess the individual in question and form an opinion. The greatest barriers which people with a disability face in our community are the negative assumptions made about them by other members of the community.[13]

In *Stephanie Travers by her next friend, Wendy Travers v State of New South Wales*[14] the magistrate allowed evidence to be given by a 12 year old child where it was alleged a school had discriminated against Stephanie Travers, who had spina bifida, by not allowing her access to the disabled toilet. However, on other occasions the child's voice is not heard at all, or worse still is lost in the bitterness of the dispute between parent and education authority.

Finally, we wish to make particular mention of the project undertaken by 16 year old Eleni Burgess, herself a wheelchair user, who recently completed a survey of wheelchair users in schools in the UK. Many of these themes emerge in the cases considered below. She comments:

> Once the ramps are built and the toilets made accessible at school, I get the impression that it is thought that integration has been achieved. My experience, however, is that access is only one aspect of integration and that there are many other important areas that need to be in place if wheelchair users in school are to be treated equally and to gain a good education.[15]

She notes a series of issues that affected disabled children in schools. These included admission to their local school and exclusion and segregation from games and sport often on overprotection or safety grounds. Transport problems were a major concern, issues here included not being able to attend after school activities, not being able to travel on buses with their friends, doors being too heavy or opening the wrong way, locked, broken or insufficient lifts and the carrying of heavy books on the back of wheelchairs. Access to overseas trips was a special problem. Facilities issues included narrow corridors, limited classroom space, heights of tables, desks and laboratory equipment. Other matters noted in

---

12 Ibid, at para. 4.1.1.

13 Ibid, at p 47.

14 [2001] FMCA 18.

15 E. Burgess, *Are We Nearly There Yet?: Do teenage wheelchair users think integration has been achieved in secondary schools in the UK? A Survey by Eleni Burgess*, Whizz-Kidz (Stockport: No Limits Millennium Award Project, 2003), at p 3.

the survey were the rescheduling of classes, poor provision of physiotherapy, lack of role models, insufficiency of education about disability and insufficiency of sex education.[16]

The United Kingdom Disability Legislation

The European Convention on Human Rights 1950 is given effect in the UK through the Human Rights Act 1998. This allows the enforcement of Article 2 of the Protocol 1, which provides that no person is to be denied the right to education. Article 14 seeks to ensure that the rights and freedoms set out in the Convention (including education) shall be secured without discrimination. The extension of the Disability Discrimination Act 1995 to education, as described below, has provided more specific remedies to disabled people and obligations on school authorities.

Defining Disability

There is a general duty owed to children by local authorities under section 17 of the Children Act 1989 to safeguard and promote the welfare of children in need, promote their upbringing by their families and provide appropriate services. This Act also defines disabled children as being in need (section 17(10)). Under section 17(11), a child is disabled if he or she is blind, deaf or dumb or suffers from mental disorder of any kind or is substantially and permanently handicapped by illness, injury or congenital deformity or other prescribed disability.

The Disability Discrimination Act 1995 describes disability in section 1 as a physical or mental impairment which has a substantial and long-term adverse effect on the person's ability to carry out normal day-to-day activities (as defined in Schedule 1). Under Schedule 1, an impairment is long-term if, inter alia, it lasts for or is likely to last for at least 12 months.

Special Educational Needs

The *Special Educational Needs Code of Practice*, referred to above, establishes the following practice for, inter alios, disabled children, who have been recognised as having needs that are additional to or different from those provided by the school. If a teacher identifies a child a having special educational needs, he or she may wish to place the child on 'school action.' This identifies the need and if the school is able, it can provide such services that would support the child. This service may be co-ordinated by the Special Education Needs Co-ordinator (SENCO) at the school and may be monitored to assess the success of this process using an Individual Education Plan (IEP). If the school finds that the

---

16 Ibid, at pp 6-16.

child has further SEN, 'school action plus' may be considered. This is where the school asks for outside bodies to provide information to enable other strategies to be put into place to support the child's further needs. If a child is placed on 'school action plus', a new IEP will be created.

If the school or parents identify that the above actions are not supporting the child, the local education authority (LEA) can be asked to assess the child for a statement, a document for which provision is made by section 324 of the Education Act 1996. Subsection (1) requires an LEA to make and maintain a statement of special educational needs where, following an assessment and any representations made by the parents, it considers that 'it is necessary for the [LEA] to determine the special educational provision which any learning difficulty [the child] may have calls for.' Under subsections (3) and (4) the statement is to contain details of the authority's assessment of the child's special educational needs and specify the special educational provision to be made for the purpose of meeting those needs. It must state generally the type of school or other institution which the LEA considers would be appropriate.

Section 316 of the 1996 Act establishes a duty to educate children who have special educational needs but no statement in mainstream schools. Those with statements must also be educated in a mainstream school, unless this is incompatible with the wishes of the parent, or the provision of efficient education for other children.[17] One concern is that the section 316 obligation for mainstreaming may create pressure to remove special schools where there still may remain a need for them for some disabled children. They provide specialist education that mainstream schools would be unable to give. It is important that all disabled children have the opportunity of inclusion, however the need for this form of special education must still be recognised.

The Special Educational Needs Tribunal (SENT) has been re-named by the Special Educational Needs and Disability Act 2001 as the Special Educational Needs and Disability Tribunal (SENDIST). An appeal can be made to this tribunal if, inter alia, parents are unhappy with the contents of a statement, or if they wish to appeal against refusal of the LEA to assess or make a statement. The appeal right also applies to amendments to statements. The tribunal's decision is binding in relation to either the LEA or the parents.

Discrimination in Schools

As discussed below, the amendments made by the 2001 Act brought education within disability discrimination law in the United Kingdom. Nevertheless, disability issues were litigated in a school context prior to this change. In *White v Clitheroe Royal Grammar School*[18] Tom White claimed that Clitheroe Royal Grammar School had discriminated by excluding him from attending a water

---

17 s 316(3).

18 Preston County Court http://www.drc-gb.org/thelaw/judgementdetails.asp?id=12.

sports holiday because of his diabetes. This claim was pursued as a breach of section 19 of the Disability Discrimination Act 1995, which made it unlawful to discriminate on disability grounds in relation to the provision of services. Another claim based on a student exchange with a German school was rejected in earlier proceedings because at that time the Act did not apply to education. This exclusion was held not to apply to the water sports holiday. The school claimed that its decision concerning Tom White was not on disability grounds but because of alleged irresponsible behaviour on a previous trip relating to his diabetes management. This reason was not accepted by Judge Ashton, it being found that the feared consequence was 'inextricably related to the disability.'[19] He also found that his 'irresponsibility' had been introduced after the decision to exclude him from the trip. [20]As to whether the decision was justified, Ashton J stated:

> I find that the initial decision was fatally flawed in the manner in which it was taken and thereafter the School adopted a defensive stance and simply confirmed the decision. There was no involvement of Tom or his parents in the decision making process, the matters held against him were never put to him for an explanation and there was no serious attempt at a risk assessment taking into account the nature of the holiday and the medical realities. A climate of blame was used to justify a decision that would avoid a repeat of the earlier frightening incident. The belief that exclusion was justified could not be said to be based on a reasonably held opinion that it was necessary in order not to endanger Tom's health or safety.[21]

The judge was also critical of a school policy which left it to the teacher to decide whether to take a disabled student on such a trip which would then be supported by the headteacher. Such a policy could not amount to justification in law because the Act itself requires a reasonably held opinion, not delegation to staff without setting decision making criteria.[22]

The Disability Discrimination Act 1995 has been amended by the Special Educational Needs and Disability Act 2001. Section 28A(1) covers admission to schools and makes it unlawful for the body responsible for a school to discriminate against a disabled child in relation to admission arrangements, the terms on which a place is offered or by refusing or deliberately omitting to accept an application. Section 28A(2) covers post enrolment discrimination and prohibits discrimination against a disabled pupil in education or associated services. Under s 28A(4) it is unlawful to discriminate against a disabled pupil by excluding him or her from the school, whether permanently or temporarily.

Discrimination is defined by section 28B as less favourable treatment for a reason relating to the disability, provided that the treatment in question cannot be shown to be justified. The section places an onus on the responsible body to

---

19 Ibid, at para 35.
20 Ibid, at para 38.
21 Ibid, at para 42.
22 Ibid, at para 46.

prove that the conduct was justified. Section 28C requires schools to take such steps as are reasonable to ensure that disabled students are not placed at a substantial disadvantage in comparison with non disabled persons. However this is somewhat weakened by section 28C(2), which provides that responsible bodies for schools are not required to remove or alter a physical feature or provide auxiliary aids or services. Australian cases dealing with unjustifiable hardship considered below may be of value to litigants seeking to discover the meaning of justified conduct and reasonableness under these two sections. Given the onus in sections 28B and 28C, schools need to consider very carefully matters such as preventing students travelling on school excursions with their classmates or denying disabled students access to the school outside teaching hours where this is not the case for non disabled pupils. Mention should also be made of section 28D, which requires local education authorities to prepare accessibility strategies for disabled students relating to the school curriculum, physical environment, and the delivery of information.

In the past, the SENT/SENDIST has considered many appeals in regard to statements. These have included matters such as LEAs seeking to discontinue a statement and parents wishing for it to continue; the support being included within a statement but not in reality occurring; and parents disagreeing with certain parts of a statement, including some of the child's needs not having been identified within the statement. As noted, the SENDIST's extended jurisdiction now enables it to deal with claims of unlawful discrimination under the relevant provisions of the 1995 Act.[23] The tribunal has not, however, been given the power to award compensation. Its main power is to make such order as it considers reasonable in the circumstances.[24] The tribunal may strike out a discrimination complaint if it does do not consider the complainant's condition to amount to a disability, but in one recent case the High Court was not satisfied that the tribunal, which had exercised this power, had made a proper assessment of a boy who had Asperger's Syndrome with features of dyspraxia and attention deficit hyperactivity disorder (ADHD) and ordered that that a fresh tribunal should re-consider the matter.[25]

The Disability Rights Commission lists recent discrimination matters that have gone to the SENDIST. These include:

- the wearing of cotton trousers by a pupil where this was against school policy and it has been alleged that the existing uniform was exacerbating a medical condition;[26]

---

23 s.28I.

24 Ibid, sub-s.(3).

25 *R (H) v Chair of the Special Educational Needs Tribunal, R School* [2004] EWHC 981.

26 http://www.drc-gb.org/thelaw/casedetails.asp?category=legal&id=398&cat=-6.

- a claim for additional time to complete an examination where a student has specific learning difficulties;[27]

- the punishment of a child with Tourette's syndrome and Attention Deficit Hyperactivity Disorder for behavioural matters relating to the disability;[28]

- the exclusion of a child with development delay and learning difficulties from various school activities including school trips and the Christmas plays. This matter went to SENDIST and various orders have been made in favour of the child;[29]

- the punishing of a child with a disability for wearing non uniform shoes;[30]

- the exclusion of a child with epilepsy.[31]

There has also been a county court decision of some interest. In *Ford-Shubrock v Governing Body of St Dominic's Sixth Form College*[32] McGrath J held in interlocutory proceedings that a 16-year-old boy, Anthony Ford-Shubrook, suffering from cerebral palsy and in a wheelchair, should be admitted to a school. The school objected on health and safety grounds, arguing that he would not safely be able to attend classes on the first floor. His parents had responded to this concern with an offer of a stair-climbing wheelchair. McGrath J found that the interim injunction should be granted because the risk of injustice if the injunction were refused sufficiently outweighed the risk of injustice if it were granted. Specifically there was a chance that the boy would miss a whole year of school, or could be delayed in gaining admission elsewhere and be forced to catch up. From the school's perspective McGrath J thought that, at most, the grant of the injunction would amount to a temporary inconvenience. Noting that the claimant had put forward convincing arguments that he had a real chance of success, the judge stated:

> The claimant has reached a certain stage in his education and in my judgment, particularly bearing in mind the disabilities which he has fought to overcome and which will face him for the rest of his life, it is important for him, he has a real need to continue the education in his chosen field and to have that education delivered at the right time.[33]

---

27 http://www.drc-gb.org/thelaw/casedetails.asp?category=legal&id=429&cat=-6.
28 http://www.drc-gb.org/thelaw/casedetails.asp?category=legal&id=517&cat=-6.
29 *Buniak v Jenny Hammond Primary School*: http://www.drc-gb.org/thelaw/casedetails.asp?category=legal&id=453&cat=-6.
30 http://www.drc-gb.org/thelaw/casedetails.asp?category=legal&id=519&cat=-6.
31 http://www.drc-gb.org/thelaw/casedetails.asp?category=legal&id=516&cat=-6.
32 Manchester County Court, MA315699 27 August, 2003.
33 Ibid, at para 29.

The decision demonstrates the critical importance of the use of interlocutory proceedings in disability cases. In this particular matter, the decision literally opened the door for the wheelchair user, thereby allowing the respective concerns of both parties to be tested in the school. Subsequently the matter was settled and an appeal against the granting of the injunction was withdrawn on the basis that funding of a temporary accessible classroom would be granted from an external source until a lift could be installed.[34]

The Australian Law

Discrimination on various grounds, including disability, is covered in State and Federal legislation in Australia. At a Federal level, the Human Rights and Equal Opportunity Commission (HREOC) is charged with the task of dealing with discrimination complaints. Our coverage concentrates on the relevant Federal legislation, the Disability Discrimination Act (DDA) 1992 (Cth), though some cases described have arisen under state legislation.

Section 4 of the Act contains a very broad definition of 'disability': this includes total or partial loss of the person's bodily or mental functions or a part of the body and the presence in the body of organisms causing or capable of causing disease or illness, malfunction, malformation and disfigurement. Importantly for present purposes is the inclusion, in the definition, of a disorder or malfunction that results in the person learning differently from a person without the disorder or malfunction, and illness or disease that affects a person's thought processes, perception of reality, emotions or judgment or that results in disturbed behaviour. Basser and Jones[35] comment positively on the flexibility in the definition. They cite the example of *Kitt v Tourism Commission*,[36] where it was found that epilepsy was not covered by the New South Wales legislation. They state:

> The broad general definition in the DDA means that there is no need to focus on the person bringing the action, and this allows decision makers to concentrate on the real issue- the actions of the alleged discriminator....Minimising the need to involve medical or other professionals in claims of discrimination is also of great significance to people with disabilities. One of the greatest hurdles confronting people with disabilities has been the medicalisation of their lives. This has led to people been confused with, and reduced to, their biological or physiological condition.[37]

---

34 http://www.drc-gb.org/thelaw/casedetails.asp?category=legal&id=445&cat=-6.

35 L.A. Basser, and M. Jones, 'The Disability Discrimination Act 1992 (Cth): A Three-Dimensional Approach to Operationalising Human Rights' (2002) *Melbourne University Law Review* 26, 254–258, at p 260.

36 (1987) EOC 92-196.

37 Above n 35, at pp 261-262.

This Act divides discrimination into two prohibited categories, direct and indirect. Direct and indirect discrimination are equally prohibited. Under section 5, direct discrimination occurs where, because of the disability, the discriminator treats or proposes to treat the aggrieved person less favourably than, in circumstances that are the same or are not materially different, the discriminator treats or would treat a person without the disability. Section 6 defines indirect discrimination as occurring when the discriminator requires the aggrieved person to comply with a requirement or condition with which a substantially higher proportion of persons without the disability comply or are able to comply, which is not reasonable having regard to the circumstances of the case, and with which the aggrieved person does not or is not able to comply.

The Act concentrates on effects; there is no need to prove any intention to discriminate.[38] Accordingly, motivations, even 'good' motivations, are irrelevant. Partial accommodation does not excuse discrimination.[39] On the other hand, schools may not have been told that a disability exists. In *Lynch v Sacred Heart College*[40] the Equal Opportunity Board of Victoria rejected a claim based on temporary impairment asserted by a student who claimed to have been sexually assaulted and subsequently was not re-enrolled in her school. The school argued that it had not been informed of the impairment, nor should it reasonably have been aware of it, and that there was nothing to connect her behaviour to her impairment. The Board accepted these arguments, ruling against the child.

In relation to discrimination in education, section 22 of the Act makes it unlawful to discriminate by refusing or failing to accept the person's application for admission as a student; or in the terms or conditions on which it is prepared to admit the person as a student. Furthermore, it is unlawful for an educational authority to discriminate against a student on the ground of the student's disability, or a disability of any of the student's associates, by denying the student access, or limiting his or her access, to any benefit provided by the educational authority; or by expelling the student; or by subjecting the student to any other detriment.

The most obvious case of direct discrimination is the refusal of a school to admit a child because of his or her disability. Cases described below demonstrate this category. A good example of indirect discrimination, provided by Blatch, is a school policy that prevents the use of computers in examinations being used to the disadvantage of a disabled child who could not write but could use a computer.[41] A case where indirect discrimination was not proven in a school context was *Martinovic v Ministry of Education*,[42] where the mother of two

---

38 *Garity v Commonwealth Bank of Australia* [1999] EOC 92-966.

39 *McNiell v Commonwealth* [1995] EOC 92-71.

40 (1995) EOC 92-724.

41 P. Blatch, 'Special Education Issues' in *School Law-1997 National Seminar Papers* (Sydney: Legal & Accounting Seminars Pty Ltd, 1997), paper 6, 1–28, at p 8.

42 (1989) EOC 92-264.

disabled boys sought special teachers at her home on an individual basis for the boys. One boy was deaf, and the other had speech problems. In relation to both children there was no evidence that any other children had been provided with one-to-one teaching by the Ministry of Education, and indeed to offer the children such a benefit would discriminate against other children with similar disabilities. Such home based teaching was not found to be in the interests of the boys and would decrease the benefits of school integration. The Equal Opportunity Board of Victoria dismissed the complaint.

The Act, in sections 37 and 38, also outlaws the harassment of a student with a disability or the associate of a person with a disability by a member of staff of a school.

Australian Discrimination Cases

It is instructive to examine a number of cases that have been litigated in Australia. There is not much case law in the UK in this field in the context of education, because disability legislation directly applicable to schools is only of recent origin. The cases below may give disabled students in Britain, their schools and indeed their lawyers an indication of the context in which disability cases may arise and the ways in which courts and tribunals deal with such matters. The cases also demonstrate some shortcomings in Australian law and the steep learning curve that schools in both countries will need to traverse in their understanding and application of disability law.

Admission and Facilities Issues

Hills Grammar School v Human Rights and Equal Opportunity Commission[43] is the best known case concerning access to school for disabled children. The applicants were the parents of a 6-year-old girl, Scarlett Finney, who had spina bifida. In early March 1997, her parents sought enrolment for her in the Hills Grammar School. The application disclosed her spina bifida, the need for level walkways and wheelchair accessibility. Later in March, the child and her parents were interviewed, when further information was given as to her condition, including additional sources of information that the school could follow up. In August 1997 the school notified the parents that her enrolment had been denied, the school stating that they did not have adequate resources to meet her special needs. The parents immediately filed a complaint with HREOC and in November and December 1998 there was a 6-day hearing, which included evidence from the girl and her mother. In July 1999, the Commissioner found that Hills Grammar had unlawfully and directly discriminated against Scarlett, and that the defence of

43 [2000] FCA 658 (18 May 2000).

unjustifiable hardship had not been made out.[44] The school immediately sought judicial review of the Commissioner's decision and orders setting it aside. In May 2000 Tamberlin J of the Federal Court refused to grant these orders and found in favour of the child. The critical aspect of the case was the definition of 'unjustifiable hardship.' Section 22(4) provides:

> (4) This section does not render it unlawful to refuse or fail to accept a person's application for admission as a student at an educational institution where the person, if admitted as a student by the educational authority, would require services or facilities that are not required by students who do not have a disability and the provision of which would impose unjustifiable hardship on the educational authority.

Commissioner Innes found that this sub-section only applied to refusal of enrolment.[45] Later he described the concept:

> As set out in the decision of *Scott v Telstra* the concept of 'unjustifiable hardship' connotes much more than just hardship on the respondent. The objects of the Act make it clear that elimination of discrimination as far as possible is the legislation's purpose. Considered in this context, it is reasonable to expect that the school should have to undergo some hardship in accepting Scarlett's enrolment. It is clear from the evidence that this would have occurred, as Scarlett required services and facilities not required by other students. The nub of the issue is whether such hardship was unjustifiable.[46]

In his finding that, on the facts, unjustifiable hardship had not been proven, the Commissioner's inquiry was a broad one, covering a range of personnel, curriculum, financial and other matters.[47] The Commissioner also considered the benefits and detriments of Scarlett attending the school. He found that the former included the school setting which would assist her learning, its multi-disciplinary approach which would help her management skills, and the integrated

---

44 *Finney v Hills Grammar School,* HREOC decision No. H98/60 (20 July 1999).

45 Ibid, at p 46. The Australian Productivity Commission has recommended that this aspect of the law be changed and that the unjustifiable hardship exception be extended to post enrolment matters: *Review of the Disability Discrimination Act 1992* Productivity Commission Draft Report (2003) at p 249. The draft *Disability Standards for Education 2004*, if approved, will make this extension: Cl 3.4.

46 Ibid, at p 48.

47 The evidence ranged from an examination of the: willingness of teachers to accept responsibility; additional training of teachers required; toileting needs and toilet modifications required; mobility; classroom assistance; accessibility of the school generally; excursion requirements; curriculum modifications required; availability of funding support; financial circumstances of the school; estimated costs incurred by the school to accommodate her; period of application for schooling at the school; information provided by the parents; level of inquiries made by the school; and availability of alternate schools.

kindergarten to year 12 approach. He noted that it would offer opportunities not available at the school she was attending. He also considered the benefits for her family, including proximity and a private non- denominational education. There were, in his opinion, benefits for the school also, including additional government funding, better accessibility for all, and better qualified teachers flowing from additional teacher training. He could see specific benefits for the school community in the inclusionary effects of Scarlett's enrolment and in having integrated schools generally.

Against these benefits he weighed the detriments. There were additional costs, but not of the magnitude argued by the school, which had been 'grossly overstated.' These included the need for a part time teacher's aide and capital costs for access modifications, though costs would be offset to some degree by government funding. Modifications to the school curriculum and school environment would be minor and of little impact on the character of the school. He found possible additional fee costs to parents of other children, but that these would be a very minor detriment to each family. Some extra work would be required of the teachers. All of these matters constituted hardship, but not unjustifiable hardship.

In his review of Commissioner Innes' reasons, Tamberlin J explained the Court's approach to the interpretation of anti-discrimination legislation. He found that the legislation is 'beneficial in character and is designed to eliminate a perceived social evil. It should therefore be approached and construed liberally and not in a technical or narrow sense.'[48] Speaking of HREOC itself, he noted that in reviewing the reasons for a decision of such an administrative decision maker 'regard must be had to substance, rather than form of reasons, having regard to the many variegated and ingenious ways in which discrimination can be achieved.'[49] The unjustifiable hardship test itself 'requires a balancing exercise between benefits and detriment to all parties in order to decide whether there is likely to be unjustifiable hardship in all the relevant circumstances.'[50]

The Commissioner was held to have applied the correct approach in finding that unjustifiable hardship had not existed. No reviewable error of law was shown in the reasons for the decision. Tamberlin J noted in particular the Commissioner's finding that the amount of money required to make the adjustments at the school was only a small fraction of the A$1.1million estimated by a consultant the school had employed to investigate the matter; furthermore, the Commissioner was not obliged to put an exact figure on this amount.[51] In particular the consultant 'did not appear to have any direct experience of the needs of a handicapped pupil' and had made certain incorrect assumptions, including the need for several accessible toilets and complete access to all parts of

48 [2000] FCA 658 (18 May 2000), at p 10.

49 Ibid.

50 Ibid.

51 [2000] FCA 658 (18 May 2000), at p 14.

the school by ramping and had costed accordingly.[52] This level of work was not required. In its curriculum the school had a policy of overall access to the school; accordingly, the school argued that the Commissioner had not properly taken into account the unjustifiable hardship it claimed would result from curriculum modifications needed to take account of the pupil's disability. The judge dismissed this claim, finding that the Commissioner had specifically found that, though some curriculum modification was needed, this was not unduly burdensome, and there would not be a great impact on the school.[53]

In a third determination, *Finney v Hills Grammar School,*[54] Scarlett Finney was awarded damages of $42,628. This was made up of $37,628 for loss of educational opportunity, based on the school's fees over a seven year period, that is, covering her primary education (a seven year period in New South Wales) and a further $5000 in general damages.

In another recent case in Australia, *Stephanie Travers by her next friend, Wendy Travers v State of New South Wales*,[55] a magistrates court made an award against a school of $6250 with costs to a disabled child who had spina bifida. It was accepted that Stephanie Travers had a disability for the purposes of the legislation. The magistrate found that the school had come to the incorrect view that she did not have a toileting problem and 'excluded from consideration as "the nearest accessible toilet," the disabled toilet in "E" block which she could have used without any reasonable apprehension of disturbance to the one other user of that toilet.'[56] She was not found to need a disabled toilet per se, but the school, in not readily making the closest toilet available to her, which happened to be the disabled toilet, discriminated against her. The school was found not to have acted maliciously, there being a misapprehension as to the pupil's needs to have a toilet available within 12 seconds of her classroom. Of interest is that the school's hesitancy in allowing her access to the disabled toilet was partly out of its concern for infection of another child with spina bifida who needed that specific toilet for catheterisation purposes. Again the magistrate found in favour of the pupil; the school's concerns about a sterile environment were not born out by expert evidence and could have been met by a lockable cupboard.[57]

Not all cases will result in successful outcomes for the child. In *L v Minister for Education in the State of Queensland*,[58] a child had an intellectual impairment which affected her emotionally, her communication skills, and her eating and hygiene. She was assessed by the department as requiring the highest level of support and was eventually enrolled in a mainstream school. Difficulties arose,

52 Ibid.

53 Ibid.

54 (2000) EOC 93-087 HREOC.

55 [2001] FMCA 18.

56 Ibid, at para. 71.

57 Ibid, at para. 67.

58 (1996) EOC 92-787.

and following a further assessment by a guidance officer, it was decided she would need special education support in another school. Further behavioural difficulties led to the child's suspension and efforts were made to relocate her to a special school. These were resisted by her mother who complained to the Anti-Discrimination Tribunal of Queensland. Evidence was given in her favour suggesting that her retention in the mainstream school would be better for her language skills and social skills, and for increasing tolerance in society towards the disabled.

The school argued there was no discrimination, claiming that the pupil's behaviour had caused the suspension, and that the outcome would have been the same as for a child without the disability. The school also argued unjustifiable hardship. The first argument was rejected, the Tribunal finding that all her actions and behaviour were characteristic of a child with that impairment, and were not to be separated from it.[59] Accordingly the school had discriminated against her. The suspension was not an action designed to protect public health. On the question of unjustifiable hardship, the Tribunal found against the child:

> I consider that the demands that would be imposed upon the teacher involved, pending resolution of L's present behavioural problems, are of themselves such as to constitute unjustifiable hardship.... Costs alone would not necessarily persuade me that unjustifiable hardship existed; the greater problem is that even with that level of resource, as long as L remains in the regular classroom, disruption of other children is inevitable, at least until her skills are improved. Even the process of intervention, with withdrawal of her from the classroom when she is noisy or requires toileting, must of itself be disruptive to other children.....[60]

A very bitter disability dispute was, however, resolved in favour of a child and her parents in *Murphy v State of New South Wales*.[61] Discrimination was found to have occurred through the actions of a school principal against both the child and her parents. The Commissioner made a finding that the communication between the parties had effectively ceased, and spoke of an 'obvious and continued acrimony between the relevant adults.' In his assessment of the mother of the child the Commissioner said:

> Ms Murphy, an obviously intelligent woman, was a powerful and articulate advocate within the school community and elsewhere for people with disabilities, especially her own daughter... She presented as one who was deeply committed to the cause of her

---

59 On this matter compare the later approach of the majority in the High Court decision in *Purvis v New South Wales (Department of Education and Training)* [2003] HCA (11 November, 2003), considered below.

60 Ibid, at p 78,821.

61 No. H98/73 HREOC 27 March 2000; http://www.hreoc.gov.au/disability_rights/decisions/comdec/2000/DD000040.htm.

> daughter's right to be educated in spite of her severe disability. She became deeply resentful of a regime which she perceived 'found us to be problem people.'[62]

The child in this case, Sian Murphy, had spinal muscular atrophy. Complaints were successfully made against the school that it had unnecessarily delayed her entrance to kindergarten by some 10 months and accordingly had discriminated against her by treating her less favourably than other children without the disability in an enrolment process. After much acrimony between the principal, Mr Houston, and the parents, a gate allowing convenient disability access was padlocked by the school. When the mother strenuously objected to these actions the school called the police and had her removed. The Commissioner was 'satisfied that the gate closure and the denial of access was treatment of Sian which was less favourable than the treatment afforded able bodied children who had a variety of alternatives provided for them so that they could access the school.'[63] A complaint of victimisation in this case, however, failed: the Commissioner was not satisfied that the acts of Mr Houston were acts of victimisation, but rather were 'the unfortunate and final reflection of an obvious inability of the school principal and his leadership to properly deal over a long period with the special needs of a seriously and progressively disabled child and the reasonable concerns of her devoted and caring parents.'[64] The parents were held to be the victims of unlawful discrimination in breach of section 24(1)(c) of the Act. Under section 22 they were held to be persons aggrieved under section 69 by the conduct of the school. An award of $25,000 was made in damages and the New South Wales Department of Education was forced to apologise in writing to the child and the parents.

Behavioural Issues and Disability

The leading Australian case on behavioural issues and disability in schools is *Purvis v New South Wales (Department of Education and Training)*.[65] This case demonstrates the point made earlier by Forlin and Forlin[66] that a critical issue is whether the behaviour is a direct result of the disability. Daniel Hoggin, the pupil in this case, had suffered a severe brain injury at 7 months. He was also a ward of the state in the foster care of Mr and Mrs Purvis. He commenced high school on 8 April 1997. He was suspended on 24 April, and then again on 9 May for abusing a teachers aide and kicking another student. A number of similar

---

62 Ibid.

63 Ibid.

64 Ibid.

65 [2003] HCA (11 November, 2003).

66 C. Forlin, C. and P. Forlin, 'The Legal Implications of Including Students with Disabilities in Regular Schools' in M. Hauritz, C. Samford & S. Blencowe, *Justice for People with Disabilities* (Sydney: Federation Press, 1998) 109–126, at p 120.

incidents occurred in June and July. On 30 July he kicked a teacher's aide and in September he punched an aide in the back. A decision was taken to enrol him in the special unit at another high school, however this was contested by his foster parents who indicated their intention to re-enrol him in the original school. The principal indicated it would exclude him 'because of his concerns for the health and safety of the staff and students at the school.'[67] The foster parents complained to HREOC, which found that discrimination had occurred in breach of sections 5 and 22(2) of the Disability Discrimination Act and awarded the complainant $49,000. This was reversed in the Federal Court. The complainants then appealed to the full Federal Court. In rejecting this appeal largely on safety grounds and duty of care grounds,[68] the Court found that the child's behaviour was a consequence of the disability rather than any part of the disability.[69] This was the issue which divided the High Court in the subsequent appeal.

The High Court, by a majority, rejected the appeal from this decision. Finding against the child, Gummow, Hayne and Heydon JJ held that there was no need to distinguish the cause of a person's disability and the effects or consequences of it. In their minds section 5 raised two questions:

> (i) How, in *those* circumstances, would the educational authority have treated a person without Daniel's disability?
> (ii) If Daniel's treatment was less favourable than the treatment that would be given to a person without the disability, was that because of Daniel's disability?[70]

They found that he was not treated less favourably. Callinan J delivered a separate judgment also rejecting the appeal. In so doing he supported the 'comparator' analysis described above.[71] Chief Justice Gleeson encapsulated the views of the majority:

> The fallacy in the appellant's argument lies in the contention that, because the pupil's violent behaviour was disturbed, and resulted from a disorder, s 5 always requires, and only permits, a comparison between his treatment and the treatment that would be given to a pupil who is not violent. Rather it requires a comparison with the treatment that would be given, in the same circumstances, to a pupil whose behaviour was not disturbed behaviour resulting from a disorder. Such a comparison requires no feat of imagination. There are pupils who have no disorder, and are not disturbed, who

---

67 *State of NSW (Dept of Education) v HREOC & Purvis obo Hoggan* (2001) EOC ¶93-171, at para 17.

68 *Purvis obo Hoggan v State of NSW (Department of Education & Training) & Anor* (2002) EOC ¶93-205 at para 25.

69 Ibid, at para 28.

70 [2003] HCA (11 November, 2003), at paras 224, 225.

71 Ibid, at para 273.

behave in a violent manner towards others. They would probably be suspended, and, if the conduct persisted, expelled, in less time than the pupil in this case.[72]

A powerful minority judgment was delivered by Kirby and McHugh JJ. The issues as they saw them were:

(i) Did 'disability' as defined in the Act include the behavioural manifestation of a disorder? These judges found that it did, and included the functional limitations that resulted from the underlying condition,[73] a proposition which they claimed had been supported by definitions of disability in international organisations such as the World Health Organisation;[74]

(ii) Did the Act contain an obligation to provide reasonable accommodation for persons with a disability? These judges followed the Federal Court in finding that it did not. This proposition was also supported in the judgment of Gummow, Hayne and Heydon JJ;

(iii) Did the comparator for determining whether there had been 'less favourable' treatment of the disabled person have that person's characteristics? The minority judgment thought not: indeed they stated that to do so would defeat the purpose of the Act.[75] They held that the appropriate comparator was *not* a student with behavioural problems,[76] and it was erroneous to attribute the behavioural characteristics of Daniel to the comparator;[77]

(iv) What is the correct test of causation in determining whether a person has been discriminated against 'on the ground of' his or her disability?[78] These judges agreed with the Commissioner who had found that, because the pupil had been treated less favourably because of his behaviour, (held to be a manifestation of his disability) he had been discriminated against on the ground of his disability.[79]

It can be seen that the majority and minority took very different views of the Australian disability legislation. No doubt schools and school teachers may gain some solace from the decision because it greatly strengthens the hand of the

72 Ibid, at para 11.
73 Ibid, at para 67.
74 Ibid, at para 74.
75 Ibid, at para 130.
76 Ibid, at para 134.
77 Ibid, at para 131.
78 Ibid, at para 26.
79 Ibid, at para 167.

school. However, it also lays a foundation for watering down Australian discrimination legislation, as was pointed out in the minority judgment.

The issues relating to disability and behaviour are not easy to resolve, as this divided decision so clearly points out. One can imagine a better time when education authorities will meet their legal obligations in such matters as wheelchair access, which are relatively clear on a factual basis: either access is provided or it is not. In relation to disabilities that are not obviously physical, additional complications arise, as seen in this judgment. Here the most difficult issue was the definition of the disability itself.

Behavioural issues also arose in the Victorian Administrative Appeals Tribunal decision in *Zygorodimos v Department of Education and Training*.[80] The Deputy President directly applied the decision in *Purvis* to a case where a boy had epilepsy. The proper comparator was held to be a boy without epilepsy who behaved in the same manner as the boy with epilepsy.[81] The boy was also profoundly deaf and was attending a school for deaf and hearing impaired children. The allegation was one of discrimination because he had been moved from one class to another. His behaviour had included throwing of objects, damaging plants, lying on the floor and refusing to get up, screaming and shouting in class, tantrums, and uncontrollable crying. There was also evidence that the teacher could not cope with the student in her class, and that this was one of the reasons why he was transferred. Discrimination was not proven on the facts and the Tribunal dismissed the complaint, not a surprising in the light of *Purvis*.

The *Purvis* test has also been recently applied in the Federal Court in relation to workplace disability discrimination. In *Y v Human Rights and Equal Opportunity Commission*[82] the person's condition had been 'described variously as an obsessive compulsive disorder, a personality disorder with behavioural implications, a paranoid psychosis and residual schizophrenia with an avoidant personality disorder.'[83] The Human Rights and Equal Opportunity Commission had found that his 'mental condition manifested itself in abusive, hostile, argumentative and over-litigious behaviour, including inappropriate behaviour towards women'; and in 'unacceptable behaviour on at least eleven occasions between 1979 and 1994' that suggested 'a reasonable belief in those who deal with' him that 'he has a propensity to violence.'[84] Finklestein J, citing *Purvis*, found that the Human Rights and Equal Opportunity Commission had erred in finding that 'to discriminate against a person suffering from a mental disorder on account of the conduct caused by the disorder was discrimination.'[85]

---

80 [2004] VCAT 128 (3 February 2004).

81 Ibid, at para.98.

82 [2004] FCA 184 (4 March, 2004).

83 Ibid, at para 1.

84 Ibid, at para 20.

85 Ibid, at para 28.

The issues surrounding disability and behaviour were canvassed in the Australian Productivity Commission's recent draft report on the *Disability Discrimination Act*. The Commission recommended that the definition of disability should be amended to ensure that it includes, inter alia, behaviour that is a symptom or manifestation of a disability.[86] This approach follows that recommended by HREOC in its submission to the Review and would, if followed in legislation, have the effect of reversing *Purvis*.[87]

Comparison with the United Kingdom The Australian outcome strengthens the hand of the school. More favour is shown to the disabled schoolchild in the UK. Comparing the UK and Australian legislation in *Purvis,* Gummow, Hayne and Heydon JJ stated:

> The principal focus of the [Australian] Act... is on ensuring equality of treatment. In this respect it differs significantly from other, more recent, forms of disability discrimination legislation. In particular... unlike the *Disability Discrimination Act* 1995 (UK) ('the 1995 UK Act'), the *Americans with Disabilities Act of 1990* ('the ADA') or the European Community Directive for 'establishing a general framework for equal treatment in employment and occupation', the Act does *not* explicitly oblige persons to treat disabled persons differently from others in the community. The Act does not, for example, contain provisions equivalent to ss 5 and 6 and ss 28B to 28G of the 1995 UK Act which expressly oblige employers and educational authorities to make 'reasonable adjustments' to accommodate disabled persons.[88]

It is at least possible that a UK court could also take the narrow definitional approach adopted in *Purvis* by a narrow selection of the comparator, though early indications discussed below suggest otherwise. The UK's Disability Discrimination Act 1995, in section 28B, uses the words 'less favourable treatment for a reason relating to the disability,' which necessitates a comparator.

The nature of the comparator was canvassed in the UK in *McA Catholic High School v Special Educational Needs and Disability Tribunal.*[89] The school appealed against a decision of the tribunal requiring the school to produce an action plan to deal with the specific needs of austistic children, or those with communication difficulties, and to establish a mentoring system. The child in question (IC) had certain behavioural difficulties and it was these that raised the comparator issue, just as in *Purvis*. The SENDIST had found 'there was discrimination against IC to the extent that he was not given the necessary personal guidance and support within the context of the School pastoral system as

86 *Review of the Disability Discrimination Act 1992*, Productivity Commission Draft Report (1993), Recommendation 9.1, p 216.

87 Ibid, at p 215.

88 [2003] HCA (11 November, 2003) at para 203.

89 [2003] EWHC 3045 (Admin).

he required.'[90] According to the tribunal, the first matter to be decided in determining unlawful discrimination against IC was to establish whether the less favourable treatment complained of was for a reason relating to the child's disability. The school denied this, on the basis that there had been no less favourable treatment because a child without any disability but manifesting the same behaviour would have been excluded permanently from the school. The tribunal found that this was an incorrect test, and noted that the question of less favourable treatment has to be answered in comparison with the school population as a whole who have not misbehaved.

The matter was appealed. In the Administrative Court, Silber J disallowed the appeal. In so doing he applied the decision in *Clark v TDG Limited (Trading as Novocold Limited)*,[91] where the comparator issue had been analysed in a disability discrimination in employment context. When this was applied in a disability in education case he agreed that the proper comparator for the disabled student was a pupil who was neither disabled nor badly behaved. Silber J, referring to the code of practice on schools issued by the Disability Rights Commission under the Act, cited the code's advice concerning the situation where a pupil with Tourette's disease has been banned from a school trip because of her abusive language: 'the comparison has to be made with others who did not use abusive language.'[92]

It can be seen that this is not the approach of the majority in *Purvis*. Indeed Gummow, Hayne and Heydon JJ acknowledged the difference in approach in the UK, and citing *Clark* state:

> In the 1995 UK Act, for example, the focus is not upon the cases of different *persons* (one disabled, one not) in the same or not materially different circumstances. As was pointed out in *Clark v TDG Ltd*, the focus of the 1995 UK Act is much narrower. It looks only to the *reason* for the treatment of the disabled person and then requires comparison with the treatment of 'others to whom that *reason* does *not* or would *not* apply' (emphasis added). That is, it requires identification of why the disabled person was treated as he or she was, and then asks would another, to whom that reason did *not* apply, have been treated in the same way?[93]

The DRC in the Tourette's example from the code of practice, cited above, expressly *and obviously* includes the involuntary swearing as a symptom of the disability. If the identification of the comparator had been as argued by the school before Silber J, the comparator would be the child without a disability who swears and is similarly excluded from school. Accordingly there would be no discrimination, producing a similar outcome to that of the majority in *Purvis*. HREOC in Australia would clearly support the DRC approach and of course

90 Ibid, at para 29.

91 [1999] ICR 951.

92 [2003] EWHC 3045 (Admin), at para 46.

93 [2003] HCA (11 November, 2003), at para 215.

Commissioner Innes made a similar finding in the initial hearing in *Purvis*. But this did not gain support in the Full Federal Court or with the majority in the High Court.

It should be noted that in the UK certain behavioural conditions are expressly excluded from the Act, including those creating a tendency to physical or sexual abuse of other persons.[94] It is submitted that the creation of such physical safety exceptions in legislation is a better approach than that adopted by the majority in *Purvis*, who had safety concerns behind their reasoning, but used those to narrow the definition of disability. The difficulty is that the majority analysis can be used to weaken discrimination legislation generally, a point made strongly in the minority judgment in *Purvis*.

We believe that the UK approach in this area is far more understanding of disability. Legal issues relating to behaviour and disability are less likely to occur in the UK because of differences in the legislation, its interpretation and the special educational needs assessment process. Furthermore the UK's Disability Discrimination Act 1995 gives the code of practice for schools a special quasi-legislative status.[95] In Australia, the government has recently released draft *Disability Standards for Education 2004* under section 31(1)(b) of the Disability Discrimination Act 1992. These standards, when promulgated, will introduce a public health exception in Section 10.4, allowing discrimination 'if the disability is an infectious disease or other condition and it is reasonably necessary to isolate or discriminate to protect the health and welfare of the student with a disability or the health and welfare of others.' It is not clear that this exception would apply to the behavioural matters discussed above: words such as those used in the UK legislation would clarify this.

The Definition of a Child and Exclusion at 18

There has been a series of cases involving disabled people who, having turned 18, have been excluded from further attendance at special schools. For example, in *Re Hamish v Minister for Education of Queensland* [96] the Minister determined that a blind and deaf person was no longer eligible to attend a school for visually handicapped children once he had turned 18. The student claimed that this exclusion was contrary to the Anti-Discrimination Act 1991 (Qld) which, in section 7(1)(f), prohibited discrimination on the ground of age. The case turned on a simple construction of the Education (General Provisions) Act 1989 (Qld), Ambrose J of the Supreme Court of Queensland holding that section 12 of that Act allowed the Minister to exclude a person at 18 years of age.

---

94 *Disability Discrimination Act* 1995 *Part 4 Code of Practice for Schools* (London: Disability Rights Commission, 2002), at p 79.

95 Disability Discrimination Act 1995, s 53(6).

96 (1996) EOC 92-806.

In an earlier decision under the same legislation, *Finn v Minister for Education*[97] the Anti-Discrimination Tribunal of Queensland had granted an interim order allowing an intellectually impaired profoundly deaf student to stay at secondary school while a discrimination complaint was being determined. As an interim matter the Tribunal only had to make its determination on the balance of convenience. In granting the order President Atkinson stated:

> It would be in keeping with the objects of the Anti-Discrimination Act for appropriate post-school options to be available to persons with Vanessa's disability as they are to others in the community. However as there are not, the only alternative is to maintain her in or return her to the school environment.[98]

The decision of Ambrose J in *Hamish* appears technically correct in law, but the facts demonstrate a serious societal shortcoming. The legislation under consideration did not take account of the educational level of the disabled person or whether that person would benefit from further education. The criterion is merely that person's age. Justification advanced for this position by the judge was essentially an economic one: 'a socially acceptable apportionment of educational resources is to be made between different groups in the community' to avoid the 'extraordinary conclusion that persons with the applicant's disability, whatever be their ages would compete with children with similar disabilities for access to special schools...'[99]

This argument ignores the fact that people with certain kinds of intellectual disabilities may not be able to attain the 'normal' knowledge levels of other 18 year olds in the same time frame, and to impose an age test on them is fundamentally unfair. It becomes even more so when evidence is given that such people are in fact, or on occasion, finally, making good educational progress which is suddenly terminated at the age of 18. In *Finn* this point was made very clear in evidence from the student's principal:

> The last two years have seen her blossom. She is extremely interested in her learning environment and very keen to explore.... There are currently no post-school options for Vanessa who lives in a government institution, but as she is at an important learning stage more input at school level would be valuable.[100]

Another decision, in *State of Victoria v Bacon & Ors*,[101] further highlights the unfairness of educational programs for the disabled that are stopped at age 18. Here the termination of the '18 Plus Transition Program' for mildly intellectually impaired students was challenged under the Equal Opportunity Act 1995 (Vict)

---

97 [1995] QADT 4.

98 Ibid, at p 3.

99 (1996) EOC 92-806, at 78, 965.

100 [1995] QADT 4, at 3.

101 [1998] VICSC 58 (30 April 1998).

on direct and indirect grounds relating to both age and impairment. The matter went to the Court of Appeal,[102] the court upholding the trial judge's finding that the termination of the transition program constituted indirect discrimination under the Victorian legislation:

> [B]y the introduction of the 'age-based policy' the appellant denied to the respondents the benefit of this essential part of the training provided because, as was common ground, they were, or were to be, excluded from the school before they could participate in it. The manner in which the denial of the benefit was effected by the appellant amounted to indirect discrimination.....because it constituted the imposition, or proposed imposition, of a requirement or condition which the respondents, because of their impairment, could not comply with; namely the requirement that to remain at the school beyond the age of 18 years, a student had to be enrolled for the VCE.[103]

An appeal on a second claim that there was direct discrimination on age was upheld by the appeal court, the court finding that all students ultimately had the 'same fate in store,' namely exclusion from the school.

School Transport Issues

This is an area likely to generate further litigation, as justifiable pressure mounts for better access to school buses, a matter raised earlier. Disability issues in relation to transport to school were considered in preliminary proceedings in *Gregor v Department of Education, Department of Infrastructure, & Hopetown Secondary College Council.*[104] Here the parent's complaint against the Department of Infrastructure and the school was that the bus route had been changed in a way that was disadvantageous to their disabled children. There was no ruling on the substantive law in the matter. In *CD on behalf of SD v JK*[105] a 9 year old boy with Down's Syndrome had been allowed to walk to school unaccompanied. The school principal decided to prevent this happening. The matter was resolved through conciliation by the introduction of an independent travel programme for the child.

The Position of the Teacher

This chapter notes but does not consider in detail the liability of teachers under cases such as *Moore v Hampshire County Council*[106] which held that where a school had been informed by a child's parent of a medical condition prohibiting participation in a sporting event, the school had to give effect to the prohibition

---

102 [1998] VICSC 58 (30 April 1998).
103 Ibid. VCE = Victorian Certificate of Education.
104 [1997]VADT 23 (19 June 1997).
105 (1994) EOC 92-558.
106 (1982) 80 LGR 418.

and would be liable for injuries even though the child had misled the school as to the currency of the condition. Similarly, in *Kretschmar v State of Queensland*[107] the school had to take precautions in regard to an intellectually disabled child in activities such as supervised games. Other issues of concern not canvassed in this chapter include the extent to which a school or teacher may become liable if an accident occurs when a disabled child is being manually handled or medication is improperly administered.

The duty of care is onerous and must be exercised in a manner which is not discriminatory.[108] Accordingly, a school which chooses to avoid its tortious liability for physical injury to a disabled child by prohibiting that child from engaging in sport runs very high risk of facing a disability discrimination action. The solution is in a carefully worked out sporting program for the child in full consultation with the child, parents and the school, and an appropriate process in the school for both informing the teachers of the program and ensuring its exercise in a safe and reasonable manner. Furthermore, some lateral thinking on the part of schools may allow safe participation by disabled children in sports programs offered to all children.

Inadequate Explanations

In *Krenske-Carter v Minister for Education*[109] the applicant claimed discrimination in the Equal Opportunity Commission of Western Australia on behalf of his daughter who suffered chronic lupus. He alleged both direct and indirect discrimination against the Minister for Education based on concerns that the daughter had not been allowed to leave the classroom to visit a nurse as necessary. Staff had claimed she had faked an attack to avoid work. Furthermore, it was alleged that bullying by other students had not been adequately dealt with. Further claims were made that she had been forced to play the victim in anti-bullying role-playing exercises and that she had been punished for a minor matter by being required to walk around a tennis court in the hot sun, exacerbating her symptoms. These claims were denied by the school. The Tribunal found that many of these complaints had arisen because her medical condition had not been adequately explained to the school. Nevertheless, the Tribunal found that the role-playing incident had constituted indirect discrimination because the principal had been appraised of bullying related to her chronic lupus at a previous school. The tennis court punishment required her to comply with a policy which would have exacerbated her condition and also constituted indirect discrimination. The student was awarded $4000 in damages.

---

107 (1989) *Australian Torts Reporter* 80-272.

108 See also English cases dealing with claims of negligent misdiagnosis of conditions such as dyslexia *Phelps v Hillingdon LBC* [2002] 2 AC 619 and *Robinson v St Helens Metropolitan Borough Counci*l [2002] EWCA Civ 109.

109 (2003) EOC 93-256, p 227.

Conclusion

Jones and Basser-Marks have commented in relation to anti-discrimination law:

> The problem remains that anti-discrimination law is reactive and does little to address the underlying causes of the problem - the negative cultural response to disability generally and to people with disabilities in particular. Anti-discrimination legislation is no more a protection against the abuse of people with disabilities than compulsory sterilisation. What is needed are strategies to change these cultural and social responses and to facilitate the inclusion of all people in our community.[110]

We would agree with their comments in relation to negative cultural responses, though we would trust that such attitudes will change more rapidly in the future than they have in the past. Naturally, law cannot be a cure-all for negative attitudes. The work of Eleni Burgess cited earlier in this chapter suggests that disabled children in wheelchairs are still encountering many physical and cultural barriers. On the other hand, the well publicised disability discrimination litigation involving the pupil in *Hills Grammar School v Human Rights and Equal Opportunity Commission* gained very strong public support in the press for that child in her battle with the school. In this way schools can be placed under enormous pressure to maintain their good standing in their communities, and cannot afford an image of exclusion. In our view, this strategy of the exercise of legal rights combined with the ready use of the press to gain publicity, provides disabled children with powerful weapons in their ongoing battle for inclusion in schools.

The approaches in Australia and the UK to issues concerning disability in schools have moved closer together with the passage of the Special Educational Needs and Disability Act 2001 in the UK. Australian case law examined in this chapter will be of some value to disabled children in the litigation which is ensuing from the passage of this legislation. In turn, Australia has much to learn from the UK approach. Specifically, the presence of SENDIST in the UK creates a specialist education tribunal which will, over time, develop high levels of expertise in dealing with the disability discrimination cases before it. However, this Tribunal does not have the power to award compensation. Australia does not have a specialist tribunal system examining disability issues in relation to schools. Furthermore, in Australia there are constitutional reasons which prevent HREOC from making binding orders. To overcome this, recent cases are being dealt with in Magistrates and Federal Courts in Australia, adding to expense and creating a

---

110 M. Jones, and L.A. Basser-Marks 'The Limitations on the Use of Law to Promote Rights: An Assessment of the *Disability Discrimination Act 1992*,' (Cth) in M. Hauritz, C. Samford and S. Blencowe (eds), *Justice for People with Disabilities* (Sydney: Federation Press, 1998), 60–84, at p 78.

far too formal atmosphere for the resolution of matters involving children compared to the right of access to tribunals in the UK.

The use of key concepts in disability legislation in both countries such as 'discrimination' and the establishment of tribunals allowing the exercise of rights are a significant step forward in recognising discrimination. These are much more orientated around the social model rather than medical model notions of need found in legislation such as the Children Act 1989. Moreover, the presence in both countries of a right to challenge has far reaching implications for a child's self-esteem and confidence. No longer are disabled children mere passive recipients of care. The recent introduction of disability rights at the school level in the UK will be of particular assistance in making disabled people aware of their rights at an early stage of their lives, and should assist their understanding of their rights later as adults. On the other hand, interpretations such as those in *Purvis* represent a backward step in the development of disability law. We trust that this approach will be reversed in Australian legislation, and prefer the UK approach to behavioural issues.

Disabled children should have the opportunity to develop social skills through the education process. In the past, opportunities for this to occur in extra curricular activities such as school trips have been denied. Rights under UK legislation, vigorously pursued, should help to ameliorate this. Those denied will now have an avenue of redress and accordingly the right of the disabled child to choose activities that he or she will enjoy should also increase.

The existence of rights in the child may remove pressures within the structure of the family because the onus may now shift to schools given the legal position they are now placed in. Many parents have been unable to continue with employment as they have been called upon to go into their child's school to attend to their needs. On occasion, parents have been requested to be carers whilst the child is at school; and often without this care, the child has been excluded from activities. Cases discussed above demonstrate the obvious proposition that many parents of disabled children have had to fight very hard for an adequate education for their children. It is of paramount importance that the creation and active pursuit of new rights in disabled children in the United Kingdom work to reduce the stress levels within family life.

For many years disabled children have had very little identity within their communities. Fundamental rights have often been ignored and the creation of disability discrimination rights must have an impact on how their rights are perceived. On a micro level, the concept of having basic *human* and *equal* rights, will surely enable them to have many opportunities that they have previously not enjoyed. Education is a fundamental process of learning on many levels and creates a basis for their future. On a macro level, the ideology of equal rights is of enormous benefit to society as a whole. Disabled children may now begin to be perceived as 'functioning members of their community.' Their image, which has previously been very negative, will surely now become more positive.

PART V
HEALTH PROMOTION

Chapter 11

School Health Education in the United States: The Law and the Public Trust

Gerald S Fain

[T]o bear the public trust, educational institutions must identify and declare those intellectual and moral purposes that they intend to strive conscientiously to fulfill.[1]

Introduction

The principal aims of health education should be the formation of good character, the acquisition of self-knowledge, and the application of good judgment in the conduct of daily life. With these, a person takes control of appetites, whether for alcohol, tobacco, or ice cream; and also establishes a reliable sense of priorities and commitments. These include a sense of civic responsibility, trustworthiness in friendship, and seriousness in love. Priorities in a healthy life clearly extend to regard for others and therefore reach beyond habits of individual risk reduction that contribute to longevity. We promote our health by refining habits of physical exercise and nutrition. We also do so by overcoming selfishness, turning to concern for others, paying attention to law and policy intended to combat dread diseases, reduce the social injustices of poverty and war, and protect the environment for ourselves and our posterity. In practice, reaching these goals as we mature depends in part on genetic make-up and predispositions, and in part on circumstances at home, in school, and in the other settings of our daily lives. The nurturing capacities of parents may matter most of all; but the complexities of social experience inside and outside the home inevitably leave their mark, for better or worse.

For most of us, a large portion of social experience in youth comes in public schools. There, health education varies dramatically, because those involved in designing and delivering health education programmes vary to the same degree. They range from highly qualified teachers to the less qualified, and include politically appointed public health officials, commercial vendors of curricula,

---

1 E. Delattre, *Education and the Public Trust*, (Washington, DC: Ethics and Public Policy Center, 1988), p XV.

textbook publishers, and members of competing special interest and advocacy groups. Motives for involvement are mixed, and not all of them put students first. This is why all of those who are directly responsible for school health education are duty bound to identify and declare those intellectual and moral purposes that they intend to strive conscientiously to fulfil. Their candour and explicitness enable the public to say Yes or No, to hold school personnel accountable for teaching and learning, and to prevent misguided or incompetent instruction of children, many of whom have no choice but to attend public schools. Without such openness by those in authority, schooling can inflict on children and youths every fad, gimmick, fashion, and popular cause that anyone is shrewd enough to market, publicise, and sell.

Purposes of Health Education

What should be the specific intellectual and moral purposes of health education? To what extent has the United States as a nation answered this question wisely and responsibly? A country's answer to the first question affects it as profoundly as its answers to questions of national security. For when the general health in a nation is neglected, when poor health is widespread because people do not learn to take responsibility for their well-being, and where the public does not widely participate in the prevention of epidemics, the public safety is severely jeopardised. How the country, the state, the local community advance the cause of good health and good health education depends in part on pertinent laws, regulations, and policies, including those that bear on schooling and school practices.

To assess recent progress at the national level, we can turn to the single most important source of information, the *National Health Education Standards: Achieving Health Literacy*.[2] The standards, published in 1995, were developed by the Joint Committee on National Heath Education Standards and published by the American Cancer Society. The group included representatives from the Association for the Advancement of Health Education, the American School Health Association, and the American Public Health Association. The standards were written with the intended purpose of providing a practical model to be used by the individual states as they developed their own curriculum standards. The standards were reviewed and made available by the federally-funded Education

---

2 Joint Committee on National Health Education Standards, *National Health Education Standards: Achieving Health Literacy*, (Atlanta: American Cancer Society, Inc., 1995), 95-50M-No.2027.

Resources Information Center (ERIC) Clearinghouse on Teaching and Teacher Education in the form of a Digest.[3]

This Digest begins by citing the Centers for Disease Control and Prevention (CDC) finding of 'six categories of behaviors that lead to intentional and unintentional injuries.'[4] They are: smoking; alcohol and other drug use; sexual behaviours leading to sexually transmitted diseases, HIV infection, and unintended pregnancy; poor nutrition, and lack of physical activity. The rationale for school health is then drawn from the conclusion that 'behaviors and attitudes about health that are initiated during childhood are responsible for most of the leading causes of death, illness, and disability in the United States today.'[5] The Digest claims that hundreds of studies are used to evaluate the effectiveness of health education, and then qualifies that claim by stating: 'effectiveness depends upon factors such as teacher training, comprehensiveness of the health programme, time available for instruction, family involvement, and community support.'[6] This work provides seven standards accompanied by 'performance indicators to help educators determine the knowledge and skills that students should possess by the end of grades 4, 8, and 11.'[7] The standards and performance indicators are as follows:

- Standard 1: Students will comprehend concepts related to health promotion and disease prevention. Performance indicators for this standard centre around identifying what good health is, recognising health problems, and ways in which lifestyle, the environment, and public policies can promote health.
- Standard 2: Students will demonstrate the ability to access valid health information and health-promoting products and services. Performance indicators focus on identification of valid health information, products, and services including advertisements, health insurance and treatment options, and food labels.
- Standard 3: Students will demonstrate the ability to practise health-enhancing behaviours and reduce health risks. Performance indicators include identifying responsible and harmful behaviours, developing health-enhancing strategies, and managing stress.
- Standard 4: Students will analyse the influence of culture, media, technology, and other factors on health. Performance indicators are

3 L. Summerfield, *National Standards for School Health Education*, (Washington, DC: ERIC Clearinghouse on Teaching and Teacher Education, 1995), Identifier: ED387483: see www.ericdigests.org/1996-2/health.html.

4 Ibid, p 1.

5 Ibid.

6 Ibid.

7 Ibid. Typically grade 4 includes students at age 9, grade 8 at age 13, and grade 11 at age 16.

related to describing and analysing how one's cultural background, messages from the media, technology, and one's friends influence health.

- Standard 5: Students will demonstrate the ability to use interpersonal communication skills to enhance health. Performance indicators relate to interpersonal communication, refusal and negotiation skills, and conflict resolution.
- Standard 6: Students will demonstrate the ability to use goal-setting and decision-making skills to enhance health. Performance indicators focus on setting reasonable and attainable goals and developing positive decision-making skills.
- Standard 7: Students will demonstrate the ability to advocate for personal, family, and community health. Performance indicators relate to identifying community resources, accurately communicating health information and ideas, and working cooperatively to promote health.[8]

Then, in 1998, the National School Boards Association and the American Association of School Administrators joined this initiative by recommending a comprehensive programme of health education in kindergarten to twelfth grade.[9] Just prior to the release of the Joint Committee standards, the American School Health Association had advocated comprehensive school health education programmes and identified ten areas of content: community health, consumer health, environmental health, personal health and fitness, family life education, nutrition and healthy eating, disease prevention and control, safety and injury prevention, prevention of substance use and abuse (alcohol, tobacco, drugs), and growth and development. They recommended a 'sequenced, and developmentally appropriate programme that is consistent with community needs and providing at least 50 hours per year of health instruction.'[10]

The major contribution from the Commission came from their standards intended for implementation at state and local levels nationwide. Yet the report also addressed methods of instruction, giving attention to parental involvement and the necessity of collaboration with other subject areas. The most effective methods of instruction in health are student-centered approaches: hands-on activities, cooperative learning techniques, and activities that include problem-solving and peer instruction to help students develop skills in decision-making, communication, setting goals, resistance to peer pressure, and stress management.[11] As with other instructional areas, the teacher should promote

---

8 L. Summerfield, above n 3, pp 2-3.

9 Typically age range from 5 to 18.

10 L. Summerfield, above n 3, p 1.

11 W. Kane, *Step-by-Step to Comprehensive School Health: the Program Planning Guide* (Santa Cruz: ETR Associates, 1993); R. Seffrin, 'The Comprehensive School

parental involvement by sending materials home, involving parents in classroom activities, and creating assignments that involve parents. Because of time limitations in the school day, some teachers find it helpful to infuse health topics into other subject areas. For example, a unit on smoking might include:[12]

- investigating the effects of smoking on body systems (science);
- developing, administering, and analysing a survey on student attitudes about smoking (mathematics);
- writing an anti-smoking advertisement (language arts);
- examining the economics of smoking in states where tobacco is a significant crop (social studies).

The anticipated approach to curriculum design described above, where parental involvement is stressed and teachers from other fields are encouraged to infuse health content into their lesson plans, reflects years of failed attempts to establish a footing for health education in public schools comparable to other subjects. As noted above, it is the limited number of minutes in the school day that leaves little time for the teaching of health. Consequently, the hope of achieving the commission standards would then be dependent upon teachers from other areas incorporating health content into their respective subjects. This strategy defeats the integrity of the health curriculum and leaves any measures of accountability unattended. How, for example, might a student get a grade in health when the lessons are somehow distributed across science, maths, language arts, and social studies? Moreover, trying effectively to implement a programme outlined in the example would by design require that teachers from the four respective content areas meet with a health teacher in advance to decide who would be responsible for teaching what parts of the health curriculum. For these reasons alone, the effective infusion of health education into other subject areas is rarely achieved. Instead, the problem of limited time in the school day combined with ongoing budget limitations has pressed the union of health and physical education. For decades American schools often gave over the teaching of health to physical education teachers. This fact has encouraged the academic staff in university-based teacher preparation programmes to combine their physical education programmes with a minor in health education. This practice is so commonplace that in some universities it is impossible to earn a teacher of health licence without completing a programme in physical education.

In the absence of active participation from the United States Department of Education, the Joint Committee intended to assert a rationale that would overcome the ongoing diffusion of responsibilities they believed threatened the

---

Health Curriculum: Closing the Gap Between State of the Art and State of the Practice' (1990) *Journal of School Health,* 60(4), 151-156.

12 D. Allensworth, 'Health Education: State of the Art' (1993) *Journal of School Health,* 63(1), 14-20.

nation's health. They did find support from the American Cancer Society; yet the influence of public health departments, commercial vendors of health curriculum, and special interest groups continued to affect local practices.

Making health education 'comprehensive' and advancing curriculum standards modestly elevated the status of the health education teacher, but not without strengthening ties to public health. The rationale for advancing school health thus came not so much from departments of education as from those in fields related to disease prevention and risk reduction. Consequently, public schools openly assumed increasing responsibility for direct instruction on matters previously considered to be private and of little academic merit. But even with open public debate and oversight of school-based practices, the instruction in health remained inconsistent from one school to another.

Responsibility for instructional and personnel decisions is normally left in the hands of individual school administrators and whichever teachers are involved. Even with National Standards, the federal government exercises no regulatory authority over health education with respect to enforcement of time devoted to teaching, qualifications of teachers, or the subject matter to be learned by students. Responsibility for living up to the public trust is simply passed on to the individual states and from there to the local authorities. This lack of accountability at the national level has permitted each state to do whatever it likes. The result is an indiscriminate array of state approved standards and local practices.[13] These problems in health education would not be solved, however, even if the federal government took control and demanded accountability. It is clear from the standards themselves that it is impossible to teach all that is stated and implied. The standards at best form the basis of a credo, but lack the specificity and logic required for a curriculum. Teachers cannot be held accountable for an impossible mission, one fundamentally dependent upon controlling the freedoms of students to engage in risk-taking behaviour. Although the mission of health education in the United States may well vary from one state to the next, the idea of school health programmes is not new, and health education is not in danger of elimination. With historic ties to the earliest cultures and religions, health education remains a noteworthy component of education in every public school in this country.

---

13 G. Fain and J. Yang, *A Study of the National Health Education Standards & State Health Curriculum Frameworks* (Boston: Boston University, unpublished research project, 2003).

A History of Public School Health Education[14]

The Ancient Greeks took seriously the vital purposes of education and considered health an essential part. Unlike viewing health as only a means to some other good (risk reduction), the Ancient Greeks took health as an end in itself. Like all other subjects worthy of effort and discipline for their own sake, it need not necessarily serve any other purpose, though it characteristically does. Aristotle's observations on one's duty to self[15] affirm this conception. We also find that every one of the long established religions gives direct instruction on health. Ancient Jews, Christians, and Muslims each gave direct instruction on matters of marital relationships, dietary practices, and duties to keep one's body and mind clean, fit, and ready to serve others. Notwithstanding ancillary doctrines of sin, religious motivation for health as an obligation to self was classical and carried considerable weight of influence.

The state, too, concerns itself with individual health, because its strength and survival as a political entity require a people capable of sustained labour who are reasonably free from illness and disease, and who respect obligations of civic order. Every country depends upon the goodwill of citizens for obedience to the laws that safeguard the public. As early as 1790 in Bavaria, Benjamin Thompson, known as Count Rumford, saw the need to provide lunch programmes for underprivileged children, as it was morally wrong to ignore hungry children; and he realised that hungry children were not easily taught. Ten years later, Johann Peter Frank wrote scientific articles on the topic of school hygiene. From then on, many public schools would be mindful of basic nutrition and disease prevention. These ideas and practices treated health as a means to other ends and established ties that would make school health the handmaiden of public health. The French, in 1833, created one of the first laws protecting children, making their public school responsible for the health of schoolchildren. Austria, Sweden, Germany, and Russia soon followed with similar laws.[16]

By this time, the earlier classical conception of health had shifted. Taking the position that public education was in the best interest of every nation, schools staffed with capable teachers became indispensable to improving the lives of children. Local schools with attendance requirements became convenient settings for a varied host of programmes targeted at the young. The most efficient way to

---

14 See, C. Willgoose, *Health Education in the Elementary School* (Philadelphia: Saunders, 1974); C. Willgoose, *Health Education in Secondary Schools* (Philadelphia: Saunders, 1972 and 1977), G. Gilbert, *Health Education: Creating Strategies for School and Community Health* (Philadelphia: Jones and Bartlett, 1995); K. Means, *A History of Health Education in the United States*, (Philadelphia: Lea and Febiger 1962).

15 *Nicomachean Ethics*: W.D. Ross's translation in *The Works of Aristotle Translated into English*, (Oxford: Oxford University Press, 1928).

16 Willgoose, *Health Education in the Elementary* School, above n 14, p 30.

reach children, and to protect them from the health risks of their day, was to go to their schools.

It would be misleading, however, to infer that all of those with influence on the founding of public education were in agreement as to the purposes of school-based health programmes. In 1842, Horace Mann, Secretary of the Massachusetts Board of Education, offered a point of view reminiscent of the position of the Ancient Greeks:

> So intimately are all parts of the human constitution connected and so vitally do the mental and moral depend upon the physical power, that we can understand either only by studying them in connection with others. For this reason, the knowledge of laws of structure, growth, development, and health of the body is essential to a comprehension of the corresponding particular in the phenomena of the mind.[17]

Mann's accomplishments marked the start of compulsory public education in the United States. The expansion of public health services came at the same time.

Massachusetts, in 1805, was the first state to enact legislation requiring hygiene as a subject in all public schools. Sixty-seven years later, the American Public Health Association was founded, followed in 1885 by the American Association of Physical Education.[18] By 1890, every state required instruction on the dangers of alcohol and narcotics. In 1894, Boston schools implemented the first regular medical inspection programme in America, followed by Chicago, New York, Philadelphia, and others. National leadership in health and physical education also grew from the influence of the Playground Association of America, formed in 1906. Joseph Lee, the 'father of the American playground movement'[19] and a Boston aristocrat, served on the Boston School Committee. At that time the school department, closely allied with settlement houses, administered public playgrounds. The first supervised playground in America was at 20 Parmenter Street in Boston, established by a committee of philanthropic women. Built in about 1886, it was a sand garden: 'Playing in the dirt is the reality of childhood.'[20] Serving Irish, Jewish and Italian immigrants, these playgrounds were the melting pots for democracy. The play leaders, who also fed and cared for the immigrant children of the settlement houses, taught civic virtue, basic hygiene, nutrition, and the benefits of physical exercise. As part of their work in physical education, Luther H Gulick and R Tait McKenzie, in 1910, stressed health information and appraisal of health attitudes and practices.[21] In this early period, physical education teachers taught the health topics. This

---

17 Ibid, p 29.

18 With some 45,000 members, mostly elementary physical education teachers, the association is named the American Alliance for Health Physical Education, Recreation and Dance (AAHPERD).

19 http://www-personal.ksu.edu/~sstevens/Joseph%20Lee.pdf, (11 October 2004).

20 http://www.bwht.org/northend1.html, (11 October 2004).

21 Willgoose, *Health Education in the Elementary* School, above n 14, p 29.

practice stifled the employment of full-time teachers of health, particularly in communities with very limited school personnel budgets.

As early as 1911, the employment of school nurses further expanded the responsibilities of schools. Nurses were to help control communicable diseases by their direct access in schools to children and youths. In 1912, the federal government established the Children's Bureau of the Federal Security Agency to address child life and welfare. In 1914, the New York City Health Department established the first local bureau of health education. Only four years later, the American Child Hygiene Association was formed. What remained undeveloped, however, was the refinement of qualifications for health teachers.

The 1920s marked the beginning of the so-called progressive era of public education. Under the influence of John Dewey, public education entered a new phase of experimentation. Formed in 1919, the Progressive Education Association stressed the development of the individual child and thereby challenged the established practices of public schooling. Drawing on ancient ideals, Dewey rejected the idea that health is a mere means to something else:

> Make health an aim; normal development cannot be had without regard to the vigor of the body—an obvious enough fact and yet one whose due recognition in practice would almost automatically revolutionize many of our educational practices.[22]

The first studies of health education, although unrelated to the mission of progressive education, came soon after, when, in 1922, Claire E Turner and Mary Spencer of Malden, Massachusetts produced the *Malden Studies in Health Education and Growth.*[23] Other public health studies would follow, as would textbooks and journals that had more to do with the health status of children than with the teaching of health as part of normal development.

Much of the history of health education reported in textbooks of that time and since blends medicine, public health, school administration, and methods of classroom instruction. In these texts one finds references to ancient Egypt, the goddess Hygeia, the Bible, the Greek physician Hippocrates, the Roman physician Galen, plagues, and impressive medical advances throughout history and continuing to this day. In 1924, the Joint Commission on Health Problems in Education, the National Education Association, and the American Medical Association, published *Health Education*. Three years later came the creation of the American School Health Association. The American Alliance for Health, Physical Education, Recreation and Dance (AAHPERD) continued throughout all these developments. It was not until 1944, however, that Bess Exton became the first full-time consultant in health education for that association. Her position was subsidised by the National Tuberculosis Association with a $5,000 grant. Over

---

22 R. Winn (ed), *John Dewey, Democracy and Education* (New York: The Free Press, 1959), p 115.

23 K. Means, above n 14, pp 170-171.

the next decade others added to this position. Affiliations were arranged with the National Education Association Joint Committee on Health Problems in Education and the American Medical Association. As early as 1935, these affiliations led to a series of meetings. Two national conferences were convened on health in colleges, the first in 1947 and the second in the early fifties.[24]

Today, AAHPERD comprises six national associations. It is the largest organisation of this kind in the United States, serving 26,000 members. AAHPERD was founded under the leadership of William Gilbert Anderson: 'Two years out of medical school and an instructor of physical training at Adelphi Academy in Brooklyn, [he] invited a group of people who were working in the gymnastic field to come together to discuss their profession.'[25]

In 1978 the U.S. Bureau of Health Manpower funded the Role Delineation Project. Conducted by the National Center for Health Education, the project was an unsuccessful attempt to sort out the overlapping duties and responsibilities of all parties working on behalf of school health programmes. This problem of duty and accountability persists today, because local schools commonly allow physical education teachers, school nurses, counselors, and representatives of special interest and advocacy groups (anti-smoking, anti-drug, anti-violence, anti-alcohol and others) to enter classrooms and school auditoriums to deliver messages on an ever growing list of topics thought pertinent to the mission of school health education.

Some 50 years after the platform set by Mann in 1842, school health tilted toward health risk reduction. Beginning in the early 1800s, public health departments and local schools in Europe and in North America agreed in this joining of purposes. Schools doing the work of public health are commonplace today. The American Medical Association, the American Public Health Association, the Educational Policies Commission of the National Education Association, and the White House Conference on Health encouraged this health education group.

This history of school health education is not, of course, limited to public education or the education of the poor. In 1818, Harvard College required all seniors to take a course in hygiene. A proper education at every level, this example was to include some attention to personal health. Today, following in this tradition, campus recreation and wellness programmes and facilities are far more prominent on some university campuses than the academic libraries.

---

24 R.K. Means and A. Nolte, 'The H in HPER' (1967) *Journal of Health, Physical Education and Recreation*, 22-23.

25 http://www.aahperd.org/aahperd/template.cfm (20 September 2004).

Public Health

Federal and state mandates now share a common ground—the purpose of health education is risk reduction. These risks are identified by departments of public health and then tied to government funding priorities, with direct consequences for public schools. The primary source for health risk reduction priorities and strategies is found in *Healthy People 2010*.[26] Comprehensive recommendations address the health risk factors associated with each cohort studied, often in settings far beyond the authorities that govern public education. The federal government now offers a total of 467 objectives in health improvement, grouped into 28 focus areas. *Healthy People 2010* represents the ideas and expertise of a diverse range of individuals and organisations concerned about the nation's health. The Healthy People Consortium—an alliance of more than 350 national organisations and 250 State public health, mental health, substance abuse, and environmental agencies—conducted three national meetings on the development of *Healthy People 2010*. In addition, many individuals and organisations gave testimony about health priorities at five *Healthy People 2010* regional meetings held in late 1998. On two occasions—in 1997 and 1998—the American public was given the opportunity to share its thoughts and ideas. More than 11,000 comments on draft materials were received by mail or via the Internet from individuals in every State, the District of Columbia, and Puerto Rico.

All the comments received during the development of *Healthy People 2010* can be viewed on the *Healthy People* website.[27] The groundwork for *Healthy People 2010* came from *1979 Healthy People,* the Surgeon General's Report on *Health Promotion and Disease Prevention*, followed by the 1980 report, *Promoting Health/Preventing Disease: Objectives for the Nation. Healthy People 2010* is designed to achieve two overarching goals: (1) Increase quality and years of healthy life; and (2) Eliminate health disparities.

While the efforts to achieve these goals target communities, thereby involving local public and private sector investments of time and money, support for schools is overwhelmed by other interests. The federal leadership responsible for implementing the objectives is the US Department of Health and Human Services. Addressing the challenge of health improvement is a shared responsibility that requires the active participation and leadership of the Federal Government, States, local governments, policy-makers, health care providers, professionals, business executives, educators, community leaders, and the American public itself. Although administrative responsibility for the *Healthy People 2010* initiative rests in the US Department of Health and Human Services, representatives of all these diverse groups shared their experience, expertise, and ideas in developing the *Healthy People 2010* goals and objectives.[28] This ten year

---

26 *Healthy People 2010:* http://www.health.gov/healthypeople/.

27 Ibid.

28 Ibid, p 2.

strategy for improving the nation's health with the 'overarching purpose of promoting health and preventing illness, disability, and premature death' is 'grounded in science, built through public consensus, and designed to measure progress.'[29] The leading health indicators identified in *Healthy People 2010* are:

1. Physical Activity
2. Overweight and Obesity
3. Tobacco Use
4. Substance Abuse
5. Responsible Sexual Behaviour
6. Mental Health
7. Injury and Violence
8. Environmental Quality
9. Immunisation
10. Access to Health Care

The *Healthy People 2010* report recommends that 'Educational and Community-Based Programs' attend to every one of the Leading Health Indicators (LHI), and gives ten objectives specifically for schools:

- 7-2 Increase the proportion of middle, junior high, and senior high schools that provide school health education to prevent health problems in the following areas: unintentional injury; violence; suicide; tobacco use and addiction; alcohol and other drug use; unintended pregnancy, HIV/AIDS, and STD infection; unhealthy dietary patterns; inadequate physical activity; and environmental health.

- 7-4 Increase the proportion of the nation's elementary, middle, junior high, and senior high schools that have a nurse-to-student ratio of at least 1:750.

- 8-20 (Developmental) Increase the proportion of the nation's primary and secondary schools that have official school policies ensuring the safety of students and staff from environmental hazards, such as chemicals in special classrooms, poor indoor air quality, asbestos, and exposure to pesticides.

- 14-23 Maintain vaccination coverage levels for children in licensed day care facilities and children in kindergarten through the first grade.

---

29 Ibid, p 1.

- 15-31 (Developmental) Increase the proportion of public and private schools that require use of appropriate head, face, eye, and mouth protection for students participating in school-sponsored physical activities.

- 19-15 (Developmental) Increase the proportion of children and adolescents aged 6 to 19 years whose intake of meals and snacks at schools contributes to good overall dietary quality.

- 22-8 Increase the proportion of the nation's public and private schools that require daily physical education for all students.

- 22-10 Increase the proportion of adolescents who spend at least 50 per cent of school physical education class time being physically active.

- 22-12 (Developmental) Increase the proportion of the nation's public and private schools that provide access to their physical activity spaces and facilities for all persons outside of normal school hours (that is, before and after the school day, on weekends, and during summer and other vacations).

- 27-11 Increase smoke-free and tobacco-free environments in schools, including all school facilities, property, vehicles, and school events.

Healthy People 2010 promises positive effects for individuals and for the country as a whole. Certainly, avoiding illness, disease, and preventable death is in the interest of individuals; we rely on government to assure access to high quality health care; protect food and water supplies; and conduct research aimed at curing or reducing the effects of illnesses and diseases. We rely on federal and state licensing and accreditation programmes to secure high quality personnel to develop and implement health strategies. The public suffers when government fails in its responsibilities.

Yet, *Healthy People 2010* is nothing more than a report filled with recommendations and strategies to employ if individuals most at risk and in large number do not change the ways in which they live. Almost every one of the targets identified in the report depends not just on effective teaching but also on the hope of lifelong behaviour change. The inference here is clear—if citizens do not take educated care of themselves, they are likely needlessly to burden the health care system. Funds are limited and so spending money to treat individuals who are sick simply because of reckless disregard for their own health diverts funds that might otherwise be available for medical research, reducing health care costs for all, food programmes for the poor, and care of the elderly. Primary prevention of preventable illness, disease, and premature death through early education combats not only these problems, but the attendant problems of reduced worker productivity and increasing numbers of days of work missed due to illness. Broader based measurable outcomes attached to quality of life (longevity, access to high quality health care, reliable and affordable sources of nutrition, clean water, and a safe environment in which to live) also turn on avoidance of waste.

Lack of attention to classroom instruction and the qualifications of health teachers in *Healthy People 2010* are noteworthy and disappointing. Even though it is uncommon for the federal government to hold local authorities accountable for methods used in teaching any subject or for teacher quality in any field, the United States Department of Education could do this within limits, if officials so desired.[30] Ignoring the methods of instruction leaves teachers of health free to agree on the topics to be covered, and share very little on when and how to teach them. The absence of governmental controls leaves each and every school the authority to decide how much time in the school day will be devoted to teaching health. Even more troubling are the remarkable variations in the quality of the instructors. Some programmes routinely enlist local police officers to teach units on drug education, or recruit representatives from any number of local advocacy groups to teach about the dangers of narcotics, alcohol, and sexual intercourse (for instance, Alcoholics Anonymous, AIDS Action Committees, Parents Against Drunk Driving and Planned Parenthood). These practices undermine health education as an element of the formal academic curriculum. Such practices would never be allowed for the teaching of mathematics or English. Until the government supports raising the standards for teachers of health, there will be no assurance that public school students will learn what they need to fulfil this two-part promise of the public trust.

The same government authorities that crafted *Healthy People 2010* know that many of those at greatest risk of preventable illness, diseases and premature death live in poverty. This relationship has long been recognised, as has the relationship between poverty and school achievement. While there is no guarantee that the rich will live longer or be better educated, the wealthy have more choices in selecting health care providers, medicines known to have beneficial preventive effects, and elective diagnostic procedures. The wealthy can also give their children academic enrichment. They typically send their children to better performing schools where high academic achievement is expected of each student. This may be why inner city schools with the highest numbers of children and youths in poverty, and therefore at high health risk, are mistakenly thought to need more health education programmes than their peers in suburban

---

[30] Reading instruction is a notable exception, where, under the federally funded *No Child Left Behind* legislation, reading instruction must be evidence based and has, therefore, stressed phonics-based instruction. In the case of health education, qualifications for teachers of health, as well as standardised assessments keyed to academic standards, could be included in existing federal law.

and private schools. The mistake is degrading to these students and their families and destructive of their education, as acting on it steals time in the school day that should be devoted to academic study.

These perceived needs stem from the view that poor children are more likely to be sexually promiscuous, have unintended pregnancies, be unaware of the dangers of sexually transmitted diseases, and inclined to use narcotics; and they embrace the wholesale purchase of risk reduction programmes that are required of each and every student. All of this assaults the character of the children who do not fit any such profile. It is simply wrong to tell any child, 'You are an "at-risk" student,' simply because the child attends an inner city public school. The roots of such prejudice aimed at the poor are long-studied and not new. The American eugenics movement, as reported by Steven Selden and detailed in public records, is among the most troubling movements in the history of this country. Prior to World War II, eugenicists held that human potential is fixed by race and other genetic factors. This prejudice led to limiting immigration of 'undesirables' from other countries, the wholesale institutionalisation of those thought to be mentally ill or mentally retarded, and in some states, legalised sterilisation. Inter-racial marriage was thought to weaken the American bloodline. State fairs featured better baby contests. With conspicuous support from politicians and academics, discrimination against people with disabilities became commonplace. Public school curricula actively taught xenophobia in some 41 states.[31]

No one objected more compellingly to the dogmas of eugenics than Ashley Montagu, author of *Man's Most Dangerous Myth: the Fallacy of Race*.[32] His work disproved eugenics but was largely ignored. Not until the bitter lessons learned from Nazi Germany's short-lived and diabolical drive to create a 'super race' were impossible to ignore did eugenics-driven theories fade from public policy. Educators pressed for giving greater weight to environmental influences, including the benefits of a proper education. They adopted a more optimistic and reliable view of human potential.

We have long known that racism and poverty can reduce expectations for student academic achievement. Public health officials continue to report on the disparities of key health indicators, based on race; but public schools are not at the forefront in solving these problems. There is also the view that nothing is more important to achieving a good and healthy life than a high quality education. After all, one can learn a great deal about avoiding communicable diseases, but never master enough of the school curriculum to earn a diploma or the prospect of a satisfying career.

---

31 S. Selden, *Inheriting Shame: The Story of Eugenics and Racism in America* (New York: Teachers College Press, 1999).

32 A. Montagu, *Man's Most Dangerous Myth: the Fallacy of Race* (New York: Columbia University Press, 1942).

We might be wiser to have public health services work more closely with families and local health care agencies and leave public schools with the responsibility for the more classical aims of education. Trends lean, however, toward including ever more comprehensive health education within public schools. This practice creates unresolved tensions, especially for schools with limited funds and struggling academic programmes, strained further by demands from the federal government to reach higher standards of academic achievement. Public health policy, like education policy, is subject to political influence. There is considerable competition for advancing one platform over another, because there are tangible benefits for the politician who successfully implements programmes that promise to improve the public health. Funding priorities wax and wane with political influence, whether for programmes to prevent HIV/AIDS, teenage pregnancy, the use of narcotics or tobacco. This trend persists, even though the most serious health problems are complex, require non-partisan cooperation, and cannot be solved easily or quickly. Funds may go to public schools, but their purpose is clearly risk reduction among the public at large and not education. This fact is confirmed by the silence of laws and regulations on methods of classroom instruction; assessment of demonstrated content mastery; and qualifications for health teachers. Health education remains less than an academic subject matter with agreed upon content to be mastered by every school child in America. It will remain so, as long as the health education curriculum is vulnerable to local influences that can adversely affect the substance of the curriculum, the effective use of time, and the quality of instruction. Dramatic variations in teacher qualifications blur the lines between instruction and counselling. If the aim is to bring about behaviour change, as opposed to content mastery, establishing a trusting relationship can be more important than the assignment of demanding homework. Health education is thus unlike any other part of the required school curriculum in America.

Classroom Instruction

The National Health Education Standards rest on a recommended sequence of instruction, developmentally appropriate and consistent with community needs. They believe that the standards can be met with 50 hours per year of instruction.[33] This means that from kindergarten to twelfth grade, students would receive 22 minutes per day of health education instruction. They also report that as little as 1.8 hours of instruction per week produced increases in health knowledge, but it took 60 hours of instruction a year to achieve maximal learning and attitude and or behaviour changes. In the same document they report that the cold fact that 'annual average number of hours spent on health education in US

33 Joint Committee on National Health Education Standards, above n 2, p 69.

Public Schools is 13.8.'[34] And at 'the secondary level, students receive an average of 9 minutes per day of health instruction.'[35]

These data come from studies completed in the mid-1990s. There are no reliable national data available today to update these findings. It is the case, however, that federal law continues to press local schools for higher achievement in academic subjects including reading, mathematics, and science. The end result is fewer minutes per day available for any subject or activity that does not directly influence performance on standardised tests. The health standards calling for a minimum of 50 hours of instruction per year, a total of 650 hours from kindergarten to twelfth grade, have no legal force, and are therefore ignored. Moreover, in states that have a required number of hours for instruction, there is no guarantee that the hours will actually be filled with health education content based on the national standards.

I have taught health education to teachers for over 25 years. From time to time, I have visited public schools observing how health education was taught, and have interviewed many teachers. Some of the schools I visit today require a total of 100 hours of instruction in health for a high school diploma. Teachers of health are rarely employed for elementary schools and are far more likely to be placed at the middle and high levels. The state requirement might be filled in either the ninth or tenth grade, and students may be required to take and pass a knowledge test designed by the teacher—that is, standardised tests are not required.

The following four accounts are representative of what I have learned and are purposefully drawn to illustrate the variations of instruction, accompanied by the inevitable implications for the public trust. Given the limited time devoted to health education in public schools, I know of teachers who believe that their first, and only, duty is to teach sex, alcohol, and drugs (SAD).[36] This SAD approach to teaching puts sex education first. In such courses students spend inordinate amounts of time learning the explicit details of male and female reproductive organs. In one ninth grade class of boys and girls (14 to 15 years of age) I heard a student ask, 'How long does it take for men to create sperm?' Another: 'What happens if your period doesn't come in 28 days?' Of the 100 hours of total instruction, some 30 to 50 hours are devoted to human reproduction, with the remainder of time given to alcohol and narcotics. These teachers know when they are employed that they cannot possibly cover the kindergarten to twelfth grade comprehensive state approved curriculum in the 100 hours allocated to health education.

---

34 Ibid.

35 Ibid.

36 This practice started some 30 years ago and was promoted by academic staff in schools of education responsible for teacher preparation in health. The National Health Standards and model curriculum promoted by the professional associations has no such priority and does not use this acronym.

By way of example, the Massachusetts Comprehensive Health Education Framework,[37] passed by law in 1999, begins with a core concept: Health Literacy/Health Self-Management Skills/Health Promotion.

The guiding principles in the framework require:

- I Sequential, pre-kindergarten to twelfth grade coordinated teaching of health, physical education, and family and consumer sciences.
- II Assessment of risks, consideration of consequences, and making healthy decisions.
- III Communication of health information.
- IV Acknowledgment of similarities and differences to create a safe and supportive environment.
- V Collaboration among components to strengthen the coordinated school health program.

The Framework content is sorted into four 'strands':

Physical Health
Social and Emotional Health
Safety and Prevention, and
Personal and Community Health.

It is clear then, by following SAD, that teachers fail to teach the state approved framework. Teachers who take human sexuality to be the start of the health curriculum may believe that by doing so they will actually lower teenage pregnancy, along with the spread of sexually transmitted diseases. No evidence supports these claims. The law makes no provision for such an emphasis.

I have also found that teachers in different schools in the same district, reporting to the same school board and superintendent, vary in the way they use instructional time. Some include time spent in physical education class as part of the State-required 100 hours for health. Schools are not held accountable in Massachusetts for student achievement in health programmes. Graduation from high school requires passing state administered tests in mathematics and English, but not in health education. The passing rate on these tests is used by the state to determine the effectiveness of the schools.

The second account is of a teacher I observed in a middle school. She was in her first year of teaching at this school and was assigned 30 students in a room with 28 desks. I sat on a radiator in the rear of the room. She told me in advance that no teacher at that school expected any of the students in her class to earn a high school diploma. She believed, however, that the students deserved her best efforts, and she faithfully taught them from the State-approved curriculum framework. Her lesson plans were completed weeks in advance and were as

---

37 http://www.doe.mass.edu/frameworks/health/1999/overview.html (13 October 2004).

thoughtfully designed as any I have reviewed. She taught units on nutrition, human anatomy, and the effects of alcohol and narcotics on the human body. The students had notebooks. She assigned homework, administered tests in class, and used the tests as means for teaching the students what they had failed to learn and needed to know. She gave grades consistent with the quality of student work. After every class, she found time to call the home of each student. She never gave up trying to reach parents or guardians, so as to report on student progress and enlist their participation in the students' education. As it happened, most of the parents were never reachable at home—at any time—but she continued to call. She was the only teacher of health in that building, and she told me that she did not mind the nearly complete absence of encouragement for her teaching from others in the school. She told me that at the end of that academic year she would find another job, one in which she hoped to be more effective in reaching children at greatest risk of suffering from the consequences of avoidable poor health.

In contrast, another middle school health teacher I observed in the classroom had many years of experience in the same school system. Often called by her supervisor to provide in-service training for new teachers, she told me of her pride in being popular with the students in the school and in being recognised by school administrators for her exemplary methods of instruction. In her classroom, she told the students that the ground rules were simple:

- You can ask me any question you want.
- I will always tell you the truth.
- You can trust me to keep confidential whatever you tell me (I will not be reporting our conversations to your parents).

The students knew that the grades in this class were meaningless, and that they would have no homework or tests. I cannot forget the first question that came from a boy who raised his hand impatiently: 'What does semen taste like?' The teacher was pleased by the question, and after class told me how it proved she had established a high level of trust with her students. They knew she would speak freely about private matters and then keep her promise of not telling their parents. She told me that this was the only way she knew to learn what was on the minds of her students. After low-level laughter from other students, she answered the question as if trying to recall the taste, and then gave a pseudo-scientific description of the chemical properties in semen. She had invited the students to invade her privacy, and for that, they mocked her competence as a teacher. She confirmed the student's suspicion that she knew the taste of semen, and then gave them a misguided 'scientific' explanation. This teacher believed that the students in her class needed to talk about sexual behaviour to learn the dangers of unprotected sexual intercourse. She would use the same strategy of instruction to cover any other topic, including narcotics, tobacco, and alcohol. Her inviting and answering the very first student question autobiographically eliminated all respect for privacy and gave her licence to pry into the lives of these young people as she had invited them to pry into hers. The main lesson she taught her students was disrespect for private life. This teacher considered herself a success because she believed she alone of the adults in the school was trusted by students. She wanted to be the 'go to' teacher for every student problem. She entirely ignored the State curriculum framework and never gave her students the benefit of a prepared lesson plan. She was indifferent to academic achievement, was never held accountable in any way by school administrators, and succeeded only in turning a classroom into bad group therapy.

Such teaching gets by in schools where parents are not involved, and where administrators cynically dismiss the potential of the students under their charge. Like this teacher, administrators betray the public trust when they intrude on the private lives of students and wrongly equate popularity in the school or community with educational effectiveness. Teachers and administrators of this stripe have abandoned, if they ever held to, the intellectual and moral purposes of education. They indulge educational laxity by taking the position that for children and youths to engage in high-risk behaviours is inevitable. Anticipating only the worst outcomes, they trade away everyone's educational opportunities for any kind of therapeutic programme that might save a child from harmful behaviour.

The fourth account points to an even more dreadful problem in the way health education is delivered to students. Arresting stories abound in the press of outrageous disregard by public school teachers and administrators for the public trust and the wellbeing of children. Sometimes, their conspicuously low expectations of students bring them to condone offensive and degrading classroom instruction. Here is another recent episode involving the perversion of the aims of health education into an excuse for the malevolent abuse of power. In this illustration, based on a factual account, a teacher distributed flavoured condoms to the 14-15 year old students in his middle school class. One of the students complained to her mother that the teacher insisted that she taste the condoms. The teacher wanted her to overcome her fear of condoms and went on to suggest that some day she might actually like to have sexual relations in this same way. This teacher had been teaching this same lesson for years and knew that he had the approval of his supervisors and health department.

Reports of such teachers frequently make national news. When these stories are made public they demoralise decent teachers and give those who never before considered such a practice reason to do the same—or worse.[38] No one can know the number of teachers who fit this last profile of a teacher's despicable abuse of students, abetted by administrative incompetence. Nonetheless, such accounts often attract national attention and undermine public confidence in local schools and teachers. Teachers like this one give parents reason to distrust the capacity of public schools to bring out the best in their children.

---

[38] A Google search for "flavored condoms" found 73,600 sites in 0.49 seconds: http://www.google.com (31 August 2004).

Lack of federal descriptive data on the qualifications of current health teachers, methods of instruction, and student achievement, make it very difficult to determine the quality of public school health education programmes today. Perhaps the splendid middle school teacher described in the second account—the one who best exemplified fidelity to the public trust—is more typical than the other two. Perhaps not. Teachers who are preoccupied with sex in health education may tell us far more about them than about their students. Our ignorance of the state of things is a sign of risk to the health of the public, if only because it confirms the absence of health education accountability to the intellectual and moral purposes of public education.

The polar opposite of this approach to teaching about human sexuality and the use of condoms is described by Edwin J Delattre. In his public presentation before the Management Team of the Chelsea Public Schools, he replies to the refrain that schools have 'a moral obligation to do everything in their power, at all times, to save lives':

> Saving lives is not the only moral concern of human beings. The prevention of needless suffering among adults, youths, children, infants and unborn babies; the avoidance of self-inflicted heartache; and the creation of opportunities for fulfilling work and for happiness in an environment of safety and justice all merit moral attention as well. And even if saving lives were our only moral concern, there is no reason to believe that distributing condoms in schools is the best way to save lives. Certainly, the distribution of condoms is an unreliable substitute for the creation of a school environment that conveys the unequivocal message that abstinence has greater life-saving power than any piece of latex can have.[39]

School Health Education Curriculum - in Perspective

Absent from the health education curricula and standards described above are areas of content vital for any well-conceived health education programme. The three illustrations that follow put current practices into a different perspective. To start, children need to be taught that they live on a planet with others. The United States Census Bureau reported a United States population of 293,785,923[40] in July of 2004. The number continues to grow, but more slowly than the reported current world population of 6,381,540,370. Those who study population can see the time when more than nine billion people will be living on Earth.[41] Imagine

---

39 E. Delattre, *Condoms and Coercion* (Chelsea, Massachusetts: Chelsea Management Team, 14 January 1992), pp 4-5.

40 http://www.census.gov/population/www (20 July 2004).

41 See population reports: *The World Health Report 2002* (Geneva: World Health Organization, 2002); UNESCO: www.unesco.org; U.S. Census Bureau: www.census.gov/; Population Reference Bureau; CARE International: www.care.org/; Earthwatch: www.earthwatch.org/; Greenpeace:

the consequences for each of us, if all of those people at some time in the future aspired to live as many Americans now live. Nine billion people, all wanting single-family homes, with indoor plumbing, electricity, telephones, televisions, air conditioning, refrigerators, microwave ovens, computers and more. Even the legendary scientist and 'despairing optimist,' Rene Dubos,[42] who believed in the power of Earth's capacity for renewal, knew that people needed to change, for there to be a hopeful future for coming generations. Jacques Cousteau,[43] likewise a conservationist, reached the same conclusions in his studies of the oceans. Living better with less is a matter of social responsibility for Americans.

The World Health Organization and UNESCO[44] are calling attention to these problems, especially as they affect the poorest countries. Most population growth is in less-developed countries where poverty and illiteracy are worst and insufficient resources are available to support a free public education for all children. Illiteracy is strongly related to morbidity and mortality and cannot be combated without greater financial support from the most developed countries. China has slowed its population growth by enforcing a one child per family law,[45] and thereby improved the quality of life for millions of people in China.[46] India and Pakistan are likewise trying to slow population growth.

Far too little money is spent on established methods of prevention and treatment for the AIDS epidemic in the Sudan. Advantaged people who spend discretionary income on trivial pursuits ought to ask themselves what they might do, what obligations they have, to help. The United Nations, The World Health Organisation, and political leaders in the United States and elsewhere have all called for greater support in fighting an epidemic that threatens to take the lives of more than 45 million people. Reduced population growth in America can be explained in part by the economic pressures on families, rather than by established social policy. Many women want to have both children and careers outside the home. This means smaller family size with the hope of higher quality and longer life.

The rate of consumption in the United States of both renewable and non-renewable resources is a sleeping giant. Population experts have for decades tried to calculate the caring capacity of the earth. It is not possible to tell whether there will come a time when there is too little clean water and clean air to sustain

---

www.greenpeace.org/international_en/; see also P. Ehrlich, *The Population Bomb* (New York: Buccaneer Books, 1971).

42 French-born (1901-1982), American Pulitzer Prize winning author, contributor Scientific American, Chairman of the Rene Dubos Center for Human Environment.

43 French born (1920-1997), and like Dubos reported a 'sickly child;' founder, The Cousteau Society, prolific author including *Jacques Cousteau: the Ocean World* (New York: Abrams Books, 1985).

44 *Encyclopedia of Life Sustaining Systems* (Oxford: Eolss Publishers): http://www.eolss.net/.

45 http://www.un.org.

46 Ibid.

human life on this planet. We are losing beyond reclamation arable land and rain forests by the day. Fossil fuels are a finite commodity. Energy efficient vehicles will likely replace gasoline powered vehicles. Environmental education programmes, based on the premise of sustainability and designed to teach children field biology, help to put health education curricula into perspective. In good environmental education, children learn the world's physical and political geography, how to read maps and descriptive statistics, and sufficient world history and systems of politics and government to make sense of the data.

The second illustration concerns the mythology of disease and treatment of illness. In America, addiction to alcohol is mistakenly considered a disease. Herbert Fingarette explains otherwise.[47] While the abuse of alcohol may well be addictive for some people, and may therefore be the cause of disease, it is not like cancer or coronary heart disease. Doctors unsuccessfully argued against those representing the twelve-step treatment programmes promoted by Alcoholics Anonymous on this very basis. The fact that health care policy in America classifies alcoholism as a disease has implications for the costs of public health services and insurance providers. Moreover, school children who are taught that willful self-destruction by alcohol and narcotics is a disease, are not being told the truth, but rather a falsehood they can easily discover for themselves, if they ever have the chance to study human pathology. Children taught this mythology may come to believe that they have no control over their appetites. This surely is a lynchpin in understanding the inherent lesson to be derived from the study of health. For if nothing more, health education is manifest in the formation of good character, the achievement of self-knowledge, and the exercise of good judgment in the matters of daily life. Knowing this alone fortifies a young person against all kinds of risks due to uncontrolled appetites, whether for alcohol, tobacco, or ice cream.

Obesity, like the abuse of alcohol, is not a disease, but rather the precondition for life-threatening diseases. Now considered by the Centers for Disease Control an epidemic in children in every state in America, obesity is the 'disease of this week.' This is to say again that health education programmes are trend driven by public health officials. The federal and state governments are now armed to fight obesity in the same ways they fought tobacco. This means media attention to the problem, lawsuits against those thought to be responsible for the epidemic,[48] and perhaps even high taxation of products thought to cause obesity. Proceeds from lawsuits and taxation can be used to fund intervention programmes. Yet, the scientific evidence concerning obesity continues to confirm the common sense explanation for the epidemic, along with a curative course of action. In the most elementary of terms Americans are fat because they eat too

47 Herbert Fingarette, *Heavy Drinking: The Myth of Alcoholism as a Disease* (Berkeley: University of California Press, 1988).

48 By example, see action by Wisconsin Governor Doyle: obesity tort reform measures http://www.heartland.org/Article.cfm?artId=14674.

much food, and most of the excess comes from carbohydrates. Slow metabolism is not at the root of the obesity epidemic in this country, and this is confirmed by the Centers for Disease Control and Prevention. They report that adult men have increased intake since 1971 by 168 calories per day, while women over that same time period have nearly doubled that number by reaching 335 more calories per day. In 1970 Americans ate 1,497 pounds, and by the year 2000 were up to 1,775 pounds.[49] Simply put, burning more calories than one consumes is the best way to stop making fat. This means children should be taught to eat a properly balanced nutritional diet and to exercise regularly.

Donald E Greydanus, Dilip R Patel, and Elizabeth K Greydanus identify twelve topics of adolescent health.[50] Obesity is at the top of the list, and accounts for 22 per cent of the prevalence. The number of obese adolescents continues to increase, with the data supporting strong correlations to economic status. Children in poverty are more likely to be obese than their affluent peers. This suggests that obesity often has to do with limited access to high quality nutrition and safe play areas for physical activity, as well as health care and other factors associated with quality of life indicators.[51] A hundred years ago, Americans knew the importance of proper nutrition and of linking schools to neighbourhood playgrounds. Without safe places to play, staffed by qualified personnel, children will needlessly continue to suffer the consequences of obesity. This epidemic is not disease-driven but socially constructed.

Absence of the Study of Neuroscience in Schools

There is yet one more vital subject to bring into consideration. This final matter concerns the benefits to health derived from the study of neuroscience. We find no mention of neuroscience in any of the curricula and standards for health education promoted by any group. Perhaps some day, instead of reading disheartening stories about sex education taught in public schools, we will be able to focus on the work of scientists like Professor Marian C Diamond. In her talks to teachers, Marian Diamond,[52] a leading brain anatomist and authority in neuroscience and cognition, explains why she prepares a cohort of university students from her courses to teach brain anatomy to students in local elementary schools. She knows that learning brain anatomy at a young age can fortify children against the health risks found in the environment, chemical agents, and

---

49 K. Newman 'Why Are We So Fat?' (2004) *National Geographic*, 206(2), pp 46-61.

50 D. Greydanus, et al, *Health and Welfare for Families in the 21st Century*, 2nd ed, (Boston: Jones and Bartlett, 2003), p 289.

51 For an overview of quality of life indicators in the United States, P. Lee (et al), *The Nation's Health*, (Boston: Jones and Bartlett, 2003).

52 Including keynote addresses at the Learning and the Brain Conferences, Boston Massachusetts: see http://www.edupr.com/.

activities of daily living. Little children should not be subjected to a diet of fast food and large servings of soft drinks. They suffer when taking in more calories than they can burn in a day, watching gratuitous violence on television, and being exposed to trauma. Elevated and sustained levels of cortisol (the stress hormone) in the brain of a young child because of environmental problems do not just interfere with behaviour and learning; they actually change the structure of the brain. In contrast, neurotransmitters (dopamine, serotonin, and norepinephrine) improve brain function and support emotional well-being. Health education of this sort is grounded in science and entirely consistent with the aims of public education. Here, attention focuses on academic content directly relevant to personal life. Students can make decisions in their own self-interest as they deepen their knowledge of the human body. Understanding brain anatomy and neuroscience in particular opens connections to everyday life. Proper nutrition, rest, daily physical activity, and positive emotional relationships direct and shape the nervous system. With trauma, anxiety, and harmful chemicals introduced, these same systems have to struggle unnecessarily to meet the demands of daily life, while the person suffers weakened capacity for impulse control, reason, and memory over a lifetime.

By example, I have found teaching adolescents about the prefrontal lobe and executive function in the brain to be an effective means for understanding responsible decision making in human beings. Studying the science of the brain introduces students to health considerations that bear on the course of a long life. They can learn early that what matters most in the long run are the abilities to remember, to reason, and to sustain the highest possible cognitive function. They learn, too, that in old age one expects to lose a cascading host of physical abilities, and that there is thus a pressing need for scientific research to combat the dreaded outcome of a living person whose brain and mind are no longer capable of expressing thought or remembering the past.

Conclusion

As a field of practice in public schools across the United States, health education is undisciplined in two crucial ways. First, it is undisciplined in the sense that the absence of rigorous standards for content and methods of instruction has resulted in chaos. Second, it is undisciplined in the sense that it remains unconnected to the academic disciplines, including history, philosophy, and literature, and the sciences, including geography, anatomy, political science, mathematics, biology, and chemistry, that would provide it with real intellectual substance.

Without addressing the lack of discipline within itself, health education cannot become a professional enterprise. It is not that the local authority of schools must be abandoned, but rather that in health education that authority needs to be exercised within a framework of professionalism that does not now exist. Were health educators to face this crisis with determination to overcome it, they would surely reverse the long slide of health education into egocentrism, preoccupation with mere risk reduction, and relative indifference to ways of life that embrace social responsibility, civic obligation, and regard for others. Instead of accepting or condoning or celebrating sensational, irresponsible, and damaging teaching, they would insist on serious methods of study and instruction, including reading, writing, laboratory experimentation, mathematical analysis, gathering of evidence and drawing of logical inferences, and other forms of discovery and understanding associated with arts and sciences. Instead of limiting health education to a narrow conception defined by public health agencies, health educators as genuine professionals would develop a field of teaching and learning that takes as its principal aims the formation of good character, the acquisition of self-knowledge, and the application of good judgment in the conduct of daily life.

Bibliography

Addaction (2004), *Collecting the Evidence: Clients' Views on Drug Services*, Addaction, London.

Allensworth, D. (1993), 'Health Education: State of the Art,' *Journal of School Health*, **63**(1), pp 14-20.

Alston, P. and Quinn, G. (1987), 'The Nature and Scope of States Parties Obligations Under the International Covenant on Economic, Social and Cultural Rights,' *Human Rights Quarterly*, **9**, pp 159-229.

Anti-Bullying Alliance (2003), *Statement of Purpose*, Anti-Bullying Alliance, London.

Arai, L. (2003), 'British Comparisons on Teenage Pregnancy and Childbearing: the Limitations of Comparisons with other European Countries,' *Critical Social Policy*, **23**, pp 89-102.

Aristotle's 'Nicomachean Ethics' in W.D. Ross (trans) (1928), *The Works of Aristotle Translated into English,* Oxford University Press, Oxford.

Association of Chief Police Officers (2003), *Cannabis Enforcement Guidance*, ACPO, London.

Avenarius, H. and Heckel, H. (2000), *Schulrechtskunde*, 7th ed, Kriftel, Luchterhand.

Babasyan, N. (1999), 'Freedom or "Life": Secular and Russian Orthodox Organizations Unite in a Struggle against Reproductive Freedom for Women,' *Izvestia,* 26 February.

Badham, B. (2004), 'Participation - for a Change: Disabled Young People Lead the Way,' *Children and Society*, **18**, pp 143 -154.

Bagley, W.C. (1979), 'Editorial' (from (1915) *School and Home Education*, **35**) in *John Dewey, the Middle Works, Volume 8: Essays on Education and Politics 1915*, Southern Illinois University Press, Carbondale.

Baker, J.P. (2003), 'The Pertussis Vaccine Controversy in Great Britain 1974-1986,' *Vaccine*, **21**, pp 4003-4010.

Basser, L.A. and Jones, M. (2002), 'The Disability Discrimination Act 1992 (Cth): A Three-Dimensional Approach to Operationalising Human Rights,' *Melbourne University Law Review,* pp 254 - 284.

Bayefsky, A. (2001), *The UN Human Rights Treaty System: Universality at the Crossroads*, Klewer Law International, The Hague.

Beck, U. (Translated by M. Ritter) (1992), *Risk Society*, Sage, London.

Beck, U. and Beck-Gernsheim, E. (2002), *Individualization: Institutionalized Individualism and its Social and Political Consequences*, Sage, London.

Beck-Gernsheim, E. (2002), 'Health and Responsibility,' in B. Adam, U. Beck and J. Van Loon (eds), *The Risk Society and Beyond: Critical Issues for Social Theory*, Sage, London, pp 122-35.

Bell, M. and Cumper, P. (2003), 'Section 28 and the Human Rights Act,' *Journal of Social Welfare and Family Law,* 25(3), pp 215-228.

Berlin, Isaiah (1969), 'Two Concepts of Liberty,' in *Four Essays on Liberty*, Oxford University Press, Oxford.

Betz, M. (1992), *The Kindergartner with AIDS and the Classroom Barrier,* PA LRP Publishing, Horsham.

Blair, A. (2002), 'Negotiating Conflicting Values: the Role of Law in Educating for Values in England and Wales,' *Education and the Law*, **14**(1-2), pp 39-56.

Blair, A. (2004), 'School Bullies Turn to Text Messages,' *The Times*, 21 June.

Blair, A. and Furniss, C. (1995), 'Sex, Lies and DfE Circular 5/94: the Legal Limits of Sex Education,' *Education and the Law*, **7**(4), pp 197-202.

Blair, A. and Stanley, N. (2004), 'Taking Risks with Sex Education,' a paper given in the education law and policy stream of the Socio-legal Studies Annual Conference, Glasgow, April.

Blatch, P. (1997), 'Special Education Issues,' *School Law:1997,* National Seminar Paper 6, Legal and Accounting Seminars Pty Ltd, Sydney, pp 1 - 28.

Boreham, R. and Shaw, A. (eds) (2001), *Smoking, Drinking and Drug Use Among Young People in England in 2000*, Department of Health, London.

Boseley, S. (2003), 'Doctors Turn on Each Other as MMR Debate Rages Again,' *The Guardian*, 1 November.

Botvin, G. (1990), 'Substance Abuse Prevention: Theory, Practice and Effectiveness,' in M. Tonry and J. Q. Wilson (eds), *Drugs and Crime*, University of Chicago Press, Chicago.

Boutenko, I. A. (1997), 'Norms of Conduct,' in I. Boutenko and K.E. Razlogov (eds), *Recent Social Trends in Russia, 1960-65*, McGill-Queen's University Press, Montreal, pp 124-127.

Boydston, J.A. (ed) (1988), *John Dewey: Middle Works, Volume 14: Human Nature and Conduct, 1922*, Southern Illinois University Press, Carbondale.

Boys, A., Marsden, J., Fountain, J., Griffiths, P., Stillwell, G. and Strang, J. (1999), 'What Influences Young People's Use of Drugs? A Qualitative Study of Decision-Making,' *Drugs: Education, Prevention and Policy*, **6**(3), pp 373-387.

Bradley, P. (2002), 'Should Childhood Immunisation be Compulsory?' *Journal of Medical Ethics*, **25**, pp 330-334.

Bridgman, J. (1996), 'Don't Tell the Children: the Department's Guidance on the Provision of Information about Contraception to Individual Pupils,' in N. Harris (ed), *Children, Sex Education and the Law*, Sex Education Forum, National Children's Bureau, London, pp 45-64.

Brunkow, A. (2001), 'Schools Rethink AIDS Ed,' *Omaha World-Herald*, 2 March.

Buckingham, D. and Bragg, S. (2004), *Young People, Sex and the Media: the Facts of Life?* Palgrave MacMillan, Basingstoke.

Bullen, E., Kenway, J. and Hey, V. (2001), 'New Labour, Social Exclusion and Educational Risk Management: the Case of the "Gymslip" Mums,' *British Educational Research Journal*, **26**(4), pp 441-456.

Burgess, E. (2003), *Are We Nearly There Ye?: Do Teenage Wheelchair Users Think Integration Has Been Achieved in Secondary Schools in the UK? A Survey,* No Limits Millennium Award Project, Stockport.

Burniston, S., Dodd, M., Elliott, L., Orr, L. and Watson, L. (2002), *Drug Treatment Services for Young People: a Research Review*, Scottish Executive Effective Interventions Unit, Edinburgh.

Burtney, E. and Duffy, M. (eds) (2004), *Young People and Sexual Health: Individual, Social and Policy Contexts*, Palgrave MacMillan, Basingstoke.

Calderone, Mary S. (1968), 'Sex Education and the Roles of School and Church,' *The Annals of the American Academy of Political and Social Sciences,* **376**, pp 53-60.

Cameron E. (1993), 'Human Rights, Racism and AIDS: the New Discrimination,' *South African Journal on Human Rights,* pp 22-9.

Cameron, E. and Swanson, E. (1992), 'Public Health and Human Rights—the AIDS Crisis in South Africa,' *South African Journal on Human Rights,* pp 200-233.

Centers for Disease Control (1981), 'Kaposi's Sarcoma and Pneumocystis Pneumonia Among Homosexual Men - New York City and California,' *Morbidity and Mortality Weekly Reporter,* **30**, p 305.

Charnitzky, J. (1996), *Facismo e Scuola: La Politica Scolastica del Regime (1922-1943)*, La Nuova Italia, Florence.

Charter, D. (1999), 'Why Schoolboy Flashman was a Happy Bully,' *The Times*, 14 December.

Chaudhary, V. (1998a), 'Children Expect Bullying at School,' *The Guardian*, 22 January.

Chaudhary, V. (1998b), 'Fear Followed Name Calling,' *The Guardian*, 22 January.

Chervyakov, V. (1996), 'Survey Supports Arguments to Start Sexuality Education in Russia,' Sexuality Information and Education Council of the US.

Chervyakov, V. and Kon, I. (1998), 'Adolescent Sexuality in Russia,' in *Aids in Europe: New Challenges for Social and Behavioural Sciences*, 2nd European Conference on the Methods of Social and Behavioural Research on AIDS, Working papers for synthesis sessions, Paris.

Chervyakov, V. and Kon, I. (2000), 'Sexual Revolution in Russia and the Tasks of Sex Education,' in T. Sandford (et al) (eds), *AIDS in Europe: New Challenges for Social Sciences*, Routledge, London, pp119 -134.

Chief Inspector of Schools in England (2004), *Standards and Quality 2002-03: Annual Report of Her Majesty's Chief Inspector of Schools,* The Stationery Office, London.

Chief Secretary to the Treasury (2003), *Every Child Matters*, The Stationery Office, London.

Childline (2003), *An Analysis of Calls to ChildLine on the Subject of Child Abuse and Neglect*, ChildLine, Scotland.

ChildLine (2004), Press release, 'Bullying - Biggest Ever Rise in Calls to ChildLine' 25 August 2004 (www.childline.org.uk).

Coates, T. (2004), 'Danger When Science Serves Theology,' *Newark Star-Ledger,* 14 September.

Coggans, N. (et al) (2003), *The Life Skills Drug Education Programme: a Review of Research*, Scottish Executive Effective Interventions Unit, Edinburgh.

Cohen, J. (1996), 'Drugs in the Classroom: Politics, Propaganda and Censorship,' *DrugLink*, March/April, pp 12-14.

Cohen, J. (2002), 'Just Say - Oh No, Not Again,' *DrugLink*, July/August, pp 13-14.

Collins, K., McAleavy G. and Adamson G. (2004), 'Bullying in Schools: a Northern Ireland Study,' *Educational Research*, **46**(1), pp 55-71.

Collishaw, S. (et al) (2004), 'Time Trends in Adolescent Mental Health,' *Journal of Child Psychology and Psychiatry,* **45**(8), pp 1350-1362.

Commission on Children and Violence (1995), *Children and Violence*, Calouste Gulbenkian Foundation, London.

Condon, J. and Smith, N. (2003), *Prevalence of Drug Use: Key Findings from the 2002/2003 British Crime Survey*, Findings 229, Home Office, London.

Coons, J.E. (1985), 'Intellectual Liberty and the Schools,' *Journal of Law, Ethics and Public Policy,* p 1.

Cooper, C. (et al) (2003), *Victimisation in the School and the Workplace: Are There Any Links?*

Council of Europe (1988), *School Health Education and the Role and Training of Teachers*, Recommendation No R (88) 7, Council of Europe, Strasbourg.

Council of Europe (1991), *Education for Health and Drug Misuse in the Member States of the Council of Europe and the European Community*, Recommendation 1169, Council of Europe, Strasbourg.

Cousteau, J. (1985), *Jacques Cousteau: The Ocean World*, Abrams Books, New York.

Craig, P. and Fairgrieve, D. (1999), 'Barrett, Negligence and Discretionary Powers,' *Public Law,* Winter, pp 626-650.

Crawford, J. (2000), 'The UN Human Rights Treaty System: a System in Crisis?' in P. Alston and J.Crawford (eds), *The Future of the UN Human Rights Treaty Monitoring*, Cambridge University Press, Cambridge, pp 1-12.

Csóti, M. (2003), *School Phobia, Panic Attacks and Anxiety in Children*, Jessica Kingsley, London.

Dallin, A. (1977) , 'Conclusions,' in D. Atkinson, A. Dallin and G. Lapidus (eds), *Women in Russia*, Stanford University Press, Stanford, p 390.

Delaney, A. (2003), 'Employee Privacy - Grasping the Nettle,' *Employment Law Bulletin*, **56**, pp 4-6.

Delattre, E. (1988), *Education and the Public Trust*, Ethics and Public Policy Center, Washington, DC.

Delattre, E. (1992), *Condoms and Coercion,* Chelsea Management Team, Chelsea, MA.

Department for Education and Employment (1994a), *Education Act 1993: Sex Education in Schools* (Circular 5/94), Department for Education and Employment, London.

Department for Education and Employment (1994b), *Pupil Behaviour and Discipline* (Circular 8/94), Department for Education and Employment, London.

Department for Education and Employment (1995), *Drug Prevention in Schools* (Circular 4/95), Department for Education and Employment, London.

Department for Education and Employment (1998), *Protecting Young People: Good Practice in Drug Education in Schools and the Youth Service*, Department for Education and Employment, London.

Department for Education and Employment (1999a), *National Healthy School Standard: Guidance*, Department for Education and Employment, London.

Department for Education and Employment (1999b), *Social Inclusion: Pupils Support* (Circular 10/99), Department for Education and Employment, London, 1999.

Department for Education and Employment (2000), *Sex and Relationship Education Guidance* (Circular 0116/2000), Department for Education and Employment, London.

Department for Education and Skills (2001), *Special Educational Needs Code of Practice* (DfES/581/2001), Department for Education and Skills, London.

Department for Education and Skills (2002), *Bullying: Don't Suffer in Silence*, Department for Education and Skills, London.

Department for Education and Skills (2003a), *Drugs: Guidance for Schools: Consultation Paper*, Department for Education and Skills, London.

Department for Education and Skills (2003b), *Revision of DfES Guidance to Schools on Drugs*, Department for Education and Skills, London.

Department for Education and Skills (2003c), *Working Together: Giving Children and Young People a Say*, Department for Education and Skills, London.

Department for Education and Skills (2004a), *Drugs: Guidance for Schools* (DfES 0092/2004), Department for Education and Skills, London.

Department for Education and Skills (2004b), *Improving Behaviour and Attendance: Guidance on Exclusion for Schools and Pupil Referral Units*, Department for Education and Skills, London.

Department of Education and Science (1987), *Sex Education at School* (Circular 11/87), Department of Education and Science, London.

Department of Health (2003a), *National HIV and Syphilis Sero-Prevalence Survey in South Africa: 2002, Department of Health, Pretoria.*

Department of Health (2003b), *School Health Policy and Implementation Guidelines, Department of Health, Pretoria.*

Dewey, J. (1934), 'Can Education Share in Social Reconstruction?' in J.A. Boydston (ed), *John Dewey: Later Works, Volume 9: 1933-1934*, Southern Illinois University Press, Carbondale.

Dewey, J., 'My Pegagogic Creed,' in *The Early Works, 1882-1898, 5: 1895-1898, Southern* Illinois University Press, Carbondale.

Di Censo et al. (2002), 'Interventions to Reduce Unintended Pregnancies Among Adolescents,' *British Medical Journal*, 324, 1426.

Disability Rights Commission (2002), *Disability Discrimination Act 1995, part 4: Code of Practice for Schools*, DRC, London.

Doek, J. (2001), 'Children and Their Right to Enjoy Health: a Brief Report on the Monitoring Activities of the Committee of The Rights of the Child,' *Health and Human Rights*, **5**(2), pp 155-173.

Dorn, N. & Murji, K. (1992), *Drug Prevention: a Review of the English Language Literature*, ISDD, London.

Dorrington R.E., Bradshaw D. and Budlender D. (2002), 'HIV/AIDS profile in the Provinces of South Africa: Indicators for 2002,' Centre for Actuarial Research, Medical Research Council, and the Actuarial Society of South Africa.

Douglas, N. (et al) (1998), *Playing it Safe: Response of Secondary School Teachers to Lesbian and Gay Pupils, Bullying, HIV and AIDS Education and Section 28*, Health and Education Research Unit, Institute of Education, University of London, London.

Douglas, N. (et al) (1999), 'Homophobic Bullying in Secondary Schools in England and Wales - Teachers' Experiences,' *Health Education*, **99**(2), pp 53-60.

DrugScope (1998), *The Right Choice: Guidance on Selecting Drug Education Materials for Schools*, DrugScope, London.

DrugScope (1999a), *The Right Approach: Quality Standards in Drug Education*, DrugScope, London.

DrugScope (1999b), *The Right Responses: Managing and Making Policy for Drug-Related Incidents in Schools*, DrugScope, London.

DrugScope (2000), *Drug Education for School Excludees: a Study of Six Local Authorities' Provision of Drug Education for Young People Not in School*, Drugscope, London.

DrugScope/Alcohol Concern (2001), *Opportunities for Drug and Alcohol Education in the School Curriculum*, DrugScope, London.

Dugard, J. (2000), 'The Role of Human Rights Treaty Standards in Domestic Law - the South African Experience, in P. Alston, and J. Crawford, (eds), *The Future of the UN Human Rights Treaty Monitoring*, Cambridge University Press, Cambridge, pp 269-286.

Ehrlich, P. (1971), *The Population Bomb*, Buccaneer Books, New York.

Fain, G. and Yang, J. (2003), *A Study of the National Health Education Standards and State Health Curriculum Frameworks*, Unpublished research project, Boston University, Boston.

Farren, S. (1995), *The Politics of Irish Education, 1920-65*, Institute of Irish Studies, The Queen's University, Belfast.

Fingarette, H. (1988), *Heavy Drinking: The Myth of Alcoholism as a Disease*, University of California Press, Berkeley.

Fisher, E. (2003), 'The Rise of the Risk Commonwealth and the Challenge for Administrative Law,' *Public Law*, Autumn, pp 455-478.

Fitzpatrick, B. (2004), 'Reformulating Sex Offences: Some Fundamental Problems in Criminal Law,' seminar, University of Leeds, School of Law, 20 April.

Fitzpatrick, M. (2001), 'Parents of Bullied Boy Win Record Payment,' *Times Educational Supplement,* 2 February.

Flood, P. J. (undated), 'Life after Communism: Democracy and Abortion in Eastern Europe and Russia,' in *University Faculty for Life*, volume 10 (http://www.uffl.org/vol10/flood10.pdf).

Flood-Page, A. (et al) (2000), *Youth Crime: Findings from a 1998/1999 Youth Lifestyles Survey*, Home Office, London.

Forero, R. (et al) (1999), 'Bullying Behaviour and Psychosocial Health Among School Students in New South Wales, Australia: Cross Sectional Survey,' *British Medical Journal,* **319**, pp 344-348.

Forlin, C. and Forlin, P. (1998), 'The Legal Implications of Including Students with Disabilities in Regular Schools,' in M. Hauritz, C. Samford and S. Blencowe, *Justice for People with Disabilities,* Federation Press, Sydney, pp 109-126.

Fortin, J. (2002), *Children's Rights and the Developing Law*, 2nd Ed, Butterworths, *London.*

Freeman, M. (2000), 'The Future of Children's Rights,' Children and *Society*, **14**, pp 277-293.

Furedi, F. (1992), *The Culture of Fear: Risk Taking and the Morality of Low Expectation*, Continuum, London.

Furniss, C. (2000), 'Bullying in Schools: It's Not a Crime- Is It?,' *Education and the Law*, **12**(1), pp 9-21.

Furniss, C. and Blair, A. (1997), 'Sex Wars: Conflict in, and Reform of, Sex Education in Maintained Secondary Schools,' *Journal of Social Welfare and Family Law*, **19**(2), pp 189-202.

Gilbert, G. (1995), *Health Education: Creating Strategies for School and Community Health*, Jones and Bartlett, Boston.

Giollitto, P. (1991), *Histoire de la Jeunesse Sous Vichy*, Perrin, Paris.

Glendenning, D. (1999), *Education and the Law*, Butterworths, Dublin.

Glendon, M.A. (1991), *Rights Talk: The Impoverishment of Political Discourse*, Free Press, New York.

Glenn, C. (1995), *Educational Freedom in Eastern Europe*, Cato Institute, Washington, DC.

Glenn, C. and De Groof, J. (2002), *Finding the Right Balance: Freedom, Autonomy, and Accountability in Education*, vol 1, Lemma, Utrecht.

Goodman, R. and Jinks, D. (2003), 'Measuring the Effects of Human Rights Treaties,' *European Journal of International Law*, **14**, pp 171-183.

Gordon, D. F. (2002), 'The Next Wave of HIV/AIDS: Nigeria, Ethiopia, Russia, India, and China,' National Intelligence Council, ICA 2002-04 D, September, downloaded from NIC public website at www.odci.gov/nic.

Greydanus, D. (et al) (2003), *Health and Welfare for Families in the 21st Century*, 2nd ed, Jones and Bartlett, Boston.

Grisin, S.A. and Wallander, C.A. (2003), *Russia's HIV/AIDS Crisis: Confronting the Present and Facing the Future,*' Center for Strategic and International Studies, Washington, DC.

Gunja, F. (2004), *Making Sense of Student Drug Testing: Why Educators Are Saying No*, American Civil Liberties Union/Drug Policy Alliance.

Hai, Y. (2003), 'Sex is Part of our Culture Now,' *The Guardian*, 17 October.

Harber, C. (2004), *Schooling as Violence,* Routledge Falmer, London.

Harris, D.J., O'Boyle, M. and Warbrick, C. (2001), *The Law of the European Convention on Human Rights*, 2nd ed, Butterworths, London.

Harris, N. (1993), 'Local Complaints Procedures under the Education Reform Act 1988,' *Journal of Social Welfare and Family Law,* 19-39.

Harris, N. (1996), 'The Regulation and Control of Sex Education,' in N. Harris (ed), *Children, Sex Education and the Law,* Sex Education Forum, National Children's Bureau, London.

Harris, N. (2000),'Liability Under Education Law in the UK—How Much Further Can it Go?' *European Journal for Education Law and Policy*, **4**(2), pp 131-140.

Harris, N. (2002), 'The Legislative Response to Indiscipline in Schools in England and Wales,' *Education and the Law*, **14**(1-2), pp 57-76.

Harris, N. (ed) (1996), *Children, Sex Education and the Law*, Sex Education Forum, National Children's Bureau, London.

Hathaway, O. (2002), 'Do Human Rights Treaties Make a Difference?' *Yale Law Journal,* **112**, pp 1935-2025.

Health and Safety Executive (1999), *Five Steps to Risk Assessment*, HSE Books, Sudbury.

Health Development Agency (2003), *National Healthy School Standard: Drug Education (Including Alcohol and Tobacco)*, Health Development Agency, London.

Health Select Committee (2003), *Sexual Health,* Third Report for Session 2002-2003, HC 69, The Stationery Office, London.

Hirsch, Jr., E. D. (1996), *The Schools We Need...And Why We Don't Have Them*, Doubleday, New York.

Home Affairs Select Committee (2002), *The Government's Drug Policy: Is It Working?* Third Report for Session 2001-2002, HC 318, The Stationery Office, London.

Home Office (1998), *Tackling Drugs to Build a Better Britain: the Government's Ten Year Strategy for Tackling Drug Misuse*, Cm 3945, The Stationery Office, London.

Home Office (2002a), *Updated Drug Strategy 2002*, Home Office, London.

Home Office (2002b), *The Government's Drug Policy: Is It Working? The Government Reply to the Third Report from the Home Affairs Committee Session 2001-2002, HC 318*, Home Office, London.

Human Rights Watch (2001a), *Hatred in the Hallways: Violence and Discrimination Against Lesbian, Gay, Bisexual and Transgender Students in US Schools,* Human Rights Watch, New York.

Human Rights Watch (2001b), *Scared at School: Sexual Violence against Girls in South African Schools,* Human Rights Watch, New York.

Human Rights Watch (2004), *Lesson Not Learned: Human Rights Abuses and HIV/AIDS in the Russian Federation*, Human Rights Watch, New York, (http://www.hrw.org/reports/2004/russia0404/4.htm).

Hunt, P. (2003), 'The UN Special Rapporteur on the Right to Health: Key Objectives, Themes, and Interventions,' *Health and Human Rights*, **7**(1), pp 1-27.

Hutchinson, D. and Tennyson, C. (1986), *Transition to Adulthood*, Further Education Unit, London.

Independent Advisory Group on Teenage Pregnancy (2003), *Second Annual Report*, Department of Health, London.

Johnson, K. (1990), 'AIDS Stricken Teacher Remembered as a Hero Memorial,' *Los Angeles Times,* 5 October.

Joint Committee on National Health Education Standards (1995), *National Health Education Standards: Achieving Health Literacy*, American Cancer Society, Inc, Atlanta.

Joint Health and Treasury Task Team (2003), *Full Report on Treatment Options to Supplement Comprehensive Care* for HIV/AIDS in the Public Health Sector, Pretoria

Jones, J. H. (1997), *Alfred C. Kinsey: A Public/Private Life*, W. W. Norton, New York.

Jones, M. and Basser-Marks, L.A. (1998), 'The Limitations on the Use of Law to Promote Rights: an Assessment of the Disability Discrimination Act 1992 (Cth)' in M. Hauritz, C. Samford and S. Blencowe, *Justice for People with Disabilities,* Federation Press, Sydney, pp 60-84.

Kaltiala, R. (et al) (1999), 'Bullying, Depression and Suicidal Ideation in Finnish Adolescents: School Survey,' *British Medical Journal*, **319**, pp 348-351.

Kane, W. (1993), *Step-by-Step to Comprehensive School Health: The Program Planning Guide*, ERT Associates, Santa Cruz.

Katz, A., Buchanan A. and Bream V. (2001), *Bullying in Britain*, Young Voice, London.

Kedzia, Z. (2003), 'United Nations Mechanisms to Promote and Protect Human Rights,' in J. Symonides (ed), *Human Rights: International Protection, Monitoring and Enforcement*, Ashgate, Aldershot, pp 3-90.

Keim, W. (1995), *Erziehung unter der Nazi-Diktatur*, Band I, Wissenschaftliche Buchgesellschaft, Darmstadt.

Kilpatrick, W. K. (1992), *Why Johnny Can't Tell Right from Wrong*, Simon and Schuster, New York.

Kirby M. (1993), 'AIDS and the Law,' *South African Journal on Human Rights,* pp1-21.

Knopp, G. (2000), *Hitlers Kinder*, Goldmann, Munich.

Kon, Igor (1995), *The Sexual Revolution in Russia*, Free Press, New York.

Lansdown, G. (2000), 'The Reporting Process Under the Convention on the Rights of the Child,' in P. Alston and J.Crawford (eds), *The Future of the UN Human Rights Treaty Monitoring*, Cambridge University Press, Cambridge, pp 113-128.

Lee, P. (et al) (2003), *The Nation's Health,* Jones and Bartlett, Boston.

Lester, W. (2004), 'Public Worries About AIDS Threat to Kids,' *Dayton Daily News,* 26 July.

Lester, W. (2004), 'Public Worries About AIDS Threat to Kids,' *Dayton Daily News*, 24 July.

Levada, Y.A. (1995), 'Homo Soveticus Five Years Later: 1989-1994 (Preliminary results of comparative research),' *Informational Bulletin of Monitoring*, January-February, p 10.

Levine, J. (2002), *Harmful to Minors: the Perils of Protecting Children from Sex*, University of Minnesota Press, Minneapolis.

Lickona, T. (1991), *Educating for Character: How Our Schools Can Teach Respect and Responsibility*, Bantam Books, New York.

Lindsay, K. (1979), 'Discrimination Law and Special Education,' *School Law:1997,* National Seminar Paper 4, Legal & Accounting Seminars Pty Ltd, Sydney, pp 1-12.

Lloyd, C. (et al) (2000), 'The Effectiveness of Primary School Drug Education,' *Drugs: Education, Prevention and Policy*, 7(2), pp 109-126.

Low, N. (undated), *Briefing Paper on Sexual Health of Young People from Black and Minority Ethnic Groups*, Teenage Pregnancy Unit, London.

Lukes, S. (1973), *Individualism*, Basil Blackwell, Oxford.

Lundy, L. (2000), *Education Law, Policy and Practice in Northern Ireland,* SLS Legal Publications, Belfast.

Mann, E. (2001), *Zehn Millionen Kinder: Die Erziehung der Jugend im Dritten Reich,* Rowohlt, Hamburg.

Marr, N. and Field, T. (2001), *Bullycid: Death at Playtime*, Success Unlimited, London.

Massachusetts State Department of Education (1999), *Massachusetts Comprehensive Curriculum Framework,* http://www.doe.mass.edu/frameworks/health/1999/.

Maugh II, T. (2002), 'The World Bleak AIDS Conference Reports Deliver a Global Reality Check Disease,' *Los Angeles Times,* 5 August.

Mawdsley, R. (1986), 'Privacy Rights of AIDS Victims,' *Education Law Reporter*, **31**, p 697.

McColgan, A. (2003), 'Do Privacy Rights Disappear in the Workplace?' *European Human Rights Law Review* (Special Issue: Privacy), pp 120-140.

McKay, A. (1999), *Sexual Ideology and Schooling*, State University of New York Press, Albany.

McManus, R. (2000), 'The House of Lords' Ruling in *Phelps v London Borough of Hillingdon* and its Implications,' *Education Law Journal,* **1**(4), pp 200-205.

Means, R. K. (1962), *A History of Health Education in the United States*, Lea & Febiger, Philadelphia.

Means, R.K. and Nolte, A. (1967), 'The H in HPER,' *Journal of Health, Physical Education and Recreation*, pp 22-23.

Meikle, J. (2004), 'Lancet Regrets MMR Report,' *The Guardian*, 21 February.

Meredith, P. (1992), *Government, Schools and the Law,* Routledge, London.

Meredith, P. (2001), 'Children's Rights and Education,' in J. Fionda (ed), *Legal Concepts of Childhood*, Hart Publishing, Oxford, pp 203-222.

Middleton, L. (1995), *Making a Difference: Social Work with Disabled Children*, Venture Press, Birmingham.

Mill, J.S. (1869), *On Liberty,* in M. Warnock (ed) (1962), *Utilitarianism,* Fontana Press, London.

Millington, P. (2003), *A History of Disability and Disabled People,* http://www.bgfl.org/dhistory/index.cfm.

Monk, D. (2001), 'New Guidance/Old Problems: Recent Developments in Sex Education,' *Journal of Social Welfare and Family Law*, **23**, pp 271-291.

Monk, D. (2002), 'Children's Rights in Education – Making Sense of Contradictions,' *Child and Family Law Quarterly*, **14**(1), pp 45-56.

Montagu, A. (1942), *Man's Most Dangerous Myth: The Fallacy of Race*, Columbia University Press, New York.

Moran, J. P. (2000), *Teaching Sex: The Shaping of Adolescence in the 20th Century*, Harvard University Press, Cambridge, MA.

Mountfield, H. (2000), 'The Implications of the Human Rights Act 1998 for the Law of Education,' *Education Law Journal,* **1**(3), pp 146-158.

Mulholland, A. (2003), 'Tackling Homophobic Bullying in Schools,' *Sex Education Matters*, Winter, pp 5-6.

Mullis, A. (2001), '*Phelps v Hillingdon London Borough Council:* A Rod for the Hunch-Backed Teacher,' *Child and Family Law Quarterly*, **13**(3), pp 331-000.

Murcott, A. and Feltham, A. (1996), 'Beliefs about Reproductive Health,' in H. Pilkington (ed), *Gender, Generation and Identity in Contemporary Russia*, Routledge, London, pp 152-53, 162-63.

Mynard, H., Joseph, S. and Alexander, J. (2000), 'Peer-Vicitmisation and Posttraumatic Stress in Adolescents,' *Personality and Individual Differences,* **29**, pp 815-821.

Napier, K. (1997), 'Chastity Programs Shatter Sex-Ed Myths,' *Policy Review*, May/June, pp 12-15.

National Centre for Social Research/National Foundation for Educational Research (2003), *Smoking, Drinking and Drug Use Among Young People in England in 2002*, The Stationery Office, London.

Navarro Sandalinas, R. (1990), *La Enseñanza Primaria Durante el Franquismo (1936-1975)*, PPU, Barcelona.

Newman, K. (2004), 'Why Are We So Fat?' *National Geographic*, **206**(2), pp 46-61.

O'Connor, L., Coggans, N. and McKellar, S. (2001), *From Policy to Practice—The New Metropolitan Police Service Strategy for School Drug Education and Support: an Evaluation of Implementation and Impact Across Five Pilot Sites*, Metropolitan Police Service, London.

Office for Standards in Education (2002a), *Drug Education in Schools: an Update*, Ofsted, London.

Office for Standards in Education (2002b), *Sex and Relationships*, Ofsted, London.

Office for Standards in Education (2003a), *Bullying: Effective Action in Secondary Schools,* HMI 465, Ofsted, London.

Office for Standards in Education (2003b), *The Education of Pupils with Medical Needs,* HMI 1713, Ofsted, London.

Office of Drug Control and Drug Prevention (2002), *Lessons Learned in Drug Abuse Prevention: a Global Review*, United Nations, New York.

Office of National Drug Control Policy (2003), *What You Need to Know About Drug Testing in Schools*, ONDCP, Washington.

Oliver, C. and Candappa, M. (2003), *Tackling Bullying: Listening to the Views of Children and Young People*, Department for Education and Skills, London.

Oliver, M. (1990), *The Politics of Disablement,* Macmillan Press Limited, London.

Olson, B.N. and Kholomogorova, A.B. (2002), 'The Professional Foster Family as One Model for Solving the Orphan Problem in Russia,' *Russian Education and Society*, **45**(6).

Olweus, D. (1993), *Bullying at School: What We Know and What We Can Do*, Blackwell, Oxford.

Osler, A. and Vincent, K. (2003), *Girls and Exclusion,* Routledge Falmer, London.

Owen, G. (2003), 'Parents Told to Pay Bullied Boy's Fees,' *The Times*, 22 February.

Paton, D. (2002), 'The Economics of Family Planning and Underage Conception,' *Journal of Health Economics*, 21(2), 207-225.

Piot, P. and Wolfensohn, J. (2003), 'Act Now or Pay Later,' *Moscow Times*, November 28, p 8.

Plant, M. and Plant, M. (1992), *Risk Takers: Alcohol, Drugs, Sex and Youth*, Routledge, London.

Popov, A. (1994), 'The USSR,' in A. Rolston and B. Eggert (eds), *Abortion in the New Europe*, Greenwood, Westport, p 274.

Poulter, S. (1998), *Ethnicity, Law and Human Rights: the English Experience,* Clarendon Press, Oxford.

Powis, B. and Griffiths, P. (2001), *Working at the Margins: an Evaluation of a Drugs-Prevention Programme for Young People Not in School*, Home Office, London.

Productivity Commission (2003), *Review of the Disability Discrimination Act 1992,* Draft Report, Productivity Commission.

Qualifications and Curriculum Authority (2003), *Drug, Alcohol and Tobacco Education: Curriculum Guidance for Schools at Key Stages 1-4*, Teachers' Booklet, Qualifications and Curriculum Authority, London.

Ramsay, M. (ed) (2003), *Prisoners' Drug Use and Treatment: Seven Research Studies*, Home Office Research Study 267, Home Office, London.

Rieff, P. (1968), *The Triumph of the Therapeutic: Uses of Faith after Freud*, Harper Torchbooks, New York.

Robinson, P. (1975), *The Modernization of Sex*, Harper and Row, New York.

Rogers, A. (1999), 'Drugs and Drugs Education in the Inner City: the Views of 12-Year-Olds and Their Parents,' *Drugs: Education, Prevention and Policy*, **6**(1), p 58.

Rotkirch, A. (2000), *The Man Question: Loves and Lives in Late 20th Century Russia*, University of Helsinki, Department of Social Policy, Research Report 1/2000, Helsinki.

Royal College of Psychiatrists (2004), *Mental Health and Growing Up. The Emotional Cost of Bullying* (3rd ed), Royal College of Psychiatrists, London.

Russo, C. (2002), 'The Family Education Rights and Privacy Act: an Update,' *School Business Affairs,* **68**(10), pp 40-43.

Russo, C. (2003), 'Recent Developments in the United States: HIV/AIDS in Schools,' *Education and the Law,* **15**(2-3), pp 171-181.

Ryan, K. and Bohlin, K.E. (1998), *Building Character in Schools: Practical Ways to Bring Moral Instruction to Life*, Jossey-Bass, New York.

Sargeant, E. (1996), 'The "Woman Question" and Problems of Maternity in Post-Communist Russia,' in R. Marsh (ed), *Women in Russia and Ukraine*, Cambridge University Press, New York, p 269.

Sarkin, J. (1999), 'The Drafting of South Africa's Final Constitution from a Human Rights Perspective,' *American Journal of Comparative Law*, **47**, pp 67-87.

Scholz, H. (1985), *Erziehung und Unterricht unterm Hakenkreuz*, Vandenhoeck, Göttingen.

Schwarz, F. and Schaffer, F. (1985), 'AIDS in the Classroom,' *Hofstra Law Review*, **14**, p 163.

Scottish Executive (2003), *Protecting Children – A Shared Responsibility*, Scottish Executive, Edinburgh.

Seffrin, R. (1990), 'The Comprehensive School Health Curriculum: Closing the Gap Between State-of-the-Art and State-of-the-Practice,' *Journal of School Health*, **60**(4), pp 151-156.

Selden, S. (1999), *Inheriting Shame: the Story of Eugenics and Racism in America*, Teachers College Press, New York.

Sex Education Forum (1996), *Forum Factsheet 10: Developing Partnerships in Sex Education: a Multicultural Approach*, Sex Education Forum, National Children's Bureau, London.

Sex Education Forum (2002), *Forum Factsheet: Faith, Values and Sex and Relationships Education*, Sex Education Forum, National Children's Bureau, London.

Shiner, M. (2000), *Doing it For Themselves: an Evaluation of Peer Approaches to Drug Prevention*, Drugs Prevention Advisory Service, Briefing Paper 6, Home Office, London.

Shiner, M. (2003), 'Out of Harm's Way? Illicit Drug Use, Medicalisation and the Law,' *British Journal of Criminology*, **43**, pp 772-796.

Shucksmith, J. (2004), '"A Risk Worth the Taking": Sex and Selfhood in Adolescence,' in E. Burtney and M. Duffy (eds), *Young People and Sexual Health: Individual Social and Policy Contexts*, Palgrave MacMillan, Basingstoke, pp 5-14.

Smith, P. and Samara, M. (2003), *Evaluation of the DfES Anti-Bullying Pack*, DfES Brief RBX06-03, Department for Education and Skills, London.

Smith, P.K. and Sharp, S. (1994), *School Bullying: Insights and Perspectives*, Routledge, London.

Social Exclusion Unit (1998), *Truancy and School Exclusion*, Cm 3957, The Stationery Office, London.

Social Exclusion Unit (1999), *Teenage Pregnancy*, Cm. 4342, The Stationery Office, London.

South African Law Reform Commission (1995), *Aspects of the Law Relating to AIDS,* (Project 85), Working Paper 58, Government Printer, Pretoria.

South African Law Reform Commission (1998), *Second Interim Report on Aspects of the Law Relating to AIDS: Pre-Employment HIV Testing,* (Project 85), Government Printer, Pretoria.

South African Law Reform Commission (1998), *Third Interim Report on Aspects of the Law Relating to AIDS: HIV/AIDS and Discrimination in Schools,* (Project 85), Government Printer, Pretoria.

Spencer, J.R. (2004), 'The Sexual Offences Act 2003: (2) Child and Family Offences,' *Crim. L.R.*, May, pp 347-360.

Starmer, K. (1999), *European Human Rights Law*, Legal Action Group, London.

Stewart, D.J. and Knott, A. E. (2002), *Schools, Courts and the Law*, Pearson Education, Frenchs Forest.

Stothard, B. (2003), 'Lies, Damned Lies and Research: Does Lifeskills Training Work?' *DrugLink*, May / June, p 18.

Studd, H. (2001a), 'Cruel Behaviour is Getting Worse,' *The Times*, 28 November.

Studd, H. (2001b), 'Bullies Drive Girl Who Saved Sister to Suicide,' *The Times*, 28 November.

Summerfield, L. (1995), *National Standards for School Health Education*, ERIC Clearinghouse on Teaching and Teacher Education, Washington, DC.

Teenage Pregnancy Unit (2001), *Guidance for Developing Contraception and Sexual Health Advice Services to Reach Black and Minority Ethnic (BME) Young People*, Teenage Pregnancy Unit, London.

Thiessen, E.J. (1993), *Teaching for Commitment: Liberal Education, Indoctrination, and Christian Nurture*, McGill-Queen's University Press, Montreal.

Thomas, G. (2002/2003), 'Random Suspicionless Drug Testing: Are Students No Longer Afforded Fourth Amendment Protections?' *New York Law School Review*, **46**, p. 821.

Thompson, D.A. (2000), 'Bullying and Harassment in and out of School,' in P. Aggleton, J. Hurry and I. Warwick (eds), *Young People and Mental Health*, John Wiley and Sons, Chichester, pp 197-210.

Todres, J. (1998), 'Emerging Limitations on the Rights of the Child: The United Nations Convention on the Rights of the Child and its Early Case Law,' *Columbia Human Rights Law Review*, **30**, pp 159-200.

Tomasevski, K. (2003), *Education Denied: Costs and Remedies*, Zed Books, London.

UNESCO (1994), *Salamanca Statement on Principles, Policy and Practice in Special Needs Education,* ED-94/WS/18, UNESCO, Paris.

UNICEF (1999), *Generation in Jeopardy: Children in Central and Eastern Europe and the Former Soviet Union,* UNICEF, Geneva..

United Nations (1993), *The Vienna Declaration and Programme of Action*, A/Conf.157/23, UN, Geneva.

United Nations (2002), *A World Fit for Children*, UNS-27/2 annex, UN, Geneva.

United Nations Commission on Human Rights (2003), *The Protection of Human Rights in the Context of Human Immunodeficiency Virus (HIV) and Acquired Immunodeficiency Syndrome (AIDS)*, Resolution 2003/47, UN, Geneva.

United Nations Committee on Economic, Social and Cultural Rights (1998), *Concluding Observations: Ireland*, CRC/C/15/Add.85, UN, Geneva.

United Nations Committee on Economic, Social and Cultural Rights (2001), *Concluding Observations: Japan*, E/C.12/1/Add.67, UN, Geneva.

United Nations Committee on Economic, Social and Cultural Rights (2002), *Concluding Observations: Poland*, E/C.12/1/Add.82, UN, Geneva.

United Nations Committee on Economic, Social and Cultural Rights, *General Comment: The Right to the Highest Attainable Standard of Health*, E/C.12/2000/4, UN, Geneva.

United Nations Committee on the Elimination of Discrimination against Women, *Women and Health*, General Recommendation No 24, Article 12, UN, Geneva.

United Nations Committee on the Elimination of Discrimination against Women, Official Records of the General Assembly, Fiftieth session, Supplement No 38, A/50/38 31, UN, Geneva.

United Nations Committee on the Rights of the Child (1995), *Concluding Observations: United Kingdom of Great Britain and Northern Ireland*, CRC/C/15/Add.34, UN, Geneva.

United Nations Committee on the Rights of the Child (2001a), *Concluding Observations: Portugal*, CRC/C/15/Add.162, UN, Geneva.

United Nations Committee on the Rights of the Child (2001b), *The Aims of Education,* General Comment No 1, UN/CRC/GC/2001/1, UN, Geneva.

United Nations Committee on the Rights of the Child (2002a), *Concluding Observations: Spain* CRC/C/15/Add.185, UN, Geneva.

United Nations Committee on the Rights of the Child (2002b), *Concluding Observations: Switzerland*, CRC/C/15/Add.182, UN, Geneva.

United Nations Committee on the Rights of the Child (2002c), *Concluding Observations: United Kingdom of Great Britain and Northern Ireland*, CRC/C/15/Add.188, UN, Geneva.

United Nations Committee on the Rights of Child (2003a), *Concluding Observations: Denmark*, CRC/C/15/Add. 151, UN Geneva.

United Nations Committee on the Rights of the Child (2003b), *Adolescent Health and Development in the context of the Convention on the Rights of the Child*, General Comment No 4, CRC/GC/2003/4, UN, Geneva.

United Nations Committee on the Rights of the Child (2003c), *Concluding Observations: Cyprus*, CRC/C/15/Add.205, UN, Geneva.

United Nations Committee on the Rights of the Child (2003d), *Concluding Observations: Greece*, CRC/C/15/Add.170, UN, Geneva.

United Nations Committee on the Rights of the Child (2003e), *Concluding Observations: Jamaica*, CRC/C/15/Add.210, UN, Geneva.

United Nations Committee on the Rights of the Child (2003f), *Concluding Observations: Libyan Arab Jamahirya*, CRC/C/15/Add.209, UN, Geneva.

United Nations Committee on the Rights of the Child (2003g), *Concluding Observations: Solomon Islands*, CRC/C/15/Add.208, UN, Geneva.

United Nations Committee on the Rights of the Child (2003h), *Concluding Observations: Sri Lanka*, CRC/C/15/Add.207, UN, Geneva.

United Nations Committee on the Rights of the Child (2003i), *Concluding Observations: Zambia*, CRC/C/15/Add.206, UN, Geneva.

United Nations Committee on the Rights of the Child (2003j), *HIV/AIDS and the Rights of the Child,* General Comment No 3, CRC/GC/2003/1, UN, Geneva.

United Nations Committee on the Rights of the Child (2004a), *Concluding Observations: Canada,* CRC/C/15/Add. 215, UN, Geneva.

United Nations Committee on the Rights of the Child (2004b), *Concluding Observations: Germany*, CRC/C/15/Add.226, UN, Geneva.

United Nations Committee on the Rights of the Child (2004c), *Concluding Observations: Guyana*, CRC/C/15/Add.224, UN, Geneva.

United Nations Committee on the Rights of the Child (2004d), *Concluding Observations: Indonesia*, CRC/C/15/Add.223, UN, Geneva.

United Nations Committee on the Rights of the Child (2004e), *Concluding Observations: Japan*, CRC/C/15/Add.331, UN, Geneva.

United Nations Committee on the Rights of the Child (2004f), *Concluding Observations: Madagascar*, CRC/C/15/Add. 218, UN, Geneva.

United Nations Committee on the Rights of the Child (2004g), *Concluding Observations: The Kingdom of the Netherlands (Netherlands and Aruba)*, CRC/C/15/Add.227, UN, Geneva.

United Nations Committee on the Rights of the Child (2004h), *Concluding Observations: New Zealand*, CRC/C/15/Add.216, UN, Geneva.

United Nations Committee on the Rights of the Child (2004i), *Concluding Observations: Pakistan*, CRC/C/15/Add.217, UN, Geneva.

United Nations Committee on the Rights of the Child (2004j), *Concluding Observations: San Marino*, CRC/C/15/Add.214, UN, Geneva.

United Nations Final Report of the Special Rapporteur of the Commission for Social Development (2003), *Monitoring the Implementation of the Standard Rules on the Equalization of Opportunities for Persons with Disabilities*, A/52/56 annex, UN, Geneva.

United Nations Population Fund (2003), *State of World Population*, United Nations Publications, New York, http://www.unfpa.org/swp/swpmain.htm.

United Nations Report of the Special Rapporteur on the Right to Education, submitted pursuant to Commission on Human Rights resolution 2002/23 (2003), *The Right to Education*, E/CN.4/2003/9, UN, Geneva.

United Nations Report of the Special Rapporteur on the Right to Education (2004), *The Right to Education*, E/CN.4/2004/45, UN, Geneva.

United Nations Report of the Special Rapporteur on the Right to Health, submitted in accordance with Commission resolution 2002/3 (2003), *The Right of Everyone to the Enjoyment of the Highest Attainable Standard of Physical and Mental Health*, E/CN.4/2003/58, UN, Geneva.

United Nations Secretary General (2002), *Strengthening of the United Nations: an Agenda for Further Change*, A/57/387, UN, Geneva.

United Nations Special Rapporteur on the Right to Education (2000), *Mission to Uganda*, E/CN.4/2000/6/Add.1, UN, Geneva.

United Nations Special Rapporteur on the Right to Education (2000), *Mission to the United Kingdom of Great Britain and Northern Ireland (England)*, E/CN.4/2000/6/Add.2, UN, Geneva.

United Nations Special Rapporteur on the Right to Education (2002), *Mission to the United States of America*, E/CN.4/2002/60/Add.1, UN, Geneva.

United Nations Special Rapporteur on the Right to Education (2003), *Mission to Indonesia*, E/CN/4/2003/9/Add.1, UN, Geneva.

United Nations Special Rapporteur on the Right to Education (2004), *Mission to the People's Republic of China*, E/CN.4/2004/45/Add.1, UN, Geneva.

US Department of Education, *No Child Left Behind*, http://www.ed.gov/nclb/landing.jhtml?src=pb.

US Department of Health and Human Services (2000), *Healthy People 2010: Understanding and Improving Health*, http://www.health.gov/healthypeople/.

Van de Braak, R. and Veazey, D. (2003), 'The AIDS Epidemic: Can It Be Contained?' *Moscow Times*, November 20, p. 8.

Van Loon, J. (2003), *Deconstructing the Dutch Utopia*, Family Education Trust, London.

Van Wyk C. (1998), 'A reply to: "Some Comments on the Discussion Paper by the South African Law Commission: Aspects of the law Relating to HIV/AIDS and Discrimination in Schools 1998 (61) THRHR p 127",' *Journal of Contemporary Roman Dutch Law,* pp 677-683.

Velleman, R., Mistral, W. and Sanderling, L. (2000), *Taking the Message Home: Involving Parents in Drug Prevention*, Drugs Prevention Advisory Service, Briefing Paper 5, Home Office, London.

Vermeersch E. (1999), 'Individual Rights Versus Societal Duties,' *Vaccine*, **17**(suppl. 3), pp S14 - S17.

Visser P.J. and Beckmann J.L. (1998), 'Some Comments on the Discussion Paper by the South African Law Commission: "Aspects of the Law Relating to AIDS: HIV/AIDS and Discrimination in Schools",' *Journal of Contemporary Roman Dutch Law,* 127-132.

Vitz, P.C. (1986), *Censorship: Evidence of Bias in Our Children's Textbooks*, Servant Publications, Ann Arbor.

Volkov, V. (1998), 'The Concept of Kul'turnost: Notes on the Stalinist Civilizing Process,' in S. Fitzpatrick (ed), *Stalinism: New Perspectives*, Routledge, London.

Voznesenskaia, I. (1991), *Zhenskii Dekameron*, Tomas, Tallin.

Warnock, M. (ed) (1962), *Utilitarianism*, Fontana Press, London.

Watkins, C. and Wagner, P. (2000), *Improving School Behaviour,* Paul Chapman, London.

Welker, M. and Pell, S. (1992), *The Formation of AIDS Policies: Legal Considerations for Schools*, National Organisation on Legal Problems of Education, Topeka.

White, D. and Pitts, M. (1998), 'Educating Young People about Drugs: a Systematic Review', *Addiction*, **93**(10), pp 1475-1487.

Wight, D., Raab, G.M., Henderson, M., Abraham, C., Buston, K., Hart, G. and Scott, S. (2002), 'Limits of Teacher Delivered Sex Education: Interim Behavioural Outcomes from a Randomised Trial,' *British Medical Journal*, **324**(7351), pp 1430-1433.

Willgoose, C. (1972 and 1977), *Health Education in Secondary Schools*, Saunders, Philadelphia.

Willgoose, C. (1974), *Health Education in the Elementary School*, Saunders, Philadelphia.

Williams, K. (et al) (1996), 'Association of Common Health Symptoms with Bullying in Primary Schools,' *British Medical Journal*, **313**, pp 17-19.

Wines, M. (2003), 'The Rise of HIV in Russia is Quickening,' *New York Times,* 22 May.

Winn, R. (ed) (1959), *John Dewey, Democracy and Education*, The Free Press, New York.

World Health Organisation (2001), *Regional Strategy on Sexual and Reproductive Health,* WHO, Copenhagen.

World Health Organisation (2002), *The World Health Report 2002*, http://www.who.int/whr/2002.

Wright, J.D. and Pearl, L. (1995), 'Knowledge and Experience of Young People Regarding Drug Misuse, 1969-1994', *British Medical Journal*, **309**, pp 20-23.

Yamaguchi, R., Johnston, L. and O'Malley, P. (2003), 'Relationship Between Student Illicit Drug Use and School Drug Testing Policies,' *Journal of School Health*, **73**(4), p 159.

Youth Justice Board for England and Wales (2002), *Positive Parenting—the National Evaluation of the Youth Justice Board's Parenting Programme*, Youth Justice Board, London.

Zirkel P. and D'Angelo, A. (2002), 'Special Education Case Law: an Empirical Trends Analysis,' *Education Law Reporter,* **161**, p 731.

Zirkel, P. (1997), 'The "Explosion" in Education Litigation: an Update,' *Education Law Reporter,* **114**, p 341.

Index